THE
BEST
OF
Gourmet

THE
BEST
OF
Gourmet

1987 EDITION

ALL OF THE BEAUTIFULLY
ILLUSTRATED MENUS FROM 1986
PLUS OVER 500 SELECTED RECIPES

FROM THE EDITORS OF GOURMET

CONDÉ NAST BOOKS
RANDOM HOUSE
NEW YORK

Copyright © 1987 Condé Nast Books

All rights reserved under International and Pan-American Copyright Conventions. Published in the United States by Random House, Inc., New York, and simultaneously in Canada by Random House of Canada Limited, Toronto.

LIBRARY OF CONGRESS CATALOGING-IN-PUBLICATION DATA
(Revised for vol. 2)

Main entry under title:
The Best of Gourmet.
    Includes indexes.
    1. Cookery, International. I. Gourmet.
TX725.A1B4827   1986   641.5   85-24458
ISBN 0-394-55258-X (v. 1)
ISBN 0-394-56039-6 (v. 2)

Most of the recipes and all the menus in this work were previously published in *Gourmet* Magazine.

Manufactured in the United States of America

98765432   24689753   23456789

First Edition

Grateful acknowledgment is made to the following for permission to reprint recipes previously published in *Gourmet* Magazine:

Faye Levy: "Fettuccine with Scallops and Peas in Saffron Butter Sauce" (page 160): "Saffron Butter Sauce" (page 160); "Noodles and Smoked Salmon with Dill Sauce" (page 161); "Pasta Gratin with Gruyère" (page 162); "Tomato Pasta with Goat Cheese and Garlic Sauce" (page 164). Copyright © 1986 by Faye Levy. Reprinted by permission of the author.

Sally Tager: "Blueberry, Green Grape, and Nectarine Compote in Lime Syrup" (page 229); "Spirited Green Fruit Compote" (page 230); "Mixed Fruit Compote with Honey and Rum" (page 230); "Orange Fruit Compote with Cognac" (page 230); "Melon Compote with Lemon Granita" (page 232); "Lemon Granita" (page 233). Copyright © 1986 by Sally Tager. Reprinted by permission of the author.

Frontispiece: "Gazpacho Ice with Cucumbers" (page 108).

PROJECT STAFF

For Condé Nast Books

Jill Cohen, Director
Jonathan E. Newhouse, Special Consultant
Ellen Bruzelius, Project Manager
Kristine Smith, Project Assistant
Diane Pesce, Composition Production Manager
Serafino J. Cambareri, Quality Control Manager

For *Gourmet* Magazine

Jane Montant, Editor-in-Chief
Evie Righter, Project Editor
Kathleen Nilon, Assistant Editor
Romulo Yanes, Staff Photographer
Irwin Glusker, Design Consultant

For Random House, Inc.

Karen Chin, Project Manager
Jayne Nomura, Project Editor
Suzanne Hastings, Editorial Coordinator

Produced in association with
Media Projects, Incorporated

Carter Smith, Executive Editor
Judy Knipe, Managing Editor
Charlotte McGuinn Freeman, Art/Permissions Editor
Michael A. Wong, Indexer
Michael Shroyer, Art/Production Director

The editors would like to thank the following people for valuable services rendered for *The Best of Gourmet—1987:* Georgia Chan Downard for her helpful and creative assistance in compiling "A Gourmet Addendum," and Blair Brown Hoyt.

The text of this book was set in Times Roman by the Composition Department of Condé Nast Publications, Inc. The four-color separations were done by The Color Company, Seiple Lithographers, and Kordet Graphics. The book was printed and bound by R. R. Donnelley & Sons. Text paper is 80-pound Mountie Gloss.

CONTENTS

INTRODUCTION

The editors of this, the second annual edition of *The Best of Gourmet*, had a happy task—improving on a success. The format of this year's edition has not been changed. We have, however, made a few additions, small touches that we believe will make this volume even more enjoyable to read and easier to use than the first.

The Best of Gourmet is divided into two parts. Part One, The Menu Collection, comprises all of the menus from the 1986 issues of *Gourmet* Magazine, including many full-color photographs. The menus are seasonal and created with an eye to the varied needs and desires of cooks everywhere—especially the Cuisine Courante combinations, designed with all the prerequisites necessary to the cook with an active lifestyle. We've created a Super Bowl supper, for example, that you can serve without missing a single play of the game. The menu features a shrimp, chicken, and vegetable curry stew that should be prepared entirely in advance.

And you will find a host of other menu ideas to inspire you and to delight your family or guests. Here's the answer to the age-old question of what to serve for lunch on a scorching summer day to refresh those sizzling spirits and senses; a dinner to celebrate the present and future pleasures heralded by the first lovely day of spring; a menu for an *intime* Thanksgiving dinner that will eliminate that holiday's major challenge for the cook—what to do with the leftovers.

On these menu pages you will see the first of this year's additions to our format. For each menu we have included page-number cross references for all of the recipes. Now, in no time at all you can refer to the recipes and decide on the menu that best suits the occasion from a practical standpoint.

Part Two, The Recipe Compendium collects all the menu recipes and provides a carefully chosen assortment of additional recipes from the magazine's other food feature columns: Gastronomie sans Argent, In Short Order, and Last Touch. Here, too, we have enhanced the format of this year's edition. The photographs—including those that appear on the front and back of the book's jacket—are cross-referenced in the recipe section, to provide you with ideas for the presentation of these dishes as well as a preview of what you will be serving.

In The Recipe Compendium, you will find recipes suited to the seasons and appropriate for entertaining or for everyday easy preparation. Our quick-to-serve soups, for example, splendid pick-me-ups anytime, include such delights as asparagus soup with sour cream and cold celery soup. And soups for other occasions are treasures as well: our Fourth of July fresh corn soup for six, suitable for any summer's day; or a splendid starter for Thanksgiving dinner, pumpkin soup topped with sage croutons.

A Gourmet Addendum contains recipes and directions for basic preparations and procedures called for in recipes elsewhere in this volume, and a little something extra—new recipes based on each of the features in the Addendum. This year's Addendum presents a first: a short primer on stockmaking. From the three basic stock recipes we have provided, you can create many classic—and innovative—soups and stews, and even a glorious seafood risotto.

The final feature of *The Best of Gourmet* is an appendix of multiple indexes, each fully cross-referenced to make locating any recipe an easy task: a General Index, a Recipe Title Index, and an Index of 45-Minute Recipes. And here, too, we have added a first: a listing of Table Setting Acknowledgments.

Gourmet Magazine, launched in 1941, is a tradition based on the pursuit of excellence. And we will continue to provide you each year with a volume that is truly *The Best of Gourmet*.

Jane Montant
Editor-in-Chief

PART ONE

THE MENU COLLECTION

The Menu Collection is a showcase of *The Best of Gourmet*—every one of Gourmet's Menus from the 1986 issues of *Gourmet* Magazine and every one ot the Cuisine Courante menus as well, accompanied by glorious full-color photographs to delight and inspire you as reader and as cook.

Here are menus for holidays; for other special occasions; for formal meals, informal get-togethers, and everyday *Gourmet* dining—a treasury of feasts for all seasons.

The Cuisine Courante menus have all been designed to provide maximum enjoyment with minimum effort. You can serve your family or guests a traditional all-American Sunday dinner of flavorful cider-braised pork with sautéed apples, for example, and still have your day of rest. Or savor the delights of an early spring dinner featuring poached salmon with cumin sauce and deep-fried celery leaves. For a midsummer's dream of a picnic, treat everyone to piquant warm-weather fare—spicy fried chicken accompanied by a colorful pasta salad with tomato, olives, and basil—complemented by cookies that you can make in minutes, pecan sand tarts *and* peanut butter chocolate chip cookies. Our gala graduation dinner for four is worthy of its own phi beta honors—creamy lemon chive pasta with asparagus, succulent boiled lobsters with tomato basil *beurre blanc*, and, for dessert, a glorious chocolate raspberry brownie torte. And there are ideas for other splendid occasions, from creating a refreshing lunch for a hot summer day, to serving an intimate weekend brunch, to hosting a tree-trimming party to ring in the gala season.

Among the Gourmet's Menus are formal menus for entertaining, *cartes* for such momentous occasions as an anniversary dinner, and holiday menus for meals that will be remembered until the season comes again.

A grand holiday dinner is one of the most delightful presents you can give your loved ones at any season of the year, and *The Best of Gourmet* Menu Collection provides opportunities for the giving of happy times all year 'round. A rack of lamb *persillé* is the centerpiece of a French-inspired Easter dinner, which also includes garlic rosemary tuiles and a salad of grilled goat cheese with spinach chiffonade. Your Thanksgiving dinner will be spectacular, whether you prepare our formal dinner for ten—boned turkey with sausage hazelnut stuffing, golden creamed onions, cranberry tart with rum cream and chocolate (and two more desserts!)—or our menu for a more relaxed but still traditional gathering of six, featuring turkey *paupiettes* with apples, onions, and cranberries. For Christmas we offer a truly elegant bill of fare: roast tenderloin of beef with wild mushroom sauce and *pommes lorette*, followed by a chocolate *dacquoise*.

And the year of Gourmet's Menus presents additional options for entertaining with style: a New Year's Day buffet, a charming meal for Valentine's Day, a cocktail party, and a trio of al fresco events—an afternoon croquet tea party, a Fourth of July celebration, and your choice of intimate terrace dinners for two.

Like the menus themselves, the Menu Collection is graced with thoughtful extras that add so much to the enjoyment of the whole. This year each menu is annotated with cross references to the page numbers on which the recipes for each of the dishes can be found in Part Two, A Recipe Compendium. And each menu includes beverage suggestions made by *Gourmet*'s wine editor, Gerald Asher, for the perfect spirited accompaniment—whether it be champagne, beer, or the wine that's just right for that stylish summer picnic.

The Menu Collection is the perfect introduction to Part Two of *The Best of Gourmet*, A Recipe Compendium of culinary delights that only begin with all of the dishes in each and every menu.

Braised Fennel with Olives

A NEW YEAR'S DAY BUFFET

Crostini, *p. 88*

Three-Mushroom Tart, *p. 96*

Schramsberg Vineyards   Oysters and Clams with Mignonnette Sauce, *p. 120*
Blanc de Blancs '82

Venegazzù dei Conti Loredan '79   Stuffed Breast of Veal, *p. 130*

Braised Fennel with Olives, *p. 172*

Gratin of Celery Root and Potato, *p. 171*

Figs Poached in Red Wine with Oranges and Mascarpone Cream, *p. 230*

Crostini

Oysters and Clams with Mignonnette Sauce

Stuffed Breast of Veal, Gratin of Celery Root and Potato

Walnut Orange Cake

SUPER BOWL SUPPER

Hot Spiced Cocktail Nut Mix, p. 86

Chick-Pea and Garlic Spread, p. 86

Heineken Beer   *Curried Shrimp, Chicken, and Vegetable Stew, p. 143*

Indian-Style Fried Bread, p. 103

Walnut Orange Cake, p. 211

Curried Shrimp, Chicken, and Vegetable Stew,
Indian-Style Fried Bread

Silver Dollar Banana Pancakes with Grape Sauce, Bacon Twists, Café au Lait

VALENTINE'S DAY

Chunky Pear Applesauce with Ginger, p. 233

Silver Dollar Banana Pancakes with Grape Sauce, p. 158

Bacon Twists, p. 133

Café au Lait, p. 239

Charles Heidsieck '79   *Green Bean and Shiitake Salad with Crisp Potato Rings, p. 195*

Volnay en Chevret '78   *Roast Duck Bourguignonne, p. 145*

Baked Polenta with Parmesan, p. 165

Coffee Dacquoise Hearts, p. 220

Roast Duck Bourguignonne, Baked Polenta with Parmesan

Coffee Dacquoise Heart

Toasted Almond Angel Food Cake

AN ALL-AMERICAN SUNDAY DINNER

Hermann J. Wiemer Vineyards
Finger Lakes
Johannisberg Riesling '84

Cider-Braised Pork Loin with Sautéed Apples, p. 132

Rutabaga Potato Purée, p. 180

Peas with Celery and Shallots, p. 176

Quick Cloverleaf Rolls, p. 98

Toasted Almond Angel Food Cake, p. 207

Cider-Braised Pork Loin with Sautéed Apples, Rutabaga
Potato Purée, Quick Cloverleaf Rolls

20

Grilled Goat Cheese with Spinach Chiffonade

EASTER DINNER

Shrimp with Papaya and Prosciutto, p. 122

Gundlach-Bundschu Winery
Sonoma Valley
Merlot '80

Rack of Lamb Persillé, p. 138

Garlic Rosemary Tuiles, p. 104

Couscous Timbales, p. 165

Saffron Turnips and Carrots, p. 184

Grilled Goat Cheese with Spinach Chiffonade, p. 150

Freemark Abbey
Edelwein Gold '82

Strawberry Mousse Cake, p. 210

Shrimp with Papaya and Prosciutto

Strawberry Mousse Cake

Rack of Lamb Persillé, Garlic Rosemary Tuiles,
Couscous Timbales

25

Honey-Glazed Pink Grapefruit with Pink Grapefruit Curd

AN EARLY SPRING DINNER

Asparagus with Sesame Mayonnaise, p. 167

Raymond Vineyards
Napa Valley
Chardonnay '83

Poached Salmon with Cumin Sauce and Deep-Fried Celery Leaves, p. 116

Steamed Red Potatoes with Dill Butter, p. 178

Red-Leaf Lettuce and Watercress Salad Mimosa, p. 192

Honey-Glazed Pink Grapefruit with Pink Grapefruit Curd, p. 232

Poached Salmon with Cumin Sauce and Deep-Fried Celery Leaves,
Steamed Red Potatoes with Dill Butter,
Red-Leaf Lettuce and Watercress Salad Mimosa

A COCKTAIL PARTY

Negroni   Baked Camembert with Hazelnut Crust, *p. 149*

                                 Sausage and Mushroom Phyllo Twists, *p. 92*

                                 Cheese Lace Crackers, *p. 102*

Spring Fever   Scallops in Saffron Mayonnaise, *p. 92*

                                 Pastry Seashells with Salmon Roe, *p. 90*

Beaujolais Kir   Shrimp and Avocado Tortilla Rounds, *p. 93*

                                 Celery Boats with Gruyère Pesto, *p. 85*

Sake Martini   Steamed Vegetables, *p. 96*

           Kalamata Dipping Sauce, *p. 96*   Chipotle Dipping Sauce, *p. 97*

Champagne Pineapple   Sweet Potato Chips, *p. 93*
   Cocktail
                                 Smoked Trout Rillettes, *p. 93*

Sake Martinis, Steamed Vegetables,
Kalamata Dipping Sauce, Chipolte Dipping Sauce

Negronis, Baked Camembert with Hazelnut Crust, Sausage and
Mushroom Phyllo Twists, Cheese Lace Crackers

Spring Fevers, Scallops in Saffron Mayonnaise, Pastry Seashells with Salmon Roe

Poached Eggs on Potato and Bacon Pancakes, Watercress Hollandaise

BRUNCH FOR FOUR

Melon Balls with Port and Lime Syrup in Melon Shells, p. 232

Cranberry-Orange Vodka Spritzers

Poached Eggs on Potato and Bacon Pancakes, p. 154

Watercress Hollandaise, p. 205

Honey and Cinnamon Drop Biscuits, p. 100

Apricot Butter, p. 100

Melon Balls with Port and Lime Syrup in Melon Shells,
Honey and Cinnamon Drop Biscuits, Apricot Butter,
Cranberry-Orange Vodka Spritzers, Potato and Bacon Pancakes

Hearts of Palm Salad with Lamb's-Lettuce

ANNIVERSARY DINNER

Roast Capon with Tarragon Sauce, Confetti Rice, Buttered Green Beans

Ananas en Surprise, Coconut Tuiles

Raspberry Hazelnut Savarin

A MAY LUNCHEON

Green Pea Consommé, p. 108

Onion Toasts, p. 109

The Hogue Cellars   *Terrine de Coquilles Saint-Jacques*, p. 122
Yakima Valley
White Riesling '84

Mixed Green Salad with Mustard Vinaigrette, p. 191

Raspberry Hazelnut Savarin, p. 212

Green Pea Consommé, Onion Toasts,
Terrine de Coquilles Saint-Jacques

Tea Sandwiches in a Bread Basket

AFTERNOON CROQUET TEA PARTIES

A Sweet Tea

Lemonade

Miniature Gingerbread Muffins, p. 100

Lemon Drop Biscuits, p. 101

Hot Brewed Tea such as
 Darjeeling or
 Earl Grey

Cinnamon Toast Rolls, p. 98

Almond Chocolate Chip Macaroons, p. 212

Lime Curd Tartlets with Fresh Fruit, p. 222

A Savory Tea

Mustard Tarragon Stuffed Eggs, p. 157

Iced Ginger "Tea"

Ham Cornets with Apple Horseradish Filling, p. 89

Tea Sandwiches in a Bread Basket, p. 94

White-Wine
 Spritzer

Layered Walnut Yogurt Terrine, p. 97

Chocolate Leaf Cookies and Fresh Fruit Kebabs, p. 214

Mustard Tarragon Stuffed Eggs, Ham Cornets with Apple Horseradish Filling

Layered Walnut Yogurt Terrine

Cinnamon Toast Rolls, Almond Chocolate Chip Macaroons,
Lime Curd Tartlets with Fresh Fruit

Creamy Lemon Chive Pasta with Asparagus

A GRADUATION DINNER

Creamy Lemon Chive Pasta with Asparagus, p. 163

Heineken Beer
or
 *Pedroncelli Winery
 Sonoma White Wine*

Boiled Lobsters with Tomato Basil Beurre Blanc, p. 120

Romaine with Anchovy Caper Vinaigrette, p. 192

Garlic Pepper Pita Toasts, p. 103

Chocolate Raspberry Brownie Torte, p. 210

Boiled Lobsters with Tomato Basil Beurre Blanc, Romaine with Anchovy
Caper Vinaigrette, Garlic Pepper Pita Toasts

Corn Soup, Corn Bread Thins

FOURTH OF JULY ALFRESCO

*Crab Claws with Thousand Island Dipping Sauce and
Horseradish Dipping Sauce*, p. 87

Corn Soup, p. 106

Corn Bread Thins, p. 100

*Bacigalupi Vineyards
Russian River Valley
Chardonnay '83*

Grilled Salmon, Shrimp, and Scallop Kebabs, p. 116

Egg Noodles with Buttered Crumbs, p. 162

Glazed Sugar Snap Peas, p. 176

Sautéed Tomatoes with Mint Butter, p. 184

Chocolate Layer Cake with Chocolate-Dipped Cherries, p. 209

48 Grilled Salmon, Shrimp, and Scallop Kebabs, Glazed Sugar Snap Peas,
Sautéed Tomatoes with Mint Butter, Egg Noodles with Buttered Crumbs

Chocolate Layer Cake with Chocolate-Dipped Cherries

Pecan Sand Tarts, Peanut Butter Chocolate Chip Cookies, Assorted Fruit

PICNIC AT THE BEACH

Dilled Clam Dip, p. 86   *Celery Sticks*

Spicy Fried Chicken, p. 142

Onion Sandwiches, p. 89

Raspberry Cooler   *Pasta Shells with*

American Beer   *Tomatoes, Olives, and Basil*, p. 196

Grated Carrot, Radish, and Chive Salad, p. 193

Pecan Sand Tarts, p. 216

Peanut Butter Chocolate Chip Cookies, p. 215

Assorted Fruit

Spicy Fried Chicken, Onion Sandwiches, Grated Carrot, Radish, and Chive Salad,
Pasta Shells with Tomatoes, Olives, and Basil, Raspberry Cooler

Chilled Cucumber Soup with Mint Ice

TERRACE DINNERS FOR TWO

Kir Royales, p. 237

Tapenade Toasts, p. 94

Gazpacho Ice with Cucumbers, p. 108

Marcarini Barolo
La Serra '80

Grilled Filets Mignons, p. 124
Garlic and Pimiento Mayonnaise, p. 124

Rosemary Potato Balls, p. 177

Summer Squash with Basil and Parmesan, p. 183

Arugula Salad, p. 190

Kahlúa Coffee Jelly with Cinnamon Cream, p. 226

Brown Sugar Wafers, p. 213

Peach Champagne Cocktails, p. 238

Prosciutto Radish Toasts, p. 90

Chilled Cucumber Soup with Mint Ice, p. 107

Eyrie Vineyards
Pinot Gris '84

Grilled Monkfish with Ratatouille, p. 114

Lemon Bulgur Timbales with Chives, p. 165

Raspberry Almond Tuile Tortes, p. 224

Gazpacho Ice with Cucumbers

Peach Champagne Cocktail, Kir Royale, Prosciutto Radish Toasts, Tapenade Toasts

Grilled Filet Mignon, Rosemary Potato Balls,
Summer Squash with Basil and Parmesan, Garlic and Pimiento Mayonnaise

Kahlúa Coffee Jelly with Cinnamon Cream, Brown Sugar Wafers, Raspberry Almond Tuile Tortes

Avocado Mousse with Radish and Coriander

LUNCH FROM A COOL KITCHEN

Avocado Mousses with Radish and Coriander, p. 168

Sesame Ginger Toasts, p. 104

Lemon and Basil Poached Chicken Breasts, p. 139

White Sangría

Smoked Mozzarella and Tomato Salad, p. 152

Strawberry Ice Cream, p. 228

Sugar Cookies, p. 218

White Sangría, Sesame Ginger Toasts, Lemon and Basil
Poached Chicken Breasts, Smoked Mozzarella and Tomato Salad

AN EARLY AUTUMN WEEKEND

Saturday Lunch

Pojer & Sandri
Alto Adige Müller-
Thurgau '83

Duck Salad with Raspberries, Oranges, Arugula, and Cracklings, p. 186

Two-Grain Salad with Green Beans and Pine Nuts, p. 198

Assorted Cheeses

Spiced Shortbread, p. 217

Saturday Dinner

Marquis d'Angerville
Meursault
Les Santenofs '82

Endive and Roquefort Spirals with Creamy Walnut Vinaigrette, p. 190

Red Snapper with Artichoke Lemon Sauce, p. 115

Sautéed Napa Cabbage and Swiss Chard, p. 170

Red Potatoes with Prosciutto and Chives, p. 177

Chocolate Coconut Phyllo Triangles
with Vanilla Ice Cream, p. 219

Sunday Brunch

Watermelon Lime Daiquiris, p. 239

Plum and Mango Bread Pudding, p. 226

Sausage Patties with Fresh Herbs, p. 134

Endive and Roquefort Spirals with Creamy Walnut Vinaigrette

Red Snapper with Artichoke Lemon Sauce, Red Potatoes with Prosciutto and Chives,
Sautéed Napa Cabbage and Swiss Chard

Duck Salad with Raspberries, Oranges, Arugula, and Cracklings,
Two-Grain Salad with Green Beans and Pine Nuts

Spinach-Stuffed Chicken Breasts with Madeira Sauce,
Saffron Rice Timbales, Zucchini and Carrot Julienne

CUISINE COURANTE

ELEGANT BUT EASY CHICKEN DINNERS

*Hill Smith Estate
Barossa Valley
Sémillon '83*

Spinach-Stuffed Chicken Breasts with Madeira Sauce, p. 140

Zucchini and Carrot Julienne, p. 185

Saffron Rice Timbales, p. 166

Plum Almond Tart, p. 224

Chiroubles '85

Blasted Cornish Hens with Basil Couscous Stuffing, p. 144

Tomatoes Stuffed with Squash, Feta, and Olives, p. 184

Steamed Green and Wax Beans, p. 173

Port-Poached Pears and Cantaloupe Compote, p. 233

Blasted Cornish Hens with Basil Couscous Stuffing,
Tomatoes Stuffed with Squash, Feta, and Olives,
Steamed Green and Wax Beans

Smoked Swiss Cheese, Apple, and Celery Salad

OCTOBER DINNER

Smoked Swiss Cheese, Apple, and Celery Salad, *p. 152*

Kallstadter Steinacker
Riesling Kabinett '83

Pork with Mustard Seed Sauce, *p. 130*

Broccoli Rabe with Lemon and Garlic, *p. 169*

Buttered Noodles with Crisp Browned Shallots, *p. 162*

Dilled Carrots and Cauliflower, *p. 170*

Apricot Cheesecake, *p. 208*

Seasonal Fruits and Nuts

Pork with Mustard Seed Sauce, Broccoli Rabe with Lemon and Garlic,
Buttered Noodles with Crisp Browned Shallots

Apricot Cheesecake

Espresso Tortoni with Chocolate-Covered Coffee Beans

MEALS TO MAKE AHEAD

Alexander Valley Vineyards
Cabernet Sauvignon '83

Spicy Lamb Stew with Sweet Potato Rosettes, p. 138

Cucumber and Radish Salad with Yogurt Coriander Dressing, p. 194

Grape, Raisin, and Vanilla Compote, p. 231

Nalle Dry Creek Valley
Zinfandel '84

Herbed Cannelloni with Prosciutto and Artichoke Hearts, p. 159

Green Bean Salad with Mustard Caper Vinaigrette, p. 196

Espresso Tortoni with Chocolate-Covered Coffee Beans, p. 227

Spicy Lamb Stew with Sweet Potato Rosettes

Golden Creamed Onions, Buttered Brussels Sprouts, Root Vegetable Purée

A COUNTRY THANKSGIVING

Hacienda Wine Cellars
Sonoma County
Sauvignon Blanc '85

Oysters on the Half Shell with
Dilled Oyster Sauce, p. 121

Chalone Vineyards
Pinot Noir '83

Boned Turkey with Sausage Hazelnut Stuffing
and Madeira Gravy, p. 146

Golden Creamed Onions, p. 174

Buttered Brussels Sprouts, p. 169

Root Vegetable Purée, p. 180

Cranberry Tart with Rum Cream and Chocolate, p. 221

Pear Mincemeat Tartlets with
Lemon Hard Sauce, p. 223

Oysters on the Half Shell with Dilled Oyster Sauce

Boned Turkey with Sausage Hazelnut Stuffing and Madeira Gravy

Cranberry Tart with Rum Cream and Chocolate, Pear Mincemeat Tartlets with Lemon Hard Sauce

Pumpkin Soup with Sage Croutons

CUISINE COURANTE

THANKSGIVING FOR A SMALL GATHERING

Pumpkin Soup with Sage Croutons, p. 111

Grgich Hills Cellars
Napa Valley
Johannisberg Riesling '85

Turkey Paupiettes with Apples, Onions,
and Cranberries, p. 148

Sweet Potato Gratin, p. 178

Parsnip and Carrot Dice, p. 175

Red Cabbage and Lettuce Salad, p. 197

1985 Muscat Canelli

Fruit and Pecan Caramel Tartlets, p. 222

Turkey Paupiettes with Apples, Onions, and Cranberries,
Parsnip and Carrot Dice, Sweet Potato Gratin

Smoked Salmon Christmas Trees, Radish and Parsley Butter Wreaths

CHRISTMAS DINNER

Taittinger Brut '79

Smoked Salmon Christmas Trees, p. 93

Radish and Parsley Butter Wreaths, p. 91

Chablis Premier Cru
Fourchaume '83

Shrimp and Artichoke Salad with Hazelnut Vinaigrette, p. 188

Laurel Glen Vineyards
Cabernet Sauvignon '81

Roast Tenderloin of Beef with Wild Mushroom Sauce, p. 126

Spinach, Pea, and Red Pepper Timbales, p. 180

Pommes Lorette, p. 176

Offley
20 Year Reserve
Tawny Port

Chocolate Dacquoise, p. 219

Apricot Macadamia Snowballs, p. 213

Roast Tenderloin of Beef with Wild Mushroom Sauce, Spinach, Pea, and Red Pepper Timbales, Pommes Lorette

Chocolate Dacquoise, Apricot Macadamia Snowballs

Baked Alaska

A TREE-TRIMMING PARTY

Scharffenberger Cellars
Sparkling Brut '83

Hot Crab, Artichoke, and Jalapeño Dip
with Pita Triangles, p. 87

Sun-Dried Tomato and Provolone Bread
with Smoked Turkey, p. 102

Radish- and Celery-Stuffed Endive Leaves, p. 91

Baked Alaska, p. 208

Hot Crab, Artichoke, and Jalapeño Dip with Pita Triangles,
Radish- and Celery-Stuffed Endive Leaves,
Sun-Dried Tomato and Provolone Bread with Smoked Turkey

THE RECIPE COMPENDIUM

The Recipe Compendium, Part Two of *The Best of Gourmet* is a treasury of culinary possibilities, from easy to elegant, from simple to challenging—over five hundred recipes divided into fourteen thoughtfully organized chapters. Each chapter—breads, soups, meats, fish and shellfish, poultry, pasta and grains, and desserts (and desserts, and desserts), to mention only a few—is subdivided into categories, and then each category's recipes are arranged alphabetically. These recipes are not only truly wonderful, they are wonderfully easy to find when you need them, even without looking at any of our excellent indexes.

All of the recipes for the dishes featured in Part One, The Menu Collection—compiled from the magazine's columns Gourmet's Menus and Cuisine Courante—are included, but those recipes are only some of the wonderful dishes presented here. An ample selection of recipes from *Gourmet* Magazine's other food features can be found as well—the best of Gastronomie sans Argent, In Short Order, and Last Touch.

This year we have cross-referenced the menu recipes by providing the page numbers on which the photos of the dishes appear. If, for example, you would like a hint on how to serve a lovely, light, chilled cucumber soup with mint ice, or rasperry almond tuile tortes for dessert, the cross reference will tell you where to look in the Menu Collection for inspiration.

The variety of recipes in each of the fourteen chapters includes old favorites, innovations, and some wonderful variations on traditional themes. Dishes very likely to become special favorites of cooks with active lifestyles are those that can be created in forty-five minutes or less. Consider our sea scallops with garlic cream on caraway biscuits: Who would have thought that such an elegant dish could be this easy? Among the many

other quickly prepared recipes you will find an interesting variation on an old but favored theme, batter-dipped French fries. And there are other quick delights—a healthful dish of mushrooms, tofu, and snow peas in soy ginger sauce, and nectarine mousse with oatmeal cookie crumbs, are examples from the wealth of options for even the busiest of cooks.

You'll also find recipes that capitalize on seasonal bounty, providing an opportunity for you to prepare the best possible version of a dish and take advantage of the low prices that are the hallmarks of bumper crops. The tomato, basil, and cheese tart that adorns our jacket front demonstrates just one of the ways to put the fruits of a tomato harvest to excellent use. Two more examples of the delectable fare you can create with this summer staple are our tangy tomato fettuccine with curry tomato sauce, or the easy and pleasing broiled tomato slices with brown sugar and sour cream—the perfect fillip for almost every grilled entrée. Shark is another tempting and equally economical ingredient, much in favor with today's discerning dieter. And oxtail is economical as well, and can serve as the foundation for many wonderful dishes, including our unusual, peppery Szechwanstyle oxtail noodle soup. An interesting aspect of the Recipe Compendium in this year's edition of *The Best of Gourmet* is a number of recipes for a variety of kebabs—even a dessert kebab of buttered rum fruits.

The final chapter of the Recipe Compendium is A Gourmet Addendum, which contains several basic procedures and recipes necessary for recipes in other chapters in the book. In addition to these, however, the Addendum provides brand-new recipes—created for this edition of *The Best of Gourmet*, and based on the recipes and procedures contained in the Addendum. After instructing you how to shuck hard-shelled clams and oysters, for example, the Addendum provides recipes for clams casino, Manhattan clam chowder, oyster and pecan stuffing, and an irresistible fried oyster sandwich on crusty Italian bread. Other features in the Addendum include methods of poaching eggs—accompanied by superb ideas for not only hot poached-egg creations but chilled poached-egg dishes as well—and a short primer on stockmaking, including recipes for chicken stock, brown stock, and white fish stock, and original and innovative recipes based on each of them.

The Addendum closes with a short but truly excellent collection of dessert recipes, some based on an airy *génoise* spongecake, others on pastry cream. The *génoise* is the foundation for a lovely English trifle and for orange tea cakes with chocolate glaze. And the pastry cream delights include a strawberry frangipane tart and raspberry Bavarian cream.

From the Hors d'Oeuvres to the Addendum, The Recipe Compendium of *The Best of Gourmet* provides the basics from which great meals are made—recipes plain and fancy, dishes for dieters and sumptuous creations for shamelessly sinful indulgence: In short, these are *The Best of Gourmet*.

HORS D'OEUVRES, CANAPÉS, AND SPREADS

BLTomatoes

10 cherry tomatoes
2 tablespoons thinly sliced scallion
4 slices of lean bacon, cooked, drained, and
　crumbled fine
¼ cup finely chopped romaine or iceberg
　lettuce
2 tablespoons mayonnaise

Cut the top ¼ inch off the tomatoes with a serrated knife, scoop out the pulp and seeds carefully, and invert the tomato shells, sprinkled lightly with salt, on paper towels to drain for 15 minutes. In a small bowl combine well the scallion, the bacon, the romaine, the mayonnaise, and salt and pepper to taste and divide the mixture among the tomato shells. Makes 10 stuffed tomatoes, serving 2 as an hors d'oeuvre.

Celery Boats with Gruyère Pesto

1 bunch of celery, separated into ribs, washed
　well, trimmed, and strings discarded
½ pound Gruyère
3 tablespoons pine nuts
½ cup packed fresh basil leaves
2 tablespoons white-wine vinegar
⅓ cup olive oil

With a small knife trim a strip down the length of the rounded side of each celery rib to form a flat bottom and cut the ribs on the diagonal into 1½-inch boats. Put the celery boats in a bowl of ice and cold water and chill them, covered, until ready to assemble the hors d'oeuvres. Cut 6 ounces of the Gruyère into 1-inch-julienne strips and grate fine the remaining 2 ounces. In a food processor or blender combine the grated Gruyère and the pine nuts and blend the mixture until it is minced fine. Add the basil and the vinegar and blend the mixture until it is a paste. With the motor running add the oil in a stream and blend the *pesto* until it is emulsified. In a bowl toss the julienne Gruyère with the *pesto* and fill the celery boats, drained and patted dry, with the mixture. *The hors d'oeuvres may be made up to 1 day in advance and kept covered and chilled.* Serve the hors d'oeuvres at room temperature. Makes about 50 hors d'oeuvres.

Cheddar Pine-Nut Bites

⅓ cup grated sharp Cheddar
2 tablespoons drained chopped pimiento-
　stuffed olives
2 tablespoons cream cheese
¼ teaspoon fresh lemon juice
¼ cup pine nuts, toasted lightly

In a bowl mash together the Cheddar, the olives, the cream cheese, and the lemon juice. Form teaspoons of the mixture into balls, coat the balls with the pine nuts, pressing the nuts into the mixture, and chill them for 20 minutes. Serves 2 as an hors d'oeuvre.

Cheddar Walnut Toasts

3 cups (½ pound) grated sharp Cheddar
½ stick (¼ cup) unsalted butter, softened
¼ cup medium-dry Sherry
½ teaspoon salt
Tabasco to taste
1½ cups walnuts, chopped fine and
   toasted lightly
four 6-inch *pita* loaves, halved horizontally,
   cut crosswise into half-moons, and
   toasted lightly

In a bowl cream together the Cheddar, the butter, the Sherry, the salt, and the Tabasco and stir in the walnuts. Spread the mixture on the *pita* and broil the toasts under a preheated broiler about 2 inches from the heat for 1 to 2 minutes, or until the topping is browned lightly and bubbly. Makes 16 hors d'oeuvres.

Chick-Pea and Garlic Spread

a 19-ounce can chick-peas, drained
½ stick (¼ cup) unsalted butter, softened
3 ounces cream cheese, softened
1 garlic clove, minced
3 tablespoons fresh lemon juice
crackers or toasted *pita* triangles as an
   accompaniment

In a food processor purée the chick-peas, add the butter, the cream cheese, the garlic, the lemon juice, and salt and pepper to taste, and blend the mixture until it is smooth. Transfer the spread to a bowl. *The spread may be made up to 1 day in advance and kept covered and chilled.* Serve the spread at room temperature with the crackers. Makes about 2½ cups.

Dilled Clam Dip

6 cherrystone clams or 2½ pounds small hard-
   shelled clams, scrubbed
⅓ cup dry white wine
4 ounces cream cheese, softened
1 garlic clove, cooked in boiling water for
   5 minutes, drained, peeled, and chopped
1 tablespoon fresh lemon juice, or to taste
1 teaspoon grated onion

1 teaspoon Worcestershire sauce
¼ teaspoon Tabasco, or to taste
3 tablespoons snipped fresh dill
celery sticks as an accompaniment

In a large saucepan combine the clams and the wine, bring the wine to a boil, and steam the clams, covered, over moderately high heat, shaking the pan several times, for 6 to 7 minutes, or until the shells have opened and the clams are just firm to the touch. Discard any unopened clams. Transfer the clams with a slotted spoon to a bowl, reserving the cooking liquid, and remove them from the shells. (The shells, separated into halves and cleaned, may be used as individual serving dishes for the dip.) Strain the reserved cooking liquid through a fine sieve lined with a double thickness of rinsed and squeezed cheesecloth into a small bowl.

In a food processor grind coarse the clams, add the cream cheese, the garlic, the lemon juice, the onion, the Worcestershire sauce, the Tabasco, and 1 to 2 tablespoons of the reserved cooking liquid, or to taste, and blend the mixture until the clams are ground fine. Season the dip with salt and pepper, transfer it to a portable container, and stir in the dill. *The dip may be made up to 1 day in advance and kept covered and chilled.* Serve the dip with the celery sticks. Makes about 1¼ cups.

Hot Spiced Cocktail Nut Mix

1 cup roasted salted cashews
1 cup roasted salted peanuts
1 cup raisins
4 cups corn chips
2 cups small oyster crackers
½ stick (¼ cup) unsalted butter
2 garlic cloves, minced and mashed to a paste
2 teaspoons ground cumin
½ teaspoon ground coriander
½ teaspoon cinnamon
½ teaspoon cayenne

In a large bowl combine the cashews, the peanuts, the raisins, the corn chips, and the oyster crackers. In a small skillet melt the butter with the garlic over moderately low heat, stirring, stir in the cumin, the coriander, the cinnamon, and the cayenne, and pour the butter mixture over the nut mixture, tossing the nut mixture to coat it thoroughly. Makes about 8½ cups.

*Hot Crab, Artichoke, and Jalapeño Dip
with Pita Triangles*

1 large green bell pepper, chopped
1 tablespoon vegetable oil
two 14-ounce cans artichoke hearts, drained
    and chopped fine
2 cups bottled mayonnaise
½ cup thinly sliced scallion
½ cup drained and chopped bottled pimiento
    or roasted red pepper
1 cup freshly grated Parmesan
1½ tablespoons fresh lemon juice, or to taste
4 teaspoons Worcestershire sauce, or to taste
3 bottled pickled *jalapeño* peppers, or to taste,
    seeded and minced (wear rubber gloves)
1 teaspoon celery salt
1 pound crab meat, thawed and drained if
    frozen, picked over
⅓ cup sliced almonds, toasted lightly
pita triangles (recipe follows)

In a small heavy skillet cook the bell pepper in the oil over moderate heat, stirring, until it is softened and let it cool. In a large bowl combine the bell pepper, the artichokes, the mayonnaise, the scallion, the pimiento, the Parmesan, the lemon juice, the Worcestershire sauce, the *jalapeño* peppers, and the celery salt, blend the mixture until it is combined well, and stir in the crab meat gently. Transfer the mixture to a buttered ovenproof chafing dish or baking dish and sprinkle it with the almonds. *The dip may be prepared up to this point 1 day in advance and kept covered and chilled.* Bake the dip in a preheated 375° F. oven for 25 to 30 minutes, or until the top is golden and the mixture is bubbly. Serve the dip with the *pita* triangles. Serves 10.

PHOTO ON PAGE 81

Pita Triangles

8 large *pita* loaves
1 stick (½ cup) unsalted butter, melted

Cut each *pita* loaf into 8 wedges and separate each wedge into 2 triangles. Arrange the triangles rough side up in one tight layer in jelly-roll pans, brush them lightly with the butter, and season them lightly with salt. Bake the triangles in the upper third of a preheated 375° F. oven for 10 to 12 minutes, or until they are crisp and light golden, and let them cool in the pans. *The triangles may be made 1 day in advance and kept covered in an airtight container at room temperature.* Makes 128 triangles.

*Crab Claws with
Thousand Island Dipping Sauce and
Tomato Horseradish Dipping Sauce*

¾ pound crab claws
For the Thousand Island dipping sauce
½ cup mayonnaise
½ cup ketchup
½ cup sour cream
1 tablespoon minced onion
1 tablespoon minced fresh parsley leaves
1 tablespoon drained sweet pickle relish
1 teaspoon Worcestershire sauce
cayenne to taste
For the tomato horseradish dipping sauce
1 cup ketchup
2 tablespoons fresh lemon juice
¼ cup drained bottled horseradish
2 tablespoons Worcestershire sauce
¼ teaspoon dried hot red pepper flakes
¼ cup minced fresh parsley leaves
½ cup minced celery
2 scallions, minced

parsley sprigs for garnish

Rinse the crab claws gently to remove any loose pieces of shell, let them drain on paper towels, and chill them, covered, on a platter.

Make the Thousand Island dipping sauce: In a bowl stir together the mayonnaise, the ketchup, the sour cream, the onion, the parsley, the relish, the Worcestershire sauce, and the cayenne until the mixture is combined well, transfer the sauce to a serving bowl, and chill it, covered, for at least 1 hour or up to 24 hours.

Make the tomato horseradish dipping sauce: In another bowl stir together the ketchup, the lemon juice, the horseradish, the Worcestershire sauce, the red pepper flakes, the parsley, the celery, and the scallions until the mixture is combined well, transfer the sauce to a serving bowl, and chill it, covered, for at least 1 hour or up to 24 hours.

Garnish the dipping sauces with the parsley sprigs and serve them with the chilled crab claws. Serves 6 as an hors d'oeuvre.

Crostini
(Assorted Italian Canapés)

a loaf of French bread,
   at least 16 inches long
olive oil for brushing
1 garlic clove, halved
1 red bell pepper, roasted
   (procedure on page 203)
   and chopped fine
½ teaspoon dried rosemary, crumbled
1½ teaspoons balsamic vinegar (available at
   specialty foods shops)
a pinch of cayenne
a ½-pound piece fresh mozzarella, halved
   lengthwise and sliced crosswise into 36
   equal pieces
¼ pound thinly sliced prosciutto, cut into
   18 equal pieces
8 anchovy fillets
chopped fresh parsley leaves
1 tablespoon drained capers

Halve the bread crosswise, cut one half crosswise into eighteen ¼-inch-thick slices, and cut the remaining half diagonally into eighteen ¼-inch-thick slices. Brush one side of each bread slice with oil, bake the slices on baking sheets in a preheated 400° F. oven for 10 minutes, or until they are golden, and rub the diagonally cut slices on both sides with the garlic while they are still warm.

In a small bowl combine the bell pepper, the rosemary, the vinegar, the cayenne, and salt and pepper to taste and toss the mixture well. Top each round toast with a slice of the mozzarella, brush the mozzarella with oil, and top each slice with ½ teaspoon of the bell pepper mixture. Arrange 1 piece of the prosciutto lengthwise on each diagonal toast, covering half the toast, and arrange 1 slice of the remaining mozzarella lengthwise on the other half of each diagonal toast. Arrange an anchovy fillet lengthwise down the middle of 8 of the diagonal toasts and brush the diagonal toasts with oil. *The* crostini *may be prepared up to this point and kept covered with plastic wrap for up to 4 hours.* Bake the *crostini* in batches on baking sheets in a preheated 400° F. oven for 8 to 10 minutes, or until the mozzarella is just melted. Sprinkle the *crostini* with the parsley and top each remaining diagonal *crostini* with 6 or 7 of the capers. Makes 36 hors d'oeuvres.

PHOTO ON PAGE 11

Cucumber Spears with Shrimp and Yogurt
Dipping Sauce

½ cup plain yogurt
¼ pound (about 8) shrimp, shelled and
   deveined
½ teaspoon drained and squeezed dry bottled
   horseradish
¼ teaspoon Worcestershire sauce
1 teaspoon snipped fresh dill
1 dill sprig for garnish
½ seedless cucumber, cut lengthwise into
   8 spears

Drain the yogurt in a fine sieve set over a bowl for 30 minutes. While the yogurt is draining, in a saucepan of boiling salted water boil the shrimp for 2 to 3 minutes, or until they are just firm, and drain them. Reserve 1 shrimp for garnish, chop the remaining shrimp fine, and in a bowl combine well the chopped shrimp, the yogurt, the horseradish, the Worcestershire sauce, the snipped dill, and salt and pepper to taste. Transfer the sauce to a serving dish, garnish it with the reserved shrimp and the dill sprig, and serve it with the cucumber spears. Serves 2.

Cucumber Tea Sandwiches with
Mint Mayonnaise

For the mint mayonnaise
2 large egg yolks
½ teaspoon Dijon-style mustard
2 tablespoons fresh lemon juice plus
   additional to taste
¾ cup loosely packed fresh mint leaves or
   2 tablespoons dried, crumbled
1 cup vegetable oil
16 very thin slices of homemade-type white
   bread, crusts discarded
1 cucumber (about ½ pound), peeled and
   sliced very thin crosswise

Make the mint mayonnaise: In a blender or food processor blend together the egg yolks, the mustard, 2 tablespoons of the lemon juice, and the mint, with the motor running add the oil in a very slow stream, and blend the mixture until it is emulsified. Season the mayonnaise with the additional lemon juice and salt and pepper and transfer it to a bowl.

Spread the mayonnaise generously on one side of

each slice of bread and arrange an even layer of cucumber slices on half the bread slices. Cover the cucumbers with the remaining bread slices and quarter the sandwiches. Makes 32 tea sandwiches.

Ham Cornets with Apple Horseradish Filling

2 Granny Smith apples
1 tablespoon fresh lemon juice
¼ teaspoon salt
1½ tablespoons drained bottled horseradish,
    or to taste
6 tablespoons sour cream
white pepper to taste
8 thin round slices of Black Forest or
    Westphalian ham (about ¼ pound), halved

Peel the apples and grate coarse 1½ of them, reserving the remaining apple half in a small bowl of cold water acidulated with the lemon juice. In a sieve toss the grated apple with the salt, let it drain for 10 minutes, and press it gently to remove some of the excess moisture. In a bowl toss the grated apple with the horseradish, the sour cream, and the white pepper. Cut the reserved apple half lengthwise into 16 thin slices and arrange 1 slice in the center of each half slice of ham so that one end of the apple extends slightly beyond the curved edge of the ham. Spoon about 2 teaspoons of the filling onto each apple slice and roll the ham into cone shapes. Makes 16 cornets.

PHOTO ON PAGE 42

Eggplant-Stuffed Mushrooms

6 large mushrooms (about 6 ounces), stems
    removed and the stems chopped fine
2 tablespoons unsalted butter
1 cup finely chopped peeled eggplant
¼ cup finely chopped onion
2 tablespoons fresh bread crumbs
2 tablespoons freshly grated Parmesan
¼ teaspoon ground cumin

In a heavy skillet cook the mushroom caps in 1 tablespoon of the butter over moderate heat, turning them, for 8 minutes and transfer them stemmed sides down to paper towels to drain. In the skillet cook the chopped stems, the eggplant, and the onion in the remaining 1 tablespoon butter, stirring, for 8 to 10 minutes, or until the vegetables are softened and all the liquid is evaporated. Transfer the mixture to a small bowl and stir in the bread crumbs, the Parmesan, the cumin, and salt and pepper to taste. Divide the filling among the caps, packing it slightly, and bake the mushrooms in a baking pan in a preheated 400° F. oven for 5 minutes. Serves 2 as an hors d'oeuvre.

Fried Okra Rounds

⅓ cup yellow cornmeal
cayenne to taste
½ pound okra, cut into ¼-inch slices,
    discarding the stems and tips
vegetable oil for deep-frying

In a shallow dish combine well the cornmeal, the cayenne, and salt to taste, coat the okra with the cornmeal mixture, tossing it, and shake off the excess cornmeal in a coarse sieve. In a large deep skillet heat 1 inch of the oil to 375° F., in it fry the okra, turning it, for 2 to 3 minutes, or until it is golden, and transfer it with a slotted spoon to paper towels to drain. Serves 2 as an hors d'oeuvre or side dish.

Onion Sandwiches

24 very thin slices of homemade-type
    white bread
about 1 cup mustard mayonnaise
    (recipe follows)
1 large mild white onion, cut crosswise into
    12 thin slices
1 cup minced fresh parsley leaves

With a 2¾-inch round cutter cut out a round from each slice of bread. Spread some of the mayonnaise generously on one side of each round, arrange a slice of onion on half the rounds, and sprinkle the onion with salt to taste. Cover the onion with the remaining rounds of bread, spread a thin layer of the remaining mayonnaise around the edges of the sandwiches, and roll the edges in the parsley. Transfer the sandwiches, covered with a dampened paper towel and plastic wrap, to a portable container. *The sandwiches may be made up to 6 hours in advance and kept wrapped well and chilled.* Makes 12 sandwiches.

PHOTO ON PAGE 51

Mustard Mayonnaise

2 large egg yolks at room temperature
4 teaspoons fresh lemon juice plus additional
    to taste
2 tablespoons Dijon-style mustard plus
    additional to taste
½ teaspoon salt plus additional to taste
1½ cups vegetable oil

In a bowl with an electric mixer or a whisk beat together the egg yolks, 4 teaspoons of the lemon juice, 2 tablespoons of the mustard, and ½ teaspoon of the salt and add ½ cup of the oil, drop by drop, beating constantly. Add the remaining 1 cup oil in a slow stream, beating constantly, and beat the mayonnaise until it is emulsified. Season the mayonnaise with the additional lemon juice, mustard, and salt. *The mayonnaise may be made up to 3 days in advance and kept covered and chilled.* Makes about 1⅔ cups.

Pastry Seashells with Salmon Roe

¾ stick (6 tablespoons) cold unsalted butter,
    cut into bits
4 ounces cold cream cheese, cut into bits
1 cup all-purpose flour
½ teaspoon salt
two 1-pound containers plain yogurt
5 ounces salmon roe
small dill sprigs for garnish

In a food processor blend the butter, the cream cheese, the flour, and the salt until the mixture forms a ball of dough. Flatten the ball and chill it, wrapped in wax paper, for 1 hour. Press small pieces of the dough into 1⅝-inch *madeleine* molds or other shell molds of the same size, pressing the dough as thin as possible and trimming away any excess dough around the edges. Chill the shells for 10 minutes, press a 2-inch square of foil into each mold to weight the dough, and bake the shells on a baking sheet in a preheated 375° F. oven for 10 to 12 minutes, or until they are pale golden. (If the dough is not pressed into the molds evenly some may brown faster than others.) Remove the shells from the molds, transfer them to racks, and let them cool. *The shells may be made in advance and kept in an airtight container for up to 2 days or frozen for several weeks.*

In the refrigerator let the yogurt drain through a sieve lined with a double thickness of rinsed and squeezed cheesecloth set over a bowl, covered with plastic wrap directly on the surface of the yogurt, for 2 days. Transfer the yogurt to a bowl and discard the liquid.

Just before serving, in each of half the shells put about ½ teaspoon of the yogurt, add about ¼ teaspoon of the roe and 1 of the dill sprigs, and top the filling with a second shell. Makes about 50 to 60 hors d'oeuvres.

PHOTO ON PAGE 31

Pears with Ham and Walnut Cream Cheese Filling

3 large firm ripe pears
¾ cup plus 2 teaspoons fresh lemon juice
1 cup chopped cooked ham
6 tablespoons thinly sliced scallion greens
½ cup walnuts, toasted lightly and chopped
½ cup cream cheese, softened

Peel the pears, halve them lengthwise, and core them, dropping them as they are cored into a bowl of ice and cold water acidulated with ¼ cup of the lemon juice. Transfer the pears with a slotted spoon, reserving the water, to a large saucepan of simmering water acidulated with ¼ cup of the remaining lemon juice and poach them for 2 to 3 minutes, or until they are just tender. Return the pears to the reserved bowl of acidulated water, let them cool for 5 minutes, and drain them. Brush the pears with ¼ cup of the remaining lemon juice and let them drain on paper towels.

In a bowl stir together the ham, the scallion greens, the walnuts, the cream cheese, and the remaining 2 teaspoons lemon juice, fill the pears with the mixture, mounding it, and broil them on the rack of a broiler pan under a preheated broiler about 4 inches from the heat for 3 to 4 minutes. Serves 6 as a first course.

Prosciutto Radish Toasts

about 2 tablespoons unsalted butter, softened
4 thin diagonal slices of French or Italian
    bread, toasted lightly and cooled
freshly ground pepper to taste
5 radishes, sliced paper thin
4 thin slices of prosciutto

Spread the butter on the toasts and sprinkle it with the pepper and salt to taste. Reserving 12 radish slices, cover the toasts with the remaining radish slices, arrange the prosciutto decoratively on them, and top each toast with 3 of the reserved radish slices. Makes 4 toasts.

PHOTO ON PAGE 54

Radish- and Celery-Stuffed Endive Leaves

¾ cup finely diced radish
¾ cup finely diced celery
4 tablespoons cottage cheese, puréed or forced
    through a fine sieve
1 teaspoon fresh lemon juice, or to taste
¼ teaspoon freshly ground white pepper, or to
    taste
30 Belgian endive leaves (separated from
    3 large Belgian endives)
30 watercress sprigs

In a bowl combine the radish, the celery, the cottage cheese, the lemon juice, and the white pepper and blend the mixture until it is combined well. *The mixture may be made 1 day in advance and kept covered and chilled.* Season the mixture with salt and fill the lower third of each endive leaf with a heaping teaspoon of it. Tuck 1 watercress sprig into the mixture on each leaf and arrange the leaves on a platter. Makes 30 hors d'oeuvres.

PHOTO ON PAGE 80

Radish and Parsley Butter Wreaths

1 stick (½ cup) unsalted butter, softened
½ cup packed fresh parsley leaves
8 large radishes, scrubbed
dill sprigs for garnish

In a food processor or blender blend the butter, the parsley, and salt to taste until the mixture is smooth and transfer the parsley butter to a pastry bag fitted with a ¼-inch star tip. Halve the radishes crosswise and trim the ends evenly so that the radishes stand upright on the trimmed ends. Pipe the parsley butter around the top of each radish half and chill the "wreaths," covered loosely, for 30 minutes, or until the butter is firm. *The wreaths may be made up to 6 hours in advance and kept covered loosely and chilled.* Transfer the wreaths to a platter and garnish the platter with "garlands" of the dill. Makes 16 hors d'oeuvres.

PHOTO ON PAGE 76

Herbed Ricotta Pine Nut Spread

½ cup whole-milk ricotta
1 small garlic clove, minced
3 tablespoons minced fresh parsley leaves
2 teaspoons minced onion
2 teaspoons fresh lemon juice
2 tablespoons pine nuts, toasted lightly and
    chopped coarse
toast points or crackers as an accompaniment

In a bowl combine well the ricotta, the garlic, the parsley, the onion, the lemon juice, and salt and pepper to taste and chill the mixture, covered, for 30 minutes. Stir in the pine nuts and serve the spread with the toast points. Serves 2 as an hors d'oeuvre.

Sardine Caper Spread

a 3¾-ounce can sardines packed in oil,
    drained
1½ ounces cream cheese, softened
1 tablespoon drained capers
½ teaspoon fresh lemon juice, or to taste
crackers or toast points as an accompaniment

In a bowl with a fork mash together the sardines, the cream cheese, the capers, the lemon juice, and pepper to taste. Serve the spread with the crackers. Makes about ½ cup, serving 2.

©HELEN FEDERICO '86

Sausage and Mushroom Phyllo Twists

½ pound pork sausage meat, crumbled
1 small onion, minced
1 garlic clove, minced
1 tablespoon unsalted butter
½ pound mushrooms, chopped fine
½ teaspoon ground cumin
a pinch of allspice
½ teaspoon dried mint,
    crumbled
¼ cup minced fresh parsley leaves
2 ounces cream cheese, softened
four 16- by 12-inch sheets of *phyllo*, stacked
    between 2 sheets of wax paper and covered
    with a dampened dish towel
¼ cup clarified butter (procedure follows)
2 tablespoons fine fresh bread crumbs

In a large skillet cook the sausage meat over moderately high heat, stirring and breaking up any large pieces, until it is cooked through and browned, transfer it to a fine sieve, and let it drain. In the skillet cook the onion and the garlic in the unsalted butter over moderately low heat until the onion is softened, add the mushrooms, and cook the mixture over moderate heat, stirring until the liquid the mushrooms give off evaporates. Add the cumin, the allspice, and the mint and cook the mixture, stirring, for 2 minutes. Transfer the mixture to a bowl, add the sausage meat, the parsley, the cream cheese, and salt and pepper to taste, and combine the mixture well.

Working quickly to keep the *phyllo* from drying out, put 1 sheet of *phyllo* on a work surface, brush it lightly with some of the clarified butter, and sprinkle it with 1 tablespoon of the bread crumbs. Lay another sheet of *phyllo* on top of the first sheet and brush it lightly with some of the remaining clarified butter. Cut the sheets into thirds lengthwise and into quarters crosswise to form 12 squares. Put a rounded teaspoon of the filling in each square, gather the corners of the *phyllo* over the filling, and twist the *phyllo* gently to seal it. Continue to make hors d'oeuvres in the same manner with the remaining *phyllo*, butter, crumbs, and filling. Bake the sausage and mushroom *phyllo* twists in jelly-roll pans in a preheated 400° F. oven for 10 to 12 minutes, or until the *phyllo* is golden brown. Arrange the twists decoratively on a serving platter. Makes 24 hors d'oeuvres.

PHOTO ON PAGE 30

To Clarify Butter

unsalted butter, cut into 1-inch pieces

In a heavy saucepan melt the butter over low heat. Remove the pan from the heat, let the butter stand for 3 minutes, and skim the froth. Strain the butter through a sieve lined with a double thickness of rinsed and squeezed cheesecloth into a bowl, leaving the milky solids in the bottom of the pan. Pour the clarified butter into a jar or crock and store it, covered, in the refrigerator. The butter keeps indefinitely, covered and chilled. When clarified, butter loses about one fourth of its original volume.

Scallops in Saffron Mayonnaise

1 pound sea scallops, cut horizontally into
    ⅓-inch rounds, rinsed, and drained
1 cup plus 1 tablespoon olive oil
⅛ teaspoon saffron threads, crumbled
1 large egg at room temperature
5 teaspoons fresh lemon juice
1 teaspoon Dijon-style mustard
¼ teaspoon salt
¼ teaspoon white pepper
about 3 heads of Bibb lettuce or other small-
    leafed lettuce, separated into leaves,
    washed, and spun dry
1 small carrot, cut into fine julienne strips
1 small bunch of chives, cut into 1-inch pieces

In a large skillet cook the scallops in 1 tablespoon of the oil, covered, over moderately high heat, shaking the skillet occasionally, for 2 to 3 minutes, or until they are just cooked through. Let the scallops cool in a bowl, covered loosely.

In a small bowl combine the saffron with 2 teaspoons hot water. In a blender or food processor blend together the egg, the lemon juice, the mustard, the salt, and the pepper, with the motor running add the remaining 1 cup oil in a slow stream, and blend the mayonnaise until it is emulsified. Stir in the saffron mixture and salt to taste.

Dip each scallop round, patted dry, into the saffron mayonnaise, coating it well, arrange it on a lettuce leaf, and garnish each hors d'oeuvre with some of the carrot and chives. (Any remaining saffron mayonnaise may be used as a dipping sauce for vegetables.) Makes about 24 hors d'oeuvres.

PHOTO ON PAGE 31

Shrimp and Avocado Tortilla Rounds

1 pound (about 25) medium shrimp
2 ripe avocados
1 teaspoon salt
cayenne to taste
2½ tablespoons fresh lemon juice, or to taste
½ cup seeded and chopped cherry tomatoes
about 50 round corn tortilla chips
about 50 flat-leafed parsley leaves for garnish
   if desired

Fill a skillet with enough salted water to reach ½ inch up the side and bring the water to a boil. Add the shrimp and simmer them, covered, shaking the skillet occasionally, for 1 to 2 minutes, or until they are pink and just firm. Transfer the shrimp with a slotted spoon to a bowl of ice and cold water, discard the shells, and halve the shrimp lengthwise, deveining them. *The shrimp may be prepared up to 1 day in advance and kept covered and chilled.*

Peel and pit the avocados and in a bowl mash them with a fork. Add the salt, the cayenne, the lemon juice, and the tomatoes and combine the mixture well.

Just before serving spread the tortilla chips with the avocado mixture, top the mixture with half a shrimp, and garnish each hors d'oeuvre with 1 of the parsley leaves if desired. Makes about 50 hors d'oeuvres.

Smoked Salmon Christmas Trees

½ pound thinly sliced smoked salmon
10 very thin slices of whole-wheat bread
3 tablespoons unsalted butter, softened
about 1 tablespoon drained capers
1 small white onion, halved and sliced thin
   lengthwise
dill sprigs for garnish

Arrange the salmon slices, overlapping them slightly, on a cutting board and with a 3¼-inch metal Christmas tree cutter cut out 10 trees, using a small sharp knife if necessary to aid in the cutting. With the cutter cut out 10 trees from the bread, spread the bread with the butter, and sprinkle the butter with pepper to taste. Top each bread "tree" carefully with a salmon "tree" and garnish the trees with caper "ornaments" and onion "icicles." *The trees may be made up to 6 hours in advance and kept covered and chilled.* Transfer the trees to a platter and garnish the platter with "garlands" of the dill. Makes 10 hors d'oeuvres.

PHOTO ON PAGE 76

Smoked Trout Rillettes

two ½-pound whole smoked rainbow trout,
   boned and head, tail, and skin discarded
1 stick (½ cup) unsalted butter at room
   temperature
2 tablespoons fresh lemon juice, or to taste
white pepper to taste
crackers or toast points as an accompaniment

Flake the trout into the container of a food processor, being very careful to remove any remaining small bones, add the butter, and blend the mixture until it is smooth. Add the lemon juice, the pepper, and salt to taste and blend the mixture until it is combined well. Transfer the mixture to a serving bowl or terrine, smooth the top, and chill the *rillettes*, covered, for at least 1 hour or overnight. Serve the *rillettes* with the crackers. Makes about 2 cups.

Sweet Potato Chips

4 (about 3 pounds) sweet potatoes or yams,
   peeled
vegetable shortening for deep-frying
coarse salt to taste

With a *mandoline* or knife cut the potatoes into ¹⁄₁₆-inch slices and pat them dry with paper towels. In a deep fryer heat enough shortening to measure 2 inches to 380° F. and in it fry the potato slices in batches, turning them, until they are golden brown. Transfer the chips with a slotted spoon to paper towels to drain and sprinkle them with the salt. Makes about 16 cups.

Tapenade Toasts

For the tapenade

¼ pound (⅔ cup) Niçoise or Kalamata olives
(available at specialty foods shops and
many supermarkets)
3 flat anchovy fillets plus 1 teaspoon of the oil
1 tablespoon drained capers
1 tablespoon olive oil

6 thin slices of French or Italian bread,
toasted lightly
2 hard-boiled quail eggs (procedure follows)
or 1 hard-boiled egg, sliced, for garnish
if desired

Make the *tapenade*: With the flat side of a heavy knife crush the olives lightly, discard the pits, and in a food processor purée the olives with the anchovies, the anchovy oil, the capers, and the olive oil, scraping down the sides often. *The* tapenade *may be made up to 5 days in advance and kept covered and chilled.*

Spread some of the *tapenade* on each slice of toast and garnish each toast with a slice of quail egg if desired. Makes 6 toasts.

PHOTO ON PAGE 54

To Hard-Boil Quail Eggs

quail eggs

In a small saucepan cover the eggs with cold water, bring the water just to a boil, and simmer the eggs for 5 minutes. Pour off the water, add cold water to the pan, and let the eggs stand until they can be handled. Shell the eggs carefully.

Tea Sandwiches in a Bread Basket

a 2½-pound round loaf of white bread, about 8
inches in diameter, preferably homemade
(recipe follows)
For the curried chicken sandwiches
2 teaspoons curry powder
2 teaspoons vegetable oil
¼ teaspoon firmly packed light brown sugar
2 teaspoons cider vinegar
1 cup minced cooked chicken
¼ cup minced celery
½ cup plus 1 tablespoon mayonnaise
(page 200)
3 tablespoons minced fresh coriander
*For the smoked salmon and cucumber
sandwiches*
1¼ sticks (10 tablespoons) unsalted butter,
softened
2 tablespoons snipped fresh dill
2 teaspoons fresh lemon juice
1 cup thinly sliced cucumber
¼ pound thinly sliced smoked salmon

watercress sprigs for garnish
cucumber rose (procedure on page 95) for
garnish if desired

On a work surface insert the tip of a sharp thin long knife into the side of the bread just above the bottom crust and push the knife into the bread until it reaches but does not pierce the opposite side. Without enlarging the slit through which the knife was inserted, work the sharp edge of the knife as far to one side as possible, remove it, and turning the blade to the other side reinsert it into the slit. Work the knife as far to the other side as possible, remove it, and repeat the procedure from the opposite side of the bread through a second slit. About 3 inches from the bottom of the bread cut off the top and reserve it for another use if desired. With a sharp thin long knife held with the tip straight down cut around the circumference of the bread about ¼ inch inside the side crust until the knife reaches but does not pierce the bottom crust. Ease out gently with your hands the center piece of bread in one piece, halve it, cutting downward, and freeze the halves, wrapped tightly in foil or plastic wrap, for at least 1 hour or up to 2 hours (this makes the bread easier to slice). Reserve the bread shell, wrapped. Lay 1 of the bread halves curved side up on a work surface and with a serrated knife cut it carefully into 8 thin slices. Repeat the procedure with the second half of the bread.

Make the curried chicken sandwiches: In a small skillet cook the curry powder in the oil over moderately low heat, stirring, for 3 minutes, stir in the brown sugar and the vinegar, and let the mixture cool to lukewarm. In a bowl toss together the chicken, the celery, the curry mixture, ½ cup of the mayonnaise, 1 tablespoon of the coriander, and salt and pepper to taste. *The chicken filling may be made up to 1 day in advance and kept cov-*

ered and chilled. Spread about ⅓ cup of the chicken filling on each of 4 slices of the bread and press 4 more slices of the bread on top of the filling. Cut each sandwich into 4 wedges, spread the remaining 1 tablespoon mayonnaise on the curved edges, and dip the curved edges in the remaining 2 tablespoons coriander.

Make the smoked salmon cucumber sandwiches: In a small bowl cream the butter with the dill, the lemon juice, and salt and pepper to taste. *The dill butter may be made up to 1 day in advance, kept covered and chilled, and softened before using*. Spread one side of the remaining 8 slices of bread with the dill butter, on 4 of the buttered slices arrange the cucumber in one layer, overlapping it slightly, and top it with the smoked salmon. Press the remaining 4 slices bread on top of the salmon and cut each sandwich into 4 wedges.

Arrange the sandwiches decoratively in the reserved bread shell and garnish the center of the basket with the watercress and the cucumber rose if desired. Makes 32 tea sandwiches.

PHOTO ON PAGE 40

Round Sandwich Loaf

2½ teaspoons (a ¼-ounce package) active
  dry yeast
3 tablespoons sugar
1 cup milk plus additional for brushing
  the loaf
2½ teaspoons salt
2 tablespoons unsalted butter
5 to 6 cups all-purpose flour

In a small bowl proof the yeast with a pinch of the sugar in ¼ cup lukewarm water for 15 minutes, or until the mixture is foamy. In a saucepan heat 1 cup of the milk with the remaining sugar, the salt, the butter, and ¾ cup water over moderate heat, stirring, until the sugar and the salt are dissolved and let the mixture cool to lukewarm. In a large bowl combine the yeast mixture with the milk mixture, add 2 cups of the flour, and whisk the mixture until it is smooth. Stir in enough of the remaining flour to form a soft but not sticky dough and knead the dough on a floured surface for 8 to 10 minutes, or until it is smooth and elastic. Put the dough in a buttered bowl, turn it to coat it with the butter, and let it rise, covered with plastic wrap, in a warm place for 1 hour and 15 minutes, or until it is double in bulk. Punch down the dough, knead it on a floured surface for

20 seconds, and fit it into a buttered 8- by 2-inch springform pan. Let the dough rise, covered loosely with plastic wrap, in a warm place for 30 minutes, or until it just rises above the rim of the pan. Brush the dough lightly with the additional milk and bake it in a preheated 400° F. oven for 30 minutes. Remove the bread from the pan, put it on a baking sheet, and bake it for 5 minutes, or until it sounds hollow when tapped. Let the bread cool completely on a rack before slicing. Makes a 2½-pound round loaf.

PHOTO ON PAGE 40

To Make a Cucumber Rose

8 to 10 paper-thin seedless cucumber slices

Cut a slit in each cucumber slice, beginning at the center and cutting through the edge, and pull the cut sides of the slits together, overlapping them to form cones. Pull 1 cone together tightly to form the center of the rose and build the rest of the rose by wrapping looser and looser cones around the center one until all the slices have been used. (The natural moisture of the cucumber will hold the rose together.)

PHOTO ON PAGE 40

Three-Mushroom Tart

pâte brisée (page 222)
raw rice for weighting the shell
1 ounce dried *porcini* mushrooms (available at
    specialty foods shops)
½ cup Sercial Madeira
1 cup finely chopped onion
3 tablespoons unsalted butter
1 pound fresh cultivated mushrooms,
    chopped fine
1½ teaspoons dried thyme, crumbled
4 ounces cream cheese
2 large eggs, beaten lightly
½ cup milk
½ package *enoki-dake* mushrooms (available
    at some supermarkets and specialty produce
    markets), the bottom ½ inch cut off and
    discarded, for garnish
fresh lemon juice for brushing the *enoki-dake*
    mushrooms
chives or scallion greens cut into long julienne
    strips for garnish

Roll the dough into a round ⅛ inch thick on a floured surface and fit it into a 10-inch tart pan with a removable fluted rim. Prick the bottom of the shell lightly and chill the shell for 1 hour. Line the shell with wax paper, fill the paper with the rice, and bake the shell in the lower third of a preheated 400° F. oven for 15 minutes. Remove the rice and paper carefully and bake the shell for 5 minutes more, or until it is pale golden.

In a small saucepan combine the *porcini*, the Madeira, and ½ cup cold water and heat the mixture over moderate heat until it is hot. Remove the pan from the heat and let the mixture stand, covered, for at least 1 hour, or until the *porcini* are softened. Drain the *porcini*, reserving the liquid, and strain the reserved liquid through a fine sieve, lined with a double thickness of rinsed and squeezed cheesecloth, into a bowl. Rinse the *porcini* to remove any grit and chop them fine.

In a large skillet cook the onion in the butter over moderately low heat, stirring, until it is softened, add the fresh cultivated mushrooms, and cook the mixture, stirring, until the liquid the mushrooms give off is evaporated. Add the *porcini*, the thyme, and the reserved liquid and cook the mixture, stirring, until the liquid is evaporated. Add the cream cheese and salt and pepper to taste, cook the mixture, stirring, until the cream cheese is melted, and let it cool. Stir in the eggs and the milk and pour the mixture into the tart shell. Arrange half the *enoki-dake* decoratively along the edge of the tart, brush them with the lemon juice, and bake the tart in a preheated 350° F. oven for 20 minutes. Arrange the remaining *enoki-dake* decoratively on top of the baked *enoki-dake*, brush them with the lemon juice, and bake the tart for 10 to 15 minutes more, or until a tester comes out clean. Let the tart cool in the pan on a rack for 10 minutes and remove the rim carefully. Transfer the tart to a platter and garnish it with the chives. Serves 12 as an hors d'oeuvre.

Steamed Vegetables

assorted small vegetables such as asparagus
    tips, *haricots verts*, beets, carrots, eggplant,
    summer squash, pattypan squash, zucchini,
    turnips, scallions, sugar snap peas, and
    small red potatoes (larger vegetables, cut
    into pieces, may be used as well)
Kalamata dipping sauce (recipe follows)
chipotle dipping sauce (page 97)

Trim, scrub, and cut the vegetables, if necessary, into similar sizes. Arrange the vegetables, salted lightly, on a steaming rack set in a kettle over boiling water and steam them, covered, until they are just tender. Transfer the vegetables with a slotted spoon as they are cooked to a bowl of ice and cold water. (The cooking times for the vegetables will vary from 1 to 2 minutes for the scallions and peas to 8 to 10 minutes for the beets and potatoes.) Drain the vegetables, pat them dry, and arrange them on a platter. Serve the vegetables at room temperature with the dipping sauces.

PHOTO ON PAGE 29

Kalamata Dipping Sauce

2 large egg yolks at room temperature
2 teaspoons red-wine vinegar
1 teaspoon Dijon-style mustard
¼ teaspoon salt
1½ cups olive oil
⅓ cup minced Kalamata or other brine-cured
    olives
3 teaspoons fresh lemon juice, or to taste
½ cup sour cream

In a bowl with an electric mixer or a whisk beat together the egg yolks, the vinegar, the mustard, and the salt, add ½ cup of the oil, drop by drop, beating, and add the remaining 1 cup oil in a stream, beating until the

mixture is emulsified. Stir in the olives, the lemon juice, the sour cream, and pepper to taste and chill the dipping sauce, covered, for at least 1 hour or overnight. Makes about 2½ cups.

PHOTO ON PAGE 29

Chipotle Dipping Sauce

2 large egg yolks at room temperature
2 teaspoons white-wine vinegar
1 teaspoon Dijon-style mustard
¼ teaspoon salt
1½ cups olive or vegetable oil or a
　combination of the two
3 canned *chipotle* chilies (available at
　Hispanic markets and some specialty foods
　shops), or to taste, minced (wear rubber
　gloves) plus 3 teaspoons of the juice, or to taste
2 teaspoons fresh lemon juice
½ cup sour cream

In a bowl with an electric mixer or a whisk beat together the egg yolks, the vinegar, the mustard, and the salt, add ½ cup of the oil, drop by drop, beating, and add the remaining 1 cup oil in a stream, beating until the mixture is emulsified. Stir in the chilies with the juice, the lemon juice, and the sour cream and chill the dipping sauce, covered, for at least 1 hour or overnight. Makes about 2¼ cups.

PHOTO ON PAGE 29

Layered Walnut Yogurt Terrine

two 1-pound containers plain yogurt
1 envelope unflavored gelatin
½ cup *crème fraîche** or heavy cream
2 teaspoons salt
3 tablespoons walnut oil*
white pepper to taste
⅓ cup plus 1 tablespoon minced scallion
　including the green part
⅓ cup plus 1 tablespoon peeled, seeded, and
　minced tomato
1 tablespoon minced walnuts
toasted French bread rounds as an accompaniment

*available at specialty foods shops

In a large sieve lined with a double thickness of rinsed and squeezed cheesecloth and set over a bowl let the yogurt drain, covered and chilled, for 8 hours and transfer it to a large bowl. In a small bowl let the gelatin soften in ¼ cup cold water for 10 minutes. In a saucepan combine the gelatin mixture with the *crème fraîche* and the salt, heat the mixture over moderately low heat, stirring, until the gelatin is just dissolved, and add it with the oil and the white pepper to the yogurt, stirring until the mixture is combined well. Line a loaf pan, 7½ by 3½ (across the top) by 2 inches, with enough plastic wrap to extend about 2 inches over the long sides, spread one third of the yogurt mixture in the pan, and sprinkle it with ⅓ cup of the scallion. Spread half the remaining yogurt mixture over the scallion, sprinkle it with ⅓ cup of the tomato, and spread the remaining yogurt mixture over the tomato. Cover the terrine with the overhanging plastic wrap and chill it for 3 hours, or until it is firm enough to be unmolded. *The yogurt terrine may be made up to this point 2 days in advance and kept covered and chilled.* Invert the terrine onto a platter, discard the plastic wrap, and garnish the terrine by sprinkling lengthwise in 3 separate bands the remaining tablespoon scallion, the remaining tablespoon tomato, and the walnuts. Serve the terrine at room temperature with the toasted French bread rounds. Serves 6 to 8.

PHOTO ON PAGE 42

Sugar-Crisp Walnuts

3 cups walnut halves
⅓ cup sugar
4 cups peanut oil

In a kettle cover the walnuts with 4 inches of water, bring the water to a boil, and boil the walnuts for 7 minutes. Drain the walnuts in a colander and refresh them under cold water until they are completely cold. Drain the walnuts well and pat them dry with paper towels. In a wok or heavy skillet combine the sugar and ⅓ cup water, bring the mixture to a boil, stirring constantly, and boil the syrup for 1 minute. Add the walnuts and cook them over high heat, stirring constantly, for 3 minutes, or until the liquid is evaporated and the walnuts are glazed. Let the walnuts cool in one layer on jelly-roll pans. Wash and dry the wok, add the oil, and heat it over moderately high heat to 380° F. In the oil fry the walnuts in 2 batches, stirring, for 4 minutes, or until they are browned, transferring them with a slotted spoon as they are fried to a marble surface or jelly-roll pans in one layer, and let them cool completely. The walnuts keep for up to 1 week in an airtight container in a cool, dry place. Makes 3 cups.

BREADS

YEAST BREADS

Caraway Rye Breadsticks

a ¼-ounce package quick-rise yeast (available
   at most supermarkets)
1 teaspoon sugar
1 teaspoon table salt
¾ cup rye flour
2 tablespoons olive oil plus additional for
   brushing the dough
about 2¼ cups all-purpose flour
an egg wash made by beating 1 egg with 1
   tablespoon water
caraway seeds and coarse salt for sprinkling
   the breadsticks

In a food processor combine the yeast, the sugar, the
table salt, and the rye flour and pulse the motor several
times to blend the mixture. With the motor running add
1 cup hot water (125° to 130° F.) and 2 tablespoons of
the oil and turn the motor off. Add 2 cups of the all-purpose flour and blend the mixture until a ball of dough
forms, adding additional all-purpose flour, 1 tablespoon at a time, if the dough seems wet or warm water,
1 tablespoon at a time, if the mixture does not gather
into a ball. Blend the dough in the processor for 10 seconds, turn it out onto a floured surface, and knead it for
3 minutes. Pat the dough into a 16- by 6-inch rectangle
on a lightly oiled surface, brush the top of the dough
with some of the additional oil, and let the dough rise,
covered loosely with plastic wrap, in a warm place for
30 minutes. Cut the dough crosswise into 4 strips and
cut each strip crosswise into 12 strips. Keeping the remaining strips covered loosely with plastic wrap, roll
1 strip between your hands into roughly a 12- to 14-inch
rope (about ⅛ to ¼ inch thick) and lay it across a lightly
oiled baking sheet. Make breadsticks with the remaining strips in the same manner, arranging them
1 inch apart on lightly oiled baking sheets. Brush the
breadsticks with the egg wash and sprinkle them with

the caraway seeds and the coarse salt. Bake the breadsticks in batches in a preheated 400° F. oven for 15 minutes, or until they are golden and crisp, and let them cool
on racks. *The breadsticks may be made up to 2 days
in advance and kept in airtight containers.* Makes
48 breadsticks.

Cinnamon Toast Rolls

¼ cup sugar
2 teaspoons cinnamon
twelve ⅜-inch-thick slices of very fresh
   homemade-type white bread, crusts
   discarded
½ stick (¼ cup) unsalted butter

In a bowl stir together well the sugar and the cinnamon. Roll out the bread ¼ inch thick between pieces of
wax paper and brush both sides of each slice with some
of the butter. Sprinkle 1 teaspoon of the cinnamon sugar
on one side of each slice, roll the bread tightly jelly-roll
fashion, beginning with a long side, and trim the ends
on the diagonal. *The rolls may be made up to this point
1 week in advance and kept wrapped tightly and frozen.*
Transfer the rolls seam side down to a baking sheet and
bake them in a preheated 350° F. oven for 15 minutes, or
until they are browned lightly. Makes 12 rolls.

PHOTO ON PAGE 43

Quick Cloverleaf Rolls

a ¼-ounce package quick-rise yeast (available
   at most supermarkets)
1 tablespoon sugar
about 3 cups all-purpose flour
¾ stick (6 tablespoons) unsalted butter
⅔ cup milk
1 large egg
1½ teaspoons salt
an egg wash made by beating 1 egg with
   1 tablespoon water

In a food processor combine the yeast, the sugar, and 1 cup of the flour and pulse the motor several times to blend the mixture. In a small saucepan melt 4 tablespoons of the butter, cut into pieces, add the milk, and heat the mixture over moderately low heat until it is 125° to 130° F. With the motor running add the milk mixture to the flour mixture, turn the motor off, and add the remaining 2 cups flour, the egg, and the salt. Blend the mixture until a ball of dough forms, adding additional flour, 1 tablespoon at a time, if the dough seems wet, or warm water, 1 tablespoon at a time, if the mixture does not gather into a ball. Blend the dough in the processor for 10 seconds, turn it out onto a floured surface, and knead it for 3 minutes. Transfer the dough to a buttered bowl and turn it to coat it with the butter. Let the dough rise, covered with plastic wrap, in a warm place for 30 minutes, or until it is double in bulk, and punch it down. Form the dough into 1-inch balls, dipping the balls as they are formed into the remaining 2 tablespoons butter, melted, and arrange the balls, buttered side up, in buttered ⅓-cup muffin tins, putting 3 balls in each tin. Let the rolls rise in a warm place for 15 minutes, brush them with the egg wash, being careful not to let it drip down the sides, and bake them in a preheated 400° F. oven for 15 to 20 minutes, or until they are golden. *The rolls may be made up to 1 day in advance and kept wrapped well in foil at room temperature. Reheat the rolls, wrapped in the foil, in a preheated 375° F. oven for 15 to 20 minutes, or until they are hot.* Makes about 12 rolls.

PHOTO ON PAGE 21

Onion and Black Pepper Flatbread

1¼ cups chopped onion
2 tablespoons olive oil plus 4 teaspoons
  additional for drizzling the dough
2½ cups all-purpose flour
2½ teaspoons (a ¼-ounce package) fast-acting
  yeast
¾ teaspoon table salt
¾ teaspoon coarsely ground pepper plus
  additional for sprinkling the dough
½ teaspoon kosher salt, or to taste

In a skillet cook 1 cup of the onion in 1 tablespoon of the oil over moderate heat, stirring occasionally, until it is golden. In a food processor combine 1 cup of the flour and the yeast, with the motor running add ¾ cup hot water (125° to 130° F.) combined with 1 tablespoon of the remaining oil, and turn the motor off. Add 1¼ cups of the remaining flour, the table salt, and ¾ teaspoon of the pepper and pulse the motor 4 times. Add the cooked onion and blend the dough until it forms a ball, incorporating more of the remaining flour if necessary, 1 tablespoon at a time, pulsing the motor until the flour is incorporated, to keep the dough from sticking. Transfer the dough to a lightly floured surface and knead it for 15 seconds. Quarter the dough, form each piece into a ¼-inch-thick round, and put the rounds on a lightly oiled baking sheet. With a finger, press indentations firmly into the dough at 2-inch intervals, drizzle the dough with the additional 4 teaspoons oil, and sprinkle it with the remaining ¼ cup onion, the additional pepper, and the kosher salt. Bake the bread in a preheated 500° F. oven for 15 to 18 minutes, or until it is golden. The bread may be kept, wrapped well, at room temperature for up to 24 hours. Makes four 5-inch breads.

Parmesan Scallion Pretzels

1 to 1½ cups all-purpose flour
½ teaspoon quick-rise yeast (available at most
  supermarkets)
½ teaspoon olive oil
1 large egg, beaten lightly with 1 tablespoon
  water
3 tablespoons freshly grated Parmesan
¼ cup thinly sliced scallion greens
kosher salt to taste

In a food processor blend ½ cup of the flour and the yeast, with the motor running add ⅓ cup hot water (125° to 130° F.), and turn the motor off. Add ½ cup of the remaining flour, the oil, 1 teaspoon of the egg mixture, the Parmesan, and the scallion and blend the mixture until it just forms a ball. Let the dough rise in the processor bowl in a warm place for 15 minutes. On a floured surface knead in enough of the remaining flour to make a smooth and elastic dough. Roll the dough into a 12- by 4-inch rectangle and with a pizza cutter or knife cut it lengthwise into 16 strips. Roll the strips gently to form ropes and on buttered baking sheets form the ropes into pretzel shapes. Brush the pretzels with some of the remaining egg mixture, sprinkle them liberally with the salt, and bake them in a preheated 400° F. oven for 12 to 15 minutes, or until they are golden. Transfer the pretzels to a rack and let them cool. The pretzels keep in an airtight container in a cool, dry place for up to 2 weeks. Makes 16 pretzels.

QUICK BREADS

Corn Bread Thins

¼ cup yellow cornmeal
¼ cup all-purpose flour
¾ teaspoon double-acting baking powder
½ teaspoon sugar
½ teaspoon salt
1 large egg, beaten lightly
6 tablespoons milk
1 tablespoon softened vegetable shortening
¼ cup sour cream
bottled roasted red bell pepper, cut into
   julienne strips, for garnish

In a bowl stir together the cornmeal, the flour, the baking powder, the sugar, and the salt, stir in the egg, the milk, and the shortening, and stir the mixture until it is combined. Spread the mixture in an even layer in a greased 9-inch round cake pan and bake it in the middle of a preheated 450° F. oven for 15 to 20 minutes, or until the top is golden. Invert the corn bread onto a cutting board and cut it into wedges. Top each wedge with a dollop of the sour cream and garnish the sour cream with the bell pepper strips. Serves 6.

PHOTO ON PAGE 46

Miniature Gingerbread Muffins

1 cup plus 2 tablespoons cake flour
   (not self-rising)
½ teaspoon double-acting baking powder
¼ teaspoon baking soda
¼ teaspoon salt
1 teaspoon ground ginger
½ stick (¼ cup) unsalted butter, softened
¼ cup firmly packed light brown sugar
¼ cup unsulfured light molasses
¼ cup buttermilk
1 large egg, beaten lightly
1 cup confectioners' sugar
crystallized ginger for garnish

Into a bowl sift together the flour, the baking powder, the baking soda, the salt, and the ginger. In another bowl with an electric mixer cream the butter, add the brown sugar, and beat the mixture until it is light and fluffy. Add the molasses, the buttermilk, and the egg and beat the mixture until it is combined well (it will look curdled). Add the flour mixture, stir the batter until it is just combined, and spoon it into buttered ⅛-cup muffin tins (gem tins), filling the tins two-thirds full. Bake the muffins in a preheated 350° F. oven for 15 minutes, or until a tester comes out clean, transfer them to a rack, and let them cool. In a small bowl stir together the confectioners' sugar and 1 tablespoon plus 2 teaspoons water until the icing is smooth. Drizzle about 1 teaspoon of the icing decoratively over each muffin and garnish the tops with a small piece of the crystallized ginger. Makes about 24 muffins.

PHOTO ON PAGE 41

Honey and Cinnamon Drop Biscuits

2 cups all-purpose flour
2½ teaspoons double-acting baking powder
1 teaspoon baking soda
1½ teaspoons cinnamon
½ teaspoon salt
1 stick (½ cup) cold unsalted butter, cut into bits
¼ cup buttermilk
2 tablespoons honey
1 large egg
⅔ cup apricot butter (recipe follows)
   as an accompaniment

Into a bowl sift together the flour, the baking powder, the baking soda, the cinnamon, and the salt, add the butter, and blend the mixture until it resembles coarse meal. In a small bowl whisk together the buttermilk, ¼ cup water, the honey, and the egg. Make a well in the center of the flour mixture, add the buttermilk mixture, and stir the mixture with a fork until it just forms a dough. Drop the dough in 3-inch mounds 2 inches apart onto an ungreased baking sheet and bake the biscuits in a preheated 425° F. oven for 10 minutes. Reduce the heat to 350° F. and bake the biscuits for 8 to 10 minutes more, or until they are golden. Serve the biscuits with the apricot butter. Makes 8 to 10 biscuits.

PHOTO ON PAGE 33

Apricot Butter

¼ pound (about 15) dried apricot halves
1 stick (½ cup) cold unsalted butter, cut into pieces

In a food processor grind the apricots to a paste, add the butter, and blend the mixture until it is smooth. Blend in salt to taste, transfer the butter to a crock, and chill it, covered. Remove the butter from the refrigerator 15 minutes before serving. Makes about ⅔ cup.

PHOTO ON PAGE 33

Lemon Drop Biscuits

1 cup all-purpose flour
1½ teaspoons double-acting baking powder
½ teaspoon salt
1 tablespoon cold unsalted butter, cut into bits
1 tablespoon freshly grated lemon rind
½ cup plus 2 tablespoons heavy cream
strawberry jam and *crème fraîche* as
    accompaniments if desired

Into a bowl sift together the flour, the baking powder, and the salt, add the butter, and blend the mixture until it resembles meal. Add the rind and the cream and stir the mixture until it is just combined. Drop the batter by rounded tablespoons onto a buttered baking sheet and bake the biscuits in a preheated 425° F. oven for 15 minutes, or until they are pale golden. Serve the biscuits with the strawberry jam and *crème fraîche* if desired. Makes about 16 biscuits.

Orange Date Scones

2 large eggs
⅓ cup heavy cream
3 tablespoons fresh orange juice
1 tablespoon freshly grated orange rind
1¾ cups all-purpose flour
1 tablespoon sugar
2½ teaspoons double-acting baking powder
¼ teaspoon salt
½ cup pitted dates, chopped

In a small bowl whisk together the eggs and the cream, reserve 1 tablespoon of the mixture, and stir in the orange juice and the rind. Into a bowl sift together the flour, the sugar, the baking powder, and the salt, add the orange juice mixture and the dates, and stir the mixture with a fork until it just forms a sticky but manageable dough. Knead the dough lightly on a floured surface for 30 seconds and pat it gently into a ¾-inch-thick round. Cut out rounds with a 2- to 2¼-inch cutter dipped in flour and arrange the scones on a buttered baking sheet. Form the scraps gently into a ball, pat the dough into a round, and cut out scones in the same man-

ner. Brush the tops of the scones with the reserved egg mixture and bake the scones in the middle of a preheated 425° F. oven for 12 to 15 minutes, or until they are golden. Makes about 12 scones.

Pumpkin Raisin Muffins

½ cup canned pumpkin purée
½ cup firmly packed light brown sugar
¼ cup vegetable oil
1 large egg
¼ cup raisins
¼ cup coarsely chopped walnuts
⅔ cup all-purpose flour
¾ teaspoon double-acting baking powder
½ teaspoon baking soda
½ teaspoon ground allspice
¼ teaspoon salt
granulated sugar for sprinkling the muffins

In a bowl whisk together the pumpkin purée, the brown sugar, the oil, and the egg until the mixture is smooth and stir in the raisins and the walnuts. Into the bowl sift together the flour, the baking powder, the baking soda, the allspice, and the salt and stir the batter until it is combined well. Divide the batter among 9 well buttered ⅓-cup muffin tins, sprinkle it with the granulated sugar, and bake the muffins in a preheated 375° F. oven for 20 to 25 minutes, or until a tester comes out clean. Turn the muffins out onto a rack and let them cool. The muffins keep in an airtight container for up to 3 days. Makes 9 muffins.

Sun-Dried Tomato and Provolone Bread with Smoked Turkey

2½ cups all-purpose flour
2 teaspoons double-acting baking powder
1¼ teaspoons salt
½ teaspoon baking soda
1 cup grated provolone (about 5 ounces)
½ cup thinly sliced scallion
2 tablespoons minced fresh parsley leaves
¾ teaspoon dried rosemary, crumbled
¾ teaspoon coarsely ground pepper
⅓ cup drained and chopped sun-dried tomatoes
    packed in oil (available at specialty foods shops),
    reserving 2 tablespoons of the oil
2 tablespoons vegetable shortening at room
    temperature
2 tablespoons sugar
2 garlic cloves, cooked in boiling water for
    15 minutes, drained, peeled, and mashed
    with a fork
2 large eggs, beaten lightly
1¼ cups buttermilk
⅓ cup pine nuts, toasted lightly
thinly sliced smoked turkey
softened butter and mayonnaise as
    accompaniments

Into a large bowl sift together the flour, the baking powder, the salt, and the baking soda, add the provolone, the scallion, the parsley, the rosemary, the pepper, and the sun-dried tomatoes, and toss the mixture well. In a small bowl whisk together the shortening, the reserved oil, and the sugar until the mixture is smooth, add the garlic, the eggs, and the buttermilk, and blend the mixture until it is combined well. Add the buttermilk mixture to the flour mixture with the pine nuts and stir the batter until it is just combined. Divide the batter among 3 greased loaf pans, 5½ by 3⅛ by 2¼ inches, smoothing the tops, and bake the loaves in the middle of a preheated 350° F. oven for 45 to 50 minutes, or until a skewer comes out clean. Let the loaves cool in the pans on a rack for 5 minutes and loosen the edges with a knife. Turn the loaves out onto the rack and let them cool completely. The bread keeps, wrapped tightly in foil and chilled, for up to 4 days. Slice the bread, arrange it decoratively on a platter with the smoked turkey, and serve the butter and mayonnaise separately. Makes 3 small loaves, serving 10.

PHOTO ON PAGE 81

CRACKERS AND FRIED BREAD

Cheese Lace Crackers

½ pound sharp Cheddar, grated
1 stick (½ cup) cold unsalted butter, cut into
    bits
½ cup all-purpose flour
1 teaspoon Worcestershire sauce
½ teaspoon salt
¼ teaspoon cayenne

In a food processor blend the Cheddar, the butter, the flour, the Worcestershire sauce, the salt, and the cayenne until the mixture forms a ball of dough. Halve the dough, putting each half on a sheet of wax paper, and with the aid of the wax paper form it into logs about 6 inches long and 1½ inches in diameter. Chill the dough, wrapped in the wax paper, for at least 2 hours, or until it is firm enough to slice. *The dough may be prepared up to this point 2 days in advance and kept covered and chilled. It may also be frozen for several weeks.* Cut the dough into ¼-inch slices, arrange the slices 2 inches apart on jelly-roll pans, and bake them in a preheated 400° F. oven for 5 to 7 minutes, or until they are golden brown around the edges. Transfer the crackers carefully with a metal spatula to racks, let them cool, and drain them on paper towels if desired. The crackers keep for up to 4 days in an airtight container. Makes about 48 crackers.

PHOTO ON PAGE 30

Dill Crackers

½ cup all-purpose flour
¼ cup toasted wheat germ
¾ teaspoon dried dill
2 tablespoons cold unsalted butter, cut into bits
kosher salt to taste

In a bowl toss together the flour, the wheat germ, and the dill and blend in the butter until the mixture resembles meal. Add 3 tablespoons ice water, toss the mixture until the water is incorporated, and form the dough into a ball. Roll the dough into a round ⅛ inch thick on a lightly floured surface, cut it into 10 rounds with a 2-inch floured cutter, and transfer the rounds to a buttered baking sheet. Prick the rounds with a fork, sprinkle them with the salt, and bake them in a preheated 400° F. oven for 10 to 12 minutes, or until they are pale golden. Makes 10 dill crackers.

Whole-Wheat Cumin Crackers

½ cup whole-wheat flour
1 tablespoon all-purpose flour
½ teaspoon double-acting baking powder
¼ teaspoon ground cumin
⅛ teaspoon table salt
1 tablespoon wheat germ
1 tablespoon cold unsalted butter
4 tablespoons milk
kosher salt to taste

Into a bowl sift together the flours, the baking powder, the cumin, and the table salt, stir in the wheat germ, and blend in the butter until the mixture resembles coarse meal. Make a well in the center, add the milk, and combine the mixture with a fork until it just forms a soft dough. Knead the dough gently on a lightly floured surface for 30 seconds and roll it out ¹⁄₁₆ inch thick. Cut out rounds of the dough with a floured 2¼-inch biscuit cutter and transfer them to buttered baking sheets. Gather the scraps, reroll the dough, and cut out more rounds in the same manner. Prick the rounds with a fork, sprinkle them with the kosher salt, and bake them in a preheated 450° F. oven for 8 to 10 minutes, or until they are golden. The crackers keep in an airtight container for up to 1 week. Makes about 30 crackers.

Indian-Style Fried Bread

2 cups all-purpose flour
2 cups whole-wheat flour
2 teaspoons salt
4 tablespoons vegetable oil
vegetable shortening for deep-frying

In a food processor combine 1 cup of the all-purpose flour, 1 cup of the whole-wheat flour, and 1 teaspoon of the salt and pulse the motor several times to blend the mixture. With the motor running add 2 tablespoons of the oil in a stream and blend the mixture for 10 seconds. With the motor running add ½ cup warm water in a stream and continue to add warm water, 1 tablespoon at a time, until a ball of dough forms. Blend the dough for 45 seconds and let the motor rest for 15 seconds. Blend the dough 4 more times in the same manner, form it into a ball, and dust it with flour. Make a second ball of dough with the remaining flours, salt, and oil in the same manner. Chill the dough, wrapped in plastic, overnight.

Let the dough stand at room temperature for 30 minutes. Cut 1 ball of dough into 16 pieces and keep the pieces covered with a dish towel. Roll 1 piece of dough on a well floured surface into a 4½-inch round and transfer it to a floured plate. Roll the remaining pieces of dough in the same manner and stack the dough rounds between sheets of wax paper. Cut and roll the remaining ball of dough in the same manner.

In a deep fryer heat enough shortening to measure 3 inches to 400° F., in it fry the rounds, 1 at a time, for 15 seconds on each side, or until the breads are puffed and golden, and transfer them to paper towels to drain. *The breads may be made up to 1 day in advance and kept wrapped in foil and chilled. Reheat the breads in the foil in a preheated 350° F. oven for 15 to 20 minutes, or until they are hot.* Makes 32 breads.

PHOTO ON PAGE 15

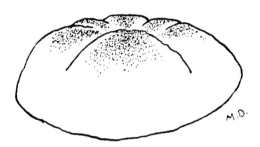

Garlic Pepper Pita Toasts

1 teaspoon minced garlic, or to taste
3 tablespoons unsalted butter
two 6-inch *pita* loaves, each cut into 8 wedges
   and each wedge separated into 2 triangles
coarsely ground pepper to taste
coarse salt to taste

In a small saucepan cook the garlic in the butter over low heat, stirring occasionally, for 5 minutes and brush the mixture lightly onto the rough side of the *pita* triangles. Arrange the triangles buttered side up in one layer on a baking sheet, sprinkle them with the pepper and the salt, and bake them in a preheated 350° F. oven for 12 to 15 minutes, or until they are crisp and light golden. Let the toasts cool on a rack and store them in an airtight container. The toasts keep in an airtight container in a dry place for up to 4 days. Makes 32 toasts.

PHOTO ON PAGE 45

Sesame Ginger Toasts

1 stick (½ cup) unsalted butter
1 teaspoon Oriental sesame oil (available at
   Oriental markets and some specialty foods
   shops and supermarkets)
1 teaspoon ground ginger
1 garlic clove, minced
1 loaf of Italian or French bread, cut crosswise
   into ½-inch slices
1 large egg, beaten lightly with ¾ teaspoon salt
½ cup sesame seeds

In a small saucepan heat the butter, the oil, the ginger, and the garlic over moderately low heat, stirring, until the butter is melted and keep the mixture warm. Brush both sides of each bread slice with some of the butter mixture, brush the crust with the egg mixture, and roll the crust immediately in the sesame seeds, shaking off the excess gently. Bake the slices on baking sheets in a preheated 400° F. oven for 10 minutes, or until they are golden, and transfer them to paper towels. The toasts may be stored in an airtight container for up to 1 week. Serves 6.

PHOTO ON PAGE 57

Garlic Rosemary Tuiles

2 large garlic cloves, unpeeled
½ stick (¼ cup) unsalted butter, softened
2 teaspoons sugar
1 large egg white at room temperature
½ teaspoon salt
4 tablespoons all-purpose flour
2 tablespoons freshly grated Parmesan
about 2 tablespoons fresh or dried rosemary
   leaves

In a small saucepan of boiling water boil the garlic, covered, for 20 minutes, drain it, and let it cool. Pat the garlic dry, peel it, and mash it to a paste with a fork. In a bowl with an electric mixer cream the butter, add the sugar, and beat the mixture until it is light and fluffy. Beat in 2 teaspoons of the garlic paste, discarding any remaining garlic paste, add the egg white and the salt, and beat the mixture at low speed for 5 seconds, or until it is just combined. (The mixture will appear lumpy and separated.) Add the flour and the Parmesan and stir the mixture until it is just combined. Transfer the mixture to a small bowl and chill it, covered, for at least 4 hours or overnight.

Arrange rounded teaspoons of the mixture 3 inches apart on buttered baking sheets, with the back of a fork dipped in cold water flatten them carefully to form 1½-inch rounds, and sprinkle the rosemary over the rounds. Bake the rounds in batches in the middle of a preheated 425° F. oven for 6 to 8 minutes, or until the edges are golden, and immediately transfer the *tuiles* with a spatula to a rolling pin, pressing them gently against the rolling pin, if necessary, to help them curve. Let the *tuiles* cool and remove them carefully from the rolling pin. *The tuiles may be made up to 1 day in advance and kept in an airtight container.* Makes about 14 *tuiles*.

PHOTO ON PAGE 24

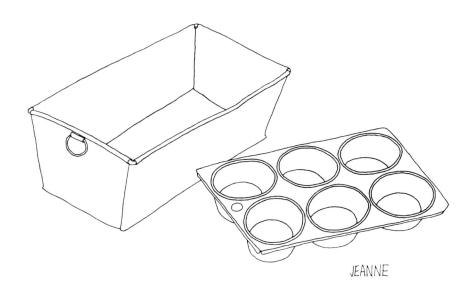

JEANNE

SOUPS

Curried Acorn Squash and Apple Soup

2½ pounds (2 small) acorn squash, scrubbed, halved, strings discarded, and the seeds removed and toasted (recipe follows) for garnish if desired
1 large onion, sliced
1 small red bell pepper, chopped coarse
3 tablespoons unsalted butter
2 large green apples, cored and cut into 1-inch pieces
1 large boiling potato, scrubbed and cut into ½-inch pieces
1 tablespoon curry powder
1 tablespoon Worcestershire sauce
1 cup heavy cream

In a large saucepan bring 4 cups water to a boil, add the squash, and boil it, covered, for 10 minutes, or until it is just tender. Transfer the squash with a slotted spoon to a colander, reserving the cooking liquid, and let the squash cool until it can be handled. Scoop out the flesh with a spoon and discard the skins.

In a kettle cook the onion and the bell pepper in the butter over moderate heat, stirring, until the onion is golden brown. Stir in the squash, the reserved cooking liquid, the apples, the potato, the curry powder, the Worcestershire sauce, 4 cups water, and salt and pepper to taste, bring the liquid to a boil, and cook the mixture, covered partially, at a slow boil, stirring occasionally, for 15 minutes, or until the potato is tender.

In a blender purée the mixture in batches, return it to the kettle, and stir in the cream and salt and pepper to taste. *The soup may be made up to 3 days in advance and kept covered and chilled.* Heat the soup over moderate heat, stirring, until it is hot, ladle it into heated bowls, and garnish it with some of the toasted seeds if desired. Makes about 12 cups, serving 8.

Toasted Acorn Squash Seeds

the seeds from 2½ pounds (2 small) acorn squash
1 tablespoon melted unsalted butter
1 teaspoon Worcestershire sauce
¼ teaspoon salt, or to taste

Rub off most of the stringy membrane clinging to the seeds and in a bowl toss the seeds with the butter, the Worcestershire sauce, and the salt. Toast the seeds in a small baking pan in a preheated 350° F. oven, stirring occasionally, for 15 minutes, or until they are golden brown, and transfer them to paper towels to drain. Makes about ⅓ cup.

Asparagus Soup with Sour Cream

1 small onion, chopped fine
1½ tablespoons unsalted butter
2 cups canned chicken broth
1 pound asparagus, trimmed, quartered lengthwise, and cut crosswise into ½-inch pieces
½ teaspoon fines herbes
¼ cup sour cream

In a saucepan cook the onion in the butter over moderately low heat, stirring, until it is softened. Add the broth, the asparagus, the fines herbes, and salt and pepper to taste, bring the broth to a boil, and simmer the mixture for 2 to 3 minutes, or until the asparagus is tender-crisp. Transfer ¼ cup of the asparagus with a slotted spoon to each of 2 soup bowls, simmer the remaining mixture for 8 to 12 minutes more, or until the asparagus is tender, and in a blender purée it with the sour cream. In a saucepan heat the soup over moderately low heat, stirring, until it is hot, but do not let it boil. Makes about 2½ cups, serving 2.

Carrot Soup with Sour Cream and Coriander

¼ cup finely chopped shallot
2 tablespoons unsalted butter
1½ cups finely chopped peeled carrot
1¾ cups canned chicken broth
1 tablespoon ground coriander
⅓ cup sour cream

In a heavy saucepan cook the shallot in the butter over moderately low heat, stirring, until it is softened. Add the carrot, the broth, the coriander, and pepper to taste, bring the liquid to a boil, and simmer the mixture for 13 to 15 minutes, or until the carrot is tender. Purée the mixture in a blender, transfer the purée to a saucepan, and stir in the sour cream and salt to taste. Heat the soup over moderately low heat, stirring, until it is hot, but do not let it boil. Makes about 2 cups, serving 2.

Curried Carrot Scallion Soup

⅓ cup thinly sliced white part of scallion plus
    thinly sliced scallion green for garnish
1 teaspoon olive oil
a pinch of curry powder
1½ cups thinly sliced peeled carrot plus finely
    grated carrot for garnish
1½ cups canned chicken broth

In a saucepan cook the white part of scallion in the oil over low heat, stirring, until it is softened, add the curry powder, and cook the mixture, stirring, for 1 minute. Add the sliced carrot and the broth, bring the liquid to a boil, and simmer the mixture for 10 to 12 minutes, or until the carrot is very tender. In a blender or food processor purée the mixture, return it to the pan, and heat the soup over moderate heat until it is hot. Ladle the soup into 2 bowls and garnish it with the scallion green and the grated carrot. Makes about 2 cups, serving 2.

Cold Celery Soup

1½ cups thinly sliced celery including the
    leaves plus additional celery leaves for
    garnish if desired
2 tablespoons unsalted butter
1¼ cups canned chicken broth
½ cup plain yogurt

In a heavy saucepan cook the sliced celery in the but-
ter over moderately low heat, stirring, for 5 minutes. Add the broth, bring the liquid to a boil, and simmer the mixture for 10 to 12 minutes, or until the celery is softened. In a blender purée the celery mixture with the yogurt and salt and pepper to taste and strain the mixture through a fine sieve into a metal bowl, pressing hard on the solids. Set the bowl into a bowl of ice and cold water and stir the soup until it is chilled. Divide the soup between 2 bowls and garnish it with the additional celery leaves if desired. Makes about 1⅓ cups, serving 2.

Chicken, Cheddar, and Cucumber Soup

3 tablespoons unsalted butter
1 pound chicken wings, cut at the joints into
    3 pieces
1 large onion, chopped
enough cucumbers (about 2 large), peeled,
    seeded, and chopped, to measure 3½ cups
2 teaspoons ground cumin
¼ teaspoon cayenne, or to taste
5 tablespoons all-purpose flour
1 cup milk
1½ cups grated sharp Cheddar

In a kettle heat 1 tablespoon of the butter over moderate heat until the foam subsides and in it brown the chicken, patted dry and seasoned with salt and pepper. Add the onion and cook the mixture, stirring, until the onion is golden. Add the remaining 2 tablespoons butter, 2½ cups of the cucumber, the cumin, the cayenne, and the flour and cook the mixture, stirring, for 3 minutes. Stir in 5 cups water, bring the liquid to a boil, stirring, and simmer the mixture, covered partially, for 1 hour. Transfer the chicken with a slotted spoon to a cutting board, discard the skin and bones, and chop the meat. Stir the milk and the Cheddar into the soup mixture and heat the mixture, stirring, until the Cheddar is just melted but do not let it boil.

In a blender purée the mixture in batches and return it to the kettle. Stir in the remaining 1 cup cucumber, the chicken meat, and salt and pepper to taste and heat the soup over moderately low heat, stirring, until it is hot. Makes about 8 cups, serving 6.

Corn Soup

1 carrot, chopped
1 rib of celery, chopped

1 onion, chopped
1 garlic clove, minced
1 small bay leaf
2 tablespoons vegetable oil
a pinch of saffron threads if desired
5 ears of corn, shucked and the corn kernels
    cut off the cobs, reserving the cobs
4 cups chicken stock (page 247) or canned
    chicken broth
¼ teaspoon cayenne, or to taste
3 tablespoons minced fresh parsley leaves

In a kettle cook the carrot, the celery, the onion, the garlic, and the bay leaf in the oil over moderately low heat, stirring, until the vegetables are softened, add the saffron if desired, and cook the mixture, stirring, for 2 minutes. Add the reserved corn cobs, the stock, and 3 cups water, bring the liquid to a boil, and simmer the mixture for 10 minutes. Add the corn kernels, simmer the mixture for 10 to 15 minutes, or until the corn kernels are very tender, and discard the bay leaf and the corn cobs. In a blender or food processor purée the mixture in batches and transfer the purée to a large saucepan. Heat the soup over moderate heat, stirring, until it is hot, add the cayenne and salt to taste, and stir in the parsley. The soup may be served hot or it may be cooled, kept covered and chilled for at least 3 hours or up to 24 hours, and served cold. Makes about 6 cups, serving 6.

PHOTO ON PAGE 46

Chilled Cucumber Soup with Mint Ice

2 cucumbers (about 1 pound), peeled and
    seeded, plus 6 thin slices of cucumber for
    garnish
⅔ cup buttermilk
3 tablespoons sour cream
2 teaspoons white-wine vinegar, or to taste
½ teaspoon salt, or to taste
6 half-spheres of mint ice (recipe follows)

Chop fine enough of the cucumber to measure ⅓ cup and reserve it. Chop the remaining cucumber, in a blender purée it with the buttermilk, the sour cream, the vinegar, and the salt until the mixture is smooth, and transfer the purée to a bowl. *The soup may be prepared up to this point 1 day in advance and kept covered and chilled.* Stir in the reserved chopped cucumber, season

the soup with salt and pepper, and divide it between 2 chilled bowls. Float 3 cucumber slices on each serving and top each slice with a half-sphere of mint ice. Serves 2.

PHOTO ON PAGE 52

Mint Ice

¼ cup firmly packed fresh mint leaves
½ teaspoon sugar

In a small saucepan bring ½ cup water to a boil, stir in the mint leaves and the sugar, and boil the mixture for 5 seconds. Strain the mixture through a fine sieve set over a bowl, reserving the mint leaves and the liquid, and let the mint leaves and the liquid cool separately to keep the mint from discoloring. In a blender purée the mint leaves with the cooking liquid, pour the purée into an ice-cube tray with the dividers in place, and freeze it. *The mint ice may be prepared up to this point 3 days in advance and kept covered and frozen.*

Transfer the mint ice cubes to a plastic bag, crush them with a mallet or rolling pin, and in a food processor grind the ice fine. The mint ice may be scooped at this point or it may be spread in a small metal pan and returned to the freezer, covered, for later use. Working quickly, with a ½-inch melon-ball cutter scoop half-spheres of the ice, packing it each time into the cutter, set the half-spheres on a metal baking pan lined with plastic wrap, and freeze them, covered with foil, for at least 1 hour *or overnight*. Leftover mint ice may be used to flavor iced tea. Makes about ½ cup.

PHOTO ON PAGE 52

Gazpacho Ice with Cucumbers

For the gazpacho ice
1 teaspoon unflavored gelatin
2 tablespoons dry white wine
½ pound tomatoes, peeled, seeded, and
    chopped
¼ cup peeled, seeded, and finely chopped
    cucumber
¼ cup finely chopped red bell pepper
2 tablespoons minced red onion
1 tablespoon olive oil
¾ teaspoon salt
½ teaspoon minced garlic
⅛ teaspoon cayenne

paper-thin slices of cucumber, soaked in a
    bowl of ice and cold water for 15 minutes,
    drained, and patted dry

Make the gazpacho ice: In a small saucepan let the
gelatin soften in the wine for 5 minutes and heat the mixture over low heat, stirring, until the gelatin is dissolved. In a blender purée the tomatoes with the
cucumber, the bell pepper, the onion, the oil, the salt,
the garlic, the cayenne, and the gelatin mixture and
freeze the purée in an ice-cream freezer according to the
manufacturer's instructions. (Alternatively, freeze the
purée in an ice-cube tray for 1 to 2 hours, or until it is
frozen, and in a food processor grind the ice until it is
smooth but still frozen.) Working quickly, with a small
oval ice-cream scoop scoop the gazpacho ice into 6
ovals, arranging them on a small metal baking pan lined
with plastic wrap, and freeze the ovals, covered with
foil, for at least 1 hour or overnight. *The gazpacho ice
may be made up to 2 days in advance and kept covered
and frozen.*

Let the gazpacho ice stand at room temperature for
5 minutes before serving. Reserving 2 cucumber slices
for garnish, arrange the remaining cucumber slices decoratively on 2 chilled salad plates, top them with the
gazpacho ice, and garnish each serving with a reserved
cucumber slice, folded decoratively. Serves 2.

PHOTO ON PAGE 53

Green Pea Consommé

1 pound peas, shelled and the pods reserved
5½ cups chicken stock (page 247) or canned
    chicken broth
½ cup dry white wine
1 cup chopped carrot
1 cup chopped onion
12 peppercorns
1½ teaspoons dried mint
6 radishes, 2 of them sliced thin and
    4 cut into julienne strips
6 lemon wedges
onion toasts (recipe follows) as an accompaniment

In a large saucepan combine the reserved pea pods,
the stock, 2½ cups water, the wine, the carrot, the onion, the peppercorns, and the mint, bring the liquid to a
boil, and simmer the mixture, covered, stirring occasionally and pressing hard on the pea pods, for 45 minutes. Strain the mixture through a fine sieve into a bowl,
pressing hard on the solids and discarding them. Strain
the stock through the sieve lined with a rinsed and
squeezed dish towel into another large saucepan and
clarify it (procedure on page 247).

In a small saucepan cook the peas in boiling salted
water to cover for 3 to 8 minutes, or until they are
tender. Drain the peas in a sieve and refresh them under
cold water.

Heat the consommé over moderate heat until it is hot
and add salt to taste. Divide the consommé among heated bowls, garnish each bowl with some of the peas and
some of the radish slices and strips, and serve the consommé with the lemon wedges and toasts. Makes about
6 cups, serving 6.

PHOTO ON PAGE 39

Onion Toasts

¾ stick (6 tablespoons) unsalted butter
1½ tablespoons finely grated onion
½ teaspoon salt, or to taste
1 teaspoon dry English mustard
6 slices of homemade-type white bread, crusts
    removed and the slices halved
    diagonally

In a small saucepan combine the butter, the onion, the salt, and the mustard and heat the mixture over moderately low heat, stirring, until the butter is melted. Arrange the bread on a baking sheet, brush both sides of it generously with the butter mixture, and bake the bread in a preheated 350° F. oven, turning it once, for 8 to 10 minutes, or until it is golden and crisp. Transfer the toasts to paper towels to drain. *The toasts may be made up to 1 day in advance and kept wrapped in foil at room temperature. Reheat the toasts on a baking sheet in a preheated 325° F. oven for 3 to 5 minutes, or until they are heated through.* Serve the toasts warm. Makes 12 toasts.

PHOTO ON PAGE 39

Ham, Lima Bean, and Carrot Soup with Orégano Croutons

¾ stick (6 tablespoons) unsalted butter
1½ teaspoons dried orégano, crumbled
8 slices of homemade-type white bread, crusts
    removed and the bread cut into ½-inch
    cubes (about 3 cups)
2 cups chopped onion
4 large carrots, halved lengthwise and sliced
    thin crosswise (about 3 cups)
5 cups chicken stock (page 247) or canned
    chicken broth
4 cups julienne strips of cooked ham
4 cups (about two 10-ounce packages) frozen
    baby lima beans
½ cup thinly sliced scallion greens

In a small saucepan melt 3 tablespoons of the butter and stir in the orégano. In a bowl drizzle the bread cubes with the butter mixture and toss them until they are coated with the mixture. Bake the croutons in a jelly-roll pan in a preheated 375° F. oven, turning them occasionally, for 10 to 15 minutes, or until they are golden, and return them to the bowl.

In a kettle cook the onion and the carrots in the re-
maining 3 tablespoons butter over moderately low heat, stirring, until the onion is softened. Stir in the stock, the ham, the lima beans, and salt and pepper to taste, bring the liquid to a boil, and simmer the mixture, stirring occasionally, for 13 to 15 minutes, or until the lima beans are tender. In a blender purée 2 cups of the lima bean mixture, add the purée and the scallion greens to the kettle, and stir the soup until it is combined well. Divide the soup evenly among heated soup bowls and serve it with the orégano croutons. Makes about 12 cups, serving 6 as a main course.

Kale Soup with Garlic Croutons

1 onion, chopped
2 tablespoons unsalted butter
2½ cups firmly packed kale leaves with the
    ribs removed, rinsed well
1 large boiling potato,
    peeled and diced
1 carrot, grated coarse
2 cups canned chicken broth
1 tablespoon fresh lemon juice
⅛ teaspoon freshly grated nutmeg
2 teaspoons olive oil
1 garlic clove, sliced
2 slices of homemade-type white bread, crusts
    removed and the bread cut into ½-inch
    squares
½ cup half-and-half

In a large heavy saucepan cook the onion in the butter over moderate heat, stirring occasionally, until it begins to brown. Stir in the kale, the potato, the carrot, the broth, 1 cup water, the lemon juice, and the nutmeg, bring the liquid to a boil, and simmer the mixture, covered, for 12 minutes.

While the mixture is cooking, in a skillet heat the oil over moderate heat until it is hot but not smoking and in it cook the garlic, stirring, for 1 minute. Add the bread squares, cook them over moderate heat, tossing them, until they are golden, and transfer the croutons to paper towels, discarding the garlic.

In a blender or food processor purée the kale mixture in batches, return the purée to the pan, and stir in the half-and-half and salt and pepper to taste. Heat the kale soup over moderate heat, stirring, until it is hot, ladle it into 2 heated bowls, and garnish it with the croutons. Serves 2.

Leek, Bacon, and Bean Soup

1¼ cups dried Great Northern beans, picked
    over and rinsed
the white part and 4 inches of the green part of
    2 pounds leeks, split lengthwise, washed
    well, and sliced thin crosswise
1 tablespoon minced garlic
½ teaspoon dried thyme, crumbled
¼ teaspoon dried sage, crumbled
2 tablespoons olive oil
½ pound sliced lean bacon, chopped
enough thin pumpernickel bread, cut into
    ¼-inch cubes, to measure 1½ cups
¼ teaspoon salt, or to taste
3 tablespoons white-wine vinegar
¼ teaspoon Tabasco

In a kettle combine the beans and 10 cups water, bring the water to a boil, and boil the beans for 2 minutes. Remove the kettle from the heat and let the beans soak in the water for 1 hour. In a large skillet cook the leeks, the garlic, the thyme, and the sage in the oil over moderately high heat, stirring, until the leeks are golden and add the mixture to the kettle. Bring the liquid to a boil and simmer the mixture, covered partially, stirring occasionally, for 1 hour and 30 minutes, or until the beans are tender.

While the beans are cooking, in a skillet cook the bacon over moderate heat, stirring, until it is crisp, transfer it with a slotted spoon to paper towels to drain, and pour off all but 2 tablespoons of the fat. Heat the fat remaining in the skillet over moderate heat until it is hot but not smoking, in it cook the bread cubes, sprinkled with the salt, tossing them, until they are crisp, and transfer the croutons with a slotted spoon to paper towels to drain.

Add to the kettle the bacon, the vinegar, and the Tabasco, stirring, season the soup with salt and pepper, and simmer it for 15 minutes. *The soup may be made up to 3 days in advance, kept covered and chilled, and reheated over moderate heat, stirring, until it is hot.* Ladle the soup into heated bowls and garnish it with the croutons. Makes about 9 cups, serving 6.

Lentil and Sauerkraut Soup

a 1½-pound smoked pork butt, soaked in
    warm water for 15 minutes and the netting
    discarded
1 pound lentils, picked over and rinsed
3 carrots, cut crosswise into ¼-inch slices
4 ribs of celery, halved lengthwise and sliced
1 large onion, chopped
2 bay leaves
1 cup drained sauerkraut
¼ cup distilled white vinegar

In a kettle combine 14 cups water, the pork butt, the lentils, the carrots, the celery, the onion, and the bay leaves, bring the water to a boil, and simmer the mixture, covered partially, for 1 hour, or until the lentils are softened. Transfer the pork butt to a cutting board, cut it into 1-inch pieces, and return it to the kettle. Add the sauerkraut, the vinegar, and salt and pepper to taste, simmer the soup, uncovered, stirring occasionally, for 30 minutes, and discard the bay leaves. *The soup may be made up to 3 days in advance, kept covered and chilled, and reheated over moderate heat, stirring, until it is hot.* Makes about 13 cups, serving 8.

Cold Cream of Mushroom Soup

½ pound mushrooms, chopped
1 leek, halved lengthwise, washed well, and
    sliced thin (about ½ cup)
1¼ cups canned chicken broth
2½ tablespoons dry vermouth
½ teaspoon minced garlic
½ teaspoon dried marjoram, crumbled
2 teaspoons fresh lemon juice
2 tablespoons minced fresh parsley leaves plus
    additional for garnish
½ cup heavy cream
½ cup milk

In a skillet combine the mushrooms, the leek, ¾ cup of the broth, the vermouth, the garlic, and the marjoram, bring the mixture to a boil, and cook it over moderately high heat, stirring, for 6 to 8 minutes, or until the liquid is almost evaporated. Transfer the mixture to a food processor or blender, add the lemon juice, the remaining ½ cup broth, and ¼ cup water, and purée the mixture. Transfer the purée to a bowl set over another bowl filled with ice and cold water, stir in 2 tablespoons of the parsley, the cream, the milk, and salt and pepper to taste, and stir the soup until it is chilled well. Divide the soup between chilled bowls and garnish it with the additional minced parsley leaves. Makes 2¼ cups, serving 2.

Szechwan-Style Oxtail Noodle Soup

4 pounds oxtails, cut into 2-inch sections and
　　trimmed
⅓ cup medium-dry Sherry
¼ cup soy sauce
six ¼-inch-thick diagonal slices of gingerroot
8 scallions
a 3½-inch cinnamon stick
1 tablespoon sugar
1 teaspoon aniseed
1 teaspoon red pepper flakes, or to taste
½ teaspoon salt
6 ounces egg noodles
Tabasco to taste

In a heavy kettle combine the oxtails, 8 cups water,
the Sherry, the soy sauce, the gingerroot, 6 of the scallions, the cinnamon stick, the sugar, the aniseed, the red
pepper flakes, and the salt, bring the liquid to a boil, and
simmer the oxtails, covered, for 3 hours and 30 minutes, or until they are very tender. Transfer the oxtails
with a slotted spoon to a bowl, let them cool until they
can be handled, and discard the bones and fat, reserving
the meat. Strain the stock through a fine sieve into a
large saucepan, spoon off the fat, and, if necessary, boil
the stock until it is reduced to about 6 cups. Add the reserved meat to the pan. *The soup may be prepared up to
this point 2 days in advance and kept covered and
chilled. Remove the congealed fat from the chilled stock
before continuing with the recipe.*

In a saucepan of boiling salted water boil the noodles
until they are just tender, drain them, and add them to
the soup. Heat the soup over moderately low heat until it
is heated through and season it with salt, pepper, and the
Tabasco. Just before serving sprinkle the soup with the
remaining 2 scallions, minced. Makes about 9 cups,
serving 6 to 8.

Pumpkin Soup with Sage Croutons

1 carrot, chopped
1 onion, chopped
1 rib of celery, chopped
1 teaspoon dried sage, crumbled
½ bay leaf
2 tablespoons unsalted butter
a 1-pound can pumpkin purée
4½ cups canned chicken broth
2 slices of homemade-type white bread,
　　buttered lightly and the crusts removed

6 very small fresh sage leaves for garnish if
　　desired

In a kettle cook the carrot, the onion, and the celery
with ¾ teaspoon of the sage, the bay leaf, and salt and
pepper to taste in the butter over moderately low heat,
stirring occasionally, until the vegetables are softened,
stir in the pumpkin, and stir in 4 cups of the broth, a little
at a time. Bring the liquid to a boil and simmer the mixture, stirring occasionally, for 15 minutes. Discard the
bay leaf and in a blender purée the mixture in batches
until it is very smooth and creamy. Return the soup to
the kettle, bring it to a simmer, stirring in enough of the
remaining ½ cup broth to thin it to the desired consistency, and season it with salt and pepper.

While the soup is cooking, cut each slice of bread into
4 squares and halve each square diagonally to form triangles. Arrange the triangles on a baking sheet, dab
them with the remaining 1 teaspoon sage, and bake the
croutons in a preheated 350° F. oven for 15 minutes, or
until they are golden.

Ladle the soup into heated bowls and garnish it with
the croutons and the sage leaves if desired. Makes about
6 cups, serving 6.

PHOTO ON PAGE 74

Romaine Soup with Basil

⅔ cup thinly sliced scallion
1 tablespoon unsalted butter
4¼ cups loosely packed thinly sliced romaine,
　　washed and spun dry
1½ cups half-and-half
½ teaspoon dried basil, crumbled

In a saucepan cook the scallion in the butter over
moderately low heat, stirring, until it is softened. Add 4
cups of the romaine, the half-and-half, 1 cup water, and
the basil, bring the liquid to a boil, and simmer the mixture for 8 to 10 minutes, or until the romaine is tender. In
a blender purée the mixture, divide the soup between 2
bowls, and garnish it with the remaining ¼ cup romaine. Makes about 2½ cups, serving 2.

Tomato Orange Gazpacho

4 large (about 2 pounds) firm-ripe tomatoes,
 peeled and seeded (procedure follows)
½ cup fresh orange juice
1 garlic clove, minced
2 tablespoons white-wine vinegar
2 teaspoons salt
2 tablespoons olive or vegetable oil
1½ teaspoons freshly grated orange rind
2 navel oranges, peel and pith cut away with a
 serrated knife and the fruit cut into
 segments and chopped
1 cucumber, peeled, seeded, and chopped fine
2 green bell peppers, chopped fine
⅓ cup finely chopped red onion, soaked in
 cold water to cover for 15 minutes and
 drained
cayenne to taste

In a blender or food processor purée 3 of the tomatoes, chopped coarse, with the orange juice, transfer the purée to a bowl, and stir in the garlic, the vinegar, the salt, the oil, the rind, the oranges, the remaining tomato, chopped fine, the cucumber, the bell peppers, the onion, the cayenne, and black pepper to taste. Chill the soup, covered, for 1 hour, or until it is cold. *The gazpacho improves in flavor if made 1 day in advance and kept covered and chilled.* Makes about 5 cups, serving 4.

To Peel and Seed Tomatoes

With a sharp knife cut a small X in the blossom end of the tomatoes. In a kettle of boiling salted water blanch the tomatoes for 10 seconds, or until the peel starts to curl at the X. Transfer the tomatoes with a slotted spoon to a bowl of ice and cold water, let them stand in the water until they are cool enough to handle, and remove the peel. Halve the tomatoes horizontally and with a small spoon scoop out the seeds.

Winter Vegetable Soup

½ cup thinly sliced white part of scallion
1½ tablespoons olive oil
2 cups canned chicken broth
1 large carrot, sliced thin
1 boiling potato, peeled and cut into
 ⅜-inch pieces
¼ teaspoon dried thyme, crumbled

1 cup small broccoli flowerets

In a large saucepan cook the scallion in the oil over moderately low heat, stirring, until it is softened. Add the broth, the carrot, the potato, and the thyme, bring the broth to a boil, and simmer the mixture for 5 minutes. Add the broccoli and salt and pepper to taste and simmer the soup for 5 to 7 minutes, or until the vegetables are tender. Makes about 3 cups, serving 2.

Yellow Split Pea Soup with Coriander

2 (about 1 pound in all) smoked ham hocks
1 pound dried yellow split peas, picked over
 and rinsed
3 slices of gingerroot each the size of a quarter
1 garlic clove, minced
3 carrots, grated
1 onion, chopped
2 teaspoons turmeric
1½ teaspoons chili powder
2 tablespoons distilled white vinegar
1½ tablespoons chopped fresh coriander
whole coriander leaves for garnish

In a kettle combine the ham hocks, 12 cups water, the split peas, the gingerroot, and the garlic, bring the water to a boil, covered, and simmer the mixture, stirring and skimming the froth occasionally, for 1 hour. Stir in the carrots, the onion, the turmeric, and the chili powder and simmer the mixture, covered, for 30 minutes. Transfer the ham hocks with a slotted spoon to a cutting board, remove the meat from the bones, and chop it. Add to the kettle the meat, the vinegar, and salt and pepper to taste and simmer the soup, uncovered, stirring occasionally, for 30 minutes. Stir in the chopped coriander and season the soup with salt and pepper. *The soup may be made up to 3 days in advance. It should be cooled, uncovered, kept covered and chilled, and reheated over moderate heat, stirring, until it is hot.* Ladle the soup into heated bowls, discarding the gingerroot, and garnish it with the coriander leaves. Makes about 16 cups, serving 10.

Cold Zucchini Soup with Scallion Sticks

¼ cup thinly sliced scallion including the
 green part
2¼ cups chopped zucchini (about ¾ pound)

1 tablespoon olive oil
1 cup canned chicken broth
¼ teaspoon dried rosemary, crumbled
2 tablespoons unsalted butter
2 tablespoons minced scallion green plus
   thinly sliced scallion green for garnish
6 slices of homemade-type white bread,
   crusts removed
½ cup half-and-half
1½ teaspoons fresh lemon juice
julienne lemon rind for garnish

In a saucepan cook the ¼ cup sliced scallion and the zucchini in the oil over moderately low heat, stirring, for 4 minutes. Add the broth and the rosemary, bring the liquid to a boil, and simmer the mixture for 8 to 10 minutes, or until the zucchini is very tender.

While the zucchini mixture is cooking, in a small saucepan melt the butter with the 2 tablespoons minced scallion green and salt to taste over moderate heat, stirring occasionally, brush the scallion butter on the bread, and cut the bread into ½-inch sticks. Toast the sticks on the rack of a broiler pan under a preheated broiler about 4 inches from the heat for 1 to 2 minutes, or until they are golden.

In a blender or food processor purée the zucchini mixture with the half-and-half, the lemon juice, and salt and pepper to taste, transfer the soup to a bowl set in a bowl of ice and cold water, and stir it until it is cold. Ladle the soup into 2 bowls and garnish it with the rind and the sliced scallion green. Serve the soup with the scallion sticks. (The scallion sticks keep, covered with plastic wrap, overnight. Reheat any leftover scallion sticks and serve them as an hor d'oeuvre.) Serves 2.

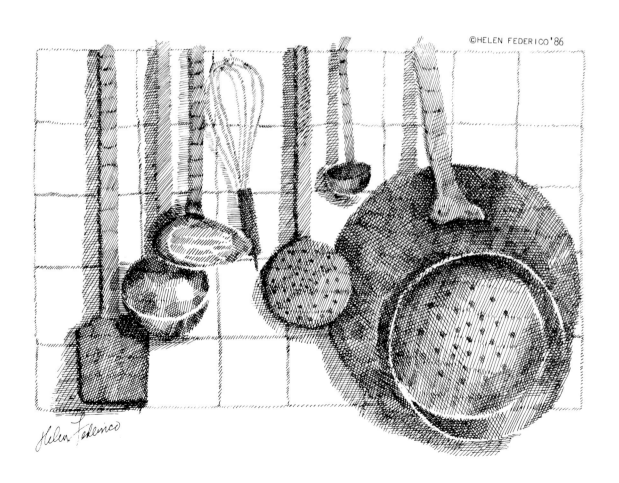

©HELEN FEDERICO '86

FISH AND SHELLFISH

FISH

Monkfish and Shrimp Kebabs

½ cup olive oil
¼ cup fresh lemon juice
3 teaspoons minced fresh thyme leaves or
    1 teaspoon dried, crumbled
2 teaspoons freshly grated lemon rind
½ teaspoon sugar
¼ teaspoon salt
¼ teaspoon freshly ground pepper
1¼ pounds monkfish fillet, trimmed and cut
    into eight 1-inch pieces
4 large shrimp (about ¼ pound), shelled and
    deveined
8 cherry tomatoes
eight 1-inch bread cubes, toasted lightly
¼ pound Feta, cut into four 1-inch cubes
1½ cups *orzo* (rice-shaped pasta)
¾ pound spinach, washed, stems discarded,
    and leaves shredded
2 tablespoons butter, softened
¼ cup minced black olives

In a bowl combine the oil, the lemon juice, the thyme, the rind, the sugar, the salt, and the pepper, add the monkfish and the shrimp, and let them marinate, covered and chilled, for 3 hours. In a shallow dish let four 12-inch wooden skewers soak in water to cover for 1 hour. Thread the skewers with the seafood, reserving the marinade, and broil the kebabs in a jelly-roll pan under a preheated broiler about 4 inches from the heat, basting them often with the reserved marinade and turning them once, for 10 minutes. Thread the tomatoes, the

bread, and the Feta on the ends of the skewers and broil the kebabs, basting them often with the reserved marinade and turning them once, for 2 to 4 minutes, or until the bread is golden brown.

While the kebabs are broiling, in a saucepan of boiling salted water cook the *orzo* for 5 minutes, add the spinach, and cook the mixture for 3 minutes, or until the *orzo* is *al dente*. Drain the mixture and in the pan toss it with the butter and salt and pepper to taste. Transfer the *orzo* mixture to a heated platter and arrange the kebabs on it. Drizzle the dish with the pan juices and sprinkle it with the olives. Serves 4.

Grilled Monkfish with Ratatouille

¾ pound monkfish fillet, trimmed of
    membranes
3 tablespoons olive oil
1 tablespoon fresh thyme leaves plus thyme
    sprigs for garnish if desired
ratatouille (page 178) as an accompaniment

With a sharp knife cut the monkfish crosswise into ⅛-inch-thick slices and arrange the slices in a shallow baking dish. Drizzle the oil over the fish, sprinkle the fish with the thyme leaves, and turn it to coat it with the oil. Let the fish marinate at room temperature for at least 1 hour or covered and chilled overnight.

Grill the fish, sprinkled with salt and pepper to taste, on an oiled rack over glowing coals or in an oiled ridged grill pan, heated over high heat until it is hot, for 1 minute on each side, or until it is firm to the touch. Spoon the *ratatouille* onto 2 heated plates, arrange the monkfish on it, and garnish each plate with the thyme sprigs if desired. Serves 2.

Louisiana-Style Red Snapper and Shrimp Court Bouillon
(Thick Seafood Soup)

1 tablespoon unsalted butter
2 tablespoons all-purpose flour
¼ cup finely chopped onion
⅓ cup finely chopped green bell pepper
a 1-pound can tomatoes including the juice
cayenne to taste
¼ pound (about 6) shrimp, shells removed in 1
   piece and reserved
½ pound red snapper fillet or any other firm-
   fleshed white fish fillet, cut into 1-inch pieces
½ cup thinly sliced scallion greens
cooked rice as an accompaniment if desired

In a large saucepan melt the butter over moderately low heat, stir in the flour, and cook the *roux*, stirring, for 6 to 8 minutes, or until it is the color of peanut butter. Add the onion and the bell pepper and cook the mixture, stirring, for 2 minutes. Add the tomatoes with the juice, the cayenne, the reserved shrimp shells, and 1½ cups water, bring the mixture to a boil, breaking up the tomatoes, and simmer it, stirring occasionally, for 20 minutes. Discard the shells, stir in the shrimp, the red snapper, the scallion, and salt to taste, and simmer the *court bouillon* for 2 to 3 minutes, or until the fish just flakes. Serve the *court bouillon* in heated bowls with the rice if desired. Makes about 4 cups, serving 2.

Red Snapper with Artichoke Lemon Sauce

¼ cup drained bottled marinated artichoke
   hearts or 3 rinsed canned artichoke hearts
1 tablespoon drained capers
1 tablespoon minced fresh mint leaves plus
   6 mint sprigs
¼ teaspoon minced garlic
1 tablespoon canned chicken broth
1 large egg yolk at room temperature
1 tablespoon fresh lemon juice
¼ cup olive oil plus additional for coating the
   red snapper
six 6- to 7-ounce red snapper fillets with
   the skin
6 thin lemon slices, quartered

In a blender purée the artichoke hearts with the capers, the minced mint, the garlic, the broth, the egg yolk, and the lemon juice, scraping down the sides with a rubber spatula, with the motor running add ¼ cup of the oil in a stream, blending the sauce until it is smooth, and add salt and pepper to taste. *The sauce will improve in flavor if made 1 day in advance and kept covered and chilled.*

Rub the red snapper fillets with the additional oil and salt and pepper to taste, wrap each fillet skin side up in a sheet of foil, and grill the fillets on a rack set 2 inches over glowing coals for 7 minutes, or until they just flake. Alternatively, bake the fillets, wrapped in foil in the same manner, on a baking sheet in a preheated 450° F. oven for 8 minutes, or until they just flake. Unwrap the packets and transfer each fillet skin side up with a slotted spatula to a plate. Spoon the sauce around the fillets and garnish them with the lemon quarters and the mint sprigs. Serves 6.

PHOTO ON PAGE 60

Red Snapper with Caper Sauce

2 tablespoons finely chopped shallot
2 tablespoons white-wine vinegar
1 tablespoon fresh lemon juice
1 large egg yolk
2 teaspoons drained capers
3 tablespoons unsalted butter, melted
two 6- to 7-ounce red snapper fillets
   with the skin
2 lemon slices

In a small saucepan combine the shallot, the vinegar, the lemon juice, 2 tablespoons water, and salt and pepper to taste, bring the mixture to a simmer, and simmer it, stirring occasionally, until the liquid is reduced to about 2 tablespoons. Transfer the mixture to a blender, add the egg yolk and the capers, and blend the mixture for 3 seconds. With the motor running add the butter, heated, in a stream, blend the sauce until it is combined well, and season it with salt and pepper.

Sprinkle the red snapper fillets lightly with salt, arrange them skin side up in a non-stick skillet, and put a lemon slice on each fillet. Cook the fillets, covered tightly, over moderately low heat for 8 to 10 minutes, or until they just flake, transfer them to heated plates, and spoon the sauce over them. Serves 2.

Poached Red Snapper with Tomato Butter Sauce

½ pound plum tomatoes, peeled, seeded,
  and chopped
1½ tablespoons chopped shallot
1 tablespoon fresh lime juice, or to taste
½ stick (¼ cup) cold unsalted butter, cut into
  8 pieces
½ cup dry white wine
4 lime slices
2 small red snapper fillets (about ¾ pound)
2 teaspoons minced fresh parsley leaves

In a blender purée the tomatoes and the shallot with the lime juice, transfer the purée to a small heavy saucepan, and cook it over moderate heat, stirring occasionally, for 10 to 12 minutes, or until it is very thick. Reduce the heat to low and whisk in the butter, 1 piece at a time, lifting the pan from the heat occasionally to cool the mixture and adding each new piece of butter before the previous one has melted completely. (The sauce should not get hot enough to liquefy. It should be the consistency of a thin hollandaise.) Reserve the sauce, covered.

In a large deep skillet combine the wine, the lime slices, and salt and pepper to taste and add the red snapper and enough water to just cover it. Bring the liquid to a simmer and simmer the mixture gently for 8 to 10 minutes, or until the fillets just flake. Transfer the red snapper carefully with a slotted spatula to paper towels to drain, discard the skin, and arrange the red snapper on 2 heated plates. Ladle the reserved sauce over the red snapper, top the red snapper with the lime slices, drained well, and sprinkle it with the parsley. Serves 2.

Grilled Salmon, Shrimp, and Scallop Kebabs

two 6-inch pieces of center-cut salmon fillet
  (about 2¾ pounds), skinned
12 medium shrimp (about ½ pound), shelled,
  leaving the last joint and the tail intact
12 sea scallops (about ¾ pound), rinsed and
  patted dry
½ cup firmly packed dark brown sugar
½ cup fresh lemon juice
dill sprigs for garnish
lemon wedges if desired

In a shallow dish let six 12-inch wooden skewers soak in water to cover for 2 hours and let them drain on paper towels. Cut each salmon fillet crosswise into six 1-inch-thick slices, discard any small bones, and beginning with the thicker end of each slice roll the slice into a coil. Thread 1 of the shrimp and 1 of the scallops onto a skewer, add 2 of the salmon coils, and add another scallop and shrimp. Make 5 more kebabs with the remaining shrimp, scallops, and salmon coils in the same manner. *The kebabs may be prepared up to this point several hours in advance and kept covered and chilled until it is time to grill them.* In a small bowl stir together the brown sugar and the lemon juice until the mixture is combined well. Season the kebabs with salt and pepper, brush them with the brown sugar mixture, and grill them over glowing coals, basting them often, for 4 to 5 minutes on each side, or until the salmon just flakes and the shrimp are pink and firm. Brush the kebabs with any remaining brown sugar mixture, garnish them with the dill sprigs, and serve them with the lemon wedges if desired. Serves 6.

PHOTO ON PAGE 48

Poached Salmon with Cumin Sauce and Deep-Fried Celery Leaves

For the deep-fried celery leaves
½ cup club soda or seltzer
⅓ cup all-purpose flour
½ teaspoon salt
½ cup packed celery leaves
vegetable oil for deep-frying

four 6-ounce center-cut salmon fillets
1 tablespoon softened unsalted butter
¼ cup minced shallot or onion
2 teaspoons ground cumin
1 teaspoon celery seeds
3 fresh or canned large plum tomatoes,
  chopped fine
⅔ cup dry white wine
⅔ cup heavy cream

Prepare the celery leaves: In a bowl whisk together the club soda, the flour, and the salt until the mixture is just combined. Dip the celery leaves into the mixture and in a deep saucepan fry them in 1½ inches of 375° F. oil in batches, turning them once, for 30 seconds. Transfer the celery leaves with a slotted spoon to paper towels to drain and keep them warm, covered.

Spread the bottom of a shallow flameproof baking dish just large enough to hold the salmon in one layer with the butter, arrange the salmon in the dish, and sprinkle it with salt and pepper to taste, the shallot, the cumin, the celery seeds, and the tomatoes. Pour the wine and ½ cup water over the salmon, bring the liquid to a boil over moderate heat, and poach the salmon, covered with buttered wax paper and foil, in a preheated 350° F. oven, turning it once, for 10 to 12 minutes, or until it just flakes. Transfer the salmon with a slotted spatula to a platter and keep it warm, covered.

Pour the poaching liquid into a saucepan and boil it until it is reduced to about ¾ cup. Add the cream, salt and pepper to taste, and any salmon juices that have accumulated on the platter and boil the mixture until it is thickened. Strain the sauce over the salmon and top it with the deep-fried celery leaves. Serves 4.

PHOTO ON PAGE 27

Spicy Stir-Fried Shark and Vegetables

For the sauce
1 cup canned chicken broth
2 tablespoons cornstarch
¼ cup soy sauce
1 tablespoon cider vinegar
3 tablespoons ketchup
1 tablespoon Worcestershire sauce
1 teaspoon sugar
1 teaspoon Oriental sesame oil (available at Oriental markets and most supermarkets)
½ teaspoon red pepper flakes

¼ cup peanut oil
2 pounds 1-inch-thick shark steaks, skinned, rinsed, patted dry, and cut across the grain into 1½- by 1-inch pieces
8 scallions, chopped fine
1 garlic clove, minced
1 tablespoon shredded peeled gingerroot
2 red bell peppers, cut lengthwise into ¼-inch strips
1¼ pounds broccoli, cut into small flowerets and the stems trimmed, peeled, and sliced thin
½ pound snow peas, strings discarded
steamed rice as an accompaniment

Make the sauce: In a bowl whisk the broth into the cornstarch, a little at a time, and whisk in the soy sauce, the vinegar, the ketchup, the Worcestershire sauce, the sugar, the sesame oil, and the red pepper flakes.

Heat a wok or large heavy skillet over moderately high heat until it is hot, add the oil, and heat it until it is hot but not smoking. In the oil fry the shark in 2 batches, stirring occasionally, for 2 to 2½ minutes, or until it is just tender when tested with a fork, transferring it with a slotted spoon to a plate as it is cooked. Add to the wok the scallions, the garlic, and the gingerroot and cook the mixture, stirring, for 1 minute. Add the bell peppers and the broccoli and cook the mixture, stirring, for 3 to 5 minutes, or until the broccoli is just tender. Stir the sauce, add it to the wok with any juices from the shark that have accumulated on the plate, and bring the mixture to a boil, stirring. Add the snow peas and the shark and cook the mixture, stirring, until the shark is heated through. Serve the dish with the rice. Serves 4 to 6.

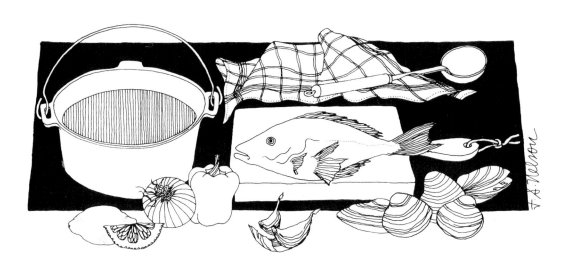

*Pan-Grilled Shark Steaks with
Rosemary Mint Butter*

For the rosemary mint butter
½ stick (¼ cup) unsalted butter, softened
¼ teaspoon pepper
½ teaspoon minced fresh rosemary leaves
1 tablespoon minced fresh mint leaves
¼ teaspoon minced garlic
½ teaspoon pepper
1 teaspoon dried rosemary, crumbled
1 teaspoon dried mint, crumbled
½ teaspoon minced garlic
¼ cup vegetable or olive oil
2 pounds 1-inch-thick shark steaks,
   skinned, rinsed, patted dry,
   and cut into serving pieces
For garnish
thin lime slices
fresh rosemary sprigs
fresh mint sprigs

Make the rosemary mint butter: In a small bowl cream the butter, add the pepper, the rosemary, the mint, and the garlic, and combine the mixture well. Spread the butter ¼ inch thick on a sheet of wax paper, cover it with another sheet of wax paper, and chill it on a flat surface until it is firm. Cut the butter with a small decorative cutter or knife into 8 to 12 pieces and keep it covered and chilled until ready to serve.

In a large bowl combine the pepper, the dried rosemary, the dried mint, the garlic, and the oil, add the shark, and toss it to coat it with the mixture. Heat a well seasoned ridged grill pan or heavy skillet over moderately high heat until it is smoking and in it grill the shark, turning it once, for 8 to 10 minutes, or until it is

tender when tested with a fork. Serve the shark whole or sliced, drizzled with any pan juices, topped with the butter, and garnished with the lime slices, rosemary sprigs, and mint sprigs. Serves 4 to 6.

*Shark with Onions, Bacon, and Potatoes
on Dandelion Greens*

2 tablespoons vegetable oil
2 pounds 1-inch-thick shark steaks, skinned,
   rinsed, patted dry, and cut into 4 pieces
½ pound sliced bacon, chopped
2 onions, sliced thin
2 boiling potatoes, peeled, cut into ¼-inch
   sticks, and reserved in a bowl of cold water
½ cup canned chicken broth
¼ cup fresh orange juice
½ teaspoon sugar
1 teaspoon Worcestershire sauce
1 pound dandelion greens, washed well,
   coarse stems discarded, and patted dry
2 tablespoons minced fresh parsley leaves
1 teaspoon freshly grated orange rind

In a large skillet heat the oil over moderately high heat until it is hot and in it cook the shark, turning it once, for 8 to 10 minutes, or until it is tender when tested with a fork. Transfer the shark to a cutting board and keep it warm, covered loosely. In the skillet cook the bacon over moderate heat, stirring, until it is crisp, transfer it with a slotted spoon to paper towels to drain, and pour all but 2 tablespoons of the fat into a small heatproof bowl, reserving it. In the fat remaining in the skillet cook the onions over moderately high heat until they are browned and transfer them with the slotted spoon to the paper towels. In the skillet cook the pota-

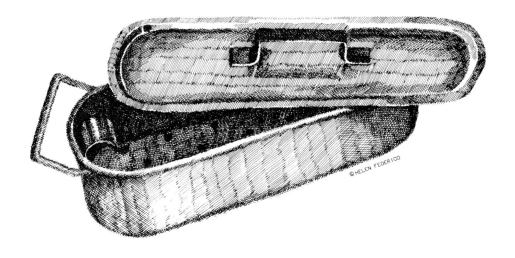

©HELEN FEDERICO

toes, drained and patted dry, in 3 tablespoons of the reserved fat over moderately high heat, stirring occasionally, until they are browned and tender and transfer them to the paper towels. Add to the skillet the broth and the orange juice, bring the liquid to a boil, scraping up the brown bits, and stir in the sugar and the Worcestershire sauce. In the skillet cook the dandelion greens in 2 batches, stirring, until they are wilted, transferring them with the slotted spoon to a heated platter as they are cooked. Add to the skillet the shark, sliced thin across the grain, the onions, and the potatoes and cook the mixture, stirring, until it is just heated through. Arrange the mixture on the dandelion greens. Sprinkle the dish with the bacon, the parsley, the rind, and salt and pepper. Serves 4 to 6.

Sautéed Swordfish and Cherry Tomatoes Filled with Parsley Purée

two 6-ounce pieces (about ¾ inch thick) of
    swordfish steak or other firm white fish
    steak or fillet
1 tablespoon soy sauce
2 tablespoons fresh lemon juice
¼ cup plus 2 tablespoons olive oil
6 cherry tomatoes
6 tablespoons canned chicken broth
1 garlic clove, chopped
1 small onion, chopped
1 cup packed fresh parsley leaves
For garnish
fresh parsley leaves and sprigs
3 lemon slices, halved

Arrange the swordfish in a shallow ceramic or glass dish. In a small bowl whisk together the soy sauce, the lemon juice, and salt and pepper to taste, add ¼ cup of the oil in a stream, whisking, and whisk the marinade until it is emulsified. Pour the marinade over the swordfish, turn the swordfish to coat it, and let it marinate, covered, turning it occasionally, for 30 minutes.

Cut the top ¼ inch off the tomatoes with a serrated knife, scoop out the pulp and seeds carefully, and invert the tomato shells on paper towels to drain. In a small saucepan stir together 1 tablespoon of the remaining oil, the broth, the garlic, the onion, the parsley, and salt and pepper to taste, bring the liquid to a boil, and simmer the mixture, covered, for 13 to 15 minutes, or until the liquid is reduced to about 1 tablespoon. Transfer the parsley mixture to a blender and purée it. Divide the parsley

purée among the tomato shells and garnish each tomato with a parsley leaf.

In a large heavy skillet heat the remaining 1 tablespoon oil over moderately high heat until it is hot but not smoking, in it brown the swordfish, drained, turning it once, for 2 minutes, and cook the swordfish over moderate heat, turning it once, for 4 to 6 minutes, or until it just flakes. Transfer the swordfish to serving plates, divide the tomatoes between the plates, and garnish each serving with a parsley sprig and half the lemon slices. Serves 2.

SHELLFISH

Deviled Crab

¼ cup minced onion
¼ cup minced green bell pepper
¼ cup minced celery
2½ tablespoons unsalted butter
½ pound lump crab meat, picked over and
    flaked
3 tablespoons mayonnaise
¼ cup thinly sliced scallion greens
3 tablespoons fine fresh bread crumbs
½ teaspoon Worcestershire sauce
2 tablespoons minced fresh parsley leaves
2 tablespoons chopped bottled roasted red
    pepper
cayenne to taste
lemon wedges for garnish
parsley sprigs for garnish

In a heavy skillet cook the onion, the bell pepper, and the celery in 1½ tablespoons of the butter over moderately low heat, stirring, until the vegetables are softened and stir in the crab meat, the mayonnaise, the scallion greens, 2 tablespoons of the bread crumbs, the Worcestershire sauce, the minced parsley, the roasted red pepper, the cayenne, and salt to taste. Divide the mixture between 2 large scallop shells or two 1-cup ramekins, sprinkle the remaining 1 tablespoon bread crumbs over it, and drizzle the crab mixture with the remaining 1 tablespoon butter, melted. Bake the mixture on the rack of a broiler pan in the upper third of a preheated 400° F. oven for 10 minutes, transfer the shells to a platter, and garnish the platter with the lemon wedges and the parsley sprigs. Serves 2.

New England Crab Cakes

½ teaspoon minced garlic
¼ cup finely chopped onion
3 tablespoons unsalted butter
¼ cup plus 2 tablespoons crushed Saltine
    crackers
1 large egg, beaten lightly
¼ cup minced fresh parsley leaves
1 teaspoon dry mustard
2 teaspoons fresh lemon juice
1 teaspoon Worcestershire sauce
⅛ teaspoon Tabasco, or to taste
1 tablespoon heavy cream
½ pound lump crab meat, picked over
all-purpose flour for coating the crab cakes
2 tablespoons vegetable oil
tartar sauce as an accompaniment
lemon wedges as an accompaniment

In a small skillet cook the garlic and the onion in 2 tablespoons of the butter over moderately low heat, stirring, for 2 minutes, or until they are softened. Transfer the mixture to a bowl, add the cracker crumbs, the egg, the parsley, the mustard, the lemon juice, the Worcestershire sauce, the Tabasco, and the cream, and combine the mixture well. Add the crab meat, stirring lightly until the mixture is just combined, and let the mixture stand, covered, for 10 minutes. Form the mixture into four ½-inch-thick cakes and coat the cakes with the flour. In a large skillet heat the oil and the remaining 1 tablespoon butter over moderately high heat until the foam subsides and in the fat cook the crab cakes, turning them once, for 3 to 5 minutes, or until they are golden brown. Transfer the cakes to paper towels to drain and serve them with the tartar sauce and lemon wedges. Makes 4 crab cakes, serving 2 as a main course.

Boiled Lobsters with Tomato Basil Beurre Blanc

four 1¼-pound live lobsters
For the beurre blanc
⅓ cup dry white wine
2 tablespoons white-wine vinegar
2 tablespoons minced shallot
1 tablespoon heavy cream
1 teaspoon tomato paste
1 stick (½ cup) unsalted butter, cut into
    8 pieces

½ cup chopped seeded tomato
2 tablespoons minced fresh basil leaves plus
    whole basil leaves for garnish

Into a large kettle of boiling salted water plunge the lobsters, cover the kettle, and return the water to a boil. Boil the lobsters for 8 minutes from the time that the water returns to a boil and transfer them with tongs to a cutting board. Cut off the claws and the legs, split the underside of the tail shells lengthwise, and reassemble the lobsters on heated plates.

Make the *beurre blanc* while the lobsters are boiling: In a small saucepan boil the wine and the vinegar with the shallot until the liquid is reduced to about 2 tablespoons and whisk in the cream and the tomato paste. Reduce the heat to low and whisk in the butter, 1 piece at a time, lifting the pan from the heat occasionally to cool the mixture and adding each new piece of butter before the previous one has melted completely. (The sauce should not get hot enough to liquefy. It should be the consistency of a thin hollandaise.) Season the sauce with salt and pepper.

Divide the tomato and the minced basil among 4 small ramekins and divide the sauce among the ramekins. Garnish the plates with the basil leaves and serve the lobsters with the sauce for dipping. Serves 4.

PHOTO ON PAGE 45

Oysters and Clams with Mignonnette Sauce

For the sauce
3 tablespoons minced shallot
½ cup red-wine vinegar
½ teaspoon salt
¾ teaspoon sugar
1½ teaspoons coarsely ground pepper
1½ tablespoons vegetable oil
¼ cup minced fresh parsley leaves

24 to 36 oysters, shucked (procedure on
    page 242), on the half shell
24 to 36 clams, shucked (procedure on
    page 241), on the half shell
fresh seaweed (available at most fish markets)
    for garnish
4 lemons, cut into wedges

Make the sauce: In a bowl stir together the shallot, the vinegar, the salt, the sugar, the pepper, and the oil and chill the sauce, covered, until serving time. *The sauce*

may be made up to this point 1 day in advance and kept covered and chilled. Just before serving stir in the parsley.

Serve the oysters and the clams on a bed of the seaweed on a platter with the sauce and the lemon wedges. Serves 12.

PHOTO ON PAGE 12

Oysters on the Half Shell with Dilled Oyster Sauce

67 oysters, shucked (procedure on page 242), reserving the liquor and 60 of the bottom shells
¾ cup olive oil or vegetable oil
2 tablespoons snipped fresh dill, plus additional to taste
1 tablespoon fresh lemon juice, plus additional to taste
60 dill sprigs for garnish
20 thin lemon slices, cut decoratively, for garnish

Rinse and dry the reserved oyster shells and arrange 6 on each of 10 oyster plates. In a blender blend the oil, the snipped dill, the lemon juice, ½ cup of the reserved oyster liquor, and 7 of the oysters until the mixture is smooth. Season the mixture with salt and the additional dill and lemon juice and thin the sauce, if desired, with more of the reserved oyster liquor. Spoon about 1½ teaspoons of the sauce into each shell, top it with one of the oysters, and garnish each oyster with a dill sprig. Arrange 2 lemon slices on each plate. Serves 10.

PHOTO ON PAGE 71

Sea Scallops with Garlic Cream Sauce on Caraway Biscuit Triangles

1 small carrot, cut into 2½-inch julienne strips
the white part of 1 leek, cut into 2½-inch julienne strips and washed well
1 cup cake flour (not self-rising)
1½ teaspoons double-acting baking powder
½ teaspoon salt
½ stick (¼ cup) cold unsalted butter
⅓ cup plus 1 tablespoon milk
1 large egg yolk
1 teaspoon caraway seeds
1 teaspoon minced garlic
½ pound small sea scallops, halved horizontally

⅓ cup heavy cream
¼ cup minced fresh parsley leaves

In a saucepan of boiling salted water boil the carrot and the leek for 5 minutes. Drain the vegetables in a sieve, refresh them under cold water, and pat them dry. Into a bowl sift together the flour, the baking powder, and the salt, add 3 tablespoons of the butter, cut into bits, and blend the mixture until it resembles coarse meal. Add ⅓ cup of the milk and stir the mixture until it just forms a dough. Gather the dough into a ball and on a floured surface roll it out ⅛ inch thick. Cut two 6-inch equilateral triangles from the dough with a sharp knife dipped in flour, transfer them to an ungreased baking sheet, and cut six 6- by ¼-inch strips to cover the edges of the triangles. In a small bowl whisk together the remaining 1 tablespoon milk and the egg yolk and brush the triangles with some of the egg wash. Fit and press the strips lightly around the edges of the triangles, trimming them at the ends, brush them with some of the remaining egg wash, and sprinkle the biscuit triangles with the caraway seeds. Bake the biscuit triangles in the middle of a preheated 450° F. oven for 10 to 12 minutes, or until they are golden, transfer them to a rack, and let them cool.

While the biscuit triangles are baking, in a skillet cook the garlic in the remaining 1 tablespoon butter over low heat, stirring, until it is softened, add the scallops, and cook the mixture over moderately high heat, stirring, for 3 minutes. Stir in the carrot and leek, the cream, the parsley, and salt and pepper to taste and cook the mixture, stirring occasionally, for 2 minutes. Transfer the scallops and the vegetables with a slotted spoon to a small bowl and boil the cream mixture over high heat, stirring, until it is reduced to about 3 tablespoons. Arrange the biscuit triangles on a platter, divide the scallop mixture between them, and serve them with the sauce. Serves 2.

Shrimp with Papaya and Prosciutto

a 1-pound papaya, peeled, halved lengthwise,
  and seeded
½ pound thinly sliced prosciutto or Black
  Forest ham, cut into ½-inch-wide strips
3 tablespoons ½-inch pieces of snipped fresh
  chives
1 tablespoon fresh lemon juice, or to taste
4 teaspoons Dijon-style mustard, or to taste
⅓ cup extra-virgin olive oil
¾ pound shrimp, shelled, leaving the tail
  intact, deveined if desired, rinsed, and
  patted dry
fresh whole chives for garnish if desired

Cut 1 of the papaya halves crosswise into 20 thin
slices and arrange 5 of the slices around the edge of 4
salad plates. Halve the remaining papaya lengthwise,
cut it crosswise into thin pieces, and in a bowl toss it
gently with the prosciutto and the snipped chives. *The
plates and the prosciutto mixture may be prepared up to
this point 4 hours in advance and kept covered and
chilled. Bring the plates and the prosciutto mixture to
room temperature before continuing with the recipe.*

In a small bowl whisk together the lemon juice, the
mustard, and salt and pepper to taste. In a large heavy
skillet heat the oil over moderately low heat until it is
very warm, add the shrimp, and season them with salt
and pepper. Cook the shrimp, covered, turning them
occasionally, for 2 to 3 minutes, or until they are just
firm to the touch, transfer them with a slotted spoon to
the prosciutto mixture, and let the oil cool until it is
lukewarm. Add the oil to the lemon juice mixture in a
stream, whisking, pour the sauce over the shrimp and
prosciutto mixture, tossing the mixture gently, and season the mixture with salt and pepper. Divide the mixture
among the plates and garnish each plate with a few
whole chives if desired. Serves 4 as a first course.

PHOTO ON PAGE 23

Terrine de Coquilles Saint-Jacques
(Scallop, Mushroom, and Tomato Terrine)

½ pound mushrooms, 5 of them halved
  lengthwise and sliced thin flat side down,
  1 of them sliced thin lengthwise, and the
  remaining chopped coarse
2 tablespoons minced shallot
3 tablespoons unsalted butter
5 tablespoons medium-dry Sherry

1 tablespoon snipped fresh dill plus dill sprigs
  for garnish
1 pound sea scallops, rinsed and patted dry well
1 teaspoon salt
¼ teaspoon freshly ground white pepper
2 cups well chilled heavy cream
½ cup diced seeded tomato, drained well on
  paper towels
about 1¼ cups spring tomato sauce
  (recipe follows)

In a skillet cook the chopped mushrooms and the
shallot in 2 tablespoons of the butter over moderately
low heat, stirring, until the liquid the mushrooms give
off is evaporated. Add 4 tablespoons of the Sherry and
cook the mixture until all of the liquid is evaporated.
Transfer the mixture to paper towels and pat it dry. Add
the remaining 1 tablespoon butter to the skillet and in it
cook all of the mushroom slices over moderately low
heat, turning them carefully, until the liquid they give
off is evaporated. Transfer the mushroom slices to paper towels and pat them dry. Press the mushroom slices
and the dill sprigs onto the bottom and sides of a buttered 1½-quart glass loaf pan.

Discard the tough muscle clinging to the side of each
scallop, if necessary, and in a food processor purée the
scallops with the salt, the pepper, and the remaining
1 tablespoon Sherry. With the motor running add the
cream in a stream and blend the mixture, scraping down
the sides of the bowl with a rubber spatula, until it is just
smooth. Transfer the purée to a bowl, fold in the mushroom shallot mixture, the tomato, and the snipped dill,
and spoon the mixture into the pan. With a knife press
the mixture carefully against the bottom and sides of the
pan to expel any air pockets and smooth the top evenly.
Cover the pan with a buttered sheet of wax paper and a
sheet of foil, put it in a baking dish just large enough to
hold it, and add enough hot water to the dish to reach
halfway up the sides of the pan. Bake the terrine in a
preheated 350° F. oven for 1 hour to 1 hour and 10 minutes, or until a skewer inserted in the center comes out
clean. Let the terrine cool in the pan for 5 minutes, invert it onto a platter, and blot up the juices around it with
a paper towel. *The terrine may be made up to 1 day in
advance. Let the terrine cool completely and keep it
covered and chilled. Before serving, invert the terrine
into the cleaned glass loaf pan, put the pan in a baking
dish filled with enough hot water to reach halfway up
the sides of the pan, and heat the terrine in a preheated*

300° F. oven for 15 minutes, or until it is heated through. Invert the terrine onto a platter. Spoon some of the tomato sauce around the terrine and serve the remaining sauce separately. Serves 6.

PHOTO ON PAGE 39

Spring Tomato Sauce

a 14-ounce can plum tomatoes including the
    juice
½ teaspoon salt, or to taste
¼ teaspoon sugar
2 tablespoons tomato paste
½ teaspoon dried basil, crumbled
⅛ teaspoon cayenne, or to taste
¾ cup peeled, seeded, and diced fresh
    tomatoes

Force the plum tomatoes with the juice through a food mill into a saucepan. Stir in the salt, the sugar, the tomato paste, the basil, and the cayenne, bring the mixture to a boil, and simmer it, stirring, for 20 minutes. Add the fresh tomatoes and cook the mixture for 5 minutes. Serve the sauce warm. Makes about 1¼ cups.

PHOTO ON PAGE 39

Spicy Fried Shrimp with Sweet-and-Sour Dipping Sauce

For the dipping sauce
1 tablespoon cornstarch
½ cup canned chicken broth
4 tablespoons distilled white vinegar
2 tablespoons sugar
2 tablespoons fresh orange juice
1 tablespoon soy sauce
1 tablespoon Scotch
1 teaspoon minced peeled fresh gingerroot
2 scallions, sliced thin

½ cup all-purpose flour
1 teaspoon salt
1 teaspoon cayenne
½ cup plus 1 tablespoon seltzer or club soda
¾ pound (about 20) shrimp, shelled and
    deveined
vegetable oil for frying

Make the dipping sauce: In a saucepan dissolve the cornstarch in the broth, add the vinegar, the sugar, the orange juice, the soy sauce, the Scotch, the gingerroot, and the scallions, and bring the liquid to a boil, stirring. Simmer the sauce, stirring, for 2 minutes and keep it warm, covered.

In a bowl stir together the flour, the salt, and the cayenne, add the seltzer, and stir the batter until it is just smooth. Dip the shrimp into the batter, a few at a time, coating them well and letting the excess drip off, and in a large deep skillet fry them in batches in 1½ inches of 375° F. oil, turning them, for 30 seconds, or until they are golden brown. Transfer the shrimp with tongs as they are browned to paper towels to drain. Divide the shrimp between 2 plates and serve them with the dipping sauce. Serves 2.

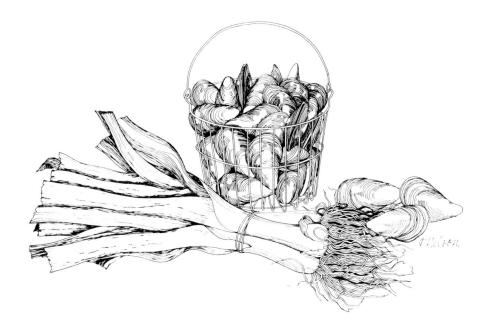

MEAT

BEEF

Guacamole Burgers

1 ripe avocado (preferably California)
1 tablespoon fresh lemon juice, or to taste
1 tablespoon minced pickled *jalapeño* chilies,
    or to taste (wear rubber gloves)
½ cup seeded and chopped tomato
3 tablespoons chopped red onion
¾ pound ground chuck
2 English muffins, split, toasted, and buttered

In a bowl mash the avocado with a fork, add the lemon juice, the *jalapeño*, the tomato, the onion, and salt and pepper to taste, and combine the *guacamole* well.

Halve the chuck, shape each half into a ¾-inch-thick hamburger patty, and sprinkle the patties with salt and pepper to taste. Broil the patties on the rack of a broiler pan under a preheated broiler about 2 inches from the heat, turning them once, for 6 minutes for medium-rare meat.

Arrange 2 muffin halves split sides up on each of 2 serving plates, set a hamburger on one of the halves on each plate, and top it with some of the *guacamole*. Serve the remaining *guacamole* separately. Serves 2.

Grilled Filets Mignons

two 1-inch-thick filets mignons, each
    weighing about 6 to 7 ounces
2 slices of lean bacon
2 teaspoons coarsely ground black pepper
2 fresh rosemary sprigs for garnish if desired
garlic and pimiento mayonnaise (recipe
    follows) as an accompaniment

Pat the filets dry on paper towels, wrap a slice of the bacon around the edge of each filet, and secure it with kitchen string. Rub 1 teaspoon of the pepper onto the cut sides of each filet and grill the filets, sprinkled with salt to taste, on an oiled grill over glowing coals for 4 to 5 minutes on each side, or until they are springy to the touch for medium-rare meat. Transfer the filets to a cutting board and discard the string and the bacon. Let the filets stand for 5 minutes and slice them thin. Arrange the slices, overlapping them slightly, on 2 heated plates and garnish each plate with a rosemary sprig if desired. Serve the filets with the garlic and pimiento mayonnaise. Serves 2.

PHOTO ON PAGE 54

Garlic and Pimiento Mayonnaise

1 garlic clove, minced
½ teaspoon salt, or to taste
1 large egg yolk
1 teaspoon fresh lemon juice, or to taste
½ cup olive oil (preferably extra-virgin,
    available at specialty foods shops and some
    supermarkets)
2 tablespoons minced drained pimiento
⅛ teaspoon cayenne

In a mortar with a pestle mash the garlic with the salt to a paste. Transfer the paste to a small bowl and whisk in the egg yolk and the lemon juice. Add ¼ cup of the oil, drop by drop, whisking constantly, add the remaining ¼ cup oil in a slow stream, whisking constantly, and season the garlic mayonnaise with lemon juice, salt, and black pepper to taste. In a food processor or blender purée the pimiento with ¼ cup of the garlic mayonnaise and the cayenne, scraping down the sides often. Spoon the garlic mayonnaise and the pimiento mayonnaise into a small serving dish. *The mayonnaise may be made up to 2 days in advance and kept covered and chilled.* Makes about ½ cup.

PHOTO ON PAGE 54

Grilled Flank Steak

a 1-pound flank steak, scored lightly
    on both sides
freshly ground pepper to taste
¼ cup olive oil
3 tablespoons fresh lemon juice

2 tablespoons soy sauce
2 garlic cloves, minced
watercress sprigs for garnish

Rub both sides of the steak with the pepper. In a shallow dish large enough to hold the steak whisk together the oil, the lemon juice, the soy sauce, and the garlic, add the steak, coating both sides well with the marinade, and let it marinate, turning it once, for 20 minutes. Remove the steak from the marinade and grill it on an oiled rack over glowing coals, brushing it occasionally with some of the marinade and turning it once, for 10 to 12 minutes for medium-rare meat. Alternatively broil the steak on the rack of a broiler pan under a preheated broiler about 4 inches from the heat, turning it once, for 12 to 15 minutes for medium-rare meat. Transfer the steak to a platter, let it stand for 10 minutes, and holding a sharp knife at a 45° angle slice it thin across the grain. Garnish the steak with the watercress sprigs. Serves 2.

Broiled Beef Rib Bones

3 tablespoons Worcestershire sauce
½ teaspoon freshly ground pepper
1 large garlic clove, minced to a paste
½ stick (¼ cup) unsalted butter, cut into bits
10 long meaty beef rib bones (cut from a rib
   roast), separated

In a small saucepan combine the Worcestershire sauce, the pepper, and the garlic, bring the mixture to a boil, and remove it from the heat. Whisk in the butter and whisk the sauce until it is smooth. Brush the ribs with the sauce and broil them on the rack of a broiling pan under a preheated broiler about 3 inches from the heat, brushing them occasionally with any remaining sauce, for 5 minutes on each side for medium-rare meat. Serves 2.

Rib-Eye Steaks with Potatoes and Green Beans in Lime Butter

1½ tablespoons unsalted butter, softened
1 teaspoon fresh lime juice
¼ teaspoon grated lime rind
¼ pound green beans, trimmed and cut into
   1-inch pieces
¼ pound small red potatoes, cut into
   ¼-inch slices
two 6-ounce 1-inch-thick rib-eye steaks

1½ teaspoons Worcestershire sauce
freshly ground pepper to taste

In a bowl with an electric mixer beat together the butter, the lime juice, the rind, and salt and pepper to taste until the mixture is combined well. In a steamer set over a saucepan of boiling water steam the beans and the potatoes for 8 to 10 minutes, or until they are tender. While the vegetables are steaming brush the steaks on both sides with the Worcestershire sauce, sprinkle them with the pepper and salt to taste, and broil them on the rack of a broiler pan under a preheated broiler about 4 inches from the heat, turning them once, for 6 minutes for medium-rare meat. Transfer the vegetables to the bowl with the lime butter, toss the mixture until the vegetables are coated well, and serve the vegetables with the steaks. Serves 2.

Tortillas with Steak, Cheese, and Salsa

4 flour tortillas
For the salsa
½ tomato, seeded and chopped
½ onion, chopped
two 2-inch pickled *jalapeño* chilies, seeded
   and chopped fine (wear rubber gloves)
½ avocado (preferably California), chopped
¼ teaspoon salt, or to taste

½ onion, sliced thin
1 tablespoon vegetable oil
½ pound boneless sirloin steak, cut across the
   grain into thin strips
¼ cup sour cream
¾ cup grated Monterey Jack

Warm the tortillas, wrapped in foil, in a preheated 200° F. oven.

Make the *salsa* while the tortillas are warming: In a small bowl stir together the tomato, the onion, the chilies, the avocado, and the salt.

In a large heavy skillet cook the onion in the oil over moderately low heat, stirring, until it is softened. Increase the heat to moderately high, add the steak, and cook it, stirring constantly, until the liquid it gives off is evaporated. Divide the sour cream among the tortillas, spreading it evenly, sprinkle it with the Monterey Jack, and top the cheese with the steak. Divide the *salsa* among the tortillas and roll up each tortilla, enclosing the filling. Serves 2.

Vermicelli with Sautéed Steak Strips and Bell Peppers

¼ pound vermicelli
1 tablespoon Oriental sesame oil (available at Oriental markets and most supermarkets)
½ pound chuck blade steaks, cut into 2- by ¼-inch strips
¾ cup ½-inch pieces of the white part of scallion
½ red bell pepper, cut into ½-inch pieces
½ green bell pepper, cut into ½-inch pieces
⅓ cup thinly sliced scallion greens
1 tablespoon soy sauce
freshly ground black pepper to taste

In a kettle of boiling salted water boil the vermicelli for 8 to 10 minutes, or until it is *al dente*, drain it in a colander, and refresh it under cold water. Drain the vermicelli well and transfer it to a platter. In a large heavy skillet heat 2 teaspoons of the oil over moderately high heat until it is hot but not smoking, in it brown the steak, patted dry, and transfer it with a slotted spatula to a plate. In the oil remaining in the skillet sauté the white scallion pieces and the bell peppers, stirring occasionally, until the vegetables are softened, stir in the steak, the scallion greens, the remaining 1 teaspoon oil, the soy sauce, and ¼ cup water, and cook the mixture, scraping up the brown bits, until it is heated through. Sprinkle the mixture with the pepper and salt to taste, spoon it over the vermicelli, and toss the mixture until it is combined. Serves 2.

Roast Tenderloin of Beef with Wild Mushroom Sauce

¼ pound shallots, minced
½ stick (¼ cup) cold unsalted butter
⅓ cup red-wine vinegar
½ ounce dried morels (available at specialty foods shops), soaked in 1 cup hot water for 30 minutes, drained, reserving the soaking liquid, washed well, and minced
1 cup dry red wine
1 cup canned beef broth
a trimmed 3-pound piece of beef tenderloin cut from the loin end, tied, at room temperature
3 tablespoons vegetable oil

In a small saucepan cook the shallots in 2 tablespoons of the butter over moderately low heat, stirring, until

they are softened, add the vinegar, and boil the mixture until the liquid is almost evaporated. Add the morels, the reserved soaking liquid, strained through a fine sieve lined with dampened paper towels, the wine, and the broth, boil the mixture until it is reduced to about 2 cups, and add salt and pepper to taste. *The sauce may be prepared up to this point 2 days in advance, cooled, kept covered and chilled, and reheated.*

Rub the tenderloin with the oil, season it with salt and pepper, and in a roasting pan roast it in a preheated 500° F. oven for 25 minutes, or until a meat thermometer registers 130° F. for medium-rare meat. Transfer the tenderloin to a cutting board and let it stand, covered loosely with foil, for 20 minutes. Whisk the pan juices into the sauce, heated if necessary, and remove the pan from the heat. Swirl in the remaining 2 tablespoons butter and transfer the sauce to a heated sauceboat. Slice the tenderloin, transfer it to a heated platter, and serve it with the sauce. Serves 8.

PHOTO ON PAGE 78

Oxtail and Okra Gumbo

For the stock
4 pounds oxtails, cut into 2-inch sections and trimmed
2 cups canned beef broth
1 onion, halved
1 carrot
1 rib of celery
2 teaspoons salt
For the gumbo
⅓ cup vegetable oil
½ cup all-purpose flour
2 cups chopped onion
2 cups chopped green bell pepper
2 cups chopped celery
a 10-ounce package frozen okra, thawed and chopped
½ teaspoon white pepper, or to taste
½ teaspoon black pepper, or to taste
½ teaspoon cayenne, or to taste
1 bay leaf
1 pound smoked sausage (such as *kielbasa*), cut crosswise into ½-inch slices
Tabasco to taste

cooked rice as an accompaniment

Make the stock: In a kettle combine the oxtails, the

broth, 8 cups water, the onion, the carrot, the celery, and the salt, bring the liquid to a boil, skimming the froth, and simmer the oxtails, covered, for 3 hours and 30 minutes, or until they are very tender. Transfer the oxtails with a slotted spoon to a bowl, let them cool until they can be handled, and discard the bones and fat, reserving the meat. Strain the stock through a fine sieve into a bowl and spoon off the fat. *The stock may be made up to 2 days in advance and the meat and the stock kept covered and chilled separately. Remove the congealed fat from the chilled stock before continuing with the recipe.*

Make the gumbo: In a heavy skillet heat the oil over moderately high heat until it is very hot but not smoking, add the flour gradually, whisking, and cook the *roux*, whisking constantly, for 2 to 5 minutes, or until it is the color of peanut butter. Scrape the *roux* immediately into a heavy kettle, add the onion, the bell pepper, and the celery, and cook the mixture over moderate heat, stirring, until the vegetables are softened slightly. Add the okra and cook the mixture, stirring, for 5 minutes. Stir in the white pepper, the black pepper, the cayenne, the oxtail stock, and the bay leaf, bring the liquid to a boil, stirring, and simmer the mixture, covered, for 30 minutes. In a skillet sauté the sausage in batches over moderately high heat, turning it, until it has released its fat and is golden brown, transferring it as it is browned to paper towels to drain. Add the sausage to the mixture and simmer the mixture, covered, for 15 minutes. Add the reserved oxtail meat and simmer the gumbo, covered, for 15 minutes. *The gumbo may be made up to 3 days in advance and kept covered and chilled.* Discard the bay leaf, season the gumbo with salt and the Tabasco, and serve it in bowls over the rice. Makes about 12 cups, serving 6 to 8.

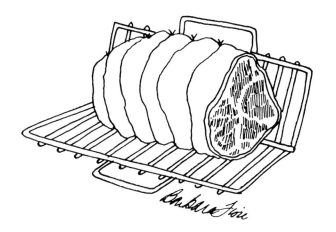

Oxtail Goulash with Caraway Noodles

1½ pounds onions, chopped
3 tablespoons vegetable oil
2 large garlic cloves, minced
2 tablespoons sweet paprika
a 1-pound can tomatoes, drained and chopped
4 pounds oxtails, cut into 2-inch sections and trimmed
1 cup canned beef broth
1 teaspoon grated lemon rind
1 teaspoon caraway seeds
1 large green bell pepper, chopped
1 large red bell pepper, chopped
1 teaspoon dried marjoram, crumbled
minced fresh parsley leaves for garnish
caraway noodles (recipe follows)

In a heavy kettle cook the onions in the oil over moderate heat, stirring, until they are golden, add the garlic, and cook the vegetables, stirring, for 1 minute. Add the paprika and cook the mixture, stirring, for 1 minute. Add the tomatoes, the oxtails, the broth, 2 cups water, the rind, the caraway seeds, and salt and pepper to taste, bring the liquid to a boil, and braise the oxtails, covered, in a preheated 350° F. oven for 3 hours. Spoon off the fat, add the bell peppers and the marjoram, and braise the mixture, covered, in the 350° F. oven for 30 minutes, or until the oxtails are very tender. *The goulash may be made up to 3 days in advance and kept covered and chilled. It improves in flavor if made at least 1 day in advance.* Before serving sprinkle the goulash with the parsley and serve it with the noodles. Serves 4 to 6.

Caraway Noodles

½ pound egg noodles
½ stick (¼ cup) unsalted butter
2 teaspoons caraway seeds
2 tablespoons minced fresh parsley leaves

In a large saucepan of boiling salted water boil the noodles, stirring occasionally, until they are just tender. Drain the noodles in a colander, refresh them under cold water, and drain them well. In a large skillet melt the butter over moderately low heat, add the noodles, the caraway seeds, the parsley, and salt and pepper to taste, and heat the mixture, stirring and tossing it, until it is heated through and combined well. Serves 4 to 6.

Curried Oxtail Stew with Spinach

4 cups chopped onion
⅓ cup vegetable oil
6 large garlic cloves, minced
a 3- by 1-inch piece of peeled gingerroot,
    minced
2 tablespoons ground coriander
1 tablespoon ground cumin
1 tablespoon turmeric
2 teaspoons sweet paprika
½ teaspoon cayenne
a 28-ounce can Italian plum tomatoes, drained
    and chopped
2 teaspoons salt
4 pounds oxtails, cut into 2-inch sections and
    trimmed
1 pound spinach
⅓ cup minced fresh coriander if desired

In a heavy kettle cook the onion in the oil over moderate heat, stirring, until it is golden, add the garlic and the gingerroot, and cook the mixture, stirring, for 1 minute. Add the ground coriander, the cumin, the turmeric, the paprika, and the cayenne and cook the mixture, stirring, for 15 seconds. Add the tomatoes, the salt, the oxtails, and 3 cups water, bring the liquid to a boil, and braise the mixture, covered, in a preheated 350° F. oven for 3 hours, or until the oxtails are tender. *The stew may be prepared up to this point 2 days in advance and kept covered and chilled. It improves in flavor if made at least 1 day in advance.*

Wash the spinach, discard the coarse stems, and drain the spinach. In a large saucepan cook the spinach in the water clinging to the leaves, covered, over moderately high heat for 2 to 3 minutes, or until it is just wilted. Drain the spinach well, pressing out any excess liquid, and chop it. Spoon off the fat from the stew, stir in the spinach and salt and pepper to taste, and simmer the stew for 5 minutes. Just before serving sprinkle the stew with the minced coriander if desired. Serves 4 to 6.

Oxtails Provençale

1½ pounds onions, chopped
3 tablespoons olive oil
5 garlic cloves
1½ cups dry white wine
a 28-ounce can Italian plum tomatoes,
    drained, reserving the juice, and chopped
    coarse

five ½-inch-wide strips of orange rind
1 bay leaf
4 teaspoons dried rosemary, crumbled
2 teaspoons salt
1 teaspoon pepper
4 pounds oxtails, cut into 2-inch sections and
    trimmed
¾ pound carrots, cut diagonally into ½-inch
    slices
1 pound small white onions, blanched in
    boiling water for 1 minute, drained, and
    peeled
½ cup drained black olives

In a heavy kettle cook the chopped onions in the oil over moderately low heat, stirring, until they are softened, add 4 of the garlic cloves, minced, and cook the mixture, stirring, for 1 minute. Add the wine, the tomatoes including the reserved juice, the rind, the bay leaf, 3 teaspoons of the rosemary, the salt, the pepper, and the oxtails, bring the liquid to a boil, and braise the mixture, covered, in a preheated 350° F. oven for 2 hours. Add the carrots and the small white onions and braise the mixture for 1 hour, or until the oxtails are tender. Discard the bay leaf and spoon off the fat. Add the olives, the remaining garlic clove, minced, the remaining 1 teaspoon rosemary, and salt and pepper to taste and simmer the stew, uncovered, on top of the stove for 5 minutes. *The stew may be made up to 2 days in advance and kept covered and chilled. It improves in flavor if made at least 1 day in advance.* Serves 4 to 6.

Deviled Oxtails

4 pounds oxtails, cut into 2-inch sections and
    trimmed
1 cup canned beef broth
1 onion, quartered
1 carrot
1 rib of celery
1 teaspoon salt
1 bay leaf
½ cup sour cream
¼ cup Dijon-style mustard
2 teaspoons Worcestershire sauce, or to taste
¼ teaspoon cayenne, or to taste
2 cups fine dry bread crumbs
½ stick (¼ cup) unsalted butter, melted

In a kettle combine the oxtails, 2 cups water, the

broth, the onion, the carrot, the celery, the salt, and the bay leaf, bring the liquid to a boil, and braise the oxtails, covered, in a preheated 350° F. oven for 2 hours and 30 minutes, or until they are tender but not falling apart. Let the oxtails cool in the liquid, uncovered. *The oxtails may be prepared up to this point 2 days in advance and kept covered and chilled. Reheat the oxtails before continuing with the recipe.*

Transfer the oxtails with a slotted spoon to paper towels, pat them dry, and trim any excess fat. In a small bowl combine well the sour cream, the mustard, the Worcestershire sauce, the cayenne, and salt and pepper to taste. Have the bread crumbs ready in a wide shallow bowl. Spread the sour cream mixture over the oxtails, coating them completely, dredge the oxtails in the bread crumbs, shaking off any excess, and arrange them in one layer in a buttered roasting pan. Drizzle the butter over the oxtails and broil the oxtails under a preheated broiler about 4 inches from the heat, turning them, for 15 minutes, or until they are golden brown and crusty. Serves 4.

Calf's Liver with Red-Wine Sauce

½ cup dry red wine
1½ tablespoons red-wine vinegar
2 garlic cloves, minced
1 teaspoon dried sage, crumbled
two ¼-inch-thick slices of calf's liver (about ½ pound)
2 slices of lean bacon, chopped
1 tablespoon finely chopped fresh parsley leaves

In a shallow baking dish combine well the wine, the vinegar, the garlic, the sage, and salt and pepper to taste, add the liver, turning it to coat it with the mixture, and let it marinate at room temperature for 30 minutes. In a large heavy skillet cook the bacon over moderate heat, stirring, until it is crisp and transfer it with a slotted spoon to paper towels to drain. Heat the bacon fat over moderately high heat until it is hot but not smoking, in it sauté the liver, drained, reserving the marinade, and patted dry, turning it once, for 2 minutes, or until it is browned on the outside but still pink within, and transfer it to a heated platter. Add the marinade to the skillet and boil it over high heat, scraping up the brown bits, until it is reduced by half. Strain the pan juices through a fine sieve over the liver and sprinkle the liver with the bacon and the parsley. Serves 2.

VEAL

Veal Paprika

8 teaspoons vegetable oil
½ pound veal cutlets, flattened ⅛ inch thick between dampened sheets of wax paper
flour seasoned with salt and pepper for dredging
1 onion, sliced thin
1 garlic clove, minced
2 teaspoons sweet paprika
½ cup plus 2 tablespoons sour cream
1 teaspoon fresh lemon juice, or to taste
2 teaspoons minced fresh parsley leaves

In a large heavy skillet heat 6 teaspoons of the oil over moderately high heat until it is hot but not smoking and in it brown the veal, patted dry and dredged in the flour, in batches, transferring it as it is browned to a plate. Discard any oil remaining in the skillet and wipe the skillet out carefully with paper towels. Add the remaining 2 teaspoons oil to the skillet and in it cook the onion over moderate heat, stirring, until it is golden. Stir in the garlic, the paprika, ½ cup of the sour cream, the veal and any juices that have accumulated on the platter, and ¾ cup water, bring the liquid to a boil, stirring, and simmer the veal, covered, for 15 to 20 minutes, or until it is tender and the sauce is thickened. Stir in the remaining 2 tablespoons sour cream, the lemon juice, and salt and pepper to taste and sprinkle the dish with the parsley. Serves 2.

Stuffed Breast of Veal

1 cup chopped onion
2 tablespoons olive oil
3 garlic cloves, minced
1 tablespoon dried marjoram, crumbled
2 teaspoons dried thyme, crumbled
3 slices of homemade-type white bread,
    crusts removed
½ cup milk
1¼ pounds hot Italian sausage, casings
    discarded
two 10-ounce packages frozen chopped
    spinach, thawed, drained, and squeezed dry
2 teaspoons salt
2 tablespoons Dijon-style mustard
3 large eggs, beaten lightly
1 cup freshly grated Parmesan
a 14-ounce can artichoke hearts, drained and
    quartered
1 whole 8- to 10-pound veal breast, halved
    crosswise by the butcher, leaving the meat
    on the bone, and a deep pocket cut
    lengthwise in each half, leaving about a
    1-inch border on 3 sides
6 hard-boiled large eggs
8 cups chicken stock (page 247) or canned
    chicken broth
2 cups dry white wine
watercress for garnish

In a skillet cook the onion in the oil over moderately low heat, stirring, until it is softened. Add the garlic, the marjoram, and the thyme, cook the mixture, stirring, for 2 minutes, and let it cool. In a bowl let the bread soak in the milk for 15 minutes, squeeze it dry, and in a large bowl combine it with the sausage, the spinach, the salt, the mustard, the beaten eggs, the Parmesan, and the onion mixture. In a food processor purée the mixture coarse in batches, pulsing the motor. (Test the seasoning by cooking a small amount of the mixture.) Transfer the mixture to a bowl and stir in the artichoke hearts.

Sprinkle the pocket of each veal breast half lightly with salt and pepper, coat the hard-boiled eggs with some of the stuffing, and spread one fourth of the remaining stuffing in each pocket. Arrange 3 of the eggs lengthwise down the center on the stuffing in each pocket, spacing them evenly, top them with the remaining stuffing, and sew the openings closed on each veal breast half with a trussing needle and kitchen string.

Wrap each half well in a large piece of cheesecloth and tie the ends of the cheesecloth with kitchen string to secure them. In a large saucepan bring the stock and the wine to a simmer. In each of 2 large baking pans arrange a veal breast half bone side up, pour half the stock mixture over each veal breast half, and braise the veal, covered tightly with foil, in a preheated 350° F. oven for 2 hours and 30 minutes to 3 hours, or until the veal is tender. (Alternatively, if your oven is not large enough to hold 2 baking pans, braise 1 veal breast half in the oven and simmer the other in a kettle, covered tightly, on top of the stove for 2 hours and 30 minutes to 3 hours, or until the veal is tender.) *The veal may be made up to 2 days in advance, let cool in the stock, and kept covered and chilled. Reheat the veal in the stock.* Transfer the veal to a cutting board, reserving the stock for another use. Cut the bones from the veal in one piece and discard them. Slice the veal thin with a serrated knife, arrange it decoratively on a heated platter, and garnish it with the watercress. Serves 12.

PHOTO ON PAGE 13

PORK

Pork with Mustard Seed Sauce

2 tablespoons vegetable oil
a 2-pound piece boneless pork loin, cut from
    the loin end
½ cup dry white wine
4 teaspoons mustard seeds, crushed lightly in
    a mortar with a pestle
2 teaspoons cornstarch dissolved in
    1 tablespoon water
1 to 1½ teaspoons Dijon-style mustard,
    or to taste
broccoli rabe with lemon and garlic
    (page 169) as an accompaniment

In a flameproof heavy casserole heat the oil over moderately high heat until it is hot but not smoking and in it brown the pork, patted dry and seasoned with salt and pepper. Transfer the pork to a plate, pour off all but 1 tablespoon of the fat in the casserole, and add the wine and the mustard seeds. Return the pork to the casserole, bring the liquid to a boil, and braise the pork, covered, in a preheated 325° F. oven for 55 minutes, or until a meat thermometer registers 155° F., for juicy, barely pink meat. Transfer the pork to a cutting board and let it stand for 10 minutes. Skim the fat from the pan juices, stir the cornstarch mixture, and stir it into the pan juices. Bring the sauce to a boil over moderately high heat, stirring, and season it with salt and pepper. Remove the casserole from the heat, whisk in the mustard, and transfer the sauce to a heated sauceboat. Slice the pork, arrange it on a heated platter, and surround it with the broccoli rabe. Serve the pork with the sauce. Serves 4.

PHOTO ON PAGE 66

Pork Chops with Bell Pepper and Tomato Sauce

1 teaspoon vegetable oil
2 shoulder pork chops (about 1¼ pounds)
1 onion, sliced thin
1 green bell pepper, cut lengthwise into ¼-inch-wide strips
a 14-ounce can Italian-style tomatoes including the juice, crushed with a fork
cooked rice as an accompaniment

In a heavy skillet heat the oil over moderately high heat until it is hot but not smoking, in it brown the pork chops, patted dry, and transfer them to a plate. Add the onion and the bell pepper to the skillet and sauté the vegetables, stirring, for 3 minutes. Stir in the tomatoes and add the pork chops and any juices that have accumulated on the plate. Bring the liquid to a boil, cook the mixture, covered, over moderate heat for 25 minutes, and season it with salt and pepper. Serve the pork chops and sauce over the rice. Serves 2.

Pork Chops with Tomatoes, Capers, and Olives

1 tablespoon olive oil
two 1-inch-thick loin pork chops (about ¾ pound)
⅓ cup finely chopped shallots
¼ cup dry white wine
a 14-ounce can plum tomatoes, drained and chopped
1 teaspoon dried basil, crumbled
a pinch of dried thyme, crumbled
6 pitted black olives, quartered
1 tablespoon drained capers
1 tablespoon unsalted butter
¼ teaspoon sugar
2 tablespoons finely chopped fresh parsley leaves

In a skillet heat the oil over moderately high heat until it is hot but not smoking, in it brown the pork chops, patted dry and seasoned with salt and pepper, and transfer them to a plate. Add the shallots to the skillet and cook them over moderate heat, stirring, until they are golden. Add the wine, the tomatoes, the basil, and the thyme and simmer the mixture, stirring occasionally, for 5 minutes. Stir in the olives, the capers, the butter, the sugar, and salt and pepper to taste, add the pork chops and any juices that have accumulated on the plate, and simmer the mixture, covered, for 5 minutes, or until the pork is no longer pink. Transfer the pork chops to a heated platter, spoon the sauce around them, and sprinkle the dish with the parsley. Serves 2.

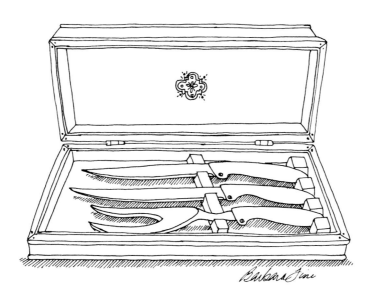

Spicy Orange Pork Kebabs

¼ cup firmly packed dark brown sugar
¼ cup red-wine vinegar
1 tablespoon soy sauce
¼ teaspoon dried hot red pepper flakes
1½ teaspoons freshly grated orange rind
1 tablespoon Worcestershire sauce
¼ cup fresh orange juice
½ stick (¼ cup) unsalted butter
1 pound sweet potatoes, cut into 1-inch-thick
    slices, cooked in boiling salted water until
    just tender, and drained
1¼ pounds boneless pork loin, cut into
    8 cubes
4 slices of lean bacon, halved crosswise
4 fresh hot red peppers
8 small red or white onions, cooked in boiling
    salted water until just tender, drained, and
    peeled
1 large navel orange, ends trimmed, the
    orange halved crosswise into 2 rounds, and
    the rounds quartered into wedges
salad greens such as watercress, spinach,
    arugula, or curly endive (chicory) as an
    accompaniment
julienne strips of orange rind for garnish

In a shallow dish let four 10-inch wooden skewers soak in water to cover for 1 hour. In a small saucepan combine the brown sugar, the vinegar, the soy sauce, the red pepper flakes, the grated orange rind, the Worcestershire sauce, the orange juice, and the butter and heat the mixture over moderate heat, stirring occasionally, until the butter is melted.

Thread the skewers with the sweet potatoes, the pork, wrapped in the bacon, the peppers, the onions, and the orange wedges, alternating the ingredients in a decorative pattern. Broil the kebabs in a jelly-roll pan under a preheated broiler about 4 inches from the heat, basting them often with the orange mixture and turning them once, for 20 to 24 minutes, or until the bacon is crisp and the vegetables are glazed.

Arrange the kebabs and the salad greens on a platter and drizzle the dish with the pan drippings, skimmed of excess fat, and any remaining orange mixture, heated. Garnish the dish with the strips of orange rind. Serves 4.

Cider-Braised Pork Loin with Sautéed Apples

2 teaspoons salt
1 teaspoon freshly ground pepper
1 teaspoon dried sage, crumbled
1 teaspoon dried thyme, crumbled
a 3-pound rib-end boneless pork loin, rolled
    and tied
2 tablespoons vegetable oil
2 cups chopped onion
4 large garlic cloves
½ cup apple cider
sautéed apples (recipe follows)
fresh sage leaves for garnish if desired

In a small bowl combine the salt, the pepper, the sage, and the thyme and on a large piece of wax paper rub the mixture on the pork, coating the pork well. Wrap the pork in the wax paper and chill it for at least 2 hours or overnight. Pat the pork dry with paper towels. In a heavy flameproof casserole heat the oil over moderately high heat until it is hot but not smoking and in it brown the pork. Transfer the pork to a plate, pour off all but 2 tablespoons of the fat, and in the fat remaining in the casserole cook the onion and the garlic over moderate

heat, stirring, for 1 minute. Return the pork to the casserole, add the cider, and bring the liquid to a boil. Braise the pork, covered, in a preheated 325° F. oven for 50 minutes to 1 hour, or until a meat thermometer registers 155° F., for juicy, barely pink meat. Transfer the pork to a heated platter, discard the string, and let the pork stand for 10 minutes. Spoon off the fat from the pan juices and in a blender or food processor purée the pan juices and solids remaining in the casserole. Season the sauce with salt and pepper and serve it in a heated sauceboat, straining it through a fine sieve if desired. Arrange the sautéed apples around the pork and if desired garnish the platter with the sage leaves. Serves 6.

PHOTO ON PAGE 21

Sautéed Apples

2 tablespoons unsalted butter
1 large Granny Smith apple, cored and cut
    into 12 wedges
1 large Red Delicious apple, cored and cut
    into 12 wedges

In a large skillet melt the butter with 2 tablespoons water over moderately low heat and in the mixture cook the apples, covered, in one layer, in batches if necessary, for 2 to 4 minutes, or until they are just tender. Increase the heat to moderate and cook the apples, seasoned with salt and pepper, uncovered, turning them, until they are tender and lightly golden.

PHOTO ON PAGE 21

Sherry Vinegared Spareribs

2 pounds lean pork spareribs, cut into
    individual ribs
3 tablespoons firmly packed light brown sugar
1½ tablespoons medium-dry Sherry
3 tablespoons cider vinegar
1 tablespoon fresh lemon juice
1 tablespoon soy sauce
¾ teaspoon Worcestershire sauce, or to taste
freshly ground pepper to taste

In a kettle blanch the ribs in boiling salted water for 30 minutes and drain them. While the ribs are cooking, in a small saucepan combine the brown sugar, the Sherry, the vinegar, the lemon juice, the soy sauce, the Worcestershire sauce, and the pepper, bring the basting sauce to a boil, stirring, and boil it until it is reduced to

about 3 tablespoons. Arrange the ribs, meaty side up, on the oiled rack of a broiler pan, brush them with some of the basting sauce, and broil them under a preheated broiler about 2 inches from the heat for 5 to 7 minutes, or until they are browned. Brush the ribs with the remaining basting sauce. Serves 2.

Fried Pork Strips with Soy Ginger Sauce

1½ pounds ½-inch-thick loin pork chops,
    boned and cut into ½-inch-wide strips
1 teaspoon Scotch
¼ cup chopped onion
2 teaspoons chopped peeled gingerroot
2 tablespoons soy sauce
2½ teaspoons distilled white vinegar
¼ teaspoon honey
2 teaspoons sugar
¼ teaspoon cornstarch
1½ tablespoons thinly sliced scallion greens
flour for dredging
vegetable oil for frying

In a bowl combine well the pork strips, the Scotch, the onion, and pepper to taste and let the pork marinate, covered and chilled, for 30 minutes. In a blender purée the gingerroot with the soy sauce, the vinegar, the honey, and the sugar and transfer the mixture to a small saucepan. Stir in the cornstarch until it is dissolved, bring the mixture to a boil over moderately high heat, stirring, and stir in the scallion greens.

Dredge the pork with any onion that adheres to it in the flour, shaking off the excess flour. In a skillet heat ½ inch of the oil over moderately high heat until it is hot but not smoking and in it fry the pork for 4 to 5 minutes, or until it is no longer pink within. Transfer the pork to paper towels to drain and serve it with the soy ginger sauce. Serves 2.

Bacon Twists

6 slices of lean bacon, halved crosswise

Twist the bacon into corkscrews, arrange it in rows on the rack of a broiler pan, and put skewers across the ends of the rows so that the bacon will not untwist while cooking. Bake the bacon in a preheated 375° F. oven for 20 minutes, or until it is crisp, and transfer it to paper towels to drain. Serves 2.

PHOTO ON PAGE 16

Sausage and Bell Pepper Hush Puppies with Mustard Sauce

¼ cup sour cream
1 tablespoon Dijon-style mustard
fresh lemon juice to taste
¼ pound *kielbasa* or other cooked smoked
    sausage, quartered lengthwise and cut
    crosswise into ¼-inch pieces
½ cup chopped red bell pepper
½ teaspoon vegetable oil plus additional for
    deep-frying
1 large egg
¼ cup milk
½ cup yellow cornmeal
¼ cup all-purpose flour
1¼ teaspoons double-acting baking powder
⅛ teaspoon cayenne, or to taste
¼ teaspoon salt
¼ cup thinly sliced scallion

In a small bowl whisk together the sour cream, the mustard, the lemon juice, and salt to taste. In a skillet cook the *kielbasa* and the bell pepper in ½ teaspoon of the oil over moderate heat, stirring occasionally, for 5 minutes, or until the bell pepper is tender-crisp. In a bowl whisk together the egg and the milk, into the bowl sift together the cornmeal, the flour, the baking powder, the cayenne, and the salt, and whisk the mixture until it is combined well. Transfer the *kielbasa* mixture with a slotted spoon to the bowl, add the scallion, and stir the batter until it is just combined. In a deep skillet or deep fryer heat 1½ inches of the additional oil to 320° F., add tablespoons of the batter, and fry them, turning them once, for 1½ to 2 minutes, or until they are golden, transferring them with a slotted spoon as they are fried to paper towels to drain. Serve the hush puppies with the mustard sauce. Makes about 10 hush puppies.

Sausage and Cabbage with Caraway

6 cups shredded cabbage
½ pound *kielbasa* or other cooked smoked
    sausage, cut into ¼-inch slices
1 teaspoon white-wine vinegar, or to taste
½ teaspoon caraway seeds

In a large saucepan of boiling salted water blanch the cabbage for 5 minutes and drain it. In a large skillet brown the *kielbasa* over moderate heat for 5 minutes

and transfer it to paper towels to drain. Pour off all but 1 tablespoon of the fat, stir in the vinegar, the cabbage, the *kielbasa*, the caraway seeds, and salt and pepper to taste, and cook the mixture, scraping up the brown bits, for 1 minute. Serves 2.

Baked Apples Stuffed with Sausage and Cranberries

1 pound bulk sausage meat
1 onion, chopped
1 teaspoon dried sage, crumbled
½ teaspoon dried thyme, crumbled
1 cup cranberries, picked over
½ cup fresh bread crumbs
3 ribs of celery, chopped fine
½ cup minced fresh parsley leaves
8 Golden Delicious apples
fresh sage leaves for garnish if desired

In a large skillet cook the sausage, crumbled, over moderate heat, breaking it up with a fork, until it is no longer pink. Stir in the onion, the dried sage, the thyme, the cranberries, and salt and pepper to taste and cook the mixture, stirring occasionally, until the cranberries just begin to pop. Stir in the bread crumbs, the celery, and the parsley and remove the skillet from the heat. *The stuffing may be prepared up to this point up to 1 day in advance and kept covered and chilled.*

Cut off the top ½ inch of the apples, core the apples with a melon-ball cutter, and scoop out the flesh, reserving it and leaving a ¾ inch shell. Chop the flesh coarse and stir it into the stuffing. Divide the stuffing among the apples, mounding it, and arrange the apples in a baking pan. Pour 1 inch hot water into the pan and bake the apples, covered tightly with foil, in a preheated 375° F. oven for 1 hour and 30 minutes, or until they are crisp-tender. Arrange the apples on a heated serving dish and garnish the dish with the sage leaves if desired. Serves 8.

Sausage Patties with Fresh Herbs

1¼ pounds ground lean pork
½ pound fresh pork fat (available at butcher
    shops)
1½ tablespoons minced fresh thyme leaves or
    2½ teaspoons dried, crumbled
1 tablespoon minced fresh sage leaves or 2
    teaspoons dried, crumbled, plus 1 sage
    sprig for garnish

½ cup minced fresh parsley leaves,
   or to taste
2 teaspoons salt
¾ teaspoon white pepper
2 tablespoons vegetable oil

In a bowl combine well the pork, the fat, the thyme, the minced sage, the parsley, the salt, and the white pepper. Divide the mixture into 18 balls and flatten the balls into patties about ½ inch thick. *The sausage patties may be made up to 1 day in advance and kept covered and chilled.* In a large skillet heat the oil over moderate heat until it is hot but not smoking, in it fry the patties in batches for 4 to 5 minutes on each side, or until they are golden brown and no longer pink within, and drain them on paper towels. Transfer the sausage patties to a serving plate and garnish them with the sage sprig. Serves 6.

©HELEN FEDERICO '86

LAMB

Lamb à la Grecque en Papillote
(*Lamb with Feta, Tomatoes,
and Olives in Parchment*)

1 tablespoon vegetable oil plus additional for
   brushing the parchment
four 1-inch-thick lean lamb shoulder chops or
   leg steaks
½ cup dry white wine
four 20- by 15-inch pieces of parchment paper
1 teaspoon minced garlic
¼ pound Feta, cut into 8 slices
3 plum tomatoes, cut into 16 slices
24 black olives (preferably Kalamata),
   sliced lengthwise
1 teaspoon fresh rosemary leaves, chopped, or
   ½ teaspoon dried, crumbled
4 sprigs of fresh rosemary for garnish
   if desired

In a large heavy skillet heat 1 tablespoon of the oil over moderately high heat until it is hot but not smoking, in it brown the lamb, patted dry and seasoned with salt and pepper, turning it once, for 3 minutes, and transfer it to a plate. Pour off the fat from the skillet, add the wine, and deglaze the skillet over high heat, scraping up the brown bits. Boil the wine until it is reduced to about 2 tablespoons and add any lamb juices that have accumulated on the plate.

Brush a 20- by 15- inch area of the work surface with the additional oil, arrange 1 of the parchment pieces on top of it, and brush it lightly with the oil. Arrange a second piece of parchment on top of the first piece, brush it lightly with the oil, and repeat the procedure with the remaining 2 parchment pieces. Fold the top piece of parchment in half by bringing the short ends together, unfold it, and arrange 1 of the chops on the parchment just to the right of the fold line. Rub the chop with ¼ teaspoon of the garlic and arrange decoratively on it 2 slices of the Feta, 4 slices of the tomato, and about 10 to 12 slices of the olives. Sprinkle the chop with ¼ teaspoon of the chopped rosemary, pour one fourth of the deglazing liquid over it, and fold the other half of the parchment over the chop. Beginning with a folded corner, twist and fold the edges together, forming a half-heart shape, and seal the end tightly by twisting it. Make *papillotes* with the remaining parchment, chops, Feta, tomatoes, olives, chopped rosemary, and deglazing liquid in the same manner. *The* papillotes *may be prepared up to this point 1 hour in advance.* Bake the *papillotes* on a baking sheet in a preheated 400° F. oven for 10 minutes, transfer them to warm plates, and cut them open. Garnish each *papillote* with a rosemary sprig if desired. Serves 4.

Lamb au Poivre

four 1-inch-thick lean lamb shoulder chops
    or leg steaks
4 teaspoons coarsely ground black pepper,
    or to taste
1 tablespoon vegetable oil
1 green bell pepper, chopped fine
1 teaspoon dried tarragon, crumbled
½ cup dry red wine
½ cup canned chicken broth
2 tablespoons unsalted butter, cut into pieces
1 tablespoon Dijon-style mustard
2 tablespoons minced fresh parsley leaves

Rub each lamb chop on both sides with a total of 1 teaspoon of the pepper and salt to taste and let the chops stand for 15 minutes. In a skillet heat the oil over moderately high heat until it is hot but not smoking and in it sauté the lamb, turning it once, for 6 to 8 minutes for medium-rare meat. Transfer the lamb with a slotted spatula to a plate and keep it warm, covered. In the fat remaining in the skillet cook the bell pepper over moderately low heat, stirring, for 3 minutes, add the tarragon and the wine, and boil the mixture until it is reduced to about 2 tablespoons. Add the broth and boil the mixture until it is reduced by half. Whisk in the butter, the mustard, the parsley, and salt to taste, add the lamb and any juices that have accumulated on the plate, and heat the mixture over moderately low heat, turning the lamb, until it is heated through, but do not let the sauce boil. Serves 4.

Lamb in Parmesan Crust with Brown Butter, Lemon, and Capers

½ cup freshly grated Parmesan
½ cup fine dry bread crumbs
2 large eggs, beaten lightly
5 tablespoons vegetable oil
four 1-inch-thick lean lamb shoulder chops or
    leg steaks
seasoned flour for dredging the chops
3 tablespoons unsalted butter, cut into pieces
1 tablespoon fresh lemon juice, or to taste
2 tablespoons drained capers

In a shallow baking dish stir together the Parmesan and the bread crumbs. In another shallow baking dish whisk together the eggs and 1 tablespoon of the oil.

Dredge the lamb in the seasoned flour, shaking off the excess, dip it in the egg mixture, letting the excess drip off, and coat it with the crumb mixture. Put the lamb on a rack set over a jelly-roll pan and chill it, uncovered, for 1 hour or, covered loosely, for up to 8 hours.

In a large skillet heat the remaining 4 tablespoons oil over moderately high heat until it is hot but not smoking, in it sauté the lamb, turning it once, for 6 to 8 minutes for medium-rare meat, and transfer it to a heated platter. Pour off the fat from the skillet, add the butter, and cook it over moderately high heat, swirling the skillet, until it is browned. Add the lemon juice and the capers and pour the sauce over the lamb. Serves 4.

Lamb London Broil with Scallion Ginger Sauce

a 2-inch-thick lamb leg steak (about 2 pounds),
    scored ¼-inch deep on both sides
¼ cup soy sauce
1 tablespoon fresh lemon juice
2 tablespoons vegetable oil
⅓ cup minced onion
1½ tablespoons grated peeled gingerroot
3 tablespoons unsalted butter at room
    temperature
1½ tablespoons minced scallion

In a shallow baking dish slightly larger than the lamb steak whisk together the soy sauce, the lemon juice, the oil, the onion, and 1 tablespoon of the gingerroot. Add the lamb, turn it to coat it well on both sides, and let it marinate, covered, turning it occasionally, at room temperature for at least 2 hours or chilled for up to 8 hours. Let the lamb come to room temperature before broiling it.

In a small bowl cream together the butter, the scallion, and the remaining ½ tablespoon gingerroot. Remove the lamb from the marinade, reserving the marinade, and broil it on the rack of a broiler pan under a preheated broiler about 4 inches from the heat, turning it once, for 16 to 18 minutes for medium-rare meat. Transfer the lamb to a platter and let it stand for 10 minutes. Pour any juices that have accumulated on the platter into a small saucepan, add 2 tablespoons of the reserved marinade, and bring the liquid to a boil. Whisk in the butter mixture and heat the sauce until it is hot, but do not let it boil. Holding a sharp knife at a 45° angle slice the lamb very thin across the grain and pour the sauce over it. Serves 4.

Sautéed Lamb with Mexican Mayonnaise

½ cup mayonnaise (page 200)
½ pound cucumbers, peeled, seeded, and
    grated coarse
2 tablespoons minced red bell pepper
½ teaspoon red pepper flakes, or to taste
1 small garlic clove, minced
½ teaspoon salt, or to taste
1½ tablespoons white-wine vinegar
¼ cup chopped fresh coriander
1 tablespoon vegetable oil
six 1-inch-thick lean lamb shoulder chops
    or leg steaks

In a bowl combine well the mayonnaise, the cucumbers, the bell pepper, the red pepper flakes, the garlic, the salt, the vinegar, and the coriander.

In a large skillet heat the oil over moderately high heat until it is hot but not smoking and in it sauté the lamb, patted dry and seasoned with salt and pepper, turning it once, for 6 to 8 minutes for medium-rare meat. Transfer the lamb with a slotted spatula to a platter and keep it warm, covered. Pour off the fat from the skillet, add ¼ cup water, and deglaze the skillet, scraping up the brown bits. Boil the liquid until it is reduced to about 1 tablespoon, stir it and any juices that have accumulated on the platter into the mayonnaise, and nap each chop with about 1½ tablespoons of the mayonnaise. Serves 6.

Middle Eastern Lamb Burgers

¾ pound lean ground lamb
¼ cup fine fresh bread crumbs
1 large egg, beaten lightly
1 teaspoon ground cumin
¾ teaspoon salt, or to taste
freshly ground pepper to taste
1 teaspoon vegetable oil
¼ cup plain yogurt
2 tablespoons thinly sliced scallion greens

In a bowl combine well the lamb, the bread crumbs, the egg, the paprika, the cumin, the salt, and the pepper and form the mixture into two ¾-inch-thick patties. In a heavy skillet heat the oil over moderately high heat until it is hot but not smoking, in it sauté the patties, turning them once, for 8 minutes for medium-rare meat, and transfer them to paper towels to drain. Arrange the burgers on 2 plates, spoon the yogurt over them, and sprinkle them with the scallion greens. Serves 2.

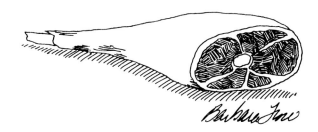

Lamb Chops with Mustard Sauce and Fried Capers

5½ tablespoons vegetable oil
four 1-inch-thick loin lamb chops
    (about 1 pound)
½ cup minced onion
1 tablespoon unsalted butter
½ cup heavy cream
1 tablespoon Dijon-style mustard
1½ teaspoons fresh lemon juice
2 tablespoons drained capers, patted dry
1 tablespoon minced fresh parsley leaves

In a heavy skillet heat 1½ tablespoons of the oil over moderately high heat until it is hot but not smoking and in it sauté the lamb chops, patted dry and seasoned with salt and pepper, turning them, for 6 to 8 minutes for medium-rare meat. Transfer the lamb chops with a slotted spatula to an ovenproof platter and keep them warm in a preheated 200° F. oven. Wipe out the skillet and in it cook the onion in the butter over moderately low heat, stirring, until it is softened. Stir in the cream and any juices that have accumulated on the platter, bring the mixture to a boil, and boil it until it begins to thicken. Remove the skillet from the heat, stir in the mustard, the lemon juice, and salt and pepper to taste, and keep the sauce warm over low heat. In a small skillet heat the remaining 4 tablespoons oil over high heat until it is hot but not smoking, in it fry the capers for 1 to 2 minutes, or until they are crisp and the buds are open, and transfer them with a slotted spoon to paper towels to drain. Strain the sauce through a fine sieve into a bowl, pressing gently on the solids, spoon it around the lamb chops, and sprinkle the chops with the capers and the parsley. Serves 2.

Rack of Lamb Persillé

2 trimmed 7-rib racks of lamb, each weighing
    about 1¼ pounds, the bones "frenched,"
    leaving 2 inches of the bones exposed, at
    room temperature
2 teaspoons Dijon-style mustard
⅓ cup minced shallot
½ stick (¼ cup) unsalted butter
¼ teaspoon dried thyme, crumbled
1 cup fine fresh bread crumbs
⅓ cup minced fresh parsley leaves
garlic rosemary *tuiles* and couscous timbales
    (pages 104 and 165) as accompaniments

Rub the fat side of each rack of lamb with the mustard. In a skillet cook the shallot in the butter over moderately low heat, stirring, for 2 minutes and remove the skillet from the heat. Add the thyme, the bread crumbs, and salt and pepper to taste and toss the mixture well. Let the mixture cool and stir in the parsley. Season the lamb with salt and pepper, pat the crumb mixture evenly over the mustard, and arrange the lamb crumb side up in a roasting pan. Roast the lamb in a preheated 450° F. oven for 30 minutes, or until a meat thermometer registers 130° to 135° F., for medium-rare meat. Transfer the lamb carefully to a work surface and let it stand for 10 minutes. Interlock the ribs together carefully and transfer the lamb to a platter. Serve the lamb with the garlic rosemary *tuiles* and the couscous timbales. Serves 4.

PHOTO ON PAGE 24

Spicy Lamb Stew with Sweet Potato Rosettes

6 tablespoons vegetable oil
3 pounds boneless lamb shoulder, trimmed
    and cut into 1-inch pieces
2 cups finely chopped onion
1 tablespoon minced garlic
2 tablespoons minced peeled fresh gingerroot
1½ tablespoons ground cumin
1 tablespoon ground coriander
¼ cup all-purpose flour
2 cups chicken stock (page 247) or canned
    chicken broth
¼ cup fresh lime juice
two 3-inch fresh green hot chilies (available at
    Hispanic markets and some supermarkets),
    seeded and minced (wear rubber gloves)
2 cups chopped drained canned Italian plum
    tomatoes

1 pound spinach, coarse stems discarded,
    washed well and drained
3 cups cauliflower flowerets
3 large sweet potatoes (about 2½ pounds)
1 russet (baking) potato
3 tablespoons unsalted butter, softened

In a 3-quart flameproof baking dish heat the oil over moderately high heat until it is hot but not smoking and in it brown the lamb, patted dry, in batches, transferring it with a slotted spoon as it is browned to a bowl. In the fat remaining in the dish cook the onion over moderately low heat, stirring occasionally, until it is softened, add the garlic and the gingerroot, and cook the mixture, stirring occasionally, for 3 minutes. Add the cumin, the coriander, and the flour and cook the mixture, stirring, for 3 minutes. Add the stock combined with 1 cup water, heated, whisking, and simmer the mixture for 5 minutes. Add the lime juice, the chilies, the tomatoes, the lamb and any juices that have accumulated in the bowl, and salt and pepper to taste and simmer the mixture, covered, skimming it occasionally, for 1 hour and 30 minutes, or until the lamb is tender.

While the mixture is simmering, in a large saucepan steam the spinach in the water clinging to the leaves, covered, over moderately high heat, stirring occasionally, for 2 to 3 minutes, or until it is just wilted. Drain the spinach in a colander, refresh it under cold water, and squeeze it dry in a kitchen towel. Add the cauliflower to the lamb mixture, simmer the mixture for 5 minutes, and stir in the spinach. *The stew may be prepared up to this point, cooled to room temperature, and kept covered well and frozen for up to 2 weeks. Let the stew thaw, covered, in the refrigerator before continuing with the recipe.*

Bake the potatoes in a preheated 425° F. oven, pricking them several times with a fork after 30 minutes, for 1 hour, or until they are very tender, and let them stand until they are cool enough to be handled. Peel the potatoes, force them through a food mill fitted with the medium disk set over a bowl, and stir in the butter and salt and pepper to taste. Transfer the mixture to a pastry bag fitted with a large decorative tip and pipe it into 2-inch rosettes around the edge of the baking dish. *The stew may be prepared up to this point, cooled to room temperature, and kept covered and chilled for up to 3 days.* Bake the stew in a preheated 400° F. oven for 20 to 30 minutes, or until it is heated through and the rosettes are browned lightly. Serves 6.

PHOTO ON PAGE 69

POULTRY

CHICKEN

*Chicken Breasts Stuffed with
Mozzarella and Canadian Bacon*

1 ounce whole-milk mozzarella, chopped
1 ounce Canadian bacon, chopped
½ teaspoon dried basil, crumbled
2 skinless boneless small whole chicken
    breasts (about 1 pound in all), flattened
    between sheets of dampened wax paper to
    ⅜ inch thick
flour seasoned with salt and pepper for
    dredging
1 large egg, beaten lightly
1 cup fine fresh bread crumbs
1½ tablespoons olive oil
1 tablespoon thinly sliced scallion greens
1½ tablespoons unsalted butter
1 tablespoon chopped fresh parsley leaves
1 teaspoon fresh lemon juice, or to taste

In a small bowl toss together the mozzarella, the bacon, and the basil, spoon the mixture onto half of each
chicken breast, and fold the other halves over it, pressing the edges together. Dredge the chicken in the flour,
shaking off any excess, dip it in the egg, coating it well,
and roll it in the bread crumbs, patting the crumbs onto it
to make them adhere. In a heavy skillet heat the oil over
moderate heat until it is hot but not smoking, in it cook
the chicken, turning it once, for 10 to 12 minutes, or until the juices run clear when the chicken is pierced with a
skewer, and transfer it to a heated platter. Wipe the skillet with paper towels and in it cook the scallion in the
butter over moderately low heat, stirring, for 2 minutes.
Add the parsley, the lemon juice, and salt and pepper to
taste and pour the sauce over the chicken. Serves 2.

Lemon and Basil Poached Chicken Breasts

three 10- to 12-ounce whole skinless boneless
    chicken breasts, halved and trimmed
6 cups canned chicken broth
⅓ cup fresh lemon juice
¼ pound fresh basil including the stems,
    rinsed, plus additional leaves for garnish
1 teaspoon freshly ground pepper
smoked mozzarella and tomato salad
    (page 152) as an accompaniment

In a kettle large enough to hold the chicken breasts in
one layer combine the broth, the lemon juice, ¼ pound
of the basil, and the pepper and bring the liquid to a boil.
Add the chicken breasts and cook them, covered, over
high heat for 4 minutes. Remove the kettle from the heat
and let the mixture stand, uncovered, until the liquid is
cooled to room temperature. Transfer the mixture to a
bowl and let it stand, covered and chilled, for at least 3
hours and up to 24 hours to allow the flavors to develop.
Remove the chicken from the broth mixture, reserving
the broth mixture for another use, and on a work surface, holding a knife at a 45° angle, slice it thin across
the grain. Arrange the chicken decoratively on a platter
with the smoked mozzarella and tomato salad and garnish the dish with the additional basil leaves. Serves 6.
PHOTO ON PAGE 57

*Spinach-Stuffed Chicken Breasts
with Madeira Sauce*

For the stuffed chicken
two 1-pound whole chicken breasts, boned but
   not skinned
1½ tablespoons crushed ice
3 tablespoons well chilled heavy cream
¼ cup firmly packed cooked,
   squeezed, and chopped spinach
   (about ½ pound fresh)
¾ teaspoon salt
¼ teaspoon crushed fennel seeds
¼ teaspoon freshly grated lemon rind
⅛ teaspoon freshly grated nutmeg
⅛ teaspoon freshly ground pepper
1 tablespoon vegetable oil
For the sauce
½ cup Sercial Madeira
¾ cup canned chicken broth
1 teaspoon arrowroot dissolved in
   1 tablespoon water

Make the stuffed chicken: Arrange the chicken breasts skin side down on a cutting board, making sure the skin is evenly stretched over the breasts, and halve them. Remove the fillet strip from each breast, discard the white tendon, and in a food processor grind the fillets. Add the ice, blend the mixture until the ice is absorbed, and with the motor running add the cream. Add the spinach, the salt, the fennel seeds, the rind, the nutmeg, and the pepper and blend the filling well, scraping down the sides.

Turn the breasts skin side up and beginning at the pointed end pull the skin back carefully, leaving the thin transparent membranes attached along a long side and leaving the skin attached at the opposite end. Spread 3 tablespoons of the spinach filling evenly over each breast, smoothing it, and stretch the skin over the filling to cover it. (Reserve the remaining spinach filling for another use such as miniature quenelles made by poaching small balls of it in clear soup, such as the chicken consommé on page 248.) Chill the chicken, wrapped tightly in plastic wrap, for 1 hour. *The chicken may be prepared up to this point 24 hours in advance and kept covered and chilled.*

In a large ovenproof skillet heat the oil over moderately high heat until it is hot but not smoking, add the chicken, skin side down, and season it with salt and pepper. Sauté the chicken for 1 to 2 minutes, or until the skin is golden brown, turn it skin side up, and bake it, covered, in a preheated 400° F. oven for 10 minutes. Transfer the stuffed chicken breasts to a cutting board and let them stand, covered loosely with foil, for 5 minutes.

Make the sauce while the chicken is standing: Pour off the fat from the skillet, add the Madeira, and boil it, scraping up the brown bits, until it is reduced to about 2 tablespoons. Add the broth and boil the mixture, stirring, for 1 minute. Stir the arrowroot mixture, add it to the skillet, whisking, and simmer the sauce, whisking, for 1 minute.

Holding a knife at a 45° angle slice the chicken crosswise and arrange the slices, overlapping them slightly, on 4 heated plates. Spoon some of the sauce around the chicken and serve the remaining sauce separately. Serves 4.

PHOTO ON PAGE 62

*Chicken Paillards with Red Bell Pepper
and Cumin Sauce*

1 whole skinless boneless chicken breast
   (about 10 ounces), halved
1 red bell pepper, quartered and the stem,
   seeds, and ribs discarded
2 garlic cloves
¼ cup canned chicken broth
¼ teaspoon ground cumin
fresh lemon juice to taste
1 tablespoon vegetable oil

Flatten the chicken breast halves between sheets of dampened wax paper until they are ¼ inch thick, transfer them to a dish, and chill them for 25 minutes. Roast the bell pepper quarters skin side up on the oiled rack of a broiler pan about 2 inches from the heat for 8 to 10 minutes, or until they are charred, transfer them to a bowl, and let them cool, covered, for 10 minutes. While the bell pepper is cooling, in a small saucepan combine the garlic and the broth, bring the broth to a boil, and boil the garlic for 3 minutes. Peel the bell pepper and in a blender purée it with the broth mixture, the cumin, the lemon juice, and salt and pepper to taste. Transfer the sauce to the pan and keep it warm, covered, over low heat. In a large heavy skillet heat the oil over moderately high heat until it is hot but not smoking and in it sauté the chicken, seasoned with salt and pepper, turning it once, for 4 to 5 minutes, or until it is just firm to the touch. Serve the *paillards* with the sauce. Serves 2.

Mixed Grill Kebabs

1 whole skinless boneless chicken breast,
    cut into 6 pieces
6 pork sausage links
½ pound chicken livers, trimmed
6 slices of lean bacon
6 large mushrooms
6 small white onions, cooked in boiling salted
    water until just tender, drained, and peeled
¼ cup fresh lemon juice
⅓ cup olive oil
1½ teaspoons minced fresh thyme leaves or
    ½ teaspoon dried, crumbled
1½ teaspoons minced fresh sage leaves or
    ½ teaspoon dried, crumbled
2 tablespoons Worcestershire sauce
1 tablespoon soy sauce
2 tablespoons Dijon-style mustard
2 garlic cloves, minced
3 tablespoons unsalted butter
½ cup fine fresh bread crumbs
¼ cup minced fresh parsley leaves
1 loaf of French or Italian bread, cut
    diagonally into six 10-inch-long slices,
    toasted, and buttered lightly

In a shallow dish let six 12-inch wooden skewers soak in water to cover for 1 hour. Thread the skewers with the chicken, the sausage, the chicken livers, wrapped in pieces of the bacon, the mushrooms, and the onions and arrange the kebabs in a jelly-roll pan. In a small bowl combine the lemon juice, the oil, the thyme, the sage, the Worcestershire sauce, the soy sauce, the mustard, and salt and pepper to taste. Broil the kebabs under a preheated broiler about 4 inches from the heat, basting them often with the lemon mixture and turning them once, for 20 minutes, or until the bacon and sausages are browned well. In a small skillet cook the garlic in the butter over moderate heat, stirring, for 2 minutes, add the crumbs and the parsley, and combine the mixture well. Sprinkle the kebabs with the crumb mixture and put them under the broiler until the crumbs are browned lightly. Arrange the toasts on plates, top them with the mixed grill kebabs, and drizzle the kebabs with the pan juices, skimmed of as much of the excess fat as possible. Serves 6.

Walnut Chicken Morsels

2 large egg whites, beaten lightly
¼ cup cornstarch
1 large garlic clove, minced
½ teaspoon salt
½ pound skinless boneless chicken breast,
    flattened ½ inch thick between sheets of
    dampened wax paper and cut into 2- by
    1-inch pieces
2 cups walnuts, chopped fine
oil for deep-frying

In a bowl blend the egg whites, the cornstarch, the garlic, and the salt until the mixture is combined well, add the chicken pieces, and toss them well with the mixture. In a shallow bowl roll the chicken in the walnuts, coating it evenly, and chill it on a plate for 30 minutes. In a deep fryer fry the chicken in batches in 375° F. oil, turning it, for 2 minutes, or until it is golden, transferring it as it is fried to paper towels to drain. Serve the chicken sprinkled with salt if desired. Makes about 36 hors d'oeuvres.

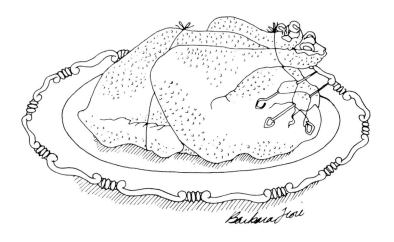

Spicy Fried Chicken

For the marinade
1 cup plain yogurt
1 tablespoon Tabasco
1½ teaspoons salt

2 pounds (about 8) chicken drumsticks, rinsed
1½ pounds (about 8) chicken wings, rinsed
For the seasoned flour
2 cups all-purpose flour
3 tablespoons sweet paprika
4 teaspoons cayenne
2 teaspoons black pepper
2 teaspoons salt
1 teaspoon dried thyme, crumbled

vegetable shortening or vegetable oil
for frying

Make the marinade: In a large wide bowl whisk together the yogurt, 1 cup water, the Tabasco, and the salt until the mixture is smooth.

Add the drumsticks and the wings to the marinade, tossing them to coat them with the marinade, and let the chicken marinate at room temperature for 1 hour *or covered and chilled overnight.*

Make the seasoned flour: In a wide shallow bowl stir together the flour, the paprika, the cayenne, the black pepper, the salt, and the thyme.

Working with 1 piece at a time remove the chicken from the marinade, letting the excess drip off, and dredge it in the seasoned flour. Arrange the chicken as it is dredged in a large shallow baking dish sprinkled with some of the seasoned flour. When all the chicken is dredged sprinkle it with the remaining seasoned flour and let it stand, turning it and patting on the flour occasionally, for 20 minutes.

In a large cast-iron or other heavy skillet heat ½ inch of the shortening over moderate heat to 350° F. and add as many pieces of chicken as will fit in one layer, crowding them slightly. Cover the skillet, reduce the heat to low, and fry the chicken for 6 minutes. Turn the chicken and fry it, covered, for 6 minutes more. Remove the lid, increase the heat to moderately high, and fry the chicken, turning it once, for 4 minutes more, or until it is golden and tender when pierced with a knife. Transfer the chicken with tongs to paper towels or brown paper bags and let it drain. Cook the remaining chicken in the same manner, let the chicken cool completely at room temperature, and transfer it to a portable container. *The chicken may be fried up to 4 hours in advance and kept at room temperature.* Serves 6.

PHOTO ON PAGE 51

Chicken Thighs
with Cream Cheese Filling

5 tablespoons minced onion
3 tablespoons minced green bell pepper
3 tablespoons unsalted butter
3 tablespoons cream cheese, softened
cayenne to taste
4 chicken thighs, boned but not skinned
   (about 1 pound), flattened between sheets of
   wax paper

In a small heavy skillet cook the onion and the bell pepper in 1½ tablespoons of the butter over moderately low heat, stirring, until the vegetables are softened. In a small bowl combine well the onion mixture, the cream cheese, the cayenne, and salt to taste. Mound one fourth of the filling on the boned side of each chicken thigh, fold the edges together to enclose the filling, and secure the edges with wooden picks. In a large heavy oven-proof skillet heat the remaining 1½ tablespoons butter over moderately high heat until the foam subsides, in it sauté the thighs, turning them, for 5 minutes, and bake them in the skillet in a preheated 350° F. oven for 15 to 17 minutes, or until the juices run clear when a thigh is pierced with a knife. Serves 2.

Sautéed Chicken Thighs
with Yellow and Green Squash

2 tablespoons fresh lemon juice
½ teaspoon dried orégano, crumbled
¼ teaspoon salt
¼ cup olive oil
4 chicken thighs (about 1 pound), boned but
   not skinned and flattened between sheets of
   plastic wrap
1 summer squash, halved lengthwise and cut
   crosswise into ¼-inch pieces
1 zucchini, halved lengthwise and cut
   crosswise into ¼-inch pieces

In a shallow dish whisk together the lemon juice, the orégano, the salt, and pepper to taste, add 2 tablespoons of the oil in a stream, whisking, and whisk the dressing until it is emulsified. Add the chicken, turning it to coat it with the marinade, and let it marinate, covered, at room temperature, turning it occasionally, for 30 minutes. In a large heavy skillet heat 1 tablespoon of the remaining oil over moderately high heat until it is hot but not smoking, in it sauté the chicken, drained, turning it once, for 6 to 8 minutes, or until the juices run clear when the meat is pricked, and transfer it to paper towels to drain.

While the chicken is sautéing, in another heavy skillet heat the remaining 1 tablespoon oil over moderately high heat until it is hot but not smoking, in it sauté the summer squash and the zucchini, stirring occasionally, for 5 to 6 minutes, or until the squash is golden brown and crisp-tender, and season the squash with salt and pepper. Serve the chicken with the squash. Serves 2.

Curried Shrimp, Chicken, and Vegetable Stew

3 onions, halved and sliced thin
3 garlic cloves, minced
3 carrots, sliced
2 ribs of celery, sliced
2 parsnips, sliced
2 red bell peppers, chopped
1 stick (½ cup) unsalted butter
3 tablespoons curry powder
1 bay leaf
½ teaspoon cayenne, or to taste
2 teaspoons ground cumin
½ teaspoon cinnamon
⅛ teaspoon allspice
½ teaspoon ground coriander
½ teaspoon black pepper
1 teaspoon salt
1 tablespoon tomato paste
a 35-ounce can plum tomatoes including the juice, chopped
5 cups chicken stock (page 247) or canned chicken broth
a 5- to 6-pound roasting chicken
⅓ cup long-grain rice
1 small head of cauliflower, cut into small flowerets

1 pound green beans, cut into 1-inch pieces
2 small zucchini, sliced
1½ pounds shrimp, shelled and deveined, leaving the tail intact if desired
¼ cup minced fresh parsley leaves
¼ cup minced fresh coriander

Accompaniments
½ pound sliced lean bacon, cooked and crumbled
6 fresh green hot chili peppers (available at specialty produce markets and many supermarkets), sliced (wear rubber gloves)
1 cup roasted salted peanuts
1 red bell pepper, cut into julienne strips
1 cup golden raisins
8 scallions, sliced thin
lime wedges if desired
plain yogurt if desired

In an 8-quart kettle cook the onions, the garlic, the carrots, the celery, the parsnips, and the bell peppers in the butter over moderate heat, stirring, until the onions are golden, stir in the curry powder, the bay leaf, the cayenne, the cumin, the cinnamon, the allspice, the ground coriander, the black pepper, and the salt, and cook the mixture over moderately low heat, stirring, for 3 minutes. Stir in the tomato paste, add the tomatoes including the juice, the stock, and 3 cups water, and bring the liquid to a boil, stirring occasionally. Add the chicken and simmer the mixture, covered, for 1 hour and 30 minutes. Transfer the chicken to a cutting board and spoon off the fat from the mixture. Discard the skin and bones from the chicken and cut the meat into 1-inch pieces, reserving it in a bowl. Bring the mixture to a boil, stir in the rice, and simmer the mixture for 10 minutes. Add the cauliflower and the green beans and simmer the mixture for 5 minutes. Add the zucchini and simmer the mixture for 2 minutes. Add the reserved chicken and the shrimp and simmer the stew until the shrimp are pink. Just before serving stir in the parsley, the fresh coriander, and salt and pepper to taste and discard the bay leaf. *The stew may be made up to 1 day in advance, kept covered and chilled, and reheated. It may also be frozen.* Serve the stew with the bacon, the chili peppers, the peanuts, the bell pepper, the raisins, the scallions, and the lime and the yogurt if desired. Serves 12.

PHOTO ON PAGE 15

ASSORTED FOWL

Roast Capon with Tarragon Sauce

For the herb butter
¼ cup minced shallot
3 tablespoons dry white wine
1 tablespoon white-wine vinegar
2 long branches of fresh tarragon or 1
    teaspoon dried, crumbled
½ stick (¼ cup) unsalted butter, softened

an 8- to 9-pound capon, thawed if frozen,
    reserving the neck and giblets (excluding
    the liver)
½ lemon, halved
1 small onion, halved
1 stick (½ cup) unsalted butter, softened
¼ pound shallots
For the sauce
¾ cup dry white wine
2 tablespoons white-wine vinegar
4 tablespoons all-purpose flour
2½ cups chicken stock (page 247) or
    canned chicken broth
1 tablespoon chopped fresh tarragon or
    1 teaspoon dried, crumbled, plus additional
    sprigs for garnish if desired

Make the herb butter: In a small saucepan combine the shallot, the wine, the vinegar, and the dried tarragon if using and boil the mixture until the liquid is evaporated. Let the mixture cool and in a small bowl blend it well with the butter and salt and pepper to taste.

Rinse the capon, pat it dry inside and out, and season the cavity with salt and pepper. Loosen the skin on the breast by slipping your fingers between the skin and the flesh at the neck opening and push your hand carefully over the breast meat, being careful not to tear the skin. Spread the herb butter on the breast meat under the skin, smoothing it evenly, and slip a branch of tarragon if using, stem end first, under the skin over each breast. Put the lemon and the onion in the cavity and truss the capon. Arrange the capon breast side up on an oiled rack in a roasting pan, rub it all over with the butter, and season it with salt and pepper. Spread the shallots and the reserved giblets in the bottom of the pan and roast the capon in a preheated 425° F. oven for 30 minutes. Reduce the heat to 325° F., baste the capon, and roast it, basting it every 15 minutes, for 1 hour and 30 minutes to

2 hours more, or until the juices run clear when the fleshy part of a thigh is pricked with a skewer and a meat thermometer inserted in the fleshy part of a thigh registers 180° F. Pour the juices that have accumulated in the cavity of the capon into the roasting pan, transfer the capon to a heated platter, and let it stand for 20 minutes.

Make the sauce: Skim the fat from the pan juices, reserving 3 tablespoons of the fat in a saucepan. Add the wine and the vinegar to the roasting pan and deglaze the pan over high heat, scraping up the brown bits. Boil the liquid until it is reduced by half, strain it through a fine sieve into a bowl, and reserve it. Stir the flour into the reserved fat in the saucepan and cook the *roux* over moderately low heat, stirring, for 3 minutes. Add the stock in a stream, whisking, the reserved wine mixture, and the fresh or dried tarragon, bring the liquid to a boil, whisking, and simmer the sauce, stirring occasionally, for 5 minutes. Season the sauce with salt and pepper and strain it into a heated sauceboat. Garnish the capon platter with the tarragon sprigs if desired. Serves 8.
PHOTO ON PAGE 36

Blasted Cornish Hens with Basil Couscous Stuffing

For the stuffing
1 garlic clove, minced
1 tablespoon unsalted butter
⅓ cup canned chicken broth
⅓ cup couscous
⅓ cup shredded fresh basil leaves
3 tablespoons pine nuts, toasted lightly

two 1½-pound Cornish hens, rinsed and
    patted dry
½ stick (¼ cup) unsalted butter, softened

Make the stuffing: In a small saucepan cook the garlic in the butter over moderately low heat, stirring, until it is softened, add the broth, and bring it to a boil. Stir in the couscous, remove the pan from the heat, and let the mixture stand, covered, for 5 minutes. Transfer the couscous to a bowl, stir in the basil, the pine nuts, and salt and pepper to taste, and let the stuffing cool.

Season the cavities of the hens with salt and pepper and fill them with the stuffing. Cover each opening with a piece of foil, truss the hens with kitchen string, and rub each hen with 1 tablespoon of the butter. In a flameproof roasting pan heat the remaining 2 tablespoons butter over moderately high heat until the foam subsides and in it sauté the hens breast side up for 1 to 2 minutes, or until the underside is golden brown. Roast the hens in a pre-heated 450° F. oven, basting them with the pan juices every 10 minutes, for 30 minutes, or until the juices run clear when the fleshy part of a thigh is pricked with a skewer. Transfer the hens to a cutting board, let them stand for 10 minutes, and discard the string and foil. Halve the hens with a sharp knife and arrange them on a heated platter. Serves 4.

PHOTO ON PAGE 63

©HELEN FEDERICO '86

Roast Duck Bourguignonne

The slow cooking in this recipe ensures that the duck will be tender, the skin crispy, and all fat will be rendered from it.

a 4½- to 5-pound duck, neck and giblets
    (excluding the liver) reserved, excess fat
    removed from the cavity, excess skin cut off
    from the neck end, and wings cut off at the
    second joint and reserved
3 cups chicken stock (page 247) or canned
    chicken broth
1 cup dry red wine
2 garlic cloves, crushed
1 bay leaf
½ teaspoon dried thyme, crumbled
1 onion, sliced
½ pound small white onions, blanched in
    boiling salted water for 2 minutes, drained,
    and peeled
1 tablespoon arrowroot
2 tablespoons Cognac
½ pound baby carrots, cooked in boiling
    salted water for 2 to 4 minutes, or until they
    are just tender, and drained
a ⅛-inch-thick slice of prosciutto, cut into
    1-inch sticks
baked polenta with Parmesan (page 165) as an
    accompaniment

Pat the duck dry, prick it all over, and rub it with salt and pepper. Roast the duck on a rack set in a roasting pan in a preheated 450° F. oven for 30 minutes, reduce the heat to 275° F., and roast the duck for 2 hours more. Drain off the fat from the pan, reserving 1 tablespoon for the green bean and *shiitake* salad with crisp potato rings (page 195), and chill the duck for at least 1 hour or up to 12 hours.

Quarter the duck, remove the breastbone and the thighbones, reserving them, and chill the duck, covered. In a saucepan combine the reserved bones with the reserved neck, giblets, and wings, the stock, the wine, and 2 cups water, bring the liquid to a boil, and simmer the mixture, skimming it, for 10 minutes. Add the garlic, the bay leaf, the thyme, and the sliced onion and simmer the mixture, adding more water if necessary to keep the bones just covered, for 4 hours. Strain the mixture into another saucepan, skim the fat from the stock, and boil the stock until it is reduced to about 2 cups. Add the small white onions, simmer the mixture, covered, for 15 minutes, or until the onions are tender, and transfer the onions with a slotted spoon to a bowl. In a small bowl whisk together the arrowroot and the Cognac, add the mixture to the boiling stock in a stream, whisking, and simmer the sauce for 1 minute. Add the onions, the carrots, and the prosciutto, cook the sauce over moderately low heat, stirring occasionally, until it is heated through, and keep it warm, covered.

Reheat the duck on the rack set in the roasting pan in a preheated 425° F. oven for 10 to 15 minutes, or until the skin is crisp, and arrange it on a platter. Transfer the vegetables with a slotted spoon to the platter, pour the sauce over the dish, and arrange some of the polenta at each end. Serves 2.

PHOTO ON PAGE 18

Boned Turkey with Sausage Hazelnut Stuffing and Madeira Gravy

a 12- to 13-pound turkey, boned and prepared
  for stuffing (procedure follows), reserving
  the neck, giblets (excluding the liver), and
  carcass for making turkey stock (page 147)
  and reserving the turkey fillets for the
  stuffing
sausage hazelnut stuffing (page 147)
1 slice of bread
2 sticks (1 cup) unsalted butter, softened
flat-leafed parsley sprigs for garnish
For the gravy
1 cup Sercial Madeira
½ cup all-purpose flour
5 cups turkey stock

Special equipment needed
a V-shaped adjustable roasting rack
a piece of cheesecloth large enough to cover
  the turkey

Arrange the turkey breast side up on a work surface, pat it dry, and pack the cavity with the stuffing, re-forming the turkey. Cover the stuffing at the opening with the slice of bread, tuck the wings under the turkey, and truss the turkey securely with the kitchen string. Set the turkey on the roasting rack in a roasting pan, spread it with 1 stick of the butter, and season it with salt and pepper. Roast the turkey in a preheated 425° F. oven for 30 minutes and reduce the heat to 325° F. Brush the turkey with the pan juices, arrange the cheesecloth, soaked in the remaining stick of butter, melted and cooled, over the turkey, and roast the turkey, basting it every 20 minutes, for 2 hours and 30 minutes, or until a meat thermometer inserted in the fleshy part of a thigh registers 185° F. Peel away the cheesecloth carefully, discard it, and transfer the turkey to a platter, reserving the pan juices in the roasting pan. Let the turkey stand for 25 minutes, discard the trussing strings, and garnish the platter with the parsley sprigs.

Make the gravy while the turkey is standing: Skim the fat from the reserved pan juices and reserve ⅓ cup of it. Add the Madeira to the pan juices and deglaze the pan over high heat, scraping up the brown bits clinging to the bottom and sides. Boil the liquid until it is reduced by half and reserve it. In a large saucepan combine the reserved fat and the flour and cook the *roux* over moderately low heat, whisking, for 3 minutes. Add the stock and the reserved Madeira mixture in a stream, whisking, bring the liquid to a boil, whisking, and simmer the gravy, stirring occasionally, for 10 minutes. Season the gravy with salt and pepper and transfer it to a heated sauceboat. Serves 10.

PHOTO ON PAGE 72

ZOÉ MAVRIDIS

To Bone, Stuff, and Truss a Turkey

1. Put the turkey, breast side down, on a work surface with the wing end away from you and with a sharp knife cut through the skin in a line along the backbone.
2. Working with one side of the turkey at a time, keeping the knife as close to the bone as possible, cut and scrape the meat free from the central bone structure. Locate the wing joint and cut it and the surrounding white tendons to free it from the central bone structure.
3. With your thumb press down on the thigh joint to dislodge it and with the knife cut it and the surrounding tendons to free it from the central bone structure.
4. Continue to cut and scrape the meat from the bones, being careful not to cut the skin when separating the breast meat from the bone. Bone the other side of the turkey in the same manner until the central bone structure is completely exposed except for a thin seam along the breastbone.
5. Holding the central bone structure up, cut the remaining breast section free from the bones, cutting into the cartilage slightly to keep from breaking the skin.
6. Spread the boned turkey open to expose the fillets

(the small pieces of meat that are attached to each breast). The fillet is recognizable by the white tendon running through it. Pull up on the tendon to help peel the fillet from each breast and reserve the fillets.

7. Season the turkey with salt and pepper, bring the cut edges of it together to re-form it, and with a trussing needle threaded with kitchen string begin sewing up the turkey at the neck end.

8. Stitch down the neck flap and continue stitching the turkey closed. If the tail (pope's nose) is still attached, cut it off.

9. Turn the turkey over carefully and continue to stitch the edges together, leaving a hole just large enough through which to stuff the turkey, and knot the string. *The turkey can be prepared up to this point 1 day in advance and kept covered and chilled.*

10. After the stuffing is packed into the turkey and covered with a slice of bread pat the turkey into shape, tuck the middle of a long piece of kitchen string under the neck end of the turkey, and bring the ends of the string up over the wings. Bring the string along the inside of the drumsticks and hook it under the end of each drumstick.

11. Using the string, pull the drumsticks together, crossing the string and knotting it.

12. Turn the turkey over carefully, secure the drumsticks to the body by crossing the string on the back, and hook the string under the wings before tying the ends together in a tight knot.

Turkey Stock

the carcass and the neck and giblets
   (excluding the liver) of 1 turkey
2 onions, halved
1 carrot
1 rib of celery, halved crosswise
1 bay leaf
1 teaspoon black peppercorns
½ teaspoon salt

Chop coarse the carcass, spread it in a flameproof roasting pan with the neck and giblets and the onions, and roast the mixture in a preheated 425° F. oven for 30 minutes, or until it is browned well. Transfer the mixture with a slotted spoon to a kettle, pour off the fat from the pan, and add 2 cups water. Deglaze the pan over high heat, scraping up the brown bits, and add the liquid to the kettle with the carrot, the celery, the bay leaf, the peppercorns, the salt, and 8 cups water, or enough just to cover the mixture. Bring the liquid to a boil, skimming the froth, and simmer the mixture, skimming the froth occasionally, for 2 hours and 30 minutes. Strain the stock through a fine sieve set over a bowl and skim the fat. *The stock may be made up to 1 day in advance and kept covered and chilled or it may be frozen for up to 2 months. If making the stock in advance, let it cool to room temperature, uncovered, before chilling or freezing it.* Makes about 5 cups.

Sausage Hazelnut Stuffing

1 pound fresh pork sausage meat
the fillets reserved from a boned turkey or
   ½ pound skinless boneless chicken breasts
½ stick (¼ cup) unsalted butter
1 pound onions, chopped
2 cups chopped celery
2 tablespoons chopped fresh sage leaves or
   1 tablespoon crumbled dried
½ pound cooked ham, cut into ¼-inch dice
3 cups dry ¼-inch bread cubes
1 cup hazelnuts, toasted and skinned
   (procedure on page 212) and chopped
1 cup minced fresh parsley leaves
3 large eggs, beaten lightly
2 teaspoons salt
1½ teaspoons freshly ground pepper

In a large skillet cook the sausage meat, crumbled, over moderate heat, stirring and breaking up the lumps, until it is no longer pink, transfer it with a slotted spoon to a large bowl, and let it cool. Remove and discard the white tendons from the turkey fillets or chicken breasts with a sharp knife and in a food processor grind the fillets coarse. Add the sausage, grind the mixture until it is blended, and transfer it to the large bowl. Pour off the fat from the skillet, add the butter, and in it cook the onions and the celery with the sage, covered, over moderately low heat, stirring occasionally, until the vegetables are softened. Let the mixture cool in the skillet, add it to the large bowl with the ham, 2 cups of the bread cubes, crushed fine in a plastic bag, the remaining 1 cup bread cubes, left whole, the hazelnuts, the parsley, the eggs, the salt, and the pepper, and combine the mixture well. *The stuffing may be prepared up to 1 day in advance and kept covered and chilled.*

PHOTO ON PAGE 72

Turkey Hash with Potatoes and Peas

1 small onion, chopped fine
1½ tablespoons unsalted butter
1 boiling potato (about ¼ pound), cut into
    ¼-inch dice and reserved in a bowl of cold
    water
1 tablespoon all-purpose flour
1 cup canned chicken broth
2 tablespoons heavy cream
½ cup frozen peas, thawed
1¼ cups diced cooked turkey breast
2 tablespoons sliced almonds, toasted lightly

In a skillet cook the onion in the butter over moderate heat, stirring occasionally, until it is just golden. While the onion is cooking, in a saucepan of boiling salted water boil the potato, drained, for 5 to 8 minutes, or until it is tender, and drain it. Stir the flour into the onion mixture and cook the *roux*, stirring, for 3 minutes. Add the broth, bring the mixture to a boil, stirring, and simmer it, stirring, for 3 minutes. Add the cream and cook the mixture over moderate heat, stirring, for 1 minute. Add the peas, the potato, and the turkey and cook the mixture, stirring, for 5 minutes, or until the sauce is absorbed. Transfer the hash to a serving dish and sprinkle it with the almonds. Serves 2.

Turkey Paupiettes with Apples, Onions, and Cranberries

For the stuffing
6 slices of whole-wheat bread, torn into ½-
    inch pieces
2 tablespoons melted unsalted butter
½ teaspoon dried marjoram, crumbled
½ teaspoon dried thyme, crumbled
1 rib of celery, chopped fine
1 garlic clove, minced
¼ Golden Delicious apple, peeled and
    chopped fine
1 small onion, chopped fine
2 tablespoons unsalted butter
½ cup canned chicken broth

three ½-pound turkey breast tenderloins
    ("cutlets"), halved horizontally, pounded
    ¼ inch thick between dampened sheets of
    wax paper, and seasoned with salt and
    pepper

2 tablespoons unsalted butter
12 small white onions,
    blanched in boiling water for 2 minutes
    and peeled
2 cups apple cider
1 cup canned chicken broth
2 tablespoons cornstarch dissolved in ¼ cup
    cold water
¾ Golden Delicious apple, sliced thin and
    kept in a bowl of 1 cup water acidulated
    with 1 teaspoon lemon juice
¼ cup cranberries, picked over
1 tablespoon minced fresh flat-leafed parsley
    leaves plus flat-leafed parsley sprigs for
    garnish

Make the stuffing: In a jelly-roll pan toss the bread with the melted butter, the marjoram, the thyme, and salt and pepper to taste and bake the mixture in a preheated 350° F. oven for 15 minutes, or until the bread is toasted lightly. In a large heavy skillet cook the celery, the garlic, the apple, and the onion in the butter over moderately low heat, stirring, until the vegetables are softened, add the broth, and bring the liquid to a boil. Stir in the bread mixture and stir the stuffing until it is combined well.

Divide the stuffing among the tenderloins, mounding it in the center, and starting with the short ends roll up the tenderloins to enclose the stuffing. Secure each end with a wooden pick and pinch the edges together to seal in the stuffing. In a large heavy skillet heat the butter over moderately high heat until the foam subsides and in it sauté the *paupiettes* and the white onions, turning them, for 8 to 10 minutes, or until the *paupiettes* are browned. Add the cider, bring the liquid to a boil, and simmer the mixture, covered, for 12 to 15 minutes, or until the turkey is tender. Transfer the *paupiettes* with a slotted spatula to a platter, removing the wooden picks, and keep them warm, covered loosely. Add the broth to the skillet and bring the liquid to a boil. Stir the cornstarch mixture, stir it into the cider mixture, and cook the sauce, stirring, until it boils and thickens. Stir in the mixture, stirring, for 3 to 5 minutes, or until the fruit is heated through, and stir in the minced parsley and salt and pepper to taste. Spoon the mixture around the *paupiettes* and garnish the dish with the parsley sprigs. Serves 6.

PHOTO ON PAGE 75

CHEESE, EGGS, AND BREAKFAST ITEMS

CHEESE

Baked Camembert with Hazelnut Crust

a round of Camembert (about 8 ounces), the
    top rind cut away and discarded, leaving the
    bottom and side rind intact
1 large egg, beaten lightly
¼ cup fine fresh bread crumbs
¼ cup finely chopped toasted and skinned
    hazelnuts (procedure on page 212)
apple slices and toasted brioche as
    accompaniments

In a shallow dish coat the Camembert well on all
sides with the egg. In another shallow dish combine the
bread crumbs and the hazelnuts, coat the Camembert
well on all sides with the mixture, patting the mixture on
to help it adhere, and chill it on a plate, covered, for
1 hour. On a baking sheet bake the Camembert rindless
side up in a preheated 400° F. oven for 15 minutes, or
until the crust is golden brown. Transfer the Camembert
carefully to a platter and serve it hot with the apple slices
and the brioche. Serves 8 to 10.

PHOTO ON PAGE 30

Tomato, Basil, and Cheese Tart

For the shell
1¼ cups all-purpose flour
¾ stick (6 tablespoons) cold unsalted butter,
    cut into bits
2 tablespoons cold vegetable shortening
¼ pound sliced lean bacon, cooked, drained,
    cooled, and crumbled
¼ teaspoon salt
raw rice for weighting the shell
For the filling
4 large (about 2 pounds) firm-ripe tomatoes,
    sliced horizontally ⅓ inch thick
1½ teaspoons salt plus additional for
    sprinkling the tomatoes
1 cup firmly packed fresh basil leaves plus
    3 basil sprigs for garnish

½ cup plus 2 tablespoons whole-milk ricotta
2 large eggs, beaten lightly
¼ pound whole-milk mozzarella, grated coarse
½ cup freshly grated Parmesan

vegetable oil for brushing the tomatoes

Make the shell: In a large bowl blend the flour, the
butter, the shortening, the bacon, and the salt until the
mixture resembles meal. Add 3 to 4 tablespoons ice water, or enough to form a dough, tossing the mixture until
the water is incorporated. Knead the dough lightly with
the heel of the hand against a smooth surface for a few
seconds to distribute the fat evenly and form it into a
ball. Flatten the dough slightly, dust it with flour, and
chill it, wrapped in wax paper, for 1 hour. Roll the
dough into a ⅛-inch-thick round on a floured surface
and fit it into a 9-inch tart pan with a removable fluted
rim. Prick the shell lightly with a fork and chill it for
30 minutes. Line the shell with foil, fill the foil with the
rice, and bake the shell in the lower third of a preheated
425° F. oven for 15 minutes. Remove the rice and foil
carefully, bake the shell for 3 to 5 minutes more, or until
it is pale golden, and let it cool in the pan on a rack.

Make the filling: Sprinkle the tomato slices on both
sides lightly with the additional salt and let them drain
on paper towels. In a food processor or blender purée
the basil leaves with the ricotta, add the eggs, and blend
the mixture until it is combined. Add the remaining
1½ teaspoons salt, the mozzarella, the Parmesan, and
freshly grated black pepper to taste and blend the mixture until it is just combined.

Pat the tomato slices dry with paper towels, line the
bottom of the shell with the tomato end pieces, and
spoon the cheese mixture over the end pieces, smoothing the mixture. Arrange the remaining tomato slices in
one layer, overlapping them slightly, over the cheese
mixture and brush them with the oil. Bake the tart in a
preheated 350° F. oven for 40 to 50 minutes, or until the
cheese mixture is set. Transfer the tart to a rack, let it
stand for 10 minutes, and garnish it with the basil sprigs.
Serve the tart hot or at room temperature. Serves 6.

PHOTO ON FRONT JACKET

Date, Bacon, and Cream Cheese Sandwiches

½ cup plus 1 tablespoon cream cheese,
    softened
⅓ cup pitted dates, chopped fine
5 slices of lean bacon, cooked until crisp,
    drained, and crumbled
12 slices of pumpernickel bread, crusts
    removed and the bread cut if necessary into
    4- by 3-inch rectangles

In a small bowl stir together the cream cheese, the dates, and the bacon until the mixture is combined well and divide the mixture among 6 slices of the bread, spreading it evenly. Top the mixture with the remaining 6 slices bread, press the bread together gently to enclose the filling, and halve each sandwich diagonally. Serves 6.

Grilled Goat Cheese with Spinach Chiffonade

½ pound spinach, stems discarded, the leaves
    washed well and spun dry
6 ounces small firm fresh goat cheese or
    crottins de chèvre, cut horizontally with a
    wet knife into ⅓-inch-thick rounds
3 tablespoons fresh bread crumbs
3 tablespoons minced walnuts
3 tablespoons walnut oil (available at specialty
    foods shops)
2 large heads of Belgian endive, trimmed and
    separated into leaves
1 tablespoon white-wine vinegar
2 tablespoons vegetable oil

Working in small batches stack about 5 to 6 spinach leaves on top of each other, with the long sides facing you roll them up jelly-roll fashion, and cut the roll on the diagonal into thin slices. Arrange the goat cheese slices on an oiled jelly-roll pan. In a small bowl combine well the bread crumbs and the walnuts. Brush the goat cheese slices with 1 tablespoon of the walnut oil, coat the tops evenly with the bread crumb mixture, and season the cheese with salt and pepper. *The goat cheese and spinach may be prepared up to this point 6 hours in advance and kept covered and chilled.*

Just before serving arrange the endive leaves in a spoke pattern on 4 salad plates. In a small bowl whisk the vinegar with salt and pepper to taste, add the vegetable oil and the remaining 2 tablespoons walnut oil in a stream, whisking, and whisk the dressing until it is

emulsified. In a large bowl toss the spinach with the dressing and divide it among the plates. Grill the goat cheese under a preheated broiler about 2 inches from the heat for 30 seconds to 1 minute, or until the crumbs are golden and the cheese is hot, and divide the rounds among the plates. Serves 4.

PHOTO ON PAGE 22

*Grilled Gouda, Salami, and Artichoke
Heart Sandwiches*

¼ cup finely chopped Gouda
2 tablespoons finely chopped sliced Genoa
    salami
3 tablespoons finely chopped drained
    marinated artichoke hearts
4 slices of homemade-type white bread, crusts
    removed
2 tablespoons unsalted butter

In a small bowl stir together the Gouda, the salami, and the artichoke hearts and divide the mixture between 2 slices of the bread, spreading it evenly. Top the mixture with the remaining 2 slices of bread and press the bread together gently to enclose the filling. In a skillet melt 1 tablespoon of the butter over moderate heat and in it cook the sandwiches for 1 minute, or until the undersides are golden. Add the remaining 1 tablespoon butter, turn the sandwiches, flattening them slightly with a spatula, and cook them for 1 minute more, or until the undersides are golden. Transfer the sandwiches to a cutting board and cut each sandwich into 4 sticks. Serves 2 as an hors d'oeuvre or light luncheon entrée.

Ham and Cheddar Puffs

½ stick (¼ cup) unsalted butter, cut into bits
½ cup all-purpose flour
2 to 3 large eggs
a pinch of freshly grated nutmeg
1 cup minced cooked ham
⅓ cup minced sharp Cheddar plus
    2½ tablespoons grated

In a saucepan bring to a boil over high heat ½ cup water with the butter and reduce the heat to low. Add the flour all at once and beat the mixture with a wooden spoon for 3 minutes. Transfer the dough to the bowl of an electric mixer and with the mixer at high speed beat in 2 of the eggs, 1 at a time, beating well after each addi-

tion. The dough should be thick enough to just hold soft peaks. If it is too stiff, break the remaining egg into a bowl, beat it lightly, and add enough of it to thin the dough to the desired consistency. Stir in the nutmeg, the ham, and the minced Cheddar.

In a buttered 9-inch round cake pan drop the dough in 8 spoonfuls in a ring around the side, mounding it slightly and leaving a ¼-inch space between the spoonfuls. Sprinkle the ring with the grated Cheddar and bake it in a preheated 425° F. oven for 40 to 45 minutes, or until it is golden brown and puffed. Break the cheese puffs apart and serve them warm. Serves 4 to 6 as a brunch dish or as an accompaniment to soup.

Leek and Gruyère Cheese Puffs

⅓ cup thinly sliced leek, washed well and
  drained
1½ tablespoons unsalted butter
¼ cup canned chicken broth
¼ cup all-purpose flour
1 large egg, beaten lightly
2 tablespoons grated Gruyère plus
  1 tablespoon cut into ¼-inch dice

In a small heavy skillet cook the leek in ½ tablespoon of the butter over moderately low heat, stirring, until it is softened. In a small heavy saucepan bring the broth and the remaining 1 tablespoon butter to a boil over high heat, reduce the heat to low, and add the leek mixture and the flour all at once. Beat the mixture with a wooden spoon for 10 minutes, remove the pan from the heat, and with an electric mixer at high speed beat in the egg, 1 tablespoon at a time, beating well after each addition. Beat in the grated Gruyère, drop 8 level tablespoons of the dough onto a buttered baking sheet, and top the dough with the diced Gruyère. Bake the dough in a preheated 400° F. oven for 18 to 20 minutes, or until the puffs are golden, and serve the puffs warm. Serves 2.

Hot Antipasto Heros

1 small onion, halved lengthwise and
  sliced thin
2 tablespoons olive oil
⅔ cup diced salami
¾ cup diced whole-milk mozzarella
¼ cup chopped drained bottled roasted
  red pepper
4 drained bottled *pepperoncini* (pickled
  Tuscan peppers, available at most
  supermarkets), chopped
6 Kalamata olives, pitted and chopped
¼ teaspoon orégano, crumbled
2 teaspoons red-wine vinegar
two 6-inch-long pieces of Italian bread

In a heavy skillet cook the onion in the oil over moderately low heat, stirring occasionally, until it is softened. While the onion is cooking, in a bowl stir together the salami, the mozzarella, the red pepper, the *pepperoncini*, the olives, the orégano, and the vinegar, stir in the onion with the oil, and combine the mixture well. Cut each piece of bread horizontally with a serrated knife without slicing all the way through, remove some of the soft inner white bread, and arrange the bread pieces cut sides up in a jelly-roll pan. Spread the antipasto mixture on both sides of each piece of bread and bake the heros in a preheated 450° F. oven for 5 minutes. Season the heros with salt and pepper and re-form them, pressing the 2 sides together. Serves 2.

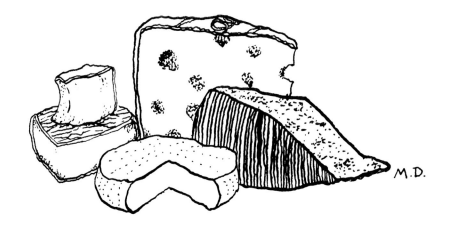

Swiss Chard Pie with Ricotta, Pine Nuts, and Raisins

1 pound Swiss chard, the ribs cut out and
   reserved and the leaves washed well and
   spun dry
1 onion, minced
2 garlic cloves, minced
2 tablespoons olive oil
1 cup ricotta
1 large egg, beaten lightly
¼ cup Kalamata or other brine-cured black
   olives, flattened slightly with the side of a
   heavy knife, pitted, and sliced thin
3 tablespoons raisins
3 tablespoons pine nuts, toasted lightly
⅓ cup freshly grated Parmesan
egg pastry dough
   (recipe follows)

Chop fine the reserved Swiss chard ribs and shred or chop the leaves. In a large skillet cook the onion and the garlic in the oil, covered, over moderately low heat, stirring occasionally, until they are softened, add the Swiss chard ribs, and cook the mixture, covered, stirring occasionally, for 5 minutes. Add the Swiss chard leaves and salt to taste and cook the mixture, covered, for 3 minutes, or until the leaves are wilted. Remove the lid and cook the mixture over moderate heat, stirring, for 2 to 3 minutes, or until almost all the liquid is evaporated. Transfer the mixture to a bowl and let it cool. Add the ricotta, the egg, the olives, the raisins, the pine nuts, the Parmesan, and salt and pepper to taste and blend the mixture well.

Roll out half the dough ⅛ inch thick on a lightly floured surface, fit it into a tart pan with a removable fluted rim, 8¾ inches across the bottom and 1 inch deep, and trim the edge, leaving a ½-inch overhang. Roll out the remaining dough ⅛ inch thick on the lightly floured surface. Spread the Swiss chard mixture evenly in the shell, cover it with the rolled-out dough, and trim the top edge, leaving a ¾-inch overhang. Fold the top overhang under the bottom overhang, tucking it inside the rim and crimping the edge decoratively to seal it. Prick the top crust all over with a fork and bake the pie in the upper third of a preheated 400° F. oven for 45 to 50 minutes, or until the crust is golden. Let the pie cool in the pan on a rack. Serve the Swiss chard pie warm or at room temperature. Serves 8 as a first course or 4 as a luncheon entrée.

Egg Pastry Dough

1¾ cups all-purpose flour plus additional for
   dusting the dough
¼ teaspoon salt
1 stick (½ cup) cold unsalted butter,
   cut into bits
1 large egg, beaten lightly

In a bowl blend 1¾ cups of the flour, the salt, and the butter until the mixture resembles coarse meal and toss the mixture with the egg and 3 to 5 tablespoons ice water, or enough to just form a dough. Knead the dough lightly with the heel of the hand against a smooth surface, distributing the butter evenly, for a few seconds and form it into a ball. Dust the dough with the additional flour, flatten it slightly, and chill it, wrapped in wax paper, for at least 1 hour or overnight.

Smoked Mozzarella and Tomato Salad

6 ounces smoked mozzarella (available at
   Italian markets and some cheese shops and
   specialty foods shops), cut into ½-inch dice
1½ pints (about 1½ pounds) cherry tomatoes,
   halved
¼ cup packed fresh basil leaves, shredded
2 tablespoons white-wine vinegar
⅓ cup olive oil

In a bowl combine the mozzarella, the tomatoes, and the basil. In a small bowl whisk together the vinegar and salt and pepper to taste, add the oil in a stream, whisking, and whisk the dressing until it is emulsified. Pour the dressing over the salad, toss the salad well, and chill it, covered, for at least 15 minutes and up to 6 hours. Serves 6.

PHOTO ON PAGE 57

Smoked Swiss Cheese, Apple, and Celery Salad

1 teaspoon caraway seeds
2 teaspoons Dijon-style mustard
2 tablespoons cider vinegar
½ cup vegetable oil
2 tablespoons minced fresh parsley leaves
¼ pound smoked or unsmoked Swiss cheese,
   cut into matchsticks
4 ribs of celery, cut into matchsticks

2 Granny Smith apples
celery leaves for garnish

In a blender blend the caraway seeds, the mustard, the vinegar, and salt and pepper to taste, with the motor running add the oil in a stream, and blend the dressing until it is emulsified. Blend in the parsley. In a bowl toss the cheese and the celery with two thirds of the dressing. In another bowl toss the apples, quartered lengthwise, cored, and sliced thin, with the remaining dressing until they are coated well. Arrange the apple slices decoratively on each of 4 salad plates and divide the cheese and celery mixture among the plates. Drizzle any remaining dressing over the salads and garnish the plates with the celery leaves. Serves 4.

PHOTO ON PAGE 64

EGGS

Baked Eggs on Eggplant
with Ham and Curry Sauce

2 tablespoons vegetable oil
2 rounds of eggplant, each 4½ inches in
     diameter and ½ inch thick
2 ounces cooked ham, chopped
2 large eggs
⅓ cup canned chicken broth
⅓ cup heavy cream
½ teaspoon curry powder
2 slices of thin-sliced homemade-type white
     bread, toasted and trimmed approximately
     to the size of the eggplant slices

freshly ground pepper to taste
2 tablespoons minced fresh parsley leaves

In a skillet heat the oil over moderate heat until it is hot but not smoking, in it cook the eggplant, turning it, for 6 to 8 minutes, or until it is browned and tender, and transfer it to a foil-lined baking pan. Arrange the ham on the edges of the eggplant slices, forming a nest, crack the eggs into the nests carefully, and bake them in a preheated 350° F. oven for 12 to 14 minutes, or until the whites are just set. While the eggs are baking, in a small heavy saucepan stir together the broth, the cream, and the curry powder, bring the liquid to a boil, and boil it until it is reduced by half. Season the sauce with salt.

Arrange the toasts on 2 serving plates, top them with the eggplant slices, and spoon the sauce around them. Season the eggs with the pepper and salt and sprinkle the parsley over them. Serves 2 as a breakfast or luncheon entrée.

Mustard Ham Custards

1 scallion, sliced thin
1½ tablespoons minced fresh parsley leaves
1 ounce sliced cooked ham, chopped
1 tablespoon unsalted butter
½ cup heavy cream
¼ cup milk
1 large egg, beaten lightly
2 teaspoons Dijon-style mustard
buttered rye toast points as an accompaniment

In a small skillet cook the scallion, the parsley, and the ham in the butter over moderately low heat, stirring, for 3 minutes. In a small bowl whisk together the cream, the milk, the egg, the mustard, and salt and pepper to taste until the mixture is just combined, stir in the ham mixture, and divide the custard between 2 buttered ¾-cup ramekins. Steam the custards, covered with rounds of wax paper, on a steamer set over boiling water for 10 to 15 minutes, or until a knife inserted in the center comes out clean. Let the custards cool on a rack for 15 minutes. Alternatively, chill the custards in a shallow pan of ice and cold water for 10 to 15 minutes, or until they are cold. Run a thin knife around the edge of each ramekin and invert the custards onto 2 small plates. Serve the custards with the toast points. Serves 2 as a first course.

Western Omelet

4 tablespoons chopped seeded green
   bell pepper
½ small onion, chopped
1 tablespoon unsalted butter
⅓ cup chopped cooked ham
3 large eggs, beaten lightly
¼ cup diced Monterey Jack

In an 8-inch non-stick skillet or omelet pan cook the
bell pepper and the onion in the butter over moderate
heat, stirring, for 2 minutes, or until the vegetables are
softened, add the ham, and cook the mixture, stirring,
for 2 minutes. Spread the mixture evenly in the skillet,
add the eggs slowly, and sprinkle the Monterey Jack
evenly over the eggs. Sprinkle the omelet with salt and
pepper to taste, cook it over over moderately low heat,
shaking the skillet occasionally, for 5 minutes, or until
the egg is set, and slide it onto a heated serving dish.
Serves 2 as a light entrée.

*Poached Eggs on Potato
and Bacon Pancakes*

½ cup chopped onion
1½ cups coarsely grated peeled russet (baking)
   potatoes (about 1½ large potatoes)
½ teaspoon salt
¼ teaspoon freshly ground pepper
2 slices of lean bacon, chopped
4 large eggs, poached (procedure on
   page 244)
1 cup watercress hollandaise
     (page 205) as an accompaniment
4 watercress sprigs for garnish

In a bowl combine well the onion, the potatoes, the
salt, and the pepper. Scatter the bacon in four 4-inch
rounds, 2 inches apart, on a non-stick griddle and arrange ½ cup of the potato mixture on top of each round,
patting it out into 4½-inch pancakes, covering the bacon
completely. Cook the pancakes on the griddle over
moderately low heat, undisturbed, for 20 minutes, increase the heat to moderate, and cook the pancakes for
5 to 10 minutes more, or until the undersides are
browned. Turn the pancakes and cook them for 10 minutes more, or until the undersides are browned. *The
pancakes may be kept warm in a preheated 250° F. oven
for up to 30 minutes.*

Remove the hot poached eggs from the water with a
slotted spoon and pat them dry carefully with paper towels. Arrange the pancakes on heated breakfast plates,
top each one with a poached egg, and spoon some of the
hollandaise over the eggs. Garnish each serving with a
watercress sprig and serve the remaining hollandaise
separately. Serves 4.

PHOTO ON PAGE 32

Ham, Pimiento, and Jalapeño Quiche

pâte brisée (page 222)
raw rice for weighting the shell
1 cup chopped cooked ham
⅓ cup chopped drained bottled pimiento,
   patted dry
1 cup grated Monterey Jack
1 tablespoon chopped bottled pickled *jalapeño*
   pepper (wear rubber gloves)
2 tablespoons minced fresh parsley leaves
2 tablespoons minced fresh coriander
1¼ cups half-and-half
2 large eggs

Roll out the dough ⅛ inch thick on a lightly floured
surface, fit it into a tart pan with a removable fluted rim,
measuring 9 inches across the bottom, and press it up
gently to form an edge extending ¼ inch above the rim.
Prick the bottom of the shell lightly with a fork and chill
the shell for 30 minutes or freeze it for 15 minutes. Line
the shell with wax paper, fill the paper with the rice, and
bake the shell on a baking sheet in the lower third of a
preheated 425° F. oven for 10 minutes. Remove the rice
and the paper carefully and bake the shell for 10 minutes
more, or until it is golden. Let the shell cool in the pan
on a rack and return it to the baking sheet.

In a small bowl toss together the ham, the pimiento,
the Monterey Jack, the *jalapeño* pepper, the parsley,
and the coriander and sprinkle the mixture evenly in the
shell. In the bowl whisk together the half-and-half and
the eggs, pour the mixture into the shell, and bake the
quiche in the middle of a preheated 375° F. oven for 35
to 40 minutes, or until a knife inserted in the custard
comes out clean. Serves 4 to 6.

*Creamed Corn, Scallion, and Roasted
Red Pepper Roulade*

1 egg sponge (recipe follows)
For the filling

a 10-ounce package frozen corn, unthawed
1 cup heavy cream
cayenne to taste
8 scallions including the green tops, sliced
  thin
1 red bell pepper, roasted (procedure on page
  203) and chopped (about ½ cup)
½ cup freshly grated Parmesan

1 tablespoon softened unsalted butter
1 tablespoon freshly grated Parmesan
3 red bell peppers, roasted (procedure on
  page 203) and chopped (about 1½ cups)
cayenne to taste
fresh parsley sprigs for garnish

While the egg sponge is baking make the filling: In a skillet combine the corn and ½ cup of the cream and simmer the mixture, stirring occasionally, for 4 minutes. Add salt to taste and cayenne, stir in the scallions and the remaining ½ cup cream, and simmer the mixture, stirring occasionally, for 5 minutes, or until it is thickened and the cream is absorbed. Stir in the roasted pepper, the Parmesan, and salt and pepper to taste.

Spread the filling over the warm egg sponge in an even layer, leaving a 1-inch border all around, roll the *roulade* jelly-roll fashion, beginning with a long side, and trim the ends on the diagonal. With the aid of the towel and the wax paper transfer the *roulade*, seam side down, to an ovenproof platter, spread it gently with the butter, and sprinkle it with the Parmesan. Bake the *roulade* in a preheated 350° F. oven for 10 minutes, or until it is heated through and the Parmesan is melted. In a food processor or blender purée the roasted peppers, add salt to taste and the cayenne, and transfer the purée to a small bowl. Slice the *roulade* on the diagonal, serve it with the purée, and garnish it with the parsley sprigs. Serves 4 as an entrée or 8 as a first course.

Egg Sponge

3 tablespoons unsalted butter
6 tablespoons all-purpose flour
1¼ cups milk
freshly grated nutmeg to taste
4 large eggs, separated, the whites at room
  temperature

½ cup freshly grated Parmesan
a pinch of cream of tartar

In a saucepan melt the butter over low heat, stir in the flour, and cook the *roux*, stirring, for 3 minutes. Remove the pan from the heat and add the milk, heated, in a stream, whisking. Simmer the mixture, whisking occasionally, for 5 minutes, add the nutmeg and salt and pepper to taste, and transfer the mixture to a large bowl. Whisk in the egg yolks, 1 at a time, whisking well after each addition, and whisk in the Parmesan. In a bowl with an electric mixer beat the egg whites with a pinch of salt until they are frothy, add the cream of tartar, and beat the whites until they just hold stiff peaks. Stir one third of the whites into the mixture and fold in the remaining whites gently but thoroughly.

Spread the sponge batter evenly in a buttered 15½- by 10½-inch jelly-roll pan lined with buttered and floured wax paper and bake it in a preheated 350° F. oven for 25 minutes, or until it is golden and firm to the touch. Cover the egg sponge with a sheet of buttered wax paper, buttered side down, and a dish towel, invert a baking sheet over the towel, and invert the egg sponge onto the baking sheet. Remove the jelly-roll pan and the wax paper carefully and trim ¼ inch from the short sides of the egg sponge. Fill the egg sponge with the filling of your choice while it is still warm and flexible. Makes 1 egg sponge.

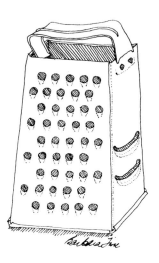

Creamed Spinach and
Crouton Roulade

For the croutons
6 slices of homemade-type white bread, crusts
    removed, cut into ½-inch cubes
½ stick (¼ cup) unsalted butter
1 garlic clove, minced

1 egg sponge (page 155)
For the filling
a 10-ounce package frozen chopped spinach,
    cooked, drained, refreshed under cold
    water, and squeezed dry
1 tablespoon softened unsalted butter
3 tablespoons heavy cream
½ cup freshly grated Parmesan

1 tablespoon softened unsalted butter
1 tablespoon freshly grated Parmesan

Spread the bread cubes in one layer in a jelly-roll pan. In a small saucepan melt the butter with the garlic, drizzle the mixture over the bread, and stir and toss the bread to coat it well. Bake the bread in one layer in a preheated 350° F. oven, turning it occasionally, for 15 to 20 minutes, or until it is golden. Transfer the croutons to paper towels to drain. *The croutons may be made 1 day in advance and stored in an airtight container.*

While the egg sponge is baking make the filling: In a food processor purée the spinach with the butter, the cream, and the Parmesan and season the filling with salt and pepper.

Spread the filling over the warm egg sponge in an even layer and sprinkle it with the croutons. Roll the *roulade* jelly-roll fashion, beginning with a long side, and trim the ends on the diagonal. With the aid of the towel and the wax paper transfer the *roulade*, seam side down, to an ovenproof platter, spread it gently with the butter, and sprinkle it with the Parmesan. Bake the *roulade* in a preheated 350° F. oven for 10 minutes, or until it is heated through and the Parmesan is melted. Serves 4 as an entrée or 8 as a first course.

Curried Potato and
Cauliflower Roulade

1 egg sponge (page 155)
For the filling
1 pound boiling potatoes, peeled, cut into ¼-
inch dice, and reserved in a bowl of cold
    water
2 cups small cauliflower flowerets
¼ cup vegetable oil
1 garlic clove, minced
1 small onion, minced
½ teaspoon fennel seeds
2 teaspoons ground coriander
¼ teaspoon cuminseed
2 teaspoons ground cumin
¼ teaspoon cayenne, or to taste
½ teaspoon turmeric
1 cup canned chicken broth
2 tablespoons fresh lemon juice
1 tablespoon minced fresh coriander leaves if
    desired

1 tablespoon softened unsalted butter
1 tablespoon freshly grated Parmesan
For the sauce
½ cup plain yogurt
½ cup sour cream
2 tablespoons minced fresh coriander leaves

While the egg sponge is baking make the filling: In a saucepan combine the potatoes, drained, with enough salted cold water to cover them and bring the water to a boil. Boil the potatoes for 2 to 3 minutes, or until they are just tender, and drain them well. In a large skillet sauté the potatoes and the cauliflower in the oil over moderately high heat, stirring, for 3 minutes, or until they are browned lightly. Reduce the heat to low, stir in the garlic, the onion, the fennel seeds, the ground coriander, the cuminseed, the ground cumin, the cayenne, the turmeric, and salt and pepper to taste, and cook the mixture, stirring, for 3 minutes. Stir in the broth, bring the liquid to a boil, and simmer the mixture, covered, for 10 to 15 minutes, or until the cauliflower is tender. Cook the mixture over moderately high heat, stirring, until any liquid is evaporated, stir in the lemon juice and the coriander leaves if desired, and season the mixture with salt and pepper.

Spread the filling over the warm *roulade* in an even layer, leaving a 1-inch border all around, roll the *roulade* jelly-roll fashion, beginning with a long side, and trim the ends on the diagonal. With the aid of the towel and the wax paper transfer the *roulade*, seam side down, to an ovenproof platter, spread it gently with the butter, and sprinkle it with the Parmesan. Bake the *rou-*

lade in a preheated 350° F. oven for 10 minutes, or until it is heated through and the Parmesan is melted.

While the *roulade* is baking make the sauce: In a small bowl stir together the yogurt, the sour cream, the coriander, and salt and pepper to taste. *The sauce may be made 1 day in advance and kept covered and chilled.* Serve the *roulade* with the yogurt sauce. Serves 4 as an entrée or 8 as a first course.

Leek and Bacon Roulade

1 egg sponge (page 155)
For the filling
½ pound sliced lean bacon, chopped
1¼ pounds leeks, green tops discarded, whites halved lengthwise, washed well, and chopped
2 tablespoons unsalted butter
½ cup heavy cream
½ cup freshly grated Parmesan
1 teaspoon caraway seeds
2 tablespoons minced fresh parsley leaves
1 tablespoon Dijon-style mustard

1 tablespoon softened unsalted butter
1 tablespoon freshly grated Parmesan

While the egg sponge is baking make the filling: In a skillet cook the bacon over moderate heat, stirring occasionally, until it is just crisp, transfer it with a slotted spoon to paper towels to drain, and pour off all but 1 tablespoon of the fat. Cook the leeks in the fat and the butter over moderately low heat, stirring, until they are softened, stir in the cream, and bring the liquid to a boil. Simmer the mixture, stirring occasionally, until it is thickened and the cream is absorbed, remove the skillet from the heat, and stir in the Parmesan, the caraway seeds, the parsley, the mustard, the bacon, and salt and pepper to taste.

Spread the filling over the warm egg sponge in an even layer, leaving a 1-inch border all around, roll the *roulade* jelly-roll fashion, beginning with a long side, and trim the ends on the diagonal. With the aid of the towel and the wax paper transfer the *roulade*, seam side down, to an ovenproof platter, spread it gently with the butter, and sprinkle it with the Parmesan. Bake the *roulade* in a preheated 350° F. oven for 10 minutes, or until it is heated through and the Parmesan is melted. Serves 4 as an entrée or 8 as a first course.

Jalapeño and Monterey Jack Soufflés

2 rounded teaspoons fine dry bread crumbs
1½ tablespoons minced shallot
1½ tablespoons unsalted butter
1½ tablespoons all-purpose flour
½ cup milk
2 large eggs, separated, the whites at room temperature
½ cup grated Monterey Jack
1 teaspoon minced pickled *jalapeño* chilies
⅛ teaspoon cream of tartar

Dust 2 well buttered 1-cup soufflé dishes with the bread crumbs. In a small heavy saucepan cook the shallot in the butter over moderately low heat, stirring, until it is softened, add the flour, and cook the *roux*, stirring, for 3 minutes. Add the milk in a stream, whisking, bring the mixture to a boil, whisking, and simmer it, stirring, for 5 minutes. Transfer the mixture to a bowl, whisk in the egg yolks, and stir in the Monterey Jack, the chilies, and salt to taste.

In a bowl beat the egg whites with a pinch of salt until they are frothy, add the cream of tartar, and beat the whites until they just hold stiff peaks. Stir one fourth of the whites into the *jalapeño* mixture and fold in the remaining whites. Divide the mixture between the soufflé dishes and bake the soufflés in a preheated 425° F. oven for 18 to 20 minutes, or until the tops are golden brown. Serves 2.

Mustard Tarragon Stuffed Eggs

6 hard-boiled large eggs
¼ cup mayonnaise
1 tablespoon Dijon-style mustard
1 teaspoon tarragon vinegar
1½ teaspoons minced fresh tarragon leaves plus 12 sprigs for garnish
1½ teaspoons minced red onion

Halve the eggs lengthwise, remove the yolks, and force them through a sieve into a bowl. Add the mayonnaise, the mustard, the vinegar, and salt and pepper to taste, stir the mixture until it is smooth, and transfer it to a pastry bag fitted with a ¼-inch star tip. Sprinkle ⅛ teaspoon of the minced tarragon into the cavity of each egg white half, pipe the yolk mixture into the whites, mounding it, and garnish each stuffed egg with some of the onion and a tarragon sprig. Makes 12 stuffed eggs.

PHOTO ON PAGE 42

BREAKFAST ITEMS

Apple Bacon Griddlecakes

⅔ cup all-purpose flour
1 tablespoon sugar
1 teaspoon double-acting baking powder
½ teaspoon baking soda
⅛ teaspoon freshly grated nutmeg
½ teaspoon salt
1 large egg
¼ cup milk
1 tart cooking apple (such as Granny Smith),
    peeled and grated coarse
4 slices of lean bacon, cooked, drained, and
    crumbled
vegetable oil for brushing the griddle
maple syrup as an accompaniment

Into a bowl sift together the flour, the sugar, the baking powder, the baking soda, the nutmeg, and the salt. In a small bowl whisk together the egg and the milk, add the mixture to the flour mixture, and stir the batter until it is just combined. Stir in the apple and the bacon. Heat a griddle or large heavy skillet over moderately high heat until it is hot, brush it lightly with the oil, and onto it drop the batter by ¼-cup measures. Cook the griddlecakes for 1 to 2 minutes, or until bubbles appear on the surface and the edges begin to brown, turn them with a metal spatula, and cook them for 1 minute more, or until they are puffed and golden. Transfer the griddlecakes to an ovenproof platter, keep them warm in a preheated 300° F. oven, and make more griddlecakes with the remaining batter in the same manner. Serve the griddlecakes with the maple syrup. Makes 6 griddlecakes, serving 2.

Silver Dollar Banana Pancakes with Grape Sauce

For the sauce
2 tablespoons unsalted butter
1 cup red grapes, quartered lengthwise and
    seeded
2 teaspoons firmly packed dark brown sugar,
    or to taste
2 tablespoons brandy
For the pancakes
¼ cup all-purpose flour
½ teaspoon double-acting baking powder
⅛ teaspoon cinnamon
1½ teaspoons firmly packed dark brown sugar
¼ cup sour cream
¼ cup milk
½ large egg, beaten lightly
½ very ripe banana, mashed
melted unsalted butter for brushing the griddle

sour cream as an accompaniment

bacon twists (page 133) as an accompaniment

Make the sauce: In a small skillet heat the butter over moderately high heat until the foam starts to subside and in it sauté the grapes, stirring occasionally, for 2 minutes. Add the brown sugar and the brandy, cook the mixture, stirring, for 2 minutes, or until most of the liquid is reduced, and keep the sauce warm.

Make the pancakes: In a bowl sift together the flour, the baking powder, the cinnamon, the brown sugar, and a pinch of salt, add the sour cream, the milk, the egg, and the banana, and stir the mixture until it is just combined. Heat a griddle over moderately high heat until it is hot and brush it with the melted butter. Drop the batter by tablespoons onto the hot griddle and cook the pancakes for 1 to 2 minutes, or until the undersides are golden brown. Turn the pancakes and cook them for 1 to 2 minutes more, or until the undersides are golden brown.

Arrange 6 of the pancakes in 2 overlapping circles on each of 2 plates, keeping the remaining pancakes warm in a preheated 250° F. oven, spoon some of the sauce over them, and top the pancakes with the sour cream. Serve the pancakes with the remaining sauce and the bacon twists. Serves 2.

PHOTO ON PAGE 16

PASTA AND GRAINS

PASTA

Herbed Cannelloni with Prosciutto
and Artichoke Hearts

For the sauce
2 cups finely chopped onion
¼ cup olive oil
3 garlic cloves, minced
a 28-ounce can Italian plum tomatoes,
    including the juice, chopped
For the filling
½ cup whole-milk ricotta
½ pound whole-milk mozzarella, grated
    coarse
½ cup freshly grated Parmesan
a 6-ounce jar marinated artichoke hearts,
    drained, reserving the marinade, and
    chopped
¼ pound thinly sliced prosciutto, chopped
    coarse

herbed pasta dough (recipe follows)
1 tablespoon olive oil
freshly grated Parmesan as an accompaniment

Make the sauce: In a saucepan cook the onion in the oil over moderately low heat, stirring, until it is softened, add the garlic, and cook the mixture, stirring, for 2 minutes. Add the tomatoes with the juice and simmer the mixture, stirring occasionally, for 30 minutes. In a food processor or blender purée the sauce with salt and pepper to taste.

Make the filling: In a bowl combine well the ricotta, the mozzarella, the Parmesan, the artichoke hearts with the reserved marinade, the prosciutto, and salt and pepper to taste.

Knead and roll the pasta dough (procedure on page 160). Cut the dough into 4-inch squares and let the pasta squares dry on a lightly floured surface for 10 minutes.

In a large kettle of boiling salted water cook the pasta squares for 4 minutes, or until they are *al dente*, and drain them in a colander. Rinse the pasta squares under lukewarm water and toss them with the oil. Mound 3 tablespoons of the filling down the center of each square, spreading it almost to the edges, and roll up the pasta squares jelly-roll fashion to enclose the filling.

In a shallow baking dish just large enough to hold the cannelloni in one layer spread one third of the sauce, arrange the cannelloni seam side down on it, and spread them with the remaining sauce. *The cannelloni may be made up to 2 weeks in advance and kept covered well and frozen or they may be made up to 2 days in advance and kept covered and chilled.* Bake the cannelloni in a preheated 400° F. oven for 20 to 40 minutes, or until they are heated through, and serve them with the Parmesan. Makes about 14 cannelloni, serving 6.

Herbed Pasta Dough

1 cup all-purpose flour
1 large egg, beaten lightly
½ teaspoon olive oil
1 tablespoon snipped fresh chives or minced
    scallion green, or to taste
1 tablespoon minced fresh parsley leaves
1 tablespoon minced fresh rosemary or 1½
    teaspoons dried, crumbled
¼ teaspoon salt

In a food processor blend the flour, the egg, the oil, the chives, the parsley, the rosemary, the salt, and 1 tablespoon water until the mixture just begins to form a ball, adding more water drop by drop if the dough is too dry. (The dough should be firm and not sticky.) Blend the dough for 15 seconds more to knead it. *The dough may be made up to 4 hours in advance and kept covered and chilled.* Let the dough rest, covered with an inverted bowl, at room temperature for 1 hour. Makes ½ pound.

Fettuccine with Scallops and Peas in Saffron Butter Sauce

2 cups shelled fresh peas (about 2 pounds
    unshelled) or a 10-ounce package frozen
    peas
1 pound fresh fettuccine or ¾ pound dried
½ stick (¼ cup) unsalted butter, cut into bits
    and softened
1¼ pounds sea scallops, rinsed, patted dry,
    and any large scallops halved
1 cup saffron butter sauce (recipe follows)

In a saucepan of boiling salted water cook the fresh peas for 3 to 10 minutes or the frozen peas for 3 to 4 minutes, or until they are just tender, and drain them well. In a kettle of boiling salted water cook the fettuccine, stirring occasionally, for 3 minutes for fresh pasta or 7 to 9 minutes for dried pasta, or until it is *al dente*, drain it well, and transfer it to a large skillet. Add the butter, the peas, and salt and pepper to taste and heat the mixture over low heat, tossing it well, until it is hot. While the pasta is cooking, arrange the scallops in a steamer set over boiling water, season them with salt and pepper, and steam them, covered, for 2 to 3 minutes, or until they are just cooked through. Add the scallops and the saffron butter sauce to the skillet and toss the mixture well. Serves 6.

Saffron Butter Sauce

¼ teaspoon crumbled saffron threads
2 tablespoons minced shallot
2 tablespoons white-wine vinegar
3 tablespoons dry white wine
3 tablespoons heavy cream
2 sticks (1 cup) cold unsalted butter, cut into
    16 pieces

In a small heavy saucepan combine the saffron, the shallot, the vinegar, and the wine, bring the liquid to a simmer, and simmer the mixture over moderate heat until it is reduced to about 2 tablespoons. Stir in the cream and simmer the mixture, whisking occasionally, until the liquid is reduced to about 2 tablespoons. *The sauce may be prepared up to this point 1 hour in advance and kept covered at room temperature. Bring the mixture to a simmer before continuing with the recipe.* Season the mixture with salt and pepper, reduce the heat to low, and whisk in the butter, 1 piece at a time, lifting the pan

from the heat occasionally to cool the mixture and adding each new piece of butter before the previous one has completely melted. (The sauce should not get hot enough to liquefy.) Remove the pan from the heat and season the butter sauce with salt and pepper. Makes about 1 cup.

Tomato Fettuccine with Curried Tomato Sauce

1 pound very ripe tomatoes, chopped coarse
2 large eggs
1 teaspoon salt
1½ cups plus 1 to 2 tablespoons all-purpose
    flour
about 2 cups curried tomato sauce (page 204)

In a saucepan simmer the tomatoes, covered, stirring occasionally, for 20 to 30 minutes, or until they are very tender, and force them through a food mill fitted with the medium disk set over a bowl. In the pan simmer the purée, stirring occasionally, for 20 to 30 minutes, or until it is reduced to about ¼ cup, and let it cool to room temperature. In a food processor blend the tomato purée, the eggs, and the salt for 5 seconds, add 1½ cups of the flour, and blend the mixture, adding the remaining flour, 1 tablespoon at a time, until it forms a soft but not sticky dough. Dust the dough lightly with flour and let it rest, covered with an inverted bowl, for 15 minutes. *The dough may be prepared up to this point and kept covered and chilled for up to 4 hours.* Makes about ¾ pound.

Knead and roll the pasta dough (procedure follows) to the second lowest notch, let the sheets of dough dry on lightly floured jelly-roll pans or hung over the top of straight-backed chairs for 15 minutes, and cut them into fettuccine (procedure on page 161).

In a kettle of boiling salted water cook the fettuccine for 3 to 4 minutes, or until it is *al dente*, drain it, and in a bowl toss it with the curried tomato sauce, heated. Serves 2 as a main course or 4 as a first course.

To Knead and Roll Pasta Dough

Set the smooth rollers of a pasta machine at the highest number. (The rollers will be wide apart.) Divide the dough into 4 pieces, flatten 1 piece into a rough rectangle, and cover the remaining pieces with an inverted bowl. Dust the rectangle with flour and feed it through the rollers. Fold the rectangle in half and feed it through

the rollers 10 more times, folding it in half each time and dusting it with flour if necessary to prevent it from sticking. Turn the dial down one notch and feed the dough through the rollers without folding. Continue to feed the dough through the rollers without folding, turning the dial one notch lower each time, until the second-lowest notch is reached. The pasta dough should be a smooth long sheet about 4 or 5 inches wide and about ¹⁄₁₆ inch thick. Roll the remaining dough in the same manner.

To Cut Fettuccine

Use the blades of a pasta machine that will cut ¼-inch-wide strips. Feed one end of a sheet of pasta dough through the blades, holding the other end straight up from the machine. Catch the strips from underneath the machine before the sheet goes completely through the rollers and put the cut strips lightly across floured jelly-roll pans or let them hang over the top of straight-backed chairs. Let the strips of pasta dry for 5 minutes.

Fusilli with Pepperoni Tomato Sauce

a 14-ounce can Italian plum tomatoes
  including the juice
½ cup chopped pepperoni
1 garlic clove, minced
2 teaspoons dried basil, crumbled
¼ teaspoon crushed red pepper flakes, or to
  taste
¼ pound *fusilli* (long corkscrew-shaped pasta)
3 tablespoons freshly grated Parmesan
2 tablespoons minced fresh parsley leaves

In a heavy saucepan combine the tomatoes with the juice, the pepperoni, the garlic, the basil, the red pepper flakes, and salt to taste, bring the liquid to a boil, breaking up the tomatoes, and simmer the mixture, stirring occasionally, for 25 to 30 minutes, or until it is thickened.

In a kettle of boiling salted water boil the *fusilli* for 15 to 17 minutes, or until it is *al dente*, drain it well, and in the pan toss it with the tomato sauce. Serve the *fusilli* sprinkled with the Parmesan and the parsley. Serves 2.

Linguine with Walnut Sauce

1 cup walnuts
½ cup half-and-half
⅓ cup packed parsley sprigs
2 tablespoons olive oil
1 large garlic clove, chopped
6 fresh basil leaves or ¾ teaspoon dried,
  crumbled
a pinch of cayenne
½ pound *linguine*

In a food processor blend the walnuts, the half-and-half, the parsley, the oil, the garlic, the basil, the cayenne, and salt to taste until the mixture is combined well. In a kettle of boiling salted water boil the *linguine* until it is *al dente*, drain it, and in a heated serving bowl toss it with the sauce. Serves 3 or 4.

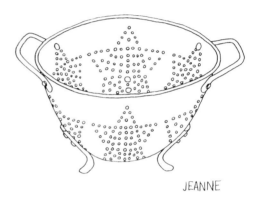

JEANNE

Noodles and Smoked Salmon with Dill Sauce

3 tablespoons minced shallot
½ cup dry white wine
1 cup heavy cream
½ pound fresh egg noodles or 6 ounces dried
2 tablespoons snipped fresh dill
¼ pound thinly sliced smoked salmon, cut
  along the grain into 2- by ⅜-inch strips

In a saucepan combine the shallot with the wine, bring the wine to a boil, and simmer the mixture until the wine is reduced to about 2 tablespoons. Stir in the cream, bring the mixture to a boil, and simmer it for 5 minutes. Keep the sauce warm, covered. In a kettle of boiling salted water cook the noodles, stirring occasionally, for 3 minutes for fresh pasta or 6 minutes for dried pasta, or until it is *al dente*. Refresh the pasta under cold water, drain it well, and transfer it to a large bowl. Bring the sauce just to a boil, remove it from the heat, and stir in the dill. Pour the sauce over the noodles and toss the mixture. With a fork stir in the salmon and season the pasta with salt and pepper. Serves 4 as a first course.

PHOTO ON PAGE 82

Buttered Noodles with Crisp Browned Shallots

vegetable oil for frying the shallots
½ pound large shallots, peeled and sliced thin
   crosswise
½ pound medium egg noodles
2 tablespoons unsalted butter, softened

In a large heavy skillet heat ½ inch of the oil over moderately high heat until it is hot but not smoking, in it fry the shallots, stirring occasionally, for 2 to 3 minutes, or until they are just golden, and transfer them with a slotted spoon to paper towels to drain. In a kettle of boiling salted water cook the noodles for 7 to 9 minutes, or until they are tender, drain them well, and return them to the kettle. Toss the noodles with the butter and salt and pepper to taste, transfer them to a heated serving dish, and sprinkle them with the shallots. Serves 4.

PHOTO ON PAGE 66

Egg Noodles with Buttered Crumbs

12 ounces wide egg noodles
1 onion, minced
1 garlic clove, minced
¾ stick (6 tablespoons) unsalted butter
¼ cup heavy cream
⅓ cup minced fresh parsley leaves,
   or to taste
a pinch of nutmeg, or to taste
¼ cup fine dry bread crumbs

In a kettle of boiling salted water cook the noodles for 7 to 8 minutes, or until they are tender, drain them in a colander, and refresh them under cold water. In the kettle cook the onion and the garlic in 4 tablespoons of the butter over moderately low heat, stirring, until the onion is softened, add the cream, and bring it to a boil. Add the noodles, drained well, the parsley, the nutmeg, and salt and pepper to taste and cook the mixture, stirring to coat the noodles with the sauce, until the noodles are hot. Transfer the mixture to a 10-inch round flameproof baking dish, sprinkle the top with the bread crumbs, and dot the crumbs with the remaining 2 tablespoons butter. Heat the dish in a preheated 400° F. oven for 10 minutes and brown the crumbs under a preheated broiler about 6 inches from the heat for 2 to 3 minutes, or until they are golden. Serves 6.

PHOTO ON PAGE 48

Ham and Pasta with Parsley Sour Cream Dressing

5 shallots, chopped fine (about ¼ cup)
1 garlic clove, chopped fine
6 tablespoons olive oil
3 tablespoons red-wine vinegar
½ cup chopped fresh parsley leaves plus
   2 tablespoons minced
½ cup sour cream
12 ounces dried egg noodles
2 cups 1-inch pieces cooked ham, ground
   coarse in a food processor
3 hard-boiled large eggs, chopped

In a small heavy skillet cook the shallots and the garlic in 1 tablespoon of the oil over moderately low heat, stirring, until the shallots are softened and in a blender purée the mixture with the remaining 5 tablespoons oil, the vinegar, the chopped parsley, the sour cream, and salt and pepper to taste. In a kettle of boiling salted water boil the noodles for 4 to 6 minutes, or until they are *al dente*, drain them in a colander, and refresh them under cold water. Drain the noodles well, in a large bowl toss them with the dressing, the ham, and the minced parsley, and sprinkle the dish with the eggs. Serves 6 to 8 as a first course.

Pasta Gratin with Gruyère

½ pound dried fettuccine
2 cups *crème fraîche* (available at specialty
   foods shops)
1 cup finely grated Gruyère
¼ teaspoon freshly grated nutmeg plus
   additional to taste
white pepper to taste
1 garlic clove, halved

In a kettle of boiling salted water cook the fettuccine, stirring occasionally, for 7 to 9 minutes, or until it is *al dente*, and drain it well. In a large bowl stir together the *crème fraîche*, ½ cup of the Gruyère, the nutmeg, the white pepper, and salt to taste. Add the fettuccine, toss the mixture, and season it with the additional nutmeg. Rub an 11-inch gratin dish with the garlic and butter it. Add the pasta mixture, sprinkle it with the remaining ½ cup Gruyère, and bake it in a preheated 400° F. oven for 15 minutes, or until the pasta has absorbed most of the *crème fraîche* and the top is golden. Serves 6 as a side dish.

Creamy Lemon Chive Pasta with Asparagus

½ pound quick fettuccine (recipe follows) or
   6 ounces dried
½ pound asparagus, trimmed, stems peeled if
   desired, and cut diagonally into ½-inch
   pieces
2 tablespoons unsalted butter, softened
¼ cup heavy cream
2 large egg yolks
½ cup freshly grated Parmesan
1 tablespoon snipped fresh chives plus
   additional for garnish
1 teaspoon freshly grated lemon rind
1 thin lemon slice, quartered, for garnish

In a kettle of boiling salted water cook the fettuccine for 3 to 4 minutes for fresh pasta or 8 to 10 minutes for dried pasta, or until it is *al dente*. Drain the pasta and put it immediately in a large bowl of cold water. In a saucepan of boiling salted water cook the asparagus for 3 to 4 minutes, or until it is just tender, drain it, and add it to the pasta.

In a large skillet cook the pasta and the asparagus, drained well, in the butter over moderately low heat, stirring, until the mixture is heated through and remove the skillet from the heat. In a small bowl whisk together the cream and the egg yolks, add the mixture and the Parmesan to the skillet, stirring to coat the pasta with the sauce, and cook the mixture over low heat, stirring, until the Parmesan is just melted. Stir in 1 tablespoon of the chives, the lemon rind, and salt and pepper to taste. Divide the pasta among heated plates, mounding it, and garnish each serving with a sprinkling of the additional chives and a lemon quarter. Serves 4.

PHOTO ON PAGE 44

Quick Fettuccine

2 large eggs
¾ teaspoon salt
about 1 cup all-purpose flour

In a food processor blend the eggs with the salt for 5 seconds, add ⅞ cup of the flour, and blend the dough, adding the remaining flour, 1 tablespoon at a time, if necessary, until it forms a ball. Dust the dough lightly with flour and let it rest, covered with a small bowl, for 15 minutes. Set the smooth rollers of a pasta machine at the highest number. (The rollers will be wide apart.) Quarter the dough, flatten 1 piece into a rough rectangle, and cover the remaining pieces with the bowl. Dust the rectangle lightly with flour and feed it through the rollers. Fold the rectangle in half and feed it through the rollers several times, dusting it with flour if necessary to prevent it from sticking, and folding it in half each time. Turn the dial down one notch and feed the dough through the rollers, dusting it with flour if necessary but without folding it. Continue to feed the dough through the rollers without folding it, turning the dial one notch lower each time, until the second-lowest notch is reached. The dough should be a smooth long strip 4 to 5 inches wide and about ¹⁄₁₆ inch thick. Roll the remaining pieces of dough in the same manner. Let the strips of dough dry on lightly floured jelly-roll pans or hung over the top of a straight-backed chair for 5 minutes, or until they feel dry to the touch but not brittle. Feed the strips, 1 at a time, through the ¼-inch cutting blades of the pasta machine: Feed one end of the strip through the blades holding the other end straight up and catch the fettuccine from underneath the machine before it goes through the rollers completely. Let the fettuccine dry on the jelly-roll pans for 5 minutes. Makes ½ pound.

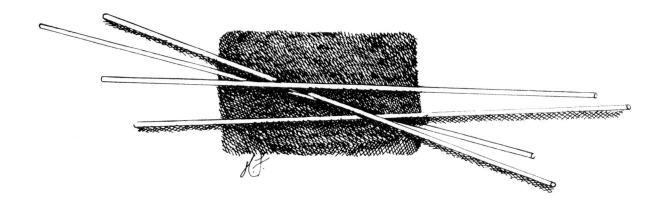

Tomato Pasta with Goat Cheese
and Garlic Sauce

1 to 1¼ cups heavy cream
8 garlic cloves, crushed lightly
2 ounces goat cheese, cut into bits
½ pound fresh tomato pasta or 6 ounces dried
   (available at specialty foods shops)
2 tablespoons minced fresh parsley leaves

In a small saucepan bring 1 cup of the cream to a boil, add the garlic, and simmer the mixture for 10 to 12 minutes, or until the garlic is softened. Transfer the garlic with a slotted spoon to a blender or food processor, add the goat cheese and ½ cup of the hot cream, and purée the mixture until it is very smooth. With the motor running add the remaining hot cream in a stream and blend the sauce until it is smooth. Return the sauce to the pan and if it is too thin simmer it until it is thick enough to coat a spoon. If the sauce is too thick add some of the remaining ¼ cup cream. *The sauce may be made up to 4 hours in advance, kept covered and chilled, and reheated over low heat with 1 to 2 tablespoons of the remaining cream to thin it.*

In a kettle of boiling salted water cook the pasta, stirring occasionally, for 3 minutes for fresh pasta or 7 to 9 minutes for dried pasta, or until it is *al dente*, and drain it well. While the pasta is cooking reheat the sauce over moderate heat, stirring, but do not let it boil. In a heated serving dish toss the pasta with the sauce and the parsley, season it with salt and pepper to taste, and serve it immediately. Serves 2 as a main course or 4 as a first course or side dish.

Black Pepper Spätzle with
Onion and Paprika Sauce

For the sauce
¼ cup finely chopped onion
1 tablespoon unsalted butter
½ teaspoon sweet paprika (preferably
   Hungarian)
1 teaspoon all-purpose flour
⅓ cup canned chicken broth
½ teaspoon white-wine vinegar

1 large egg
¼ cup milk
½ teaspoon salt
1 teaspoon freshly ground pepper

¾ cup all-purpose flour
2 teaspoons minced fresh parsley leaves

Make the sauce: In a small saucepan cook the onion in the butter with the paprika over moderately low heat, stirring, until it is softened, stir in the flour, and cook the *roux*, stirring, for 3 minutes. Add the broth and the vinegar, simmer the sauce, stirring, for 2 minutes, and keep it warm, covered.

In a bowl whisk together the egg, the milk, 1 tablespoon water, the salt, and the pepper, add the flour, and beat the mixture with a wooden spoon until it is just smooth. Transfer the batter to a pastry bag fitted with a ⅜-inch plain tip. In a large deep skillet bring 2 inches salted water to a bare simmer. Holding the pastry bag in one hand with the tip resting just over the rim of the skillet and working quickly, cut off ¼-inch segments of the batter from the pastry tip with a knife, letting the batter drop into the water. When all of the batter is used, cook the *Spätzle* for 5 minutes, or until it is *al dente*, drain it in a sieve, and rinse it quickly under cold water. Add the *Spätzle* to the sauce, cook the mixture over moderate heat, stirring, until it is heated through, and stir in the parsley. Serves 2.

GRAINS

Barley Pilaf with Pine Nuts

½ cup chopped onion
3 cloves
½ bay leaf
1 tablespoon olive oil
½ cup pearl barley
⅛ teaspoon cinnamon
2 tablespoons pine nuts,
   toasted lightly
1½ tablespoons minced
   fresh parsley leaves

In a small heavy saucepan cook the onion, the cloves, and the bay leaf in the oil over moderate heat, stirring, until the onion is browned. Stir in the barley, the cinnamon, 1 cup water, and salt and pepper to taste, bring the water to a boil, and simmer the mixture, covered, for 30 to 35 minutes, or until the liquid is absorbed and the barley is tender. Discard the cloves and the bay leaf and with a fork stir in the pine nuts and the parsley. Serves 2.

Bulgar Pilaf with Cashews

1 small onion, sliced thin
1 tablespoon unsalted butter
½ cup *bulgur* (processed cracked wheat, available at natural foods stores and some supermarkets)
¾ cup canned chicken broth
3 tablespoons chopped unsalted dry-roasted cashews
1 tablespoon thinly sliced scallion greens

In a small heavy saucepan cook the sliced onion in the butter over moderately low heat, stirring occasionally, until it is softened, stir in the *bulgur*, and cook the mixture, stirring, for 1 minute. Add the broth, bring the liquid to a boil, and cook the mixture, covered, over low heat for 10 minutes, or until the liquid is absorbed. Fluff the pilaf with a fork, transfer it to a serving bowl, and sprinkle it with the cashews and the scallion greens. Serves 2.

Lemon Bulgur Timbales with Chives

2 tablespoons thinly sliced white part of scallion
1 tablespoon unsalted butter
½ cup *bulgur* (processed cracked wheat, available at natural foods stores, specialty foods shops, and some supermarkets)
1½ teaspoons freshly grated lemon rind
¾ cup canned chicken broth
2 tablespoons snipped fresh chives plus chive blades for garnish if desired
1 decoratively cut lemon slice, halved, for garnish if desired

In a small saucepan cook the scallion in the butter over moderately low heat, stirring, until it is softened, add the *bulgur* and the rind, and cook the mixture, stirring, for 1 minute. Add the broth, bring it to a boil, and simmer the mixture, covered, for 10 minutes, or until all the liquid is absorbed. Fluff the *bulgur* with a fork, stir in the snipped chives, and let the mixture stand, covered, off the heat for 5 minutes. Season the *bulgur* with salt and pepper and pack it into 2 buttered ½-cup timbale molds. Invert the *bulgur* timbales onto individual serving dishes and garnish each timbale with a halved lemon slice and a few chive blades if desired. Serves 2.

Couscous Timbales

⅓ cup thinly sliced scallion
1 tablespoon unsalted butter
¾ teaspoon ground cumin
¼ teaspoon turmeric
⅛ teaspoon cinnamon
a 14-ounce can Italian plum tomatoes, drained, chopped fine, and drained again
¼ cup dried currants
¾ cup couscous
3 tablespoons minced fresh parsley leaves
4 flat-leafed parsley sprigs for garnish if desired

In a skillet cook the scallion in the butter over moderately low heat, stirring, for 1 minute and stir in the cumin, the turmeric, the cinnamon, the tomatoes, the currants, and 1 cup plus 2 tablespoons water. Bring the liquid to a boil, stir in the couscous, and let the mixture stand, covered, off the heat for 5 minutes, or until the couscous has absorbed the liquid. Pack the couscous into 4 well buttered ½-cup timbale molds. *The couscous may be prepared and molded up to 2 hours in advance and kept at room temperature. Reheat the timbales, covered with foil, in a preheated 350° F oven for 10 minutes.* Invert the timbales onto a platter and garnish each timbale with a parsley sprig if desired. Serves 4.

PHOTO ON PAGE 24

Baked Polenta with Parmesan

½ teaspoon salt
½ cup yellow cornmeal (not stone-ground)
2 tablespoons unsalted butter
3 tablespoons freshly grated Parmesan

In a heavy saucepan bring 2 cups water to a boil, add the salt and the cornmeal in a very slow stream, whisking constantly, and cook the mixture over moderately low heat, stirring, for 15 minutes, or until it is very thick. Stir in the butter and pepper to taste, spoon the polenta into a buttered 9-inch pie plate, and smooth the top. Sprinkle the Parmesan over the top and chill the mixture, covered, for at least 30 minutes or up to 12 hours. Bake the polenta in a preheated 400° F. oven for 25 minutes, brown it lightly on the rack of a preheated broiler about 4 inches from the heat, and cut it into wedges. Serves 2.

PHOTO ON PAGE 18

Brown Rice Pilaf with Dates and Carrots

1 small onion, halved lengthwise and sliced
thin crosswise (about ¾ cup)
1 carrot, halved lengthwise and sliced thin
crosswise (about ½ cup)
1 cup long-grain brown rice
1 tablespoon olive oil
¼ cup pitted dates, chopped
1 teaspoon freshly grated lemon rind
1½ cups canned chicken broth
¼ cup sliced almonds, toasted lightly
2 tablespoons thinly sliced scallion greens
lemon juice to taste

In a large heavy saucepan cook the onion, the carrot,
and the rice in the oil over moderately low heat, stirring,
for 1 minute. Stir in the dates, the rind, the broth, ½ cup
water, and salt and pepper to taste, bring the liquid to a
boil, and simmer the mixture, covered, for 45 to 50 minutes, or until the liquid is absorbed and the rice is tender.
Fluff the pilaf with a fork, transfer it to a serving dish,
and sprinkle it with the almonds and the scallion greens.
Season the pilaf with the lemon juice. Serves 4 to 6.

Confetti Rice

4 tablespoons vegetable oil
2 teaspoons cuminseed
6 scallions, the white part and the green part
sliced thin separately
2 cups unconverted long-grain rice
2½ teaspoons salt
1 green bell pepper, diced
1 red bell pepper, diced
1 yellow bell pepper, diced

In a large saucepan heat 3 tablespoons of the oil over
moderate heat until it is hot but not smoking and in it
cook the cuminseed, stirring, for 10 seconds, or until it
is fragrant. Add the white part of the scallions and the
rice and cook the mixture, stirring, for 2 minutes. Add
3½ cups water and the salt, bring the liquid to a boil, and
simmer the rice, covered, for 18 to 20 minutes, or until
it is tender and the liquid is absorbed. In a large skillet
heat the remaining 1 tablespoon oil over moderately
high heat until it is hot but not smoking and in it sauté the
diced bell peppers, stirring, for 2 minutes, or until they are
just tender. Add the bell peppers to the rice with 2 tablespoons scallion greens and toss the mixture. Serves 8.

PHOTO ON PAGE 36

Saffron Rice Timbales

⅓ cup minced onion
1½ tablespoons unsalted butter
⅛ teaspoon crumbled saffron threads
⅔ cup long-grain rice
1¼ cups canned chicken broth
3 tablespoons drained and finely chopped
pimiento

In a small saucepan cook the onion in the butter over
moderately low heat, stirring, until it is softened, add
the saffron and the rice, and cook the mixture, stirring,
for 1 minute, or until the rice is coated well with the butter. Add the broth, bring the liquid to a boil, and simmer
the rice, covered, for 18 minutes, or until all the liquid is
absorbed. Stir in the pimiento, remove the pan from the
heat, and let the rice stand, covered, for 5 minutes. Pack
the rice into 4 buttered ½-cup timbale molds and invert
the timbales onto heated plates. Serves 4.

PHOTO ON PAGE 62

Mushroom Risotto

2½ cups canned beef broth
¼ cup finely chopped onion
2 tablespoons unsalted butter
¼ pound mushrooms (about 5), sliced
¾ cup long-grain rice
2 tablespoons medium-dry Sherry

In a saucepan bring the broth to a simmer and keep it
at a bare simmer. In a heavy saucepan cook the onion in
1 tablespoon of the butter over moderately low heat,
stirring, until it is softened. While the onion is cooking,
in a small skillet cook the mushrooms in the remaining
1 tablespoon butter over moderately low heat, stirring
occasionally, until they are just golden. Add the rice to
the onion mixture, stirring with a wooden spatula until
it is coated well with the butter, add the Sherry, and
cook the mixture over moderately high heat, stirring,
until the Sherry is absorbed. Add about ½ cup of the
simmering broth and cook the mixture, stirring, until
the broth is absorbed. Continue adding the broth, about
½ cup at a time, stirring constantly and letting each por-
tion be absorbed before adding the next. With the last ½
cup broth add the mushrooms, stirring, cook the mixture until the broth is absorbed and the rice is *al dente*,
and season the risotto with freshly ground black pepper.
Serves 2.

VEGETABLES

Artichoke Bottoms Filled with Herbed Carrots

2 artichokes, trimmed into bottoms
  (procedure follows)
2 tablespoons olive oil
¼ cup dry white wine
1½ cups canned chicken broth
1 teaspoon fresh lemon juice
½ teaspoon dried orégano, crumbled
½ teaspoon dried marjoram, crumbled
½ teaspoon dried thyme, crumbled
½ cup thinly sliced carrots
1 tablespoon minced fresh parsley leaves

With a spoon scrape the chokes from the artichoke bottoms and return the artichoke bottoms to the acidulated water. In a saucepan combine the oil, the wine, the broth, the lemon juice, the orégano, the marjoram, the thyme, and salt and pepper to taste and bring the liquid to a boil. Add the artichokes, drained, and simmer them for 15 minutes. Add the carrots and simmer the vegetables for 5 to 10 minutes, or until the artichokes are tender. Transfer the artichokes concave side up to serving plates and mound half the carrots in each bottom. Spoon the cooking liquid over the artichokes and sprinkle the carrots with the parsley. Serves 2 as a first course.

To Trim Artichokes into Artichoke Bottoms

large artichokes
1 lemon, halved

Break off and discard the stems of the artichokes. Bend the outer leaves back until they snap off close to the base and remove several more layers of leaves in the same manner until the pale inner leaves are reached. Trim the bases and sides with a stainless steel knife, cut through each artichoke 1½ inches from the bottom, and rub the cut surfaces with 1 of the lemon halves, dropping the artichoke bottoms as they are trimmed into a bowl of cold water acidulated with the juice of the remaining lemon half.

Asparagus with Sesame Mayonnaise

⅓ cup mayonnaise (page 200)
2 tablespoons sour cream
¼ teaspoon Oriental sesame oil (available at
  Oriental markets and most supermarkets)
1½ pounds asparagus, trimmed and the stems
  peeled
1 tablespoon sesame seeds, toasted lightly

In a bowl stir together the mayonnaise, the sour cream, the oil, and salt and pepper to taste until the mixture is combined well. In a large skillet of boiling salted water cook the asparagus for 3 to 5 minutes, or until they are just tender, and drain them well. Serve the asparagus warm or at room temperature topped with the sesame mayonnaise and sprinkled with the sesame seeds. Serves 4.

Avocado Mousses with Radish and Coriander

1½ teaspoons unflavored gelatin
2 avocados (preferably California)
2 teaspoons fresh lime juice
⅛ teaspoon cayenne, or to taste
2 tablespoons minced fresh coriander plus 6
　　leaves for garnish
¼ cup minced radish plus thin slices for
　　garnish
½ teaspoon salt, or to taste
⅓ cup well chilled heavy cream
sesame ginger toasts (page 104) as an
　　accompaniment

In a very small saucepan sprinkle the gelatin over 2 tablespoons cold water and let it soften for 10 minutes. Heat the mixture over low heat, stirring, until the gelatin is dissolved and remove the pan from the heat. Peel and pit 1 of the avocados and in a food processor purée it with the lime juice, scraping down the sides. Transfer the mixture to a bowl, stir in the gelatin mixture thoroughly, and stir in the cayenne, the minced coriander, the minced radish, and the salt, combining the mixture well. In a chilled bowl beat the cream until it just holds stiff peaks and fold it into the avocado mixture. Arrange a coriander leaf and some of the radish slices decoratively in the bottom of each of six ⅓-cup ramekins, fill the ramekins with the avocado mixture, smoothing the tops, and chill the mousses, covered, for 2 hours, or until they are set. *The mousses may be made up to 8 hours in advance and kept covered tightly and chilled.* Just before serving run a thin knife around the edge of each ramekin and invert the mousses onto small plates. Peel, pit, and cut into 12 slices the remaining avocado and garnish each serving with 2 of the slices and a radish slice, halved. Serve the mousses with the sesame ginger toasts. Serves 6 as a first course.

PHOTO ON PAGE 56

Beet and Horseradish Purée

2¼ pounds beets, scrubbed and trimmed,
　　leaving 2 inches of the stem ends intact
2 teaspoons freshly grated horseradish or
　　2 tablespoons drained bottled, or to taste
2 teaspoons red-wine vinegar

In a large saucepan combine the beets and enough water to cover them by 1 inch, bring the water to a boil, and simmer the beets, covered, for 20 to 40 minutes (depending on their size), or until they are very tender. Drain the beets, reserving 1 tablespoon of the cooking liquid, and slip off the skins and stems. In a food processor purée the beets with the reserved cooking liquid, the horseradish, the vinegar, and salt and pepper to taste. *The purée may be made up to 1 day in advance and kept covered and chilled.* In a heavy saucepan reheat the purée over low heat, stirring constantly, until it is hot. Makes about 3 cups.

Bell Pepper Filled with Shrimp, Feta, and Pasta Salad

4 whole scallions plus 2 tablespoons thinly
　　sliced scallion greens
2 teaspoons white-wine vinegar
4 teaspoons olive oil
¼ pound (about 12) small shrimp, shelled and
　　deveined
3 tablespoons *orzo* (rice-shaped pasta)
4 tablespoons crumbled Feta
1 large green bell pepper, quartered and the
　　stem, seeds, and ribs discarded

Trim the root ends and the loose green parts of the whole scallions, leaving about 4 inches of firm scallion. Fringe the green ends with a sharp knife by cutting two 3-inch slits and rolling the scallion 90° for the second slit. Drop the scallion brushes as they are cut into a bowl of ice and cold water and chill them to curl the ends while making the salad.

In a small bowl whisk together the vinegar and salt and pepper to taste, add the oil, whisking, and whisk the dressing until it is emulsified. In a saucepan of boiling salted water boil the shrimp for 20 to 30 seconds, or until they are just firm to the touch, and drain them. Reserve 2 of the shrimp, halved lengthwise, for the garnish and chop the remaining shrimp. In a large saucepan of boiling salted water boil the *orzo* for 10 to 12 minutes, or until it is *al dente*. Drain the *orzo* in a sieve, refresh it under cold water, and drain it well. In a bowl combine the chopped shrimp, the *orzo*, the Feta, the sliced scallion greens, and salt and pepper to taste. Whisk the dressing, add it to the shrimp mixture, and toss the salad well. Divide the salad among the pepper quarters, top each quarter with 1 of the reserved shrimp halves, and transfer the filled bell pepper quarters to a platter. Garnish the platter with the scallion brushes,

drained well and patted dry carefully. Serves 2 as a light luncheon entrée.

Roasted Broccoli with Sesame Dressing

½ pound large broccoli flowerets including
   3 inches of the stem
1½ tablespoons olive oil
2 tablespoons fresh lemon juice
1 teaspoon Oriental sesame oil (available at
   Oriental markets and most supermarkets)
2 teaspoons soy sauce
1½ tablespoons vegetable oil
1 teaspoon sesame seeds, toasted lightly
½ teaspoon ground ginger
¼ teaspoon minced garlic
a pinch of sugar

In a bowl toss the broccoli with the olive oil until it is coated well and roast it in a jelly-roll pan in a preheated 500° F. oven, turning it occasionally with tongs, for 10 to 12 minutes, or until it is crisp-tender. While the broccoli is roasting, in a blender blend the lemon juice, the sesame oil, the soy sauce, the vegetable oil, the sesame seeds, the ginger, the garlic, and the sugar until the dressing is smooth. Transfer the broccoli to a serving dish or salad bowl and pour the dressing over it. Serves 2.

Deep-Fried Broccoli Flowerets in Beer Batter with Soy Curry Sauce

¼ cup all-purpose flour
¼ cup plus 1 tablespoon beer
1 garlic clove, peeled
1 teaspoon unsalted butter
¼ teaspoon curry powder
¾ teaspoon firmly packed dark brown sugar
1½ teaspoons red-wine vinegar
1 teaspoon fresh lemon juice
½ teaspoon soy sauce
vegetable oil for deep-frying
12 small broccoli flowerets

In a small bowl whisk together the flour and the beer and let the batter stand for 30 minutes. In a small saucepan of boiling water boil the garlic for 5 minutes and drain it. Mince the garlic and mash it to a paste with the blade of a knife. In the pan melt the butter over moderately low heat and in it cook the curry powder, stirring, for 1 minute. Stir in the garlic paste, the brown sugar, the vinegar, the lemon juice, and the soy sauce and transfer the sauce to a small dish.

In a deep heavy skillet heat 1 inch of the oil to 375° F. Whisk the beer batter, dip the broccoli flowerets into it, knocking off the excess batter, and fry them in the oil for 1½ to 2 minutes, or until they are golden. Transfer the broccoli flowerets to paper towels to drain and serve them with the soy curry sauce. Serves 2 as a first course.

Broccoli Rabe with Lemon and Garlic

1½ pounds pencil-thin broccoli rabe, washed
   and any yellow leaves and coarse stem ends
   discarded
2 teaspoons minced garlic
3 tablespoons unsalted butter
2 tablespoons minced fresh parsley leaves
2 teaspoons freshly grated lemon rind

In a heavy kettle cook the broccoli rabe in the water clinging to the leaves, covered, over moderately high heat, stirring occasionally, until the stems are just tender. While the broccoli rabe is cooking, in a small skillet cook the garlic in the butter over moderately low heat, stirring occasionally, for 3 minutes. Drain the broccoli rabe, transfer it to a bowl, and pour the garlic mixture over it. Add the parsley and salt and pepper to taste, toss the mixture gently until it is combined well, and sprinkle it with the lemon rind. Serves 4.

PHOTO ON PAGE 66

Buttered Brussels Sprouts

3 pounds (about 3 pints) Brussels sprouts,
   trimmed and halved lengthwise
3 tablespoons unsalted butter, cut into pieces
   and softened

In a steamer set over boiling water steam the Brussels sprouts, covered, for 7 to 8 minutes, or until they are just tender, transfer them to a bowl, and toss them with the butter and salt and pepper to taste until they are coated well. Serves 10.

PHOTO ON PAGE 70

Braised Red Cabbage with Chestnuts

1½ pounds red cabbage, cored and sliced thin
¼ cup vegetable oil
¾ cup canned beef broth
¼ cup red-wine vinegar
30 chestnuts, roasted and peeled (procedure
    follows) and chopped coarse
2 tablespoons sugar
2 tablespoons unsalted butter, softened

In a large skillet stir-fry the cabbage in the oil over moderately high heat for 3 minutes. Stir in the broth, the vinegar, the chestnuts, and salt and pepper to taste, bring the liquid to a boil, and simmer the mixture, covered, for 10 minutes. Stir in the sugar, simmer the mixture, covered partially, stirring occasionally, for 20 to 30 minutes, or until the cabbage is tender and the liquid is almost evaporated, and stir in the butter. Serves 6 to 8.

To Roast and Peel Chestnuts

With a sharp knife score each chestnut ¼ inch deep all around. Spread the chestnuts, no more than 1 pound at a time, in one layer in a jelly-roll pan and roast them in a preheated 400° F. oven for 20 minutes, or until the shells are just opened. Holding the chestnuts in a potholder or thick towel, peel off both layers of skin with a knife while the chestnuts are still hot. Roast and peel the remaining chestnuts in the same manner.

Sautéed Napa Cabbage and Swiss Chard

½ stick (¼ cup) unsalted butter
2 tablespoons vegetable oil
1 tablespoon minced peeled fresh gingerroot
1 large head of Napa cabbage (celery
    cabbage, about 1¾ pounds), ribs discarded
    and the leaves shredded or chopped
2 bunches (about 1¾ pounds) of Swiss chard,
    ribs discarded and the leaves shredded
    or chopped

In a very large skillet heat the butter and the oil over moderately high heat until the foam starts to subside and in the fat cook the gingerroot, stirring, for 30 seconds. Add the cabbage, the chard, and salt and pepper to taste and cook the mixture, stirring, for 3 minutes, or until the vegetables are wilted. (The skillet will be very crowded until the vegetables start to wilt.) Serves 6.

PHOTO ON PAGE 60

Dilled Carrots and Cauliflower

2 tablespoons unsalted butter
1 teaspoon sugar
½ teaspoon salt
white pepper to taste
1 small head of cauliflower, cut into
    1-inch flowerets
6 carrots, cut into 2-inch matchsticks
3 tablespoons snipped fresh dill plus dill
    sprigs for garnish

In a heavy skillet combine the butter, the sugar, the salt, the white pepper, and ¼ cup water and bring the mixture to a simmer, stirring until the butter is melted. Add the cauliflower and simmer it, covered, stirring occasionally, for 10 to 12 minutes, or until it is just tender. Transfer the cauliflower with a slotted spoon to the center of a serving dish and keep it warm. Add the carrots to the skillet and simmer them, covered, stirring occasionally, for 5 minutes, or until they are just tender. Transfer the carrots with a slotted spoon to the serving dish, arranging them around the cauliflower, and spoon any pan juices over the vegetables. Sprinkle the vegetables with the snipped dill and salt and pepper to taste and garnish the dish with the dill sprigs. Serves 4.

Caramelized Carrots and Onions

1 cup thinly sliced onion
3 carrots, cut into matchsticks (about 2 cups)
2 tablespoons unsalted butter

In a large heavy saucepan cook the onion and the carrots in the butter over moderate heat, stirring occasionally, for 20 to 25 minutes, or until the vegetables are golden, and season the vegetables with salt and pepper. Serves 2.

Carrots with Candied Pecans

3 tablespoons unsalted butter
2 tablespoons light corn syrup
1 tablespoon plus 2 teaspoons sugar
¼ teaspoon cinnamon
½ cup pecans

1 pound carrots, cut diagonally into
  ⅛-inch slices
white pepper to taste
1 teaspoon freshly grated orange rind

In a small heavy saucepan melt 1 tablespoon of the butter, stir in the corn syrup, 1 tablespoon of the sugar, the cinnamon, and a pinch of salt, and bring the mixture to a boil. Simmer the syrup for 5 minutes. While the syrup is cooking heat the pecans in a small baking pan in a preheated 250° F. oven for 5 minutes. Pour the syrup over the pecans and bake the mixture, stirring every 20 minutes, for 1 hour. Scrape the pecan mixture into a buttered baking pan, let it cool for 3 minutes, and separate the pecans with 2 forks. Let the pecans cool completely. *The pecans may be prepared up to 1 day in advance.* In a large skillet melt the remaining 2 tablespoons butter with the remaining 2 teaspoons sugar, 3 tablespoons water, the white pepper, and salt to taste. Stir in the carrots, bring the liquid to a boil, and cook the carrots, covered, over moderate heat for 5 minutes. Stir in the rind and cook the carrots, uncovered, for 3 to 4 minutes, or until they are crisp-tender. Transfer the carrots to a heated serving dish and sprinkle them with the candied pecans. Serves 4 to 6.

Baked Cauliflower

2 cups 2-inch cauliflower flowerets
1 tablespoon olive oil
fresh lemon juice to taste

In a bowl toss the cauliflower with the oil until it is coated well and bake it in a jelly-roll pan in a preheated 500° F. oven, turning it occasionally, for 8 to 12 minutes, or until it is crisp-tender. Serve the cauliflower flowerets with the lemon juice and salt and pepper to taste. Serves 2.

Gratin of Celery Root and Potato

2½ cups heavy cream
2½ cups milk
2 teaspoons salt
½ teaspoon freshly ground pepper
¼ teaspoon freshly grated nutmeg
2 pounds celery root
2 pounds boiling potatoes

¾ stick (6 tablespoons) unsalted butter, sliced
  thin and chilled
1 tablespoon chopped fresh parsley leaves for
  garnish

In a saucepan combine the cream, the milk, the salt, the pepper, and the nutmeg, heat the mixture over moderate heat until it is hot, and keep it warm. Peel and slice thin half the celery root and half the potatoes, preferably using a *mandoline*, and in a well buttered 14-inch gratin pan layer the potatoes and celery root alternately, starting and ending with the potatoes. Pour half the cream mixture over the vegetables and arrange half the butter on top. Fill another well buttered 14-inch gratin pan with the remaining potatoes, celery root, cream mixture, and butter in the same manner. Bring the cream mixture in the gratin pans to a simmer on top of the stove and bake the gratins in a preheated 375° F. oven for 50 minutes, or until the vegetables are tender. Sprinkle the parsley decoratively on the gratins. Serves 12.

PHOTO ON PAGE 13

Corn with Bacon and Bell Peppers

2 slices of lean bacon
¼ cup chopped onion
1 cup corn (cut from about 2 ears of corn)
½ small red bell pepper, chopped
½ small green bell pepper, chopped
2 teaspoons white-wine vinegar
⅛ teaspoon cayenne, or to taste

In a small skillet cook the bacon over moderately low heat, turning it, until it is crisp and transfer it to paper towels to drain. Pour off all but 1 tablespoon of the fat and in the fat remaining in the skillet cook the onion, stirring, until it is softened. In a saucepan of boiling water boil the corn for 2 minutes, add the bell peppers, and boil the vegetables for 1 minute. Drain the vegetables well and transfer them to a bowl. Add the onion, the bacon, crumbled, the vinegar, the cayenne, and salt to taste and toss the mixture until it is combined well. Serves 2.

Chinese-Style Spicy Pickled Cucumbers

1 pound small pickling (Kirby) cucumbers,
  scrubbed, cut lengthwise into 8 wedges, and
  seeded, or 1 seedless cucumber, cut
  crosswise into 2-inch sections and each
  section cut lengthwise into 8 wedges
1½ teaspoons salt
4 teaspoons sugar
2 tablespoons rice vinegar* or white-wine
  vinegar
3 tablespoons Oriental sesame oil*
1 tablespoon vegetable oil
a 1-inch cube of peeled fresh gingerroot, cut
  into fine julienne strips
1 teaspoon red pepper flakes

*available at Oriental markets and many
  specialty foods shops and supermarkets

In a bowl toss the cucumber wedges with the salt and let them stand for 20 minutes. Drain the cucumbers in a colander, rinse them under cold water, and pat them dry on paper towels. In a bowl dissolve the sugar in the vinegar, stirring, add the cucumbers, and toss them to coat them with the mixture.

In a wok or small skillet heat the sesame oil and the vegetable oil over moderately high heat until the oil is just smoking, add the gingerroot and the red pepper flakes, and stir-fry the mixture for 5 to 10 seconds, or until the red pepper flakes are several shades darker. Remove the wok from the heat and let the oil cool to room temperature. Pour the spiced oil over the cucumbers, toss the mixture well, and let it marinate at room temperature for 1 hour. *The pickles may be made up to 4 days in advance and kept covered and chilled, stirring occasionally.* Makes about 2½ cups.

Fried Eggplant with Yogurt Cumin Sauce

½ cup plain yogurt
½ teaspoon ground cumin, or to taste
1 garlic clove, cooked in boiling water for
  5 minutes, drained, chopped, and mashed
  to a paste
1 large egg
3 tablespoons milk
6 ounces eggplant, peeled and cut into
  ½-inch-thick rounds
all-purpose flour for dredging
fine fresh bread crumbs for dredging
vegetable oil for frying

In a bowl whisk together the yogurt, the cumin, the garlic, and salt and pepper to taste and chill the sauce, covered, for 20 minutes. In a shallow dish whisk together the egg, the milk, and salt and pepper to taste. Dredge the eggplant in the flour, shaking off the excess, dip it in the egg mixture, and dredge it in the bread crumbs, patting the crumbs on to help them adhere. In a large skillet heat ½ inch of the oil over moderate heat until it is hot but not smoking, in it fry the eggplant in batches, turning it, for 3 to 4 minutes, or until it is tender and golden, and transfer it to paper towels to drain. Serve the fried eggplant with the yogurt cumin sauce. Serves 2.

Braised Fennel with Olives

2 large onions, chopped coarse
½ cup olive oil
4 garlic cloves, minced
two 28-ounce cans plum tomatoes, drained,
  reserving 1 cup of the juice, and chopped
1½ cups chicken stock (page 247) or canned
  chicken broth
3 pounds small fennel bulbs, trimmed,
  quartered, and kept in a bowl of water
  acidulated with the juice of ½ lemon
2 teaspoons freshly grated orange rind
1½ cups pitted and sliced imported brine-
  cured black olives
2 teaspoons fennel seeds
1 tablespoon fresh lemon juice
3 large sprigs of fennel top for garnish

In a kettle cook the onions in the oil over moderately low heat, stirring, until they are softened, add the garlic, and cook the mixture, stirring, for 3 minutes. Add the tomatoes and the reserved juice, the stock, the fennel bulbs, drained, the rind, the olives, the fennel seeds, and salt and pepper to taste, bring the liquid to a boil, and simmer the mixture, covered, for 15 minutes. Simmer the mixture, uncovered, stirring occasionally, for 30 minutes, or until the fennel is very tender and the liquid is reduced by half. Stir in the lemon juice and salt and pepper to taste. *The fennel may be made up to 2 days in advance and kept covered and chilled.* Serve the fennel hot or at room temperature garnished with the fennel sprigs. Serves 12.

PHOTO ON PAGE 10

Green Beans with Sunflower Seeds and Hot Vinegar Dressing

½ pound green beans, trimmed
1½ tablespoons unsalted shelled
 sunflower seeds
2 teaspoons olive oil
2 teaspoons red-wine vinegar

In a saucepan of boiling salted water boil the beans for 5 to 7 minutes, or until they are crisp-tender, and drain them well. While the beans are cooking, in a skillet cook the sunflower seeds in the oil over moderate heat, stirring, for 3 minutes, or until they are golden, add the beans, the vinegar, and salt and pepper to taste, and cook the mixture, stirring, for 1 minute. Serves 2.

Steamed Green and Wax Beans

¾ pound combined green and wax beans,
 trimmed as desired
1 tablespoon unsalted butter, softened

In a steamer set over boiling water steam the beans, covered, for 4 minutes, or until they are crisp-tender, remove the steamer basket, and in a bowl toss the beans with the butter and salt and pepper to taste. Serves 4.

PHOTO ON PAGE 63

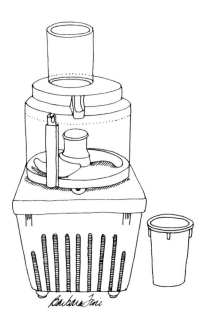

Buttered Green Beans

1¾ pounds green beans, trimmed
½ stick (¼ cup) unsalted butter

In a kettle of boiling salted water boil the green beans for 5 to 7 minutes, or until they are crisp-tender, transfer them with a slotted spoon to a bowl of ice and cold water, and let them stand for 2 to 3 minutes, or until they are cooled completely. Drain the beans and pat them dry. *The beans may be prepared up to this point 4 hours in advance and kept chilled, wrapped in plastic wrap.* In a large skillet heat the butter over moderate heat until the foam begins to subside, add the beans with salt and pepper to taste, and cook them, tossing them, for 2 to 3 minutes, or until they are heated through and coated well with the butter. Serves 8.

PHOTO ON PAGE 36

Leek and Green Pea Purée

1½ pounds leeks, the tough green tops
 discarded, halved lengthwise, washed well,
 and sliced thin (about 8 cups)
½ stick (¼ cup) unsalted butter
1 teaspoon dried savory, crumbled
½ teaspoon dried thyme, crumbled
1 boiling potato (about ¼ pound), peeled, cut
 into ½-inch pieces, and reserved in a bowl
 of cold water
a 10-ounce package frozen peas, thawed
¼ cup canned chicken broth or water

In a large skillet cook the leeks in the butter with the savory and the thyme, covered, over moderately low heat, stirring occasionally, for 30 minutes, or until the leeks are softened but not browned. While the leeks are cooking, in a saucepan of boiling salted water boil the potato, drained, for 4 minutes, add the peas, and cook the vegetables for 2 minutes, or until they are tender. Drain the potato and pea mixture well and add it to the leeks, stirring until the vegetables are combined well. While the vegetables are still hot force them through a food mill fitted with the medium disk into a saucepan or purée them in a food processor and add the broth and salt and pepper to taste, combining the mixture well. *The purée may be made up to 1 day in advance and kept covered and chilled.* In a heavy saucepan reheat the purée over low heat, stirring constantly, until it is hot. Makes about 3¼ cups.

*Mushrooms, Tofu, and Snow Peas
in Soy Ginger Sauce*

1 small onion, halved lengthwise and sliced
    thin crosswise
1 tablespoon vegetable oil
¼ pound mushrooms, sliced thin
1 garlic clove, minced
2 teaspoons minced peeled fresh gingerroot
¾ teaspoon cornstarch dissolved in 2
    tablespoons cold water
3 tablespoons soy sauce
½ pound firm tofu, drained, wrapped in a
    double thickness of paper towels for 15
    minutes, and cut into ¼-inch-thick slices
¼ pound snow peas, strings discarded
cooked rice as an accompaniment

In a skillet brown the onion in the oil over moderately
high heat, stirring occasionally, add the mushrooms,
and sauté the mixture, stirring, until the mushrooms are
tender. Add the garlic and the gingerroot and sauté the
mixture, stirring, for 1 minute. Stir the cornstarch mixture, add it to the skillet with the soy sauce, the tofu, and
½ cup water, and simmer the mixture, stirring gently
and turning the tofu to coat it with the sauce, for 2 to 3
minutes, or until the sauce is thickened. Stir in the snow
peas, cook the mixture, stirring gently, for 30 seconds,
and serve the tofu mixture over the rice. Serves 2.

Barbara Fiore

Mustard-Batter Onion Rings

1 large onion (about ½ pound), cut into
    ⅜-inch slices
½ cup all-purpose flour
1 teaspoon salt
½ teaspoon freshly ground pepper
2 tablespoons spicy brown mustard
½ cup plus 1 tablespoon seltzer or club soda
vegetable shortening or oil for deep-frying

Separate the onion slices into rings and in a bowl let
the rings soak in ice and cold water for 15 minutes.
While the onion rings are soaking, in a small bowl
whisk together the flour, the salt, the pepper, the mustard, and the seltzer until the batter is smooth. Dip the
onion rings, drained and patted dry, into the batter,
coating them well and letting the excess drip off, and in
a deep fryer fry them in batches in 3 inches of 375° F.
shortening, turning them, for 3 minutes, or until they
are golden brown. Transfer the onion rings with a slotted spoon as they are browned to paper towels to drain
and season them with salt if desired. Serves 2.

Golden Creamed Onions

3 pounds (about 50) small white onions,
    blanched in boiling water for 2 minutes,
    drained, and peeled
2 tablespoons unsalted butter
1 teaspoon sugar
¾ teaspoon salt
⅔ cup heavy cream
⅔ cup minced fresh parsley leaves

In a deep skillet large enough to hold the onions in
one layer combine the onions, the butter, the sugar, the
salt, and enough water to cover the onions by ½ inch,
bring the water to a boil, and boil the onions until the
liquid is almost evaporated. Cook the onions over moderate heat, swirling the skillet, until they turn golden
and begin to brown. Add the cream, bring the liquid to a
boil, and boil the mixture, stirring occasionally, until
the sauce is thickened slightly. Season the mixture with
salt and pepper and stir in the parsley. *The onion mixture
may be prepared 1 day in advance, kept covered and
chilled, and reheated in a skillet over moderately low
heat, stirring, until it is hot.* Serves 10.

PHOTO ON PAGE 70

Onions in Mushroom Cream Sauce

2 pounds small onions, each about
    1½ inches in diameter, peeled
½ pound mushrooms
3 tablespoons unsalted butter
2 tablespoons all-purpose flour
½ cup heavy cream
2 tablespoons medium-dry Sherry
½ cup minced fresh parsley leaves

Put the onions in a large saucepan with enough salted
cold water to cover them by 1 inch, bring the water to a

boil, and simmer the onions for 15 minutes, or until they are just tender. Drain the onions, reserving the cooking liquid. *The onions may be prepared up to 1 day in advance and kept covered and chilled.* In a food processor mince the mushrooms fine and in a large skillet cook them in the butter over moderate heat, stirring, until the liquid they give off is evaporated. Stir in the flour and cook the mixture over moderately low heat, stirring, for 3 minutes. Whisk in 1 cup of the reserved cooking liquid and the cream and simmer the sauce, stirring occasionally, for 10 minutes, or until it is thickened. *The sauce may be prepared up to 1 day in advance and kept covered and chilled.* Add the Sherry, the parsley, the onions, and salt and pepper to taste and cook the mixture until the onions are heated through. Serves 8 to 10.

Parsley Pancakes with Basil Creamed Corn Sauce

1 cup corn (cut from about 2 ears of corn)
2 teaspoons unsalted butter
½ cup heavy cream
½ cup all-purpose flour
1½ teaspoons double-acting baking powder
¼ teaspoon salt
1 large egg yolk
1½ tablespoons vegetable oil plus additional
   for brushing the skillet
1 tablespoon minced fresh parsley leaves
½ cup seltzer or club soda
¼ cup loosely packed fresh basil leaves, shredded

In a small saucepan combine the corn, the butter, and the cream, bring the liquid to a boil, and simmer the mixture, stirring occasionally, for 6 to 8 minutes, or until the corn is tender. Keep the sauce warm, covered, over very low heat.

Into a bowl sift together the flour, the baking powder, and the salt. In a small bowl whisk together the egg yolk, 1½ tablespoons of the oil, and the parsley, add the mixture to the flour mixture with the seltzer, and stir the batter until it is just combined. Heat a large heavy skillet or griddle over moderately high heat until it is hot, brush it lightly with the additional oil, and pour the batter into it, using 1 tablespoon batter for each pancake. Cook the pancakes for 45 seconds to 1 minute, or until the edges begin to brown and bubbles appear on the surface, turn them with a metal spatula, and cook them for 20 to 30 seconds more, or until they are golden. Transfer the pancakes to an ovenproof platter, keep them warm in a

preheated 325° F. oven, and make pancakes with the remaining batter in the same manner. Divide the pancakes between 2 plates, stir the basil into the sauce, and spoon the sauce around the pancakes. Makes sixteen 2-inch pancakes, serving 2 for brunch.

Parsnip and Carrot Dice

1 small onion, minced
2 tablespoons unsalted butter
6 carrots, cut into ¼-inch dice
6 parsnips, cut into ¼-inch dice
½ cup canned chicken broth
2 teaspoons Dijon-style mustard
1 tablespoon heavy cream
2 tablespoons minced fresh parsley leaves

In a large saucepan cook the onion in the butter over moderately low heat, stirring, until it is softened, add the carrots, the parsnips, and salt and pepper to taste, and stir the vegetables to coat them with the butter. Add the broth, bring the liquid to a simmer, and cook the vegetables, covered, over moderate heat for 5 to 7 minutes, or until they are tender. In a small bowl stir together the mustard and the cream and stir the mustard mixture into the vegetable mixture with the parsley and salt and pepper to taste. Serves 6.

PHOTO ON PAGE 75

Parsnip Saffron Purée

1½ pounds parsnips, peeled and cut into
   1-inch pieces
2 tablespoons unsalted butter
½ cup half-and-half
a pinch of crumbled saffron threads, or to taste
1 teaspoon fresh lemon juice, or to taste

In a saucepan combine the parsnips and enough cold water to cover them by 1 inch, bring the water to a boil, and simmer the parsnips, covered, for 8 to 10 minutes, or until they are very tender. Drain the parsnips well, while they are still hot force them through a food mill fitted with the medium disk into the pan, and stir in the butter, the half-and-half, the saffron, the lemon juice, and salt and pepper to taste. *The purée may be made up to 1 day in advance and kept covered and chilled.* In a heavy saucepan reheat the purée over low heat, stirring constantly, until it is hot. Makes about 2½ cups.

Peas and Lima Beans with Scallions and Parsley

½ cup frozen baby lima beans
¾ pound fresh peas, shelled (about 1 cup),
    or 1 cup frozen peas
1 teaspoon unsalted butter
2 tablespoons heavy cream
1½ tablespoons minced scallion greens
1 tablespoon minced fresh parsley leaves
fresh lemon juice to taste

In a small saucepan bring ¼ cup water to a boil and add the lima beans. Return the water to a boil, simmer the lima beans, covered, for 8 to 10 minutes, or until they are tender, and drain them. In a saucepan of boiling salted water boil the peas for 3 to 5 mintues, or until they are just tender, and drain them. In the small pan stir together the butter, the cream, the scallion greens, and the parsley and boil the mixture, stirring, until it is thickened. Stir in the lima beans, the peas, the lemon juice, and salt and pepper to taste. Serves 2.

Peas with Celery and Shallots

1 cup thinly sliced celery
⅓ cup minced shallot
3 tablespoons unsalted butter
two 10-ounce packages frozen peas, thawed
½ teaspoon sugar
½ teaspoon celery seeds if desired
2 tablespoons minced celery leaves

In a heavy saucepan cook the sliced celery and the shallot in the butter, covered, over low heat, stirring occasionally, for 5 minutes, or until the celery is softened. Add the peas, 2 tablespoons water, the sugar, the celery seeds if desired, and salt and pepper to taste and simmer the mixture, covered, for 3 minutes, or until it is hot. Sprinkle the mixture with the celery leaves and toss it. Serves 6.

Glazed Sugar Snap Peas

1½ pounds sugar snap peas, strings discarded
2 tablespoons unsalted butter, softened

In a kettle of boiling salted water cook the peas for 1 to 2 minutes, or until they are crisp-tender, drain them, and return them to the kettle with the butter and salt and pepper to taste. Toss the peas to coat them with the butter. Serves 6.

PHOTO ON PAGE 48

Batter-Fried French Fries

½ cup all-purpose flour
½ cup beer (not dark)
½ small onion, minced
1 small garlic clove, minced
½ teaspoon paprika
¼ teaspoon turmeric
a pinch of ground ginger
1 baking potato (about ½ pound)
vegetable oil for deep-frying

In a bowl whisk together the flour, the beer, the onion, the garlic, the paprika, the turmeric, the ginger, and salt and pepper to taste until the batter is combined well. Peel the potato and cut it lengthwise into ¼-inch strips. Add the potato to the batter and stir the mixture carefully until the potato is coated well. In a large deep skillet heat 1 inch of the oil to 375° F. and in it fry the potato strips in batches, letting the excess batter drip into the bowl first, for 4 to 5 minutes, or until they are golden. Transfer the fries with a slotted spoon to a jelly-roll pan lined with paper towels to drain, season them with salt, and keep them warm in a preheated 250° F. oven. Serves 2.

Pommes Lorette (Fried Puffed Potato Strips)

2 pounds Idaho potatoes, scrubbed well
½ stick (¼ cup) unsalted butter,
    cut into pieces
¼ teaspoon salt, or to taste
½ cup all-purpose flour
2 large eggs
vegetable oil for deep-frying

Bake the potatoes in a preheated 425° F. oven for 30 minutes, prick them with a fork, and bake them for

30 minutes more, or until they are very tender. Let the potatoes cool just until they can be handled. Halve the potatoes lengthwise, scoop out the flesh into the bowl of an electric mixer, reserving the shells for another use, and mash it while it is still warm with salt to taste. In a small heavy saucepan bring to a boil ½ cup water with the butter and the salt. Reduce the heat to moderate, add the flour all at once, and beat the mixture with a wooden paddle until it leaves the sides of the pan and forms a ball. Transfer the flour mixture to the bowl with the potatoes and with the electric mixer at high speed beat in the eggs, 1 at a time, beating the mixture until it is combined well. Transfer the mixture to a large pastry bag fitted with a ½-inch star tip. In a large deep heavy skillet heat 1½ inches of the oil to 380° F., pipe six to eight 3-inch lengths of the potato mixture into the oil, and fry the potatoes, turning them, for 1 minute and 30 seconds to 2 minutes, or until they are crisp and golden. Transfer the potatoes as they are fried to paper towels to drain and transfer them to a fine meshed rack set in a jelly-roll pan so that they won't become soggy. Fry the remaining potato mixture in the same manner, making sure that the oil returns to 380° F. before frying each batch. *The potatoes may be made up to 1 day in advance and kept covered loosely at room temperature. Reheat the potatoes on the rack in a preheated 500° F. oven for 5 to 10 minutes, or until they are heated through and crisp.* Sprinkle the potato strips with salt to taste if desired. Serves 8.

PHOTO ON PAGE 78

Potato Celery Root Purée

2 pounds boiling potatoes, peeled and cut into
  1-inch pieces
1 pound celery root, peeled and cut into
  1-inch pieces
5 tablespoons unsalted butter, cut into pieces
½ cup milk
2 teaspoons fresh lemon juice
1 teaspoon salt, or to taste
freshly ground pepper to taste

In a large saucepan combine the potatoes and enough salted cold water to cover them by 2 inches, bring the water to a boil, and boil the potatoes, covered, for 4 minutes. Add the celery root, simmer the vegetables, covered, for 10 to 15 minutes, or until they are very tender, and drain them well. While the vegetables are still hot force them through a food mill fitted with the medium disk into a saucepan, add the butter, the milk, the lemon juice, the salt, and the pepper, and stir the purée well. *The purée may be made up to 1 day in advance and kept covered and chilled.* In a heavy saucepan reheat the purée over low heat, stirring constantly, until it is hot. Makes about 5½ cups.

Rosemary Potato Balls

1 pound boiling potatoes
1 tablespoon unsalted butter
1 tablespoon olive oil
1 teaspoon chopped fresh rosemary leaves

Peel the potatoes and put them in a bowl of cold water. With a ½-inch melon-ball cutter cut out balls from the potatoes, reserving the scraps for another use. In a small saucepan of boiling salted water simmer the potato balls for 5 to 6 minutes, or until they are just tender, drain them well, and pat them dry. *The potatoes may be prepared up to this point 1 day in advance and kept covered and chilled.* In a skillet heat the butter and the oil over moderately high heat until the foam subsides and in the fat sauté the potatoes with the rosemary and salt and pepper to taste, stirring, for 3 to 5 minutes, or until they are golden. Serves 2.

PHOTO ON PAGE 54

Red Potatoes with Prosciutto and Chives

2 pounds small red potatoes, quartered
½ stick (¼ cup) unsalted butter, cut into bits
  and softened
½ cup canned chicken broth
1 tablespoon white-wine vinegar
¼ cup snipped fresh chives
½ pound thinly sliced prosciutto, chopped fine

In a saucepan combine the potatoes with enough salted cold water to cover them by 2 inches, bring the water to a boil, and simmer the potatoes for 8 to 12 minutes, or until they are just tender. Drain the potatoes and in a bowl toss them gently with the butter, the broth, and the vinegar. Add the chives, the prosciutto, and salt and pepper to taste and toss the mixture gently until it is combined well. Serves 6.

PHOTO ON PAGE 60

Steamed Red Potatoes with Dill Butter

2 tablespoons softened unsalted butter
1 tablespoon snipped fresh dill
¾ pound small red potatoes, unpeeled

In a small bowl cream together the butter, the dill, and salt and pepper to taste. In a steamer set over boiling water steam the potatoes, covered, for 12 to 14 minutes, or until they are tender, slice them, and serve them topped with the dill butter. Serves 4.

PHOTO ON PAGE 27

Sweet Potato Bacon Fritters

1 cup plus 2 tablespoons all-purpose flour
1 teaspoon double-acting baking powder
½ teaspoon salt
⅔ cup milk
2 large eggs, beaten lightly
2 tablespoons unsalted butter, melted and
  cooled
4 slices of lean bacon, cooked, drained,
  and crumbled
2 cups coarsely grated sweet potato
vegetable oil for deep-frying
maple syrup as an accompaniment

Into a bowl sift together the flour, the baking powder, and the salt, add the milk, the eggs, and the butter, and whisk the batter until it is combined well. Stir in the bacon and the sweet potato. In a deep skillet or deep fryer heat 2 inches of the oil to 375° F., add rounded tablespoons of the batter, and fry the fritters, turning them once, for 2 to 3 minutes, or until they are golden. Transfer the fritters with a slotted spoon as they are fried to a jelly-roll pan lined with paper towels to drain, keep them warm in a preheated 250° F. oven, and make fritters with the remaining batter in the same manner. Serve the fritters with the maple syrup. Serves 2 for brunch.

Sweet Potato Gratin

1 garlic clove, minced
3 tablespoons unsalted butter
1 tablespoon all-purpose flour
1 cup heavy cream
4 sweet potatoes (about 2¼ pounds), peeled
  and cut crosswise into ¼-inch-thick rounds
¼ cup fine fresh bread crumbs
¼ cup freshly grated Parmesan

In a small skillet cook the garlic in 2 tablespoons of the butter over moderately low heat, stirring, until it is softened, add the flour, and cook the mixture, stirring, for 3 minutes. Stir in the cream and bring the mixture just to a simmer, stirring occasionally. Arrange the potatoes in layers in a well buttered 11½-inch gratin dish, seasoning them with salt and pepper, pour the cream mixture over them, and bake the gratin in a preheated 325° F. oven for 1 hour, or until the potatoes are tender. Remove the gratin from the oven, baste the top with the cream mixture, and sprinkle it with the bread crumbs and the Parmesan. Drizzle the gratin with the remaining 1 tablespoon butter, melted, bake it in the 325° F. oven for 15 minutes more, and put it under a preheated broiler about 4 inches from the heat for 1 to 2 minutes, or until the top is browned. Serves 6.

PHOTO ON PAGE 75

Spiced Sweet Potatoes with Apples and Raisins

½ cup raisins
1 tablespoon Grand Marnier
1 pound (about 3) sweet potatoes, peeled and
  cut crosswise into ⅓-inch slices
1 Granny Smith apple
½ stick (¼ cup) unsalted butter
¼ teaspoon cinnamon
¼ cup fresh orange juice

In a small bowl let the raisins soak in ¼ cup water combined with the Grand Marnier for 20 minutes. In a steamer set over simmering water steam the sweet potatoes, covered, for 15 to 20 minutes, or until they are just tender. In a large skillet cook the apple, cored, quartered, and cut into ¼-inch slices, in 2 tablespoons of the butter over moderate heat, stirring, for 2 minutes. Stir in the cinnamon and the orange juice and cook the apple, covered, for 5 minutes more. Stir in the sweet potatoes, the raisin mixture, and salt to taste, simmer the mixture, uncovered, for 3 minutes, and swirl in the remaining 2 tablespoons butter. Serves 4 to 6.

Ratatouille

2 tablespoons olive oil
1 small eggplant, cut into ¼-inch dice
  (about ¾ cup)
⅓ cup minced white onion
1 garlic clove, minced

1 small zucchini, scrubbed and cut into ¼-inch
   dice (about ¾ cup)
1 small red bell pepper, cut into
   ¼-inch dice (about ½ cup)
1½ tablespoons fresh thyme leaves
½ pound tomatoes, peeled, seeded, and cut
   into ¼-inch dice (about 1 cup)

In a large skillet heat the oil over moderately high
heat until it is hot but not smoking, in it sauté the eggplant, stirring, for 3 minutes, or until it is golden, and
transfer it with a slotted spoon to a bowl. Add the onion
to the skillet and cook it over moderately low heat, stirring, until it is softened. Add the garlic and cook the
mixture, stirring, for 1 minute. Add the zucchini, the
bell pepper, 1 tablespoon of the thyme, and salt to taste
and cook the mixture over moderate heat, stirring, for
4 minutes. Add the tomatoes and the eggplant and cook
the mixture, stirring, for 3 to 5 minutes, or until the vegetables are just tender. Season the *ratatouille* with salt
and pepper and stir in the remaining 1½ teaspoons
thyme. *The ratatouille may be made up to 2 days in advance and kept covered and chilled. Reheat the ratatouille in a skillet over moderately low heat.* Makes
about 2 cups.

Ratatouille Kebabs
(*Herbed Eggplant, Pepper,*
Zucchini, and Onion Kebabs)

four 3-inch eggplants, halved lengthwise,
   cooked in boiling salted water until just
   tender, and drained
1 red bell pepper, cut into 1-inch pieces,
   cooked in boiling water for 2 minutes,
   and drained
1 yellow bell pepper, cut into
   1-inch pieces, cooked in boiling water for
   2 minutes, and drained
1 green bell pepper, cut into 1-inch pieces,
   cooked in boiling water for 2 minutes,
   and drained
1 zucchini, scrubbed, cut crosswise into
   1-inch pieces, cooked in boiling salted
   water until just tender, and drained
8 small white onions, cooked in boiling salted
   water until just tender, drained, and peeled
½ cup olive oil
4 garlic cloves, minced, or to taste

1½ teaspoons minced fresh thyme leaves or
   ½ teaspoon dried, crumbled
1½ teaspoons minced fresh orégano leaves or
   ½ teaspoon dried, crumbled
1½ teaspoons minced fresh basil leaves or
   ½ teaspoon dried, crumbled
2 cups canned tomato purée
2 tablespoons sugar
2 tablespoons fresh lemon juice
1 pound *fusilli* (corkscrew-shaped pasta)

In a shallow dish let four 12-inch wooden skewers
soak in water to cover for 1 hour. Thread the skewers
with the eggplant, the red, yellow, and green bell peppers, the zucchini, and the onions and arrange the kebabs in a jelly-roll pan. In a saucepan combine the oil,
the garlic, the thyme, the orégano, the basil, and salt
and pepper to taste and cook the mixture over moderately low heat, stirring, for 5 minutes. Stir in the tomato
purée, the sugar, the lemon juice, and salt and pepper to
taste and bring the sauce to a simmer. Broil the kebabs
under a preheated broiler about 4 inches from the heat,
basting them often with the tomato sauce and turning
them once, for 12 minutes, or until they are browned
and glazed.

   While the kebabs are broiling, cook the *fusilli* in a
kettle of boiling salted water until it is *al dente*, drain it,
and toss it with any remaining tomato sauce. Transfer
the *fusilli* to a heated large serving dish, top it with the
kebabs, and pour the pan juices over the dish. Serves 4.

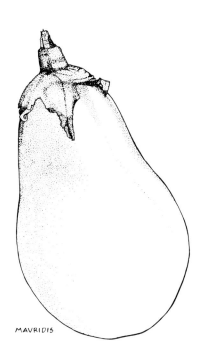

MAVRIDIS

Root Vegetable Purée

3 pounds large boiling potatoes
1½ pounds turnips, peeled and
    cut into ½-inch pieces
¾ pound carrots, sliced thin
¾ stick (6 tablespoons) unsalted butter, cut
    into pieces and softened
⅓ cup heavy cream if desired

In a large saucepan combine the potatoes, peeled and quartered, with enough salted cold water to cover them by 1 inch, bring the water to a boil, and simmer the potatoes for 10 to 15 minutes, or until they are tender. While the potatoes are cooking, in a steamer set over boiling water steam the turnips and the carrots, covered, for 15 minutes, or until they are very tender, and purée them in a food processor. Drain the potatoes in a large colander, let them stand for 5 minutes, and force them through a ricer or purée them in a food mill fitted with the medium disk into the saucepan. Add the butter, stirring until it is melted into the purée, add the turnip and carrot purée, and season the mixture with salt and pepper. Stir in the cream if desired and heat the purée over moderately low heat, stirring, until it is hot. *The purée may be made 1 day in advance and kept covered and chilled. Reheat the purée in the top of a double boiler set over simmering water, stirring, until it is hot.* Transfer the purée to a heated serving dish and, if desired, smooth it and then mark it decoratively with a rubber spatula. Makes about 7 cups, serving 10.

PHOTO ON PAGE 70

Rutabaga Potato Purée

2 pounds rutabaga, peeled and cut into
    1-inch cubes
1 pound boiling potatoes, peeled, cut into
    1-inch cubes, and reserved in a bowl of cold
    water
½ stick (¼ cup) unsalted butter, cut into pieces
    and softened

In a large saucepan combine the rutabaga with enough salted cold water to cover it by 2 inches, bring the water to a boil, and boil the rutabaga, covered, for 40 minutes, or until it is just tender. Add the potatoes, drained, simmer the vegetables, covered, for 10 to 15 minutes, or until they are very tender, and drain them well in a large sieve or colander. While the vegetables are still hot force them through a ricer or food mill into the pan or mash them with a potato masher in the pan, add the butter and salt and pepper to taste, and stir the purée well. Reheat the purée, if necessary, over low heat, stirring constantly, until it is hot, transfer it to a heated serving dish, and spread it decoratively with a rubber spatula. Serves 6.

PHOTO ON PAGE 21

Spinach, Anchovy, and Parmesan Purée

2½ pounds spinach with the stems intact,
    washed well
2 cups firmly packed parsley leaves,
    rinsed well
8 flat anchovy fillets, or to taste
2 garlic cloves, minced
½ cup freshly grated Parmesan
2 teaspoons fresh lemon juice, or to taste

In a kettle combine the spinach and the parsley, pour enough boiling water over the greens to barely cover them, and return the water to a boil. Transfer the greens immediately to a colander, drain them, pressing firmly with the back of a spoon to remove some of the water, and purée them in a food processor. Add the anchovies, the garlic, ⅓ cup of the Parmesan, the lemon juice, and salt and pepper to taste and purée the mixture until it is very smooth. *The purée may be made up to this point 1 day in advance and kept covered and chilled.* In a heavy saucepan reheat the purée over low heat, stirring constantly, until it is hot. Transfer the purée to a small flameproof baking dish, sprinkle it with the remaining Parmesan, and put it under a preheated broiler about 4 inches from the heat for 1 to 2 minutes, or until the Parmesan begins to bubble. Makes about 3 cups.

Spinach, Pea, and Red Pepper Timbales

1 large red bell pepper, cut into ¼-inch pieces
1 tablespoon unsalted butter
a 10-ounce package frozen chopped spinach,
    thawed, drained, and squeezed dry
a 10-ounce package frozen peas, thawed
    and drained
1 teaspoon dried chervil
¾ cup canned chicken broth
1 tablespoon sugar

freshly ground black pepper to taste
3 large eggs, beaten lightly

In a small skillet cook the bell pepper in the butter over moderately low heat, stirring, until it is softened, remove the skillet from the heat, and let the mixture cool. In a food processor purée the spinach, the peas, and the chervil with the broth, the sugar, the black pepper, and salt to taste. In a bowl combine well the purée, the bell pepper mixture, and the eggs and divide the mixture among 8 buttered ½-cup timbale molds. Put the molds in a baking pan, add enough hot water to the pan to reach halfway up the sides of the molds, and bake the timbales in a preheated 400° F. oven for 35 minutes, or until a knife comes out clean. *The timbales may be made 1 day in advance and kept covered and chilled. To reheat the timbales unmold them into a glass baking dish large enough to just hold them, add about 2 tablespoons hot water to the dish, or enough to barely cover the bottom, and reheat the timbales, covered with foil, in a preheated 500° F. oven for 15 minutes.* Invert the timbales onto a platter. Serves 8.

PHOTO ON PAGE 78

Squash, Apple, and Onion Tart with Sage
For the shell
pâte brisée (page 222)
raw rice for weighting the shell
For the filling
2 tablespoons vegetable oil
1½ pounds onions, halved lengthwise and
   sliced thin
2 garlic cloves, minced

2 teaspoons minced fresh sage or ¾ teaspoon
   dried, crumbled
¼ teaspoon dried thyme, crumbled
¼ cup heavy cream
1 large Golden Delicious apple
½ pound butternut squash, peeled, halved
   lengthwise, seeded, and sliced thin
   crosswise

½ stick (¼ cup) cold unsalted butter, sliced
   very thin
sage sprigs for garnish if desired

Make the shell: Roll out the dough ⅛ inch thick on a lightly floured surface and fit it into a 9½-inch-square flan form set on a baking sheet, leaving a ½-inch overhang. Fold the overhang inward onto the sides of the shell and press it firmly against the flan form. Prick the shell lightly with a fork and chill it for 30 minutes or freeze it for 15 minutes. Line the shell with foil, fill the foil with the rice, and bake the shell in the lower third of a preheated 425° F. oven for 15 minutes. Remove the rice and foil carefully and bake the shell for 5 to 8 minutes more, or until it is golden. Let the shell cool in the flan form on the baking sheet.

Make the filling: In a large heavy skillet heat the oil over moderately high heat until it is hot but not smoking, stir in the onions and the garlic with salt and pepper to taste, and cook the mixture, covered, over low heat, stirring occasionally, for 20 to 25 minutes, or until the onions are softened. Add the minced sage, the thyme, and the cream, bring the liquid to a boil, and simmer the mixture, stirring occasionally, for 3 to 5 minutes, or until it is thickened. Let the onion mixture cool. *The onion mixture may be prepared up to 1 day in advance and kept covered and chilled.* Spread the onion mixture evenly in the shell. Peel and halve the apple lengthwise, core it with a melon-ball cutter, and slice it very thin crosswise. Arrange the apple and the squash slices decoratively over the onion mixture, overlapping them, season them with salt, and top them with the butter.

Bake the tart in the upper third of a preheated 375° F. oven for 15 minutes, cover the tart with foil, and bake it for 30 minutes more, or until the squash is tender. Let the tart cool in the flan form on the baking sheet set on a rack and transfer it to a platter, removing the flan form. Serve the tart warm or at room temperature garnished with the sage sprigs if desired. Serves 8 to 10 as a first course or 4 to 6 as a luncheon entrée.

Acorn Squash with Raisins and Walnuts

a ¾- to 1-pound acorn squash, halved
   crosswise and seeds and strings discarded
2 tablespoons coarsely chopped walnuts
2 tablespoons raisins
2 teaspoons firmly packed dark brown sugar
1 tablespoon unsalted butter, softened

Sprinkle the squash cavities with salt and pepper to taste. Slice off the ends of the squash to form flat bottoms and arrange the squash cut sides down in a well buttered shallow baking pan large enough to just hold it. Prick the squash skin lightly with a sharp knife and bake the squash in a preheated 425° F. oven for 25 to 30 minutes, or until it is tender. While the squash is baking, in a small bowl combine well the walnuts, the raisins, the brown sugar, the butter, and salt to taste. Invert the squash halves in the pan, fill the cavities with the raisin mixture, and bake the squash for 10 minutes more. Serves 2.

Maple-Glazed Acorn Squash

1 small acorn squash, quartered, seeded,
   peeled, and cut crosswise into ½-inch slices
2 tablespoons maple syrup
a pinch of ground mace
2 tablespoons dark rum

In a small heavy saucepan combine the squash, the maple syrup, the mace, the rum, and ¼ cup plus 2 tablespoons water, bring the liquid to a boil, and simmer the mixture for 15 to 17 minutes, or until the squash is tender. Transfer the squash with a slotted spoon to a heated serving dish, boil the cooking liquid until it is thickened, and pour it over the squash. Serves 2.

*Butternut Squash Tartlets with Cheese Lattice
and Sunflower Seed Crust*

For the shells
sunflower seed pastry dough (recipe follows)
raw rice for weighting the shells
For the filling
1 cup puréed steamed butternut squash
   (procedure on page 183)
¼ cup heavy cream
1 large egg, beaten lightly
¾ teaspoon salt, or to taste

¼ teaspoon pepper, or to taste
about ¼ pound thinly sliced Gruyère,
   cut into thirty-six ⅛-inch strips,
   for the lattice

Make the shells: Roll out the dough ⅛ inch thick on a lightly floured surface and with a 4½-inch round cutter cut out 6 rounds, gathering and rerolling the scraps as necessary. Press each round into a fluted metal tartlet pan, 3¼ inches across the bottom and ⅝ inch deep, prick the shells lightly with a fork, and chill them for 30 minutes or freeze them for 15 minutes. Line the shells with foil, fill the foil with the rice, and bake the shells in a jelly-roll pan in the lower third of a preheated 425° F. oven for 15 minutes. Remove the rice and foil carefully and bake the shells for 5 to 7 minutes more, or until they are golden. Let the shells cool in the pans on a rack. *The shells may be made 1 day in advance and kept in an airtight container at room temperature.*

Make the filling: In a food processor or bowl with a whisk blend the squash with the cream, the egg, the salt, and the pepper.

Divide the squash filling among the tartlet shells, smoothing it, and arrange 6 strips of Gruyère, trimming them to fit, in a lattice pattern on each tartlet. Place the tartlets on a jelly-roll pan and bake in the middle of a preheated 375° F. oven for 20 to 25 minutes, or until the filling is puffed slightly and the cheese is melted, and serve them immediately. Serves 6 as a first course or side dish.

Sunflower Seed Pastry Dough

¼ cup salted roasted sunflower seeds
1 cup all-purpose flour plus additional for
   dusting the dough
¾ stick (6 tablespoons) cold unsalted butter,
   cut into bits

In a food processor grind fine the sunflower seeds with 1 cup of the flour, add the butter, and blend the mixture until it just resembles coarse meal. Transfer the mixture to a bowl and toss it with 2 to 3 tablespoons ice water, or enough to just form a dough. Knead the dough lightly with the heel of the hand against a smooth surface, distributing the butter evenly, for a few seconds and form it into a ball. Dust the dough with the additional flour, flatten it slightly, and chill it, wrapped in wax paper, for at least 1 hour or overnight.

To Steam and Purée Winter Squash

butternut squash, acorn squash,
　　or pumpkin

Cut the squash into 2-inch pieces, discard the seeds and strings, and in a steamer set over boiling water steam the squash, covered, checking the water level every 10 minutes and adding more water as necessary, for 30 to 40 minutes, or until it is very tender. Let the squash cool until it can be handled, scrape the flesh from the skins into a food processor, discarding the skins, and purée it. If the purée is watery, drain it in a sieve lined with paper towels set over a bowl for 10 to 15 minutes. One pound raw squash makes about 1 cup purée.

Summer Squash with Basil and Parmesan

½ pound summer squash, trimmed and cut
　　crosswise into ¼-inch slices
1 tablespoon olive oil
2 tablespoons shredded fresh basil leaves
1 tablespoon freshly grated Parmesan

In a steamer set over boiling water steam the squash, covered, for 2 minutes, or until it is just tender, and transfer it to a bowl. Drizzle the squash with the oil, sprinkle it with the basil, and season it with salt and pepper. Let the squash cool to room temperature. *The squash may be made up to 1 day in advance and kept covered and chilled. Let the squash come to room temperature before serving.* Serve the squash sprinkled with the Parmesan. Serves 2.

PHOTO ON PAGE 54

Summer Squash with Rosemary

2 teaspoons olive oil
¾ pound summer squash, cut into ¼-inch
　　rounds
½ teaspoon dried rosemary,
　　crumbled
2 teaspoons fresh lemon juice,
　　or to taste

In a large heavy skillet heat the oil over moderately high heat until it is hot but not smoking and in it sauté the squash, stirring, for 5 to 6 minutes, or until it is golden brown and just tender. Stir in the rosemary, the lemon juice, and salt and pepper to taste. Serves 2.

Fried Tofu with Vegetables in Sweet-and-Sour Sauce

½ pound tofu, drained, patted dry, and cut
　　into 1½-inch squares ½-inch thick
3½ tablespoons soy sauce
¾ teaspoon cornstarch dissolved in 3
　　tablespoons cold water plus additional
　　cornstarch for dredging
1 large egg, beaten lightly
vegetable oil for frying
1 carrot, sliced thin lengthwise and cut
　　diagonally into ½-inch pieces (about ½ cup)
1 small garlic clove, minced
2 tablespoons distilled white vinegar
1½ teaspoons sugar
2 ounces snow peas, trimmed, strings
　　discarded, and cut diagonally into ½-inch
　　pieces (about ½ cup)

In a shallow dish combine the tofu with 3 tablespoons of the soy sauce, turning it to coat it with the soy sauce, and let it marinate at room temperature, turning it occasionally, for 15 minutes. Pat the tofu dry, dredge it in the additional cornstarch, coating it completely, and dip it in the egg, letting the excess drip off. In a large heavy skillet heat ¼ inch of the oil to 350° F., in it fry the tofu in batches, turning it once, for 6 to 8 minutes, or until it is golden, and transfer it to paper towels to drain. Keep the tofu warm on an ovenproof platter in a preheated 225° F. oven.

Pour off all but 1 tablespoon of the oil in the skillet and in it cook the carrot and the garlic, covered, over moderately low heat for 5 minutes. In a small bowl stir together the remaining 1½ teaspoons soy sauce, the vinegar, and the sugar until the sugar is dissolved, add the sauce to the skillet with the snow peas, and cook the mixture over moderately high heat, stirring, for 1 minute. Stir the cornstarch mixture, add it to the skillet, and bring the liquid to a boil, stirring. Boil the vegetable mixture, stirring, for 1 minute and spoon it around the tofu. Serves 2.

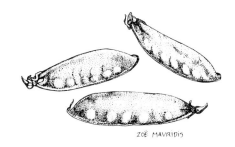

ZOÉ MAVRIDIS

183

Broiled Tomato Slices with Brown Sugar and Sour Cream

1 cup sour cream
2 teaspoons firmly packed dark brown sugar
2 teaspoons Dijon-style mustard, or to taste
¼ teaspoon salt
3 large (about 1½ pounds) firm-ripe tomatoes, sliced horizontally ⅓ inch thick

In a bowl stir together the sour cream, the brown sugar, the mustard, and the salt. Arrange the tomato slices in one layer in a jelly-roll pan and top each slice with a rounded tablespoon of the sour cream mixture, spreading the mixture almost to the edges. Broil the tomatoes under a preheated broiler about 4 inches from the heat for 5 to 6 minutes, or until the topping begins to brown. Serves 4 to 6.

Tomatoes Stuffed with Squash, Feta, and Olives

4 small tomatoes (about 1¼ pounds)
1 teaspoon salt
¼ pound zucchini, scrubbed and trimmed
¼ pound yellow summer squash, scrubbed and trimmed
¼ cup Kalamata or other brine-cured black olives, crushed lightly with the flat side of a knife, pitted, and sliced thin
3 tablespoons crumbled Feta
1 large egg yolk, beaten lightly
vegetable oil for brushing the tomatoes

Cut a thin slice from the stem end of each tomato and with a melon-ball cutter or small spoon scoop out the seeds and inner pulp, leaving a ¼-inch-thick shell. Sprinkle the tomatoes with ¼ teaspoon salt, invert them onto paper towels, and let them stand for 20 minutes. In a food processor fitted with the grating blade or with a hand-held grater grate the zucchini and the summer squash coarse. In a colander toss the squash with the remaining ¾ teaspoon salt and let it stand for 20 minutes. Rinse the squash under cold water, squeeze it dry in a kitchen towel, and in a bowl combine it well with the olives, the Feta, and the egg yolk. Stuff the tomatoes with the squash mixture, mounding it, put them in an oiled small baking dish, and brush the outsides of the tomatoes with the oil. Bake the tomatoes in a preheated 450° F. oven for 10 minutes. (The tomatoes may be baked with the hens during the last 10 minutes of roasting.) Serves 4.

PHOTO ON PAGE 63

Sautéed Tomatoes with Mint Butter

2 pounds small tomatoes, quartered
½ stick (¼ cup) unsalted butter
1 tablespoon dried mint, crumbled, or 3 tablespoons minced fresh mint leaves, or to taste

In a large skillet cook the tomatoes in the butter with the mint and salt and pepper to taste over moderate heat, stirring, until they are just heated through. Serves 6.

PHOTO ON PAGE 48

Saffron Turnips and Carrots

¾ pound (about 3) small turnips, peeled and cut lengthwise into ¾-inch wedges
½ pound thick carrots, peeled, cut crosswise into 1½-inch sections, and the sections cut lengthwise into ½-inch wedges
2 tablespoons unsalted butter
¼ teaspoon crumbled saffron threads
½ cup canned chicken broth

With a sharp paring knife trim the turnip and carrot wedges, rounding the sharp edges, and in a large skillet combine them with the butter, the saffron, and the broth. Bring the liquid to a boil and simmer the mixture, covered, stirring occasionally, for 7 to 8 minutes, or until the vegetables are just tender. Remove the lid, simmer the mixture, uncovered, stirring occasionally, until almost all the liquid is evaporated and the vegetables are coated with the butter, and season the vegetables with salt and pepper. Serves 4.

Vegetable Custard

1 large egg
¾ cup heavy cream
2 tablespoons minced fresh parsley leaves
½ teaspoon snipped fresh dill
½ teaspoon salt
¼ teaspoon freshly ground pepper
1 teaspoon white-wine vinegar

¼ cup thinly sliced leek, washed well and
  patted dry
¼ cup coarsely grated carrot
¼ cup coarsely grated Gruyère or Swiss
  cheese

In a small bowl whisk together the egg, the cream, the
parsley, the dill, the salt, the pepper, and the vinegar,
stir in the leek, the carrot, and the Gruyère, and transfer
the mixture to a well buttered 7¾-inch (2½-cup) gratin
dish. Bake the custard in a preheated 400° F. oven for 20
to 25 minutes, or until a knife inserted in the center
comes out clean. Let the custard cool on a rack for 5
minutes. Serves 2 as a first course.

Zucchini and Carrot Julienne

½ pound carrots, trimmed and peeled
½ pound zucchini, scrubbed and trimmed
2 tablespoons unsalted butter
1½ teaspoons fresh lemon juice, or to taste

With a *mandoline* or very sharp knife cut the carrots
and the zucchini separately into ⅛-inch-thick julienne
strips, about 2 inches long. In a steamer set over boiling
water steam the carrots, covered, for 2 to 3 minutes, or
until they are crisp-tender, and transfer them to a bowl.
In the steamer set over boiling water steam the zucchini,
covered, for 30 seconds to 1 minute, or until it is crisp-
tender, and transfer it to the bowl of carrots. *The vegetables may be prepared up to this point 8 hours in advance
and kept covered and chilled.* In a skillet melt the butter
over moderate heat, add the vegetables, drained if necessary, the lemon juice, and salt and pepper to taste, and
cook the mixture, stirring gently, for 1 to 2 minutes, or
until the vegetables are heated through. Serves 4.

PHOTO ON PAGE 62

Zucchini, Bell Pepper, and Olive Jumble

1 red bell pepper, cut into ½-inch pieces
1 tablespoon unsalted butter
½ pound zucchini, scrubbed, trimmed, halved
  lengthwise, and cut into ¼-inch slices
8 Kalamata olives, cut into strips

In a skillet cook the bell pepper in the butter, covered,
over moderately low heat, stirring occasionally, for 5
minutes, add the zucchini and the olives, and cook the
mixture, covered, stirring occasionally, for 5 to 7 minutes, or until the zucchini is tender. Season the jumble
with salt and pepper. Serves 2.

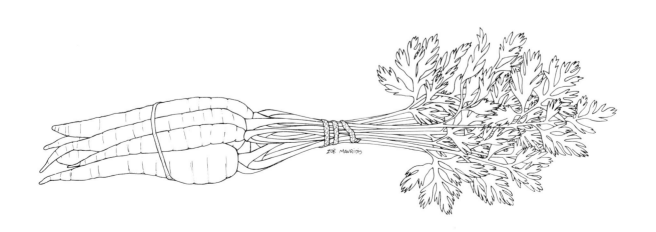

SALADS AND SALAD DRESSINGS

ENTRÉE SALADS

Cobb Salad

1 bunch of watercress, coarse stems
  discarded, rinsed, spun dry, and chopped
  fine (about 1½ cups)
1 small head of iceberg lettuce, rinsed, spun
  dry, and chopped fine (about 5 cups)
½ small head of curly endive (chicory),
  rinsed, spun dry, and chopped fine
  (about 3 cups)
1 small head of romaine, rinsed, spun dry,
  and chopped fine (about 5 cups)
3 tablespoons snipped fresh chives
3 cups canned chicken broth
1 bay leaf
4 parsley sprigs
2 whole skinless boneless chicken breasts
  (about 1½ pounds), halved
3 tablespoons fresh lemon juice
¾ cup plus 4 teaspoons olive oil
1 avocado (preferably California)
6 hard-boiled large eggs, chopped fine
1 cup crumbled Roquefort
3 tablespoons red-wine vinegar
5 plum tomatoes, peeled, seeded, and
  chopped fine
6 slices of lean bacon, cooked until crisp,
  drained, and crumbled

In a large salad bowl combine well the watercress,
the iceberg lettuce, the curly endive, the romaine, and
the chives and chill the greens, covered. In a skillet
bring the broth to a boil with the bay leaf, the parsley
sprigs, and salt and pepper to taste, add the chicken in
one layer, and cook it at a bare simmer, turning it once,
for 7 minutes. Remove the skillet from the heat and let
the chicken cool in the broth for 20 minutes. Transfer
the chicken to a cutting board, pat it dry, and dice it fine.
In a bowl whisk together 2 tablespoons of the lemon
juice, 4 teaspoons of the oil, and salt to taste, add the
chicken, and toss the mixture well. Peel, pit, and dice
fine the avocado. In a small bowl toss the avocado with
the remaining 1 tablespoon lemon juice and salt to taste.
In a bowl toss the eggs with the Roquefort. In another
bowl whisk together the vinegar and salt and pepper to
taste, add ½ cup of the remaining oil in a stream, whisking, and whisk the dressing until it is emulsified.

Drizzle the remaining ¼ cup oil over the greens and
toss the mixture until it is coated well. Arrange the
chicken, the avocado, the egg mixture, the tomatoes,
and the bacon decoratively on the greens. To serve,
whisk the dressing, pour it over the mixture, and toss the
salad well. Serves 8 to 10.

Duck Salad with Raspberries, Oranges, Arugula, and Cracklings

three 4½-pound ducks, excess fat discarded
  from the cavity, excess skin cut off and
  discarded from the neck end, and the neck
  and giblets reserved for another use
⅓ cup raspberry vinegar (available at specialty
  foods shops)
2 teaspoons Dijon-style mustard
2 tablespoons crème de cassis
3 tablespoons fresh lemon juice

¾ cup vegetable oil

3 navel oranges, peel and pith cut away with a
serrated knife, the fruit sliced thin crosswise
and halved

1 pint raspberries

2 bunches of *arugula*, tough stems discarded,
rinsed and spun dry

¾ cup finely chopped scallion

Pat the ducks dry, prick them all over, and rub them
with salt and pepper. Roast the ducks on racks in roasting pans in a preheated 450° F. oven for 20 minutes, reduce the heat to 300° F., and roast the ducks for 1 hour
and 30 minutes more. Let the ducks cool until they can
be handled or chill them, covered, overnight, pull off
the skin carefully, reserving it, and remove the meat
from the bones. *The duck meat and skin may be pre-*
pared up to this point 2 days in advance and kept cov-
ered and chilled.

In a bowl whisk together the vinegar, the mustard,
the *crème de cassis,* the lemon juice, and salt and pepper
to taste, add the oil in a stream, whisking, and whisk the
dressing until it is emulsified.

Scrape off any fat from the duck skin and bake the
skin in one layer in a jelly-roll pan in a preheated 350° F.
oven for 10 to 15 minutes, or until it is crisp. Transfer
the cracklings to paper towels to drain, sprinkle them
with salt to taste, and crumble them.

On a large platter arrange the orange slices, the raspberries, and the *arugula* decoratively. In a bowl toss the
duck meat, chopped, with ¾ cup of the dressing, the
scallion, one fourth of the cracklings, and salt and pepper to taste and mound the salad on the platter. Drizzle
the remaining dressing over the *arugula* and fruit and
serve the remaining cracklings separately. Serves 6.

PHOTO ON PAGE 61

Curly Endive Salad with Melon, Ham, and Green Beans

2 ounces green beans, trimmed and cut into
1-inch pieces (about ½ cup)

2 teaspoons red-wine vinegar

¼ teaspoon Sherry if desired

2 tablespoons olive oil

3 cups loosely packed curly endive (chicory)
leaves, rinsed, spun dry, and torn into
bite-size pieces

½ cup chopped cantaloupe

¼ cup chopped cooked ham

In a large saucepan of boiling salted water boil the
green beans for 6 to 8 minutes, or until they are crisp-
tender, drain them in a sieve, and refresh them under
cold water. In a small bowl whisk together the vinegar,
the Sherry if desired, and salt and pepper to taste, add
the oil, whisking, and whisk the dressing until it is emulsified. In a bowl combine the curly endive, the cantaloupe, the ham, and the green beans, add the dressing,
and toss the salad until it is combined. Serves 2.

Lobster Salad with Basil and Lemon Vinaigrette

two 1¼- to 1½-pound live lobsters

½ pound peas, shelled (about ½ cup)

½ cup diagonally sliced celery

1 tablespoon minced fresh basil leaves

1 tablespoon freshly grated lemon rind

3 tablespoons fresh lemon juice

⅓ cup olive oil

white pepper to taste

For garnish

4 small lettuce leaves

4 lemon slices

4 tomato slices

Into a kettle of boiling salted water plunge the lobsters and boil them, covered, for 8 minutes from the
time the water returns to a boil. Transfer the lobsters
with tongs to a cutting board and let them cool until they
can be handled. Break off the claws at the body, crack
them, and remove the meat, cutting it into ¾-inch
pieces. Halve the lobsters lengthwise along the undersides, remove the meat from the tails, and cut it into
¾-inch pieces. In a large bowl combine the claw meat
and the tail meat. Break off the legs carefully at the
body, reserving them for another use, remove the meat
from the body cavities near the leg joints, and add it
to the bowl.

In a small saucepan of boiling salted water cook the
peas for 5 to 8 minutes, or until they are just tender,
drain them, and refresh them under cold water. Pat the
peas dry and add them to the lobster meat. Stir in the celery, the basil, and the lemon rind. In a small bowl whisk
the lemon juice with a pinch of salt, add the oil in a
stream, whisking, and whisk the dressing until it is
emulsified. Drizzle the mixture with the dressing, toss it
gently to coat it well, and add salt and white pepper to
taste. Divide the salad between 2 salad plates and garnish it with the lettuce and the lemon and tomato slices.
Serves 2.

Penne Salad with Salami and Basil Caper Dressing

1 pound *penne* (quill-shaped macaroni)
enough sliced Genoa salami (about ¼ pound),
   cut into 1- by ½-inch strips, to measure 1 cup
½ cup chopped drained bottled pimiento
⅓ cup minced fresh parsley leaves
¼ cup thinly sliced scallion greens
2½ tablespoons drained bottled capers
2 tablespoons white-wine vinegar
2 teaspoons dried hot red pepper flakes
1½ cups loosely packed fresh basil leaves
½ cup olive oil

In a kettle of boiling salted water boil the *penne* for 13 to 15 minutes, or until it is tender, drain it in a colander, and refresh it under cold water. Drain the *penne* well and in a large bowl combine it with the salami, the pimiento, the parsley, and the scallion. In a blender or food processor blend the capers, the vinegar, the red pepper flakes, the basil, and salt to taste, with the motor running add the oil in a stream, and blend the dressing until it is emulsified. Pour the dressing over the *penne* mixture, season the mixture with salt, and toss the salad well. Serves 6 to 8.

Grilled Shark Salad
with Rouille Mayonnaise

For the rouille mayonnaise
1 large egg at room temperature
6 teaspoons fresh lemon juice
1 teaspoon Dijon-style mustard
¼ teaspoon minced garlic
¾ teaspoon sweet paprika
¼ teaspoon cayenne
¼ teaspoon turmeric
1 cup olive or vegetable oil
¼ teaspoon cuminseed

4 slices of homemade-type white bread, cut
   into ½-inch cubes
2 tablespoons olive oil
1 head of romaine, rinsed, patted dry, and
   torn into bite-size pieces
1 pint cherry tomatoes
1 cucumber, seeded and cut into bite-size
   pieces
1 red bell pepper, cut into thin strips
2 pounds 1-inch-thick shark steaks, skinned,

rinsed, patted dry, and cut into 4 pieces

Make the *rouille* mayonnaise: In a blender or food processor blend the egg, the lemon juice, the mustard, the garlic, the paprika, the cayenne, and the turmeric, with the motor running add the oil in a stream, and blend the mayonnaise until it is emulsified. Blend in the cuminseed, salt and pepper to taste, and enough warm water to thin the mayonnaise to the desired consistency. Transfer the mayonnaise to a small bowl and keep it covered and chilled until ready to serve.

In a small baking pan toss the bread cubes with 1 tablespoon of the oil, toast them in a preheated 350° F. oven for 10 to 12 minutes, or until they are golden, and transfer them to a rack. On a platter arrange decoratively the romaine, the tomatoes, the cucumber, and the bell pepper and chill the vegetables, covered, while cooking the shark.

Rub the shark with the remaining tablespoon oil and pepper to taste and grill it over glowing coals, turning it once, for 8 to 10 minutes, or until it is tender when tested with a fork. (Or heat a ridged grill pan over moderately high heat until it is smoking and in it grill the shark, turning it once, for 8 to 10 minutes, or until it is tender when tested with a fork.) Transfer the shark to a cutting board and slice it thin across the grain. Arrange the shark on the platter, drizzle it with any juices from the cutting board, and serve the salad sprinkled with the croutons and drizzled with the *rouille* mayonnaise. Serves 4 to 6.

Shrimp and Artichoke Salad with Hazelnut Vinaigrette

6 tablespoons hazelnut oil (available at
   specialty foods shops)
1 cup dry white wine
3 cups canned chicken broth
3 tablespoons fresh lemon juice
6 large artichokes, trimmed into bottoms
   (procedure on page 167), reserving some of
   the small outer leaves in acidulated water
   for garnish
24 shrimp (about 1 pound), shelled
2 tablespoons Sherry vinegar, or to taste

In a kettle combine 4 tablespoons of the oil, the wine, the broth, the lemon juice, the artichoke bottoms, and the reserved leaves, bring the liquid to a boil, and simmer the artichoke bottoms and the leaves, turning the bottoms once, for 30 minutes, or until they are tender.

Transfer the artichoke bottoms and the reserved drained leaves with a slotted spoon to a cutting board, reserving the cooking liquid, and let the bottoms cool until they can be handled. Remove the chokes with a spoon, discarding them, cut the bottoms into ⅓-inch slices, and keep the bottoms and the leaves covered with plastic wrap. Boil the reserved cooking liquid until it is reduced to about 1½ cups and let it cool. In a saucepan of boiling water cook the shrimp for 1 to 2 minutes, or until they are just firm to the touch, drain them in a colander, and refresh them under cold water. Drain the shrimp and pat them dry. Halve the shrimp lengthwise and devein them. Stir the vinegar into the reserved cooking liquid, whisk in the remaining 2 tablespoons oil, and in a large shallow dish toss the artichoke bottoms and leaves with ¾ cup of the dressing. In a bowl toss the shrimp with the remaining dressing. *The salad may be prepared up to this point 1 day in advance and kept covered and chilled. Let the ingredients return to room temperature before serving.* Divide the artichoke bottoms among 8 salad plates, top each serving with 6 shrimp halves, and garnish the salads with the artichoke leaves. Serves 8.

moderately high heat, stirring, for 30 seconds to 1 minute, or until the sole is just cooked. Line 2 plates with the lettuce leaves and divide the sole mixture between them. Whisk the dressing and drizzle it over the salads. Serves 2.

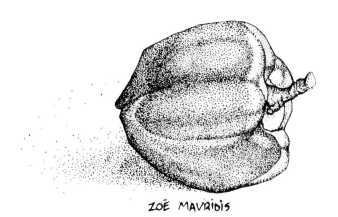

ZOË MAVRIDIS

Warm Sole Salad with Bell Pepper Tomato Dressing

For the dressing
¼ cup chopped green bell pepper
1 cup chopped tomato
1 tablespoon olive oil
½ teaspoon red wine vinegar, or to taste

½ cup finely chopped green bell pepper
⅔ cup finely chopped onion
2 tablespoons unsalted butter
¾ pound sole fillets, cut into ½-inch pieces
6 tablespoons fine dry bread crumbs
cayenne to taste
Boston or Bibb lettuce leaves for lining
   the plates

Make the dressing: In a blender or food processor purée the bell pepper and the tomato with the oil, the vinegar, and salt and pepper to taste, scraping down the sides, and strain the dressing through a fine sieve into a bowl, discarding the solids.

In a skillet cook the bell pepper and the onion in the butter over moderately low heat, stirring, until the vegetables are softened, stir in the sole, the bread crumbs, the cayenne, and salt to taste, and cook the mixture over

Warm Spinach Salad with Chicken and Walnuts

2 cups firmly packed spinach leaves, washed
   well and spun dry
3 slices of red onion, halved
1 navel orange, peel and pith cut away with a
   serrated knife and the orange cut into
   sections
3 tablespoons olive oil
¼ cup walnuts, chopped coarse
1 whole skinless boneless chicken breast,
   trimmed and cut into 1-inch pieces
2 tablespoons fresh orange juice
2 tablespoons white-wine vinegar

In a shallow serving dish or on a platter combine the spinach leaves, the onion, and the orange sections. In a skillet heat 2 tablespoons of the oil over moderately high heat until it is hot but not smoking and in it sauté the walnuts, stirring, for 1 minute. Add the chicken and sauté it, stirring, until it is just firm to the touch. Stir in the remaining 1 tablespoon oil, the orange juice, the vinegar, and salt and pepper to taste and cook the mixture, stirring, for 30 seconds. Spoon the chicken mixture and juices over the spinach mixture and toss the salad until it is combined well. Serves 2.

White Bean and Tuna Salad

1 tablespoon white-wine vinegar
1 teaspoon fresh lemon juice
2 tablespoons olive oil
¼ cup seeded and chopped tomatoes
2 tablespoons thinly sliced scallion
½ cup drained canned white beans, rinsed and
    drained well
a 7-ounce can tuna (preferably packed in oil),
    drained and broken into chunks
lettuce leaves for garnish if desired

In a small bowl whisk together the vinegar, the lemon juice, and salt and pepper to taste, whisk in the oil, and whisk the dressing until it is emulsified. In a bowl combine the tomatoes, the scallion, the beans, and the tuna, add the dressing, and with a fork toss the mixture gently until it is combined well. Serve the salad on the lettuce if desired. Serves 2.

SALADS WITH GREENS

Arugula Salad

¼ teaspoon Dijon-style mustard
1 teaspoon balsamic vinegar (available at
    specialty foods shops and many
    supermarkets) or red-wine vinegar
2 tablespoons olive oil
1 small bunch of *arugula*, stems discarded,
    washed well, and spun dry

In a small bowl whisk together the mustard, the vinegar, and salt and pepper to taste, add the oil in a stream, whisking, and whisk the dressing until it is emulsified. Add the *arugula*, tossing it to coat it with the dressing, and divide the salad between 2 chilled salad plates. Serves 2.

Caesar Salad

3 garlic cloves
¾ teaspoon salt
9 tablespoons olive oil
5 slices of homemade-type white bread, crusts
    discarded and the bread cut into ½-inch
    squares (about 2½ cups)
2 large eggs

2 tablespoons fresh lemon juice
1 teaspoon Worcestershire sauce
2 heads of romaine, rinsed, spun dry, and torn
    into bite-size pieces (about 16 cups)
½ cup freshly grated Parmesan
drained flat anchovy fillets if desired

In a mortar with a pestle mash the garlic to a paste with the salt, stir in 4 tablespoons of the oil, and force the mixture through a fine sieve into a bowl. In a jelly-roll pan bake the bread squares in the middle of a preheated 350° F. oven for 10 minutes, add them to the garlic mixture, and toss them until they are coated well with the mixture. Return the croutons to the pan, bake them for 3 minutes, or until they are golden, and let them cool in the pan on a rack.

In a saucepan of boiling water boil the eggs in the shell for 1 minute and drain them. In a salad bowl drizzle the remaining 5 tablespoons oil, the lemon juice, and the Worcestershire sauce over the romaine and sprinkle the mixture with the Parmesan, the croutons, and salt and pepper to taste. Break the eggs over the salad, toss the salad until it is combined well, and serve it with the anchovies if desired. Serves 6 to 8.

Endive and Roquefort Spirals with Creamy Walnut Vinaigrette

¾ pound Roquefort at room temperature
¾ stick (6 tablespoons) unsalted butter,
    softened
6 ounces cream cheese, softened
3 large Belgian endive
2 teaspoons egg yolk
2 tablespoons white-wine vinegar
¼ cup walnut oil (available at specialty foods
    shops)
½ cup vegetable oil
2 tablespoons chopped walnuts, toasted lightly
6 small watercress sprigs for garnish
½ McIntosh apple, kept in a small bowl of 1
    cup water acidulated with 1 teaspoon lemon
    juice

In a food processor blend the Roquefort, the butter, and the cream cheese until the mixture is smooth. Cut ¼ inch from the bottom of each endive and separate the leaves, reserving the tight inner core of each endive for another use. Spread each leaf ¼ inch thick with the

Roquefort mixture and reconstruct each endive by pressing the leaves back together, Roquefort side in. Chill the endive rolls, wrapped tightly in plastic wrap, for at least 1 hour and 30 minutes, or until the Roquefort mixture is firm. *The endive rolls may be made up to 4 hours in advance and kept wrapped and chilled.*

In a small bowl whisk together the egg yolk, the vinegar, and salt and pepper to taste, add the oils in a stream, whisking, and whisk the dressing until it is emulsified. *The dressing may be made up to 6 hours in advance and kept covered and chilled.*

Slice each endive diagonally about ½ inch thick. On each of 6 chilled salad plates pour about 2 tablespoons of the dressing and top it with 2 endive spirals. Sprinkle each plate with 1 teaspoon of the walnuts and garnish it with a watercress sprig and 3 apple slices, cut lengthwise from the apple. Serves 6.

PHOTO ON PAGE 60

Escarole Salad with Honey Lime Dressing

1 teaspoon onion juice, made by pressing
  2 tablespoons chopped onion through a
  garlic press and straining the juice
1 teaspoon Dijon-style mustard
1 teaspoon fresh lime juice
½ teaspoon honey
2 tablespoons olive oil
4 cups loosely packed torn escarole leaves,
  rinsed and spun dry
1 hard-boiled large egg, sieved

In a small bowl whisk together the onion juice, the mustard, the lime juice, the honey, and salt and pepper to taste, whisk in the oil, and whisk the dressing until it is emulsified. In a bowl toss the escarole with the dressing until it is coated well, divide the salad between 2 salad plates, and sprinkle it with the sieved egg. Serves 2.

Green Goddess Salad

1 cup mayonnaise (page 200)
4 flat anchovy fillets, drained and minced
⅓ cup minced fresh parsley leaves
1½ tablespoons snipped fresh chives
2 teaspoons tarragon vinegar
2 teaspoons fresh tarragon leaves or ¼ teaspoon
  dried, crumbled

2 teaspoons fresh lemon juice
1 scallion, sliced thin
enough mixed greens such as Boston lettuce, curly
  endive (chicory), and romaine (about 3 small
  heads), rinsed, spun dry, and torn into bite-size
  pieces, to measure 18 cups
1¼ pounds tomatoes, cut into wedges (about 4 cups)

In a bowl whisk together the mayonnaise, the anchovies, the parsley, the chives, the vinegar, the tarragon, the lemon juice, the scallion, and salt and pepper to taste and chill the dressing, covered, for at least 3 hours or overnight. In a large salad bowl combine the greens and the tomatoes, spoon the dressing over the mixture, and toss the salad well. Serves 8 to 10.

Mixed Green Salad with Mustard Vinaigrette

2 tablespoons Sherry vinegar (available at
  specialty foods shops) or red-wine vinegar
1 teaspoon coarse-grained mustard
2 teaspoons minced fresh parsley leaves
5 tablespoons olive oil
1 head of romaine, torn into pieces, rinsed,
  and spun dry
1 head of Bibb lettuce, torn into pieces,
  rinsed, and spun dry
1 bunch of watercress, rinsed, spun dry, and
  the coarse stems discarded
½ small red onion, sliced thin

In a small bowl whisk together the vinegar, the mustard, the parsley, and salt and pepper to taste, add the oil in a stream, whisking, and whisk the dressing until it is emulsified. In a salad bowl toss together the romaine, the Bibb lettuce, the watercress, and the onion. Just before serving pour the vinaigrette over the salad and toss the salad well. Serves 6.

Red-Leaf Lettuce and Watercress Salad Mimosa

2 tablespoons white-wine vinegar
1 teaspoon Dijon-style mustard
1 teaspoon dried tarragon, crumbled
6 tablespoons olive oil
1 small head of red-leaf lettuce, separated into leaves, rinsed, and spun dry
1 bunch of watercress, coarse stems discarded and the leaves and tender stems rinsed and spun dry
2 hard-boiled large eggs

In a small bowl whisk together the vinegar, the mustard, the tarragon, and salt and pepper to taste, add the oil in a stream, whisking, and whisk the dressing until it is emulsified. Line a salad bowl with the larger lettuce leaves, tear the smaller leaves into pieces, and arrange them in the center. Spread the watercress in a circle on the torn leaves, separate the cooked egg yolks from the cooked whites, and sieve them decoratively in the center. Just before serving pour the dressing over the salad and toss the salad well at the table. Serves 4.

PHOTO ON PAGE 27

Romaine with Anchovy Caper Vinaigrette

3 tablespoons balsamic vinegar (available at specialty foods shops and some supermarkets)
1 tablespoon minced drained anchovy fillets
1 teaspoon fennel seeds, crushed
⅓ cup olive oil
1 head of romaine, separated into leaves, rinsed, spun dry, and torn into bite-size pieces
¼ cup minced fresh parsley leaves
1 tablespoon drained capers

In a small bowl whisk together the vinegar, the anchovies, the fennel seeds, and salt and pepper to taste, add the oil in a stream, whisking, and whisk the vinaigrette until it is emulsified. In a salad bowl toss the romaine with the vinaigrette and sprinkle the salad with the parsley, the capers, and salt and pepper to taste. Serves 4.

PHOTO ON PAGE 45

Romaine with Walnut Vinaigrette and Sautéed Feta

1 teaspoon red-wine vinegar
2 tablespoons chopped walnuts
1½ tablespoons olive oil
2 ounces Feta, cut into 1- by ½-inch pieces
all-purpose flour for dredging
1 large egg, beaten lightly
1 cup fine fresh bread crumbs
1½ tablespoons unsalted butter
4 cups torn romaine, rinsed and spun dry

In a blender blend the vinegar, the walnuts, the oil, and salt and pepper to taste until the dressing is emulsified and transfer the dressing to a small bowl. Dredge the Feta in the flour, brushing off the excess, dip it in the egg, and roll it in the bread crumbs, patting the crumbs gently onto the sides. In a heavy skillet heat the butter over moderate heat until the foam subsides, in it cook the Feta, turning it, for 3 to 5 minutes, or until it is golden, and transfer it to paper towels to drain. Whisk the dressing and in a bowl toss it with the romaine. Divide the salad between 2 plates and on it arrange the warm Feta. Serves 2.

Spinach Salad with Roquefort Dressing

3 slices of lean bacon, cut into ¾-inch pieces
1 tablespoon red-wine vinegar
⅓ cup crumbled Roquefort
4 cups loosely packed trimmed and torn spinach leaves, washed and spun dry

In a skillet cook the bacon over moderate heat, stirring, until it is crisp, transfer it with a slotted spoon to paper towels to drain, and reserve 1 tablespoon of the fat. In a small bowl whisk together the vinegar, ¼ cup of the Roquefort, mashed, and pepper to taste, whisk in the reserved fat, and whisk the dressing until it is emulsified. In a bowl toss together the spinach, the remaining Roquefort, and the dressing, divide the salad between 2 salad plates, and sprinkle the bacon over it. Serves 2.

Watercress and Water Chestnut Salad with Walnut Vinaigrette

¼ cup drained canned whole water chestnuts
2 teaspoons red-wine vinegar
2 tablespoons olive oil
enough watercress, coarse stems discarded,
    rinsed and spun dry, to measure 3½ cups
    loosely packed
2 tablespoons chopped walnuts, toasted lightly
    and chopped fine

In a saucepan of boiling salted water blanch the water chestnuts for 15 seconds, drain them in a sieve, and refresh them under cold water. Drain the water chestnuts well and slice them thin. In a small bowl whisk together the vinegar and salt and pepper to taste, whisk in the oil, and whisk the dressing until it is emulsified. Stir in the water chestnuts and let them marinate for 20 minutes. In a bowl combine the watercress and the walnuts, add the water chestnuts with the dressing, and toss the salad until it is combined. Serves 2.

VEGETABLE SALADS AND SLAWS

Beets and Carrots in Cabbage Leaves with Dill Seed Vinaigrette

¼ pound small beets, the stems trimmed
    to 1 inch
2 teaspoons white-wine vinegar
1 teaspoon dill seed
2 tablespoons olive oil
1½ cups thinly sliced green cabbage plus
    2 small leaves for lining the plates
¼ pound carrots, cut into 1½- by ¼-inch sticks

In a saucepan of boiling water boil the beets for 25 to 30 minutes, or until they are tender, drain them, and let them cool until they can be handled. (To prevent a loss of flavor be careful not to pierce the beets more than once when testing them for doneness.)

While the beets are cooking, in a small bowl whisk together the vinegar, the dill seed, and salt and pepper to taste, whisk in the oil, and whisk the dressing until it is emulsified. In a large saucepan of boiling salted water blanch the cabbage leaves for 30 seconds. Transfer the leaves with a slotted spoon to a sieve, refresh them under cold water, and pat them dry, being careful not to tear them. In the pan of boiling salted water boil the carrots for 3 to 5 minutes, or until they are just tender. Transfer the carrots with the slotted spoon to the sieve, refresh them under cold running water, and transfer them to paper towels to drain. In the pan of boiling salted water boil the sliced cabbage for 3 to 5 minutes, or until it is tender. Drain the cabbage in the sieve, refresh it under cold running water, and transfer it to paper towels to drain.

Peel the beets and cut them into ¼-inch-thick sticks. Transfer the cabbage leaves to salad plates, in each leaf mound half the sliced cabbage, and arrange half the beets and carrots on top. Whisk the dressing and drizzle it over the vegetables. Serves 2.

Grated Carrot, Radish, and Chive Salad

1 pound carrots, peeled and grated coarse in a
    food processor
¾ pound radishes, trimmed and grated coarse
    in a food processor
3 tablespoons fresh lemon juice
½ teaspoon sugar
½ cup olive oil
4 tablespoons snipped fresh chives

In a bowl toss together the carrots and the radishes. In a small bowl whisk together the lemon juice, the sugar, and salt and pepper to taste, add the oil in a stream, whisking, and whisk the dressing until it is emulsified. Stir in the chives, pour the dressing over the mixture, and toss the salad until it is combined. Season the salad with salt and pepper and transfer it to a portable container. *The salad may be made up to 6 hours in advance and kept covered and chilled.* Serves 6.

PHOTO ON PAGE 51

Coleslaw with Almonds and Horseradish Dressing

2 teaspoons white-wine vinegar

3 tablespoons olive oil

1½ teaspoons drained bottled horseradish

3 cups thinly sliced cabbage

2 tablespoons sliced almonds, toasted lightly

⅓ cup thinly sliced red onion

In a small bowl whisk together the vinegar and salt and pepper to taste, add the oil in a stream, whisking, and whisk the dressing until it is emulsified. Whisk in the horseradish. In a bowl toss the cabbage, the almonds, and the onion with the dressing. Serves 2.

Coleslaw with Celery Seed and Sour Cream Dressing

⅔ cup quick mayonnaise (page 200)

½ cup sour cream

2 tablespoons cider vinegar

1 tablespoon honey

2 tablespoons minced onion

6 cups finely shredded green cabbage

4 cups finely shredded red cabbage

1 teaspoon celery seeds

In a bowl whisk together the mayonnaise, the sour cream, the vinegar, the honey, and the onion. In a large bowl toss together the green cabbage, the red cabbage, and the celery seeds. Pour the dressing over the mixture, add salt to taste, and toss the salad well. Serves 4 to 6.

*Composed Salad with Sunflower Seed
and Parsley Sauce*

5 tablespoons unsalted sunflower seeds,
     toasted lightly

¼ cup packed fresh parsley leaves

1 tablespoon white-wine vinegar

2 tablespoons olive oil

2 small tomatoes, sliced

2 hard-boiled large eggs, sliced

½ cup asparagus tips, cooked in boiling salted
     water until tender and drained

In a blender blend the sunflower seeds, the parsley, the vinegar, the oil, 3 tablespoons water, and salt and pepper to taste until the mixture is smooth, adding more water if a thinner consistency is desired. Divide the tomatoes, the eggs, and the asparagus tips between plates and drizzle the salads with the sauce. Serves 2.

*Cucumber and Radish Salad with
Yogurt Coriander Dressing*

3 cups plain yogurt

2 teaspoons salt

1 tablespoon fresh lemon juice

1 tablespoon vegetable oil

3 pounds cucumbers, peeled, halved
     lengthwise, seeded, and sliced diagonally
     ¼ inch thick

1 cup sliced radishes

2 tablespoons chopped fresh coriander,
     or to taste

In a large sieve lined with a double thickness of rinsed and squeezed cheesecloth and set over a bowl let the yogurt drain for 10 minutes. Transfer the yogurt to a bowl, add the salt, the lemon juice, and the oil, and stir the dressing until it is combined well. *The dressing may be made up to 1 day in advance and kept covered and chilled.* In a bowl toss together the cucumbers, the radishes, the dressing, and the coriander and let the salad stand for 10 minutes before serving. Serves 6.

*Oriental Cucumber and Noodle Salad with
Spicy Peanut Sauce*

2 pounds (about 4) cucumbers, peeled, halved
     lengthwise, seeded, and cut diagonally into
     ⅛-inch slices

2 teaspoons salt

For the peanut sauce

½ cup smooth peanut butter

2 tablespoons soy sauce

4 teaspoons fresh lemon juice

1 garlic clove, blanched in boiling water for
     3 minutes, drained, peeled, and minced

a ¾-inch cube of peeled fresh gingerroot,
     minced

½ teaspoon red pepper flakes

¼ teaspoon sugar

½ pound dried Oriental noodles (available at
     Oriental markets, natural foods stores, and
     many supermarkets) or spaghetti

2 tablespoons vegetable oil

2 tablespoons thinly sliced scallion greens

2 tablespoons crushed roasted peanuts

In a bowl toss the cucumber slices with the salt and let them stand for 20 minutes.

Make the peanut sauce while the cucumbers are standing: In a blender blend the peanut butter, the soy sauce, the lemon juice, the garlic, the gingerroot, the red pepper flakes, the sugar, and ½ cup water until the mixture is smooth.

In a kettle of boiling salted water boil the noodles for 3 to 10 minutes, or according to the package instructions, until they are just tender, drain them in a colander, and rinse them under cold water. Drain the noodles well again, transfer them to a platter, and toss them with the oil. Drain the cucumbers in the colander, rinse them under cold water, and pat them dry on paper towels. Arrange the cucumbers on the noodles, pour the peanut sauce over them, and sprinkle the salad with the scallion greens and the peanuts. Serve the salad immediately. Serves 6 as a first course.

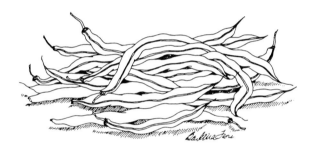

Creamy Cucumber Salad with Cumin

2 pounds (about 4) cucumbers, peeled, halved
    lengthwise, seeded, and cut diagonally into
    ½-inch slices
2 teaspoons salt
⅓ cup sour cream
¼ cup plain yogurt
2 tablespoons distilled white vinegar
4 teaspoons ground cumin
¼ cup olive or vegetable oil
1½ teaspoons cuminseed

In a bowl toss the cucumber slices with the salt and let them stand for 20 minutes.

While the cucumbers are standing, in a bowl whisk together the sour cream, the yogurt, the vinegar, and the ground cumin, add the oil in a stream, whisking, and whisk the mixture until it is emulsified. In a small dry skillet toast the cuminseed over moderate heat, stirring, for 3 to 5 minutes, or until it is fragrant and several shades darker, and transfer it to a small dish. Drain the cucumbers in a colander, rinse them under cold water, and pat them dry on paper towels. Add the cucumbers to

the sour cream mixture with 1 teaspoon of the toasted cuminseed and salt and pepper to taste, stirring to combine the salad well, transfer the salad to a serving bowl, and sprinkle it with the remaining ½ teaspoon toasted cuminseed. Serves 4.

*Green Bean and Shiitake Salad
with Crisp Potato Rings*

1 tablespoon melted duck fat (reserved from
    roast duck *bourguignonne*, page 145) or
    melted unsalted butter
1 boiling potato (about ¾ pound)
2 ounces fresh *shiitake* mushrooms (Oriental
    black mushrooms, available at Oriental
    markets), stems discarded and caps sliced
    thin with a sharp knife held at
    a 45° angle
4 tablespoons vegetable oil
½ teaspoon minced garlic
2 teaspoons Sherry vinegar (available at
    specialty food shops)
¼ pound green beans, trimmed, "frenched" or
    cut into thin strips, cooked in boiling salted
    water for 3 minutes, refreshed in a bowl of
    ice and cold water, and drained

In a large shallow baking dish brush two 5-inch circles with 1½ teaspoons of the fat and chill the fat until it is hardened. Peel the potato into an even cylindrical shape and slice it paper thin crosswise, preferably using a *mandoline*. In the bottom of the baking dish arrange the potato slices, overlapping, to form a 4-inch ring on each circle of hardened fat, leaving a 1-inch border all around, brush the slices with the remaining 1½ teaspoons fat, and chill them for 30 minutes (the potatoes will discolor slightly). Bake the potato rings in a preheated 425° F. oven for 15 minutes, or until they are crisp and brown. While the potatoes are baking, in a skillet cook the mushrooms in 2 tablespoons of the oil over moderately high heat, stirring, for 3 minutes, or until they are browned lightly, add the garlic and salt and pepper to taste, and cook the mixture, stirring, for 1 minute. In a large bowl whisk together the vinegar and salt and pepper to taste, add the remaining 2 tablespoons oil in a stream, whisking, and add the green beans, patted dry, and the mushroom mixture. Toss the salad well, divide it between 2 plates, and arrange a potato ring carefully on top of each salad. Serves 2.

Green Bean Salad with Mustard Caper Vinaigrette

2 pounds green beans, trimmed
2 tablespoons drained capers
1 tablespoon fresh lemon juice, or to taste
1 tablespoon Dijon-style mustard, or to taste
½ cup olive oil
2 hard-boiled large eggs

In a kettle of boiling salted water boil the green beans for 5 minutes, or until they are crisp-tender, and drain them. Refresh the green beans in a bowl of ice and cold water, drain them, and pat them dry. *The beans may be prepared up to this point 1 day in advance and kept covered and chilled.* In a blender purée the capers with the lemon juice, the mustard, and 2 tablespoons water, with the motor running add the oil in a stream, and blend the dressing until it is emulsified. *The dressing may be made up to 1 day in advance and kept covered and chilled.* In a large serving bowl toss together the green beans, the dressing, and pepper to taste and sieve the hard-boiled eggs over the top. Serves 6.

Hearts of Palm Salad with Lamb's-Lettuce

two 14-ounce cans hearts of palm, drained
1½ cups thinly sliced celery
1 cup thinly sliced radish
½ cup minced red onion, soaked in a bowl of
    ice water for 15 minutes and drained well in
    a fine sieve
½ cup thinly sliced Kalamata or other brine-
    cured black olives
For the dressing
1 large egg yolk
3 tablespoons fresh lemon juice, or to taste
½ cup olive oil

¼ pound lamb's-lettuce (*mâche*, available at
    specialty produce markets) or other small
    tender lettuce leaves

In a saucepan of boiling water blanch the hearts of palm for 1 minute, drain them, and cut them crosswise on the diagonal into ¼-inch slices, discarding any tough edges. In a bowl toss together the hearts of palm gently with the celery, the radish, the onion, and the olives.

Make the dressing: In a metal bowl whisk the egg yolk with the lemon juice and salt and pepper to taste, set the bowl over very low heat, and heat the mixture,

whisking, for 1 to 2 minutes, or until it is frothy and thickened slightly. Remove the bowl from the heat, add the oil in a slow stream, whisking constantly, and whisk the dressing until it is emulsified.

Drizzle the dressing over the salad and toss the salad gently with salt and pepper to taste. Arrange the lamb's-lettuce in a ring around the edge of 8 salad plates and divide the salad among the plates, mounding it slightly. Serves 8.

PHOTO ON PAGE 34

Pasta Shells with Tomatoes, Olives, and Basil

½ pound dried small pasta shells
1 tablespoon white-wine vinegar
1 tablespoon vegetable oil
1 cup pitted ripe black olives, cut crosswise
    into rings
1 pint cherry tomatoes, quartered lengthwise
1 small green bell pepper, chopped fine
½ cup thinly sliced celery
½ cup thinly sliced scallion
⅓ cup shredded fresh basil leaves, or to taste
⅔ cup mayonnaise (page 200)
1 tablespoon fresh lemon juice, or to taste

In a kettle of boiling salted water boil the pasta shells, stirring occasionally, for 12 to 14 minutes, or until they are tender, drain them in a colander, and refresh them under cold water. Drain the shells well again, in a bowl toss them with the vinegar and the oil, and add the olives, the tomatoes, the bell pepper, the celery, the scallion, and the basil. In a small bowl whisk together the mayonnaise, the lemon juice, and 2 tablespoons water, pour the dressing over the mixture, and toss the salad gently until it is combined. Season the salad with salt and pepper and transfer it to a portable container. *The salad may be made up to 1 day in advance and kept covered and chilled.* Just before serving toss the salad again. Serves 6.

PHOTO ON PAGE 51

Potato Radish Salad with Russian Dressing

¾ pound boiling potatoes, peeled and cut into
    ½-inch pieces
⅓ cup mayonnaise
½ teaspoon finely grated onion or to taste
¼ teaspoon Worcestershire sauce
2½ teaspoons ketchup
½ teaspoon drained bottled horseradish

2 tablespoons finely chopped sweet gherkin
3 radishes, sliced thin

In a large saucepan of simmering salted water cook the potatoes for 6 to 8 minutes, or until they are tender, and drain them in a colander. Refresh the potatoes under cold water, drain them well, and transfer them to a bowl. In a small bowl whisk together the mayonnaise, the onion, the Worcestershire sauce, the ketchup, the horseradish, the gherkin, and salt and pepper to taste, add the dressing and the radishes to the potatoes, and stir the mixture gently until it is combined. Serves 2.

Red Cabbage and Lettuce Salad

1½ tablespoons red-wine vinegar
½ teaspoon Dijon-style mustard
⅓ cup vegetable oil
2 cups finely shredded red cabbage
2 cups finely shredded iceberg lettuce

In a salad bowl whisk together the vinegar, the mustard, and salt and pepper to taste, add the oil in a stream, whisking, and whisk the dressing until it is emulsified. Add the cabbage and the lettuce and toss the salad to coat it with the dressing. Serves 6.

Herbed Tomato and Crouton Salad

1¼ cups olive or vegetable oil

3 garlic cloves, minced
5 cups ½-inch cubes of country-style
   or Italian bread
3 tablespoons red-wine vinegar
1½ teaspoons Dijon-style mustard, or to taste
3 pounds firm-ripe tomatoes, chopped
½ cup finely chopped fresh mint leaves
½ cup finely chopped scallion greens
½ cup minced fresh parsley leaves

In a small bowl combine the oil and the garlic, let the mixture stand for 30 minutes, and strain the oil into a bowl, discarding the garlic. Toast the bread cubes in one layer on a baking sheet in a preheated 350° F. oven, turning them occasionally, for 15 minutes, or until they are golden brown. Drizzle ½ cup of the garlic-flavored oil over the croutons, toss the mixture well, and let the croutons cool to room temperature. In another small bowl whisk together the vinegar, the mustard, and salt and pepper to taste, add the remaining ¾ cup garlic-flavored oil in a stream, whisking, and whisk the dressing until it is emulsified. In a large bowl toss together the croutons, the tomatoes, the mint, the scallion, the parsley, and salt and pepper to taste, drizzle the mixture with the dressing, and toss the salad well. The salad may be served at this point if a crunchy texture is desired. The longer the salad stands, the softer the croutons become, as the bread absorbs the dressing. Serve the salad at room temperature. Serves 8 to 10.

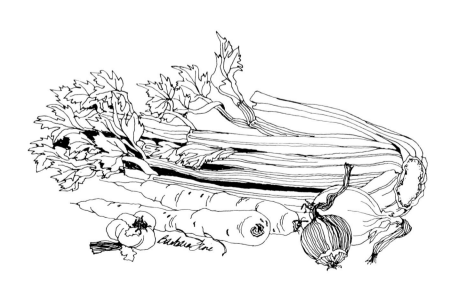

GRAIN SALADS

Tabbouleh
(Bulgur, Vegetable, and Mint Salad)

1 cup *bulgur* (cracked wheat)
1½ teaspoons salt
3 tablespoons fresh lemon juice
¼ cup olive oil
½ teaspoon minced garlic
1½ cups minced fresh mint leaves
1 cup minced fresh parsley leaves
3 plum tomatoes, chopped fine
½ cup peeled, seeded, and finely chopped
   cucumber
2 tablespoons minced scallion
½ cup drained canned chick-peas, rinsed

In a bowl let the *bulgur* soak in boiling water to cover with the salt for 1 hour, drain it, and in a towel squeeze it dry. In another bowl toss the *bulgur* with the lemon juice, the oil, and the garlic and let it marinate, covered, at room temperature for at least 1 hour or chilled for up to 3 hours. Add the mint, the parsley, the tomatoes, the cucumber, the scallion, the chick-peas, and salt and pepper to taste and toss the salad well. Serves 4.

Two-Grain Salad with Green Beans and Pine Nuts

1 cup barley (not quick-cooking)
1 cup *bulgur* (available at natural foods stores,
   specialty foods shops, and some supermarkets)
¼ cup fresh lemon juice
1 teaspoon Dijon-style mustard
¾ cup olive oil
1 pound green beans, trimmed
½ cup pine nuts, toasted lightly

In a saucepan combine the barley with 6 cups boiling salted water and simmer it for 40 minutes, or until it is cooked but still *al dente*. Drain the barley in a colander, rinse it, and drain it well. In a bowl combine the *bulgur* with 1½ cups boiling salted water and let the mixture stand, fluffing it with a fork occasionally, for 20 to 30 minutes, or until all the water is absorbed. Add the barley and toss the mixture until it is combined well.

In a small bowl whisk together the lemon juice, the mustard, and salt and pepper to taste, add the oil in a stream, whisking, and whisk the dressing until it is

emulsified. Add the dressing to the grain mixture and toss the mixture until it is combined well. *The mixture may be prepared up to this point 1 day in advance and kept covered and chilled.*

In a kettle of boiling salted water cook the green beans for 4 to 5 minutes, or until they are just tender, refresh them under cold water, and drain them well. Slice the beans thin crosswise, add them to the grain mixture with the pine nuts and salt and pepper to taste, and toss the salad until it is combined well. Serves 6 to 8.

PHOTO ON PAGE 61

SALAD DRESSINGS

Camembert Dressing

¼ cup white-wine vinegar
½ pound ripe Camembert, rind discarded and
   cheese at room temperature
¼ cup dry white wine
1 small garlic clove, minced
1 large egg
1 teaspoon Worcestershire sauce
1¾ cups olive oil

In a food processor blend the vinegar, the Camembert, and a pinch of salt until the mixture is smooth and blend in the wine, the garlic, the egg, and the Worcestershire sauce. With the motor running add the oil in a stream, blend the dressing until it is emulsified, and add salt and pepper to taste. Transfer the dressing to a bowl and chill it, covered, for 2 hours. Makes about 2½ cups.

Creamy Roquefort Dressing

½ cup crumbled Roquefort
1½ cups sour cream
¼ cup half-and-half
2 tablespoons mayonnaise
1 tablespoon olive oil
2 tablespoons white-wine vinegar
cayenne to taste

In a blender or food processor blend the Roquefort, the sour cream, the half-and-half, the mayonnaise, the oil, and the vinegar until the dressing is smooth and add the cayenne and salt to taste. Makes about 2¼ cups.

Creamy Sesame Dressing

½ pound farmer cheese
¼ cup Oriental sesame oil (available at
 Oriental markets and most supermarkets)
1 small garlic clove, minced
1 tablespoon fresh lemon juice
⅓ cup loosely packed fresh coriander
⅛ teaspoon red pepper flakes
½ cup half-and-half
2 tablespoons sesame seeds, toasted lightly

In a food processor or blender blend the farmer cheese, the oil, the garlic, the lemon juice, the coriander, and the red pepper flakes until the mixture is smooth. With the motor running add the half-and-half in a stream and blend the dressing until it is combined. Transfer the dressing to a bowl and stir in the sesame seeds and salt and pepper to taste. Makes about 1½ cups.

Curried Cottage Cheese Dressing with Bacon

⅓ cup crumbled cooked bacon (about ¼ pound
 uncooked)
1 cup cottage cheese
3 tablespoons half-and-half
¼ cup olive oil
2 tablespoons fresh lemon juice
2 teaspoons curry powder
½ teaspoon ground cumin
¼ cup bottled mango chutney
cayenne to taste

In a food processor blend the bacon, the cottage cheese, the half-and-half, the oil, the lemon juice, the curry powder, the cumin, and the chutney until the dressing is smooth and add the cayenne and salt to taste. Use the dressing for fruit or chicken salads. Makes about 1½ cups.

Gruyère Pesto Dressing

¼ pound Gruyère, grated fine
⅓ cup pine nuts, toasted lightly
½ cup loosely packed fresh basil leaves
6 tablespoons white-wine vinegar
¾ cup olive oil

In a food processor blend the Gruyére, the pine nuts, and the basil until the mixture forms a paste and blend in the vinegar. With the motor running add the oil in a stream, blend the dressing until it is emulsified, and add salt and pepper to taste. Serve the dressing with sliced tomatoes. Makes about 2 cups.

Herbed Cream Cheese Dressing

8 ounces cream cheese, softened
½ cup sour cream
½ cup loosely packed fresh parsley leaves
½ cup loosely packed fresh dill sprigs, coarse
 stems discarded
½ cup chopped scallion
1 tablespoon white-wine vinegar
¼ cup vegetable oil
2 teaspoons Worcestershire sauce
2 tablespoons half-and-half or milk

In a food processor blend the cream cheese, the sour cream, the parsley, the dill, and the scallion until the mixture is smooth. With the motor running add the vinegar, the oil, the Worcestershire sauce, the half-and-half, and salt and pepper to taste and blend the dressing until it is combined well. Makes about 2 cups.

Mint Yogurt Dressing

½ cup plain yogurt
½ cup cottage cheese
⅓ cup firmly packed fresh mint leaves
½ teaspoon ground cumin
⅛ teaspoon cayenne
½ teaspoon salt
3 tablespoons vegetable oil
2 tablespoons fresh lemon juice

In a blender blend together the yogurt, the cottage cheese, the mint, the cumin, the cayenne, the salt, the oil, and the lemon juice until the mixture is smooth. Makes about 1 cup.

Mayonnaise

2 large egg yolks at room temperature
2 teaspoons wine vinegar
1 teaspoon Dijon-style mustard,
    or to taste
¼ teaspoon salt
white pepper to taste
1½ cups olive oil, vegetable oil, or a
    combination of both
fresh lemon juice to taste
cream to thin the mayonnaise
    if desired

Rinse a mixing bowl with hot water and dry it well. In the bowl combine the egg yolks, 1 teaspoon of the vinegar, the mustard, the salt, and the white pepper, beat the mixture vigorously with a whisk or with an electric mixer at high speed until it is combined, and add ½ cup of the oil, drop by drop, beating constantly. Add the remaining 1 teaspoon vinegar and the remaining 1 cup oil in a stream, beating constantly. Add the lemon juice and white pepper and salt to taste and thin the mayonnaise, if desired, with a small quantity of cream or water. Makes about 2 cups.

Quick Mayonnaise

1 large egg at room temperature
5 teaspoons fresh lemon juice
1 teaspoon Dijon-style mustard
¼ teaspoon salt
¼ teaspoon white pepper
1 cup olive oil, vegetable oil, or a
    combination of both

In a food processor or blender with the motor on high blend the egg, the lemon juice, the mustard, the salt, and the white pepper, add the oil in a stream, and turn the motor off. Makes about 1 cup.

Caesar Vinaigrette

3 tablespoons white-wine vinegar
1 tablespoon Dijon-style mustard
½ cup olive oil
1 teaspoon anchovy paste
1 tablespoon drained capers
1 large egg yolk
½ cup freshly grated Parmesan

In a small bowl whisk together the vinegar, the mustard, and a pinch of salt, add the oil in a stream, whisking, and whisk the dressing until it is emulsified. Whisk in the anchovy paste, the capers, and the egg yolk, whisk the dressing until it is combined well, and whisk in the Parmesan and salt and pepper to taste. Makes about 1¼ cups.

Roquefort Vinaigrette

¼ cup red-wine vinegar
¼ teaspoon salt
½ cup olive oil
2 tablespoons heavy cream
½ cup crumbled Roquefort
fresh lemon juice to taste

In a small bowl whisk together the vinegar and the salt, add the oil in a stream, whisking, and whisk the dressing until it is emulsified. Whisk in the cream, the Roquefort, the lemon juice, and pepper to taste and whisk the vinaigrette until it is combined well. Makes about 1¼ cups.

SAUCES

SAVORY SAUCES AND MARINADES

Creamy Anchovy Sauce

1 large garlic clove, unpeeled
1 large egg
2 teaspoons fresh lemon juice
2 teaspoons anchovy paste
¼ cup canned beef broth
¾ cup vegetable oil

In a small saucepan of boiling water boil the garlic for 8 minutes, peel it, and chop it fine. In a blender or food processor blend the garlic, the egg, the lemon juice, the anchovy paste, and the broth until the mixture is combined and with the motor running add the oil in a slow stream, blending the sauce until it is emulsified. *The sauce may be made up to 1 day in advance and kept covered and chilled.* Serve the sauce with cold meats. Makes about 1 cup.

Spicy Apricot Basting Sauce

1 cup apricot jam
½ cup distilled white vinegar
3 tablespoons Worcestershire sauce
2 tablespoons Dijon-style mustard
2 tablespoons honey
2 teaspoons dried hot red pepper flakes

In a saucepan combine the jam, the vinegar, the Worcestershire sauce, the mustard, the honey, the red pepper flakes, and salt to taste and gently simmer the mixture, stirring, until the jam and the honey are dissolved. Use the sauce to baste ham steaks, chicken, or shrimp during the last third of its grilling time. Makes about 1¾ cups.

Carrot Coriander Sauce

4 carrots, cut into 1-inch slices
1 teaspoon salt
2 teaspoons fresh lemon juice
½ cup plain yogurt
1½ tablespoons minced fresh coriander

In a small saucepan combine the carrots, the salt, and 1 cup water, bring the water to a boil, and cook the carrots, covered, over moderately high heat for 10 minutes, or until they are very tender. Drain the carrots, reserving 3 tablespoons of the cooking liquid, and in a food processor or blender purée them with the reserved liquid and the lemon juice until the mixture is very smooth. Transfer the purée to a bowl, stir in the yogurt, the coriander, and salt and pepper to taste, and chill the sauce, covered, for 20 minutes. *The sauce may be made up to 2 days in advance and kept covered and chilled.* Serve the sauce with cold chicken or fish. Makes about 1⅓ cups.

Hot Pepper Basting Sauce

2 large red bell peppers, roasted (procedure on page 203)
2 pickled 1-inch *jalapeño* peppers, halved lengthwise and seeded (wear rubber gloves)
3 tablespoons fresh lime juice
½ teaspoon ground cumin
2 tablespoons firmly packed dark brown sugar
2 tablespoons vegetable oil

In a blender purée the roasted bell peppers, the *jalapeño* peppers, the lime juice, the cumin, the brown sugar, the oil, and salt to taste. Use the sauce to baste shrimp, beef, or chicken during the last third of its grilling time. Makes about 1 cup.

Lemon and Thyme Marinade

½ cup fresh lemon juice
1 tablespoon plus 1 teaspoon freshly grated
   lemon rind
¼ cup chopped fresh thyme leaves
¼ cup minced shallot
2 teaspoons salt
1 teaspoon freshly ground pepper
½ cup vegetable oil

In a bowl stir together the lemon juice, the rind, the thyme, the shallot, the salt, and the pepper until the salt is dissolved and whisk in the oil. Use the marinade to marinate scallops, shrimp, fish, chicken, or lamb, covered, at room temperature for 1 hour. Makes about 1⅓ cups.

Lemon, Dill, and Caper Cream Sauce

2 tablespoons fresh lemon juice
2 tablespoons snipped fresh dill
½ cup heavy cream
1 tablespoon chopped drained capers

In a bowl stir together the lemon juice and the dill. Add the cream, a little at a time, stirring with a wooden spoon, and stir the mixture until it thickens slightly. Stir in the capers and salt and pepper to taste and chill the sauce, covered, for 1 hour. *The sauce may be made up to 1 day in advance and kept covered and chilled.* Stir the sauce to combine it before serving. Serve the sauce with cold chicken or fish. Makes about ¾ cup.

Lime Date Basting Sauce

½ cup chopped onion
½ cup chopped green bell pepper
¾ cup pitted dates, chopped
2 teaspoons vegetable oil
½ cup fresh lime juice
½ cup plus 2 tablespoons fresh orange juice
¼ teaspoon freshly grated lime rind

In a saucepan cook the onion, the bell pepper, and the dates in the oil over moderately low heat, stirring, for 5 minutes. Add the lime juice, the orange juice, the rind, and salt and pepper to taste, bring the liquid to a boil, and simmer the mixture, stirring occasionally, for 10 to 12 minutes, or until the bell pepper is very tender. In a blender or food processor purée the mixture and force the purée through a fine sieve with a spatula into a small bowl. (The sauce will be tart.) Use the sauce to baste pork or chicken during the last third of its cooking time. Makes about 1 cup.

Maple Apple Marinade

1 cup maple syrup
½ cup apple juice
1 cup cider vinegar

In a saucepan combine the syrup, the apple juice, and the vinegar, bring the mixture to a boil, and simmer it for 45 minutes, or until it is reduced to about 2 cups. Use the marinade to marinate pork or chicken, covered and chilled, overnight. Makes about 2 cups.

Mint and Yogurt Marinade

¼ cup minced fresh mint leaves
1 teaspoon sugar
1 teaspoon minced garlic
2 teaspoons fresh lemon juice
2 tablespoons vegetable oil
1 cup plain yogurt

In a bowl with a fork mash the mint with the sugar and the garlic and stir in the lemon juice, the oil, the yogurt, and salt to taste. Use the marinade to marinate lamb, beef, or chicken, covered and chilled, overnight. Makes about 1 cup.

Mint Pesto
(Mint, Walnut, and Parmesan Sauce)

4 cups firmly packed fresh mint leaves
2 tablespoons chopped walnuts
½ teaspoon salt
½ teaspoon minced garlic
½ cup olive oil
½ cup freshly grated Parmesan

In a blender or food processor purée the mint, the walnuts, the salt, the garlic, and the oil, scraping down the sides of the container with a rubber spatula. Transfer the purée to a bowl and stir in the Parmesan. Serve the *pesto* tossed with pasta or as a sauce for sliced tomatoes or grilled lamb or chicken. Makes about ¾ cup.

Savory Mint Sauce

½ cup distilled white vinegar
3 tablespoons sugar
⅓ cup minced fresh mint leaves

In a saucepan combine the vinegar and the sugar, cook the mixture over moderately low heat, stirring, until the sugar is dissolved, and remove the pan from the heat. Add the mint, let the sauce stand for 1 hour, and serve it heated, with lamb. Makes about ½ cup.

Mustard and Bourbon Marinade

½ cup Dijon-style mustard
¼ cup plus 2 tablespoons bourbon
¼ cup soy sauce
½ cup firmly packed dark brown sugar
2 teaspoons Worcestershire sauce
⅓ cup minced scallion

In a bowl stir together the mustard, the bourbon, the soy sauce, the brown sugar, the Worcestershire sauce, and the scallion. Use the marinade to marinate shrimp or scallops, covered, at room temperature for 1 hour, or beef, chicken, or pork, covered and chilled, overnight. Baste the shellfish or meat with the marinade as it is grilled. Makes about 1⅓ cups.

Spicy Oriental Peanut Sauce

⅓ cup smooth peanut butter
1 teaspoon sugar
1 tablespoon fresh lemon juice
1 large garlic clove, minced
1 tablespoon soy sauce
¼ teaspoon chili oil (available at Oriental markets and some supermarkets), or to taste
⅓ cup canned chicken broth

In a food processor or blender blend the peanut butter, the sugar, the lemon juice, the garlic, the soy sauce, and the oil until the mixture is smooth and with the motor running add the broth in a stream, blending the sauce until it is combined well. *The sauce may be made up to 2 days in advance and kept covered and chilled.* Serve the sauce with cold chicken. Makes about ¾ cup.

Red Pepper and Basil Sauce

2 red bell peppers, roasted (procedure follows) and chopped, or a 7-ounce jar of roasted red peppers, drained and chopped
¼ teaspoon Tabasco, or to taste
½ teaspoon white-wine vinegar
2 tablespoons heavy cream
¼ cup finely chopped fresh basil leaves

In a food processor or blender purée the roasted peppers, add the Tabasco, the vinegar, and salt to taste, and blend the mixture, scraping down the sides occasionally, until it is combined. Transfer the purée to a small bowl and whisk in the cream and the basil. *The sauce may be made up to 3 days in advance and kept covered and chilled.* Serve the sauce with cold fish, meats, or poultry. Makes about 1 cup.

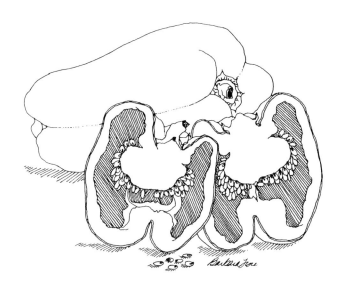

To Roast Bell Peppers or Chili Peppers

Using a long-handled fork char the peppers over an open flame, turning them, for 2 to 3 minutes, or until the skins are blackened. (Or broil the peppers on the rack of a broiler pan under a preheated broiler about 2 inches from the heat, turning them every 5 minutes, for 15 to 25 minutes, or until the skins are blistered and charred.) Transfer the peppers to a bowl and let them steam, covered, until they are cool enough to handle. Keeping the peppers whole, peel them starting at the blossom end, cut off the tops, and discard the seeds and ribs (wear rubber gloves when handling chili peppers).

Tahini Sauce

1 cup drained canned chick-peas, rinsed
3 tablespoons well stirred *tahini* (sesame seed
    paste, available at specialty foods shops and
    some supermarkets)
1 large garlic clove, minced
2 tablespoons fresh lemon juice
½ teaspoon ground cumin
a pinch of cayenne, or to taste
⅓ cup canned chicken broth

In a food processor or blender blend the chick-peas, the *tahini*, the garlic, the lemon juice, the cumin, and the cayenne until the mixture forms a paste. With the motor running add the broth in a stream, blending the sauce until it is smooth, and add salt and pepper to taste. *The sauce may be made up to 1 week in advance and kept covered and chilled.* Stir the sauce to combine it before serving. Serve the sauce with cold chicken. Makes about 1¼ cups.

Curried Tomato Sauce

1½ cups finely chopped onion
¼ cup vegetable oil
4 garlic cloves, minced
2 teaspoons minced peeled fresh gingerroot
1 tablespoon plus 1 teaspoon curry powder
½ teaspoon ground cumin
2 pounds firm-ripe tomatoes, peeled and
    seeded (procedure on page 112) and
    chopped fine
¼ cup chopped fresh coriander

In a skillet cook the onion in the oil over moderately low heat, stirring occasionally, until it is softened, add the garlic, the gingerroot, the curry powder, and the cumin, and cook the mixture, stirring, for 3 minutes. Add the tomatoes, cook the mixture, stirring occasionally, for 5 minutes, and stir in the coriander and salt and pepper to taste. Makes about 2 cups.

Quick Tomato Barbecue Sauce

1 onion, quartered
1 tablespoon minced garlic
1 dill pickle, chopped
1½ cups distilled white vinegar
¼ cup firmly packed dark brown sugar
2 tablespoons Dijon-style mustard
2 tablespoons Worcestershire sauce
2 teaspoons Tabasco
1 cup ketchup
¼ cup vegetable oil

In a blender purée the onion, the garlic, and the pickle with the vinegar, add the brown sugar, the mustard, the Worcestershire sauce, the Tabasco, the ketchup, and the oil, and blend the mixture until it is smooth. Transfer the mixture to a saucepan and simmer it, stirring occasionally, for 20 minutes, or until it is reduced to about 2 cups. Use the sauce to baste shrimp, beef, or chicken during the last third of its grilling time. Makes about 2 cups.

Spicy Tomato Barbecue Sauce

2 cups chopped onion
¼ cup vegetable oil
4 garlic cloves, minced
⅓ cup unsulfured dark molasses
1¼ cups ketchup
⅓ cup dill pickle juice
2 tablespoons Dijon-style mustard
1 cup cider vinegar
2 tablespoons Worcestershire sauce
2 teaspoons Tabasco
1½ teaspoons cayenne, or to taste

In a saucepan cook the onion in the oil over moderately low heat, stirring, until it is softened, add the garlic, and cook the mixture, stirring, for 2 minutes. Add the molasses, the ketchup, the pickle juice, the mustard, the vinegar, the Worcestershire sauce, the Tabasco, the

cayenne, and salt to taste and simmer the mixture, stirring occasionally, for 30 minutes. Transfer the mixture to a blender or food processor and purée it. Use the sauce to baste beef, chicken, or pork during the last third of its grilling time. Makes about 2½ cups.

Spicy Tomato Salsa

½ pound plum tomatoes, peeled, seeded, and chopped (about 1¼ cups)
⅓ cup finely chopped red onion
2 tablespoons finely chopped green bell pepper
1½ tablespoons minced and seeded (wear rubber gloves) canned pickled *jalapeño* chilies
2 tablespoons chopped Kalamata or other brine-cured olives
1 tablespoon fresh lime juice
1 tablespoon olive oil

In a bowl combine well the tomatoes, the onion, the bell pepper, the *jalapeño* chilies, the olives, the lime juice, and the oil and season the *salsa* with salt and pepper. *The salsa may be made up to 30 minutes in advance and kept covered.* Serve the *salsa* with cold fish, meats, or poultry. Makes about 1½ cups.

Watercress Hollandaise

1 cup packed rinsed watercress leaves
1 stick (½ cup) unsalted butter
2 large egg yolks
4 teaspoons fresh lemon juice
2 teaspoons Dijon-style mustard
¼ teaspoon salt, or to taste
⅛ teaspoon freshly ground white pepper, or to taste

In a small saucepan cook the watercress in 2 tablespoons water over high heat until it is just wilted and drain it in a sieve. Refresh the watercress under cold water and squeeze out the excess liquid. In another small saucepan melt the butter over moderate heat and keep it warm.

In a blender blend the egg yolks, the lemon juice, the mustard, the watercress, the salt, and the pepper for 5 seconds, turn the motor off, and scrape down the sides of the blender. With the motor running add the butter in

a stream and season the hollandaise with salt and pepper. *The hollandaise may be kept warm in a bowl, covered with a buttered round of wax paper, in a pan of warm water for up to 20 minutes.* Makes about 1 cup.

PHOTO ON PAGE 32

DESSERT SAUCES AND TOPPINGS

Almond Praline with Amaretto

6 ounces unblanched whole almonds
2 cups sugar
Amaretto to taste

Spread the almonds in one layer in a well buttered 10-inch round cake pan. In a large heavy skillet cook the sugar with 3 tablespoons water over moderately high heat, stirring constantly with a fork, until it melts and is a golden brown caramel and pour the caramel over the almonds evenly. Let the caramel cool and harden, break the praline into large pieces, and in a food processor or blender grind it coarse. Serve the praline over vanilla or peach ice cream and drizzle it with the Amaretto. The praline keeps, chilled, in an airtight container indefinitely. Makes about 3 cups.

Butterscotch Marshmallow Sauce

1 cup firmly packed light brown sugar
2 tablespoons light corn syrup
2 tablespoons unsalted butter
½ cup heavy cream
¼ teaspoon salt
1 teaspoon vanilla
1 cup miniature marshmallows

In a heavy saucepan combine the brown sugar, the corn syrup, the butter, the cream, and the salt, bring the mixture to a boil, stirring until the sugar is dissolved, and boil it, undisturbed, until it registers 235° F. on a candy thermometer. Stir in the vanilla and let the mixture cool for 10 minutes. Stir in the marshmallows and serve the sauce warm over vanilla, coffee, or chocolate ice cream. The sauce keeps, covered and chilled, for up to 1 week. Reheat the sauce before serving. Makes about 2 cups.

Caramelized Coconut Crumble

1 cup packaged sweetened flaked coconut
¼ cup firmly packed dark brown sugar
2 tablespoons unsalted butter, melted
coffee or vanilla ice cream as an
    accompaniment, if desired.

In a jelly-roll pan toss together the coconut and the brown sugar until they are combined well, drizzle the mixture with the butter, and toss the mixture to combine it thoroughly. Spread the mixture in an even layer and bake it in a preheated 350° F. oven, stirring occasionally, for 8 to 10 minutes, or until the coconut is golden brown and crisp. Serve the coconut crumble over the vanilla or coffee ice cream. The crumble keeps, cooled completely, in an airtight container for up to 1 week. Makes about 2¼ cups.

Chocolate-Covered Peanut Crunch

1 cup salted roasted peanuts
2 cups sugar
4 ounces semisweet chocolate, melted
chocolate or vanilla ice cream
    as an accompaniment, if desired.

Spread the peanuts in one layer in a well buttered 9-inch round cake pan. In a large heavy skillet cook the sugar with 3 tablespoons water over moderately high heat, stirring constantly with a fork, until it melts and is a golden brown caramel and pour the caramel over the peanuts evenly. Drizzle the top with the chocolate, chill the mixture until the caramel is hardened and the chocolate is set, and chop it coarse. Serve the peanut crunch over the vanilla or chocolate ice cream. The crunch keeps, chilled, in an airtight container for several weeks. Makes about 2½ cups.

Double Orange Sauce with Chocolate

a 12-ounce jar sweet orange marmalade
2 tablespoons unsalted butter
¼ cup Grand Marnier
1 tablespoon fresh lemon juice, or to taste
2 ounces semisweet chocolate, chopped

In a saucepan combine the marmalade, the butter, the Grand Marnier, and the lemon juice, bring the mixture to a simmer, stirring, and simmer it, stirring occasionally, for 5 minutes. Transfer the sauce to a bowl and chill it, covered, for 1 hour. Serve the sauce over vanilla or chocolate ice cream and sprinkle it with the chocolate. The sauce keeps, covered and chilled, for up to 1 week. Makes about 1 cup.

Peppermint Chip Fudge Sauce

½ stick (¼ cup) unsalted butter
1 cup sugar
¼ teaspoon salt
½ cup heavy cream
6 ounces unsweetened chocolate, chopped
3 tablespoons crème de menthe
½ cup coarsely crushed peppermint hard candies

In a heavy saucepan cook the butter, the sugar, the salt, and the cream over moderately low heat, stirring, until the sugar is dissolved. Remove the pan from the heat and let the mixture cool for 10 minutes. Stir in the chocolate, stir the sauce until the chocolate is melted and the sauce is smooth, and stir in the crème de menthe. Serve the sauce warm over chocolate ice cream and sprinkle it with the peppermint. The sauce keeps, covered and chilled, for up to 1 week. Reheat the sauce in the top of a double boiler set over barely simmering water before serving. Makes about 1¾ cups.

DESSERTS

CAKES

Toasted Almond Angel Food Cake

For the cake
1 cup cake flour (not self-rising)
1⅔ cups sugar
1¾ cups egg whites (about 13 large egg
    whites) at room temperature
½ teaspoon salt
1 teaspoon cream of tartar
1 teaspoon almond extract, or to taste
For the icing
1 cup sugar
1 tablespoon light corn syrup
2 large egg whites at room temperature
¼ teaspoon cream of tartar
½ teaspoon vanilla, or to taste

1½ cups toasted sliced almonds

Make the cake: Sift the flour 3 times onto a sheet of wax paper. In the sifter combine the sifted flour and ⅔ cup of the sugar and sift the mixture onto another sheet of wax paper. In a large bowl with an electric mixer beat the egg whites until they are broken up, add the salt and the cream of tartar, and beat the whites until they are frothy. Beat in the remaining 1 cup sugar, a little at a time, and the almond extract and beat the whites until they hold soft peaks. Sift one fourth of the flour mixture over the whites, folding it in gently but thor-oughly, and continue to sift and fold the remaining flour mixture into the whites in the same manner. Spoon the batter into a very clean, ungreased tube pan, 10 by 8¼ by 4¼ inches, preferably with a removable bottom, smoothing the top, and rap the pan on a hard surface twice to remove any air bubbles. Bake the cake in the middle of a preheated 300° F. oven for 1 hour, or until it is springy to the touch and a tester comes out clean. If the pan has feet invert the pan over a work surface; oth-erwise invert the pan over the neck of a bottle. Let the cake cool for at least 1 hour or overnight. Run a thin knife in a sawing motion around the edge of the pan and the tube to loosen the cake from the pan and invert the cake onto a cake stand. Slip strips of wax paper under the edge of the cake to cover the cake stand.

Make the icing: In a small saucepan combine the sug-ar, the corn syrup, and ¼ cup water, bring the mixture to a boil, covered, stirring occasionally to dissolve the sugar, and boil the syrup, uncovered, until it registers 240° F. on a candy thermometer. While the syrup is boiling, in a heatproof bowl with an electric mixer beat the egg whites with a pinch of salt and the cream of tar-tar until they are frothy and as soon as the syrup reaches 240° F. add it to the whites in a thin stream, beating con-stantly. Beat in the vanilla and beat the icing until the bowl is no longer hot. (If the icing is too stiff beat in 1 to 2 tablespoons hot water, or enough to form a fluffy, spreadable icing.)

Spread the icing over the top and sides of the cake, including the inner cavity, cover the cake with the al-monds, and remove the wax paper strips carefully.

PHOTO ON PAGE 20

Apricot Cheesecake

6 ounces dried apricots plus 8 additional
    dried apricots
⅓ cup graham cracker crumbs
¾ cup plus 1 teaspoon sugar
1 tablespoon unsalted butter, softened
2 tablespoons plus 2 teaspoons apricot brandy
¾ pound cream cheese, softened
2 large eggs
½ cup sour cream
¼ cup apricot jam

In a saucepan combine 6 ounces of the apricots with 1½ cups water and bring the water to a boil. Simmer the mixture, covered partially, for 45 minutes, or until the apricots are soft and the liquid is almost evaporated, and let it cool. In a food processor blend the graham cracker crumbs, 2 tablespoons of the sugar, and the butter and pat the mixture onto the bottom and 1 inch up the side of a buttered 5-inch springform pan, 3½ inches deep.

In the food processor purée the cooked apricots and the cooking liquid with the apricot brandy until the mixture is smooth. Add the cream cheese, the eggs, and ½ cup plus 2 tablespoons of the remaining sugar and blend the mixture until it is smooth. Pour the mixture into the shell and bake the cake in the middle of a preheated 375° F. oven for 30 minutes. Let the cheesecake stand in the pan on a rack for 5 minutes. (The cake will not be set.)

In a bowl combine the sour cream with the remaining 1 teaspoon sugar, spread the mixture evenly on the cake, and bake the cake for 5 minutes more. Let the cake cool completely in the pan on a rack (it will continue to set as it cools) and chill it, covered loosely, overnight. Remove the side of the pan and transfer the cake to a stand.

In a small saucepan heat the apricot jam, stirring, until it is just heated through, force it through a fine sieve into a small bowl, and spoon most of it on the top of the cheesecake. Arrange the additional apricots, sliced, around the top of the cheesecake and brush them lightly with the remaining apricot jam.

PHOTO ON PAGE 67

Baked Alaska

1½ quarts coffee ice cream, softened slightly
1 chocolate fudge sheet cake (recipe follows)
For the meringue

12 large egg whites
½ teaspoon salt
3 cups sugar
4 tablespoons dark rum

Line a 15½- by 10½-inch jelly-roll pan with foil and put it in the freezer for 15 minutes. In a food processor purée the ice cream until it is just smooth, working quickly spread it evenly in the chilled pan, and freeze it for 2 hours, or until it is frozen hard. Freeze the chocolate fudge sheet cake in its pan, covered loosely with plastic wrap, for at least 1 hour, or until it is firm. *The ice cream and the cake may be made 1 day in advance and kept covered with plastic wrap and frozen.*

Working quickly cut the ice cream and the cake lengthwise through the foil into 3 strips each, invert an ice cream strip onto a large ovenproof platter, peeling off the foil, and invert a cake strip onto it, peeling off the foil. Continue to layer alternating strips of the ice cream and cake in the same manner. Freeze the dessert, covered with plastic wrap, on the platter for at least 1 hour, or until it is frozen. *The dessert may be prepared up to this point 1 day in advance and kept covered and frozen.*

Make the meringue: In the large bowl of an electric mixer stir together the egg whites, the salt, and the sugar, set the bowl over a pan of simmering water, and stir the mixture until the sugar is dissolved. Remove the bowl from the pan and with the mixer beat the meringue until it holds soft glossy peaks. Add 1 tablespoon of the rum and beat the meringue until it holds stiff glossy peaks. Working quickly with a rubber spatula spread the top and sides of the frozen dessert with a generous layer of the meringue, covering it completely. Transfer the remaining meringue to a pastry bag fitted with a large star tip and pipe it generously and decoratively on and around the dessert. Bake the dessert in a preheated 450° F. oven for 4 to 5 minutes, or until the meringue is golden brown. While the baked Alaska is browning, in a small saucepan heat the remaining 3 tablespoons rum over low heat until it is warm. Remove the baked Alaska from the oven, ignite the rum, and pour it quickly over the dessert. Serves 10.

PHOTO ON PAGE 80

Chocolate Fudge Sheet Cake

2½ ounces unsweetened chocolate, chopped
1 stick (½ cup) unsalted butter
1 cup firmly packed dark brown sugar

2 large eggs
1 cup cake flour (not self-rising)
½ teaspoon baking soda
½ teaspoon salt
⅓ cup milk
½ teaspoon vanilla

Line a lightly greased 15½- by 10½-inch jelly-roll pan with foil, grease the foil, and dust it with flour, knocking out the excess.

In a small heavy saucepan melt the chocolate with 2 tablespoons of the butter, ¼ cup of the brown sugar, and 1 tablespoon water over moderately low heat, stirring the mixture until it is smooth, and let the mixture cool. In a bowl with an electric mixer cream the remaining 6 tablespoons butter, softened, with the remaining ¾ cup brown sugar until the mixture is light and fluffy, beat in the eggs, 1 at a time, beating well after each addition, and beat in the chocolate mixture. Into a bowl sift together the cake flour, the baking soda, and the salt, add the flour mixture to the chocolate mixture in batches alternately with the milk, stirring, and stir the batter until it is combined well. Stir in the vanilla, pour the batter into the prepared pan, spreading it evenly, and bake the cake in the middle of a preheated 350° F. oven for 12 to 14 minutes, or until it begins to pull away from the sides of the pan and a tester comes out clean. Let the cake cool completely in the pan on a rack.

Chocolate Layer Cake
with Chocolate-Dipped Cherries

For the cake layers
2 cups all-purpose flour
1½ teaspoons baking soda
¾ teaspoon double-acting baking powder
1 teaspoon salt
2 cups sugar
½ stick (¼ cup) unsalted butter, softened
2 large eggs
4 ounces unsweetened chocolate, melted
   and cooled
1 cup sour cream
1 teaspoon vanilla
For the filling
⅔ cup black cherry preserves
2 tablespoons fresh lemon juice
For the chocolate-dipped cherries and the icing
an 8-ounce jar maraschino cherries with
   stems, drained and rinsed

⅓ cup cherry brandy
16 ounces semisweet chocolate, melted
   and cooled
1 cup sour cream at room temperature
½ teaspoon vanilla

Make the cake layers: Into a small bowl sift together the flour, the baking soda, the baking powder, and the salt. In a large bowl with an electric mixer beat together the sugar and the butter until the mixture is light and fluffy, add the eggs, 1 at a time, beating well after each addition, and beat in the chocolate, the sour cream, the vanilla, and ⅔ cup water. Add the flour mixture and beat the batter at high speed for 3 minutes. Line the bottoms of 3 buttered 8-inch round cake pans with rounds of wax paper, butter the rounds, and dust the pans with flour, shaking out the excess. Divide the batter evenly among the pans and bake the layers in the middle of a preheated 350° F. oven for 35 to 40 minutes, or until a cake tester comes out clean. Let the layers cool in the pans on racks for 10 minutes. Run a thin knife around the edge of each pan, invert the layers onto the racks, and let them cool completely.

Make the filling: In a blender or food processor purée the preserves with the lemon juice until the filling is smooth and transfer the filling to a small bowl.

Make the chocolate-dipped cherries and the icing: Arrange the cherries in a small shallow dish, pour the brandy over them, and let the cherries macerate in the freezer for 30 minutes. Drain the cherries, reserving the brandy for another use if desired, and dip them, 1 at a time, into the chocolate, letting the excess drip off. Arrange the dipped cherries stem end up in a pan lined with wax paper and chill them until it is time to decorate the cake. In a bowl beat together the remaining chocolate, the sour cream, a pinch of salt, and the vanilla until the icing is combined well. The icing should be very glossy. If the sour cream is too cold the icing will become too firm; if this happens, beat in 1 to 2 tablespoons hot water to soften the icing.

Assemble the cake: On a cake stand arrange 1 cake layer, spread the top with ⅓ cup of the filling, and top the filling with a second layer. Spread the second layer with the remaining filling and top the filling with the remaining layer. Spread the outside of the cake with the chocolate icing, arrange some of the chocolate-dipped cherries in a circle on top, and serve the remaining cherries separately.

PHOTO ON PAGE 49

Chocolate Raspberry Brownie Torte

2 ounces unsweetened chocolate, chopped
1 stick (½ cup) unsalted butter, cut into pieces
⅔ cup all-purpose flour
¼ teaspoon salt
½ teaspoon double-acting baking powder
2 large eggs
½ cup granulated sugar
½ cup seedless raspberry jam
2 teaspoons *eau-de-vie de framboise*
  (raspberry brandy)
1 ounce semisweet chocolate, chopped
confectioners' sugar for sifting over the torte
chocolate ice cream as an accompaniment
  if desired

In the top of a double boiler set over barely simmering water melt the unsweetened chocolate with the butter, stirring, until the mixture is smooth. In a small bowl combine the flour, the salt, and the baking powder. In a bowl whisk together the eggs, the granulated sugar, the jam, the *eau-de-vie de framboise*, the semisweet chocolate, and the melted chocolate mixture and whisk in the flour mixture. Line a buttered 9-inch round pan with a round of wax paper, butter the paper, and pour the batter into the pan. Bake the torte in a preheated 350° F. oven for 25 to 30 minutes, or until a cake tester inserted in the center comes out with crumbs on it. Let the torte cool in the pan on a rack for 5 minutes, invert it onto the rack, and remove the paper. Invert the torte onto another rack and let it cool top side up. Sift the confectioners' sugar lightly over the torte and serve the torte with the ice cream if desired.

Strawberry Mousse Cake

For the cake
⅓ recipe *génoise* batter (use ⅓ of the ingredients,
  page 252)
⅓ cup rum syrup (recipe follows)
9 or 10 fresh strawberries, trimmed and
  halved lengthwise
strawberry mousse filling (page 211)

about ½ pint fresh strawberries
¼ cup red currant jelly
1 fresh mint sprig

Make the cake: Line the bottom of a buttered 8-inch springform pan with wax paper, butter the paper, and dust the pan with flour, knocking out the excess. Pour the *génoise* batter into the pan, smoothing the top, and bake it in the middle of a preheated 350° F. oven for 20 to 25 minutes, or until the top is golden and a tester comes out clean. Let the cake cool in the pan on a rack for 5 minutes, remove the sides of the pan, and invert the cake onto the rack. Remove the wax paper carefully and let the cake cool completely. *The génoise may be made up to 1 day in advance and kept wrapped in plastic wrap at room temperature.* Halve the cake horizontally with a serrated knife, arrange one half cut side up on a 7-inch cardboard round covered tightly with foil, and brush some of the rum syrup over the cake. Set the cake on the cardboard round on the bottom of the springform pan, wrap a 3-inch-wide doubled sheet of foil tightly around the layer to form a cylindrical collar, and secure the foil with tape. Replace the sides of the pan around the foil and arrange the strawberries around the edge of the cake layer, cut sides flush with the foil collar and pointed ends up.

Pour the strawberry mousse filling over the cake layer and strawberries, smoothing the top, cover it with the remaining cake layer cut side down, and brush the cake with the remaining rum syrup to taste. Chill the cake, covered, for at least 4 hours or overnight. Remove the sides of the pan and the foil collar carefully. Arrange some of the strawberries, trimmed and sliced thin, in a decorative pattern on the cake. In a small saucepan melt the jelly with 1 tablespoon water over low heat, stirring, and brush the glaze over the strawberries, the cake layers, and the mousse. *The cake may be made up to this point 3 hours in advance and kept covered loosely and chilled.* Just before serving transfer the cake from the cardboard to a cake plate, arrange a strawberry, cut almost but not completely through into thin slices, leaving the stem end intact, and fanned open, in the center, and garnish it with the mint sprig. Arrange the remaining strawberries, trimmed and sliced thin, around the edge of the cake plate.

PHOTO ON PAGE 25

Rum Syrup

4 tablespoons sugar
4 tablespoons dark rum

In a small saucepan combine the sugar, 3 tablespoons water, and the rum, bring the mixture to a boil, stirring until the sugar is dissolved, and let the syrup cool to room temperature. The syrup keeps, covered and chilled, indefinitely. Makes about ⅓ cup.

Strawberry Mousse Filling

a 10-ounce package frozen strawberries in syrup, thawed and drained, reserving the syrup
1 envelope unflavored gelatin
2 tablespoons dark rum, or to taste
¾ cup heavy cream

In a food processor purée the strawberries coarse. In a small saucepan sprinkle the gelatin over the reserved strawberry syrup combined with the rum, let it soften for 5 minutes, and heat the mixture over moderately low heat, stirring, until the gelatin is dissolved. With the motor running add the gelatin mixture in a stream to the strawberry purée and blend the mixture until it is combined. Transfer the strawberry mixture to a metal bowl set in a larger bowl of ice and cold water and stir the mixture until it is cold and thickened slightly, but do not let it begin to set. In a chilled bowl beat the cream until it holds soft peaks and fold it into the strawberry mixture. *Do not make the filling in advance.*

Walnut Orange Cake

2 cups sugar
2 sticks (1 cup) unsalted butter, softened
2 large eggs
2 cups all-purpose flour
½ teaspoon salt
1 teaspoon double-acting baking powder
½ teaspoon cinnamon
1 cup sour cream
1 teaspoon vanilla
2 tablespoons orange-flavored liqueur
1¼ cups finely chopped walnuts
1 tablespoon freshly grated orange rind
For garnish
about 2 teaspoons confectioners' sugar
walnut halves
honey for brushing the walnut halves
1 navel orange, peel and pith cut away with a serrated knife and discarded and the orange cut into segments

In a bowl with an electric mixer cream together the sugar and the butter until the mixture is light and fluffy, beat in the eggs, 1 at a time, and beat the mixture until it is combined well. Into a small bowl sift together the flour, the salt, the baking powder, and the cinnamon. In another small bowl stir together the sour cream, the vanilla, and the liqueur. Add the flour mixture and the sour cream mixture alternately to the butter mixture, a little at a time, beating, and beat the batter until it is combined well. Beat in the walnuts and the rind and spoon the batter into a buttered and floured 10-inch (3-quart) Bundt pan. Bake the cake in a preheated 350° F. oven for 1 hour, or until a skewer comes out clean. Let the cake cool in the pan on a rack for 20 minutes, turn it out onto the rack, and let it cool completely.

Transfer the cake to a plate, sift the confectioners' sugar over it lightly, and arrange the walnuts, brushed with the honey, and the orange segments around the cake decoratively.

PHOTO ON PAGE 14

Raspberry Hazelnut Savarin

For the cake
2½ teaspoons (a ¼-ounce package)
    active dry yeast
2 tablespoons sugar
⅓ cup milk
1¼ cups all-purpose flour
⅓ cup finely chopped toasted and skinned
    hazelnuts (procedure follows)
2 large eggs
¼ teaspoon salt
7 tablespoons unsalted butter, cut into 7 pieces
    and softened
For the syrup
½ cup sugar
⅓ cup Frangelico (hazelnut-flavored liqueur)
For the glaze
¼ cup seedless raspberry preserves
2 tablespoons Frangelico
2 tablespoons sugar

½ pint raspberries
3 kiwis, peeled, cut into wedges lengthwise,
    and sliced thin crosswise

Make the cake: In the bowl of an electric mixer proof the yeast with the sugar in the milk, heated to lukewarm, for 5 minutes, or until it is foamy. Stir in ¼ cup of the flour until the mixture is smooth and let the mixture rise, covered, in a warm place for 20 minutes. Add the hazelnuts and beat the mixture until it is combined well. In a small bowl whisk together lightly the eggs and the salt and add the mixture and the remaining 1 cup flour to the yeast mixture alternately in 2 batches, beating well after each addition. Beat in the butter, 1 piece at a time, beating well after each addition, and beat the batter, scraping down the sides of the bowl, for 3 minutes. Spoon the batter into a buttered and floured 1-quart savarin mold or ring mold, smoothing the top, and let it rise, covered with plastic wrap, for 30 minutes, or until it is ½ inch from the top of the mold. Bake the cake in a preheated 350° F. oven for 25 to 30 minutes, or until the top is browned well. Let the cake cool in the mold on a rack for 15 minutes.

Make the syrup: In a small saucepan combine the sugar and 1 cup water, bring the mixture to a boil, stirring until the sugar is dissolved, and simmer it for 3 minutes. Remove the pan from the heat and stir in the Frangelico.

Make the glaze: In a small saucepan combine the preserves, the Frangelico, and the sugar, bring the mixture to a boil, stirring, and simmer it, stirring, for 2 minutes.

Run a thin sharp knife around the center and side of the mold, invert the cake onto the rack, and set the rack over a jelly-roll pan. Spoon the Frangelico syrup, heated, over the cake, reusing the syrup that drips into the pan, until it is all absorbed. Let the cake stand for 15 minutes and brush the raspberry glaze, heated, carefully over it. *The cake may be made and soaked in the Frangelico syrup up to 1 day in advance and kept on the rack over the jelly-roll pan covered with a large bowl. The cake may be brushed with the raspberry glaze up to 1 hour before serving.* Transfer the savarin to a serving dish and decorate it with some of the raspberries and kiwis. In a bowl toss together the remaining raspberries and kiwis and serve the fruit with the savarin. Serves 6 to 8.

PHOTO ON PAGE 38

To Toast and Skin Hazelnuts

Toast the hazelnuts in one layer in a baking pan in a preheated 350° F. oven for 10 to 15 minutes, or until they are colored lightly and the skins blister. Wrap the nuts in a dish towel and let them steam for 1 minute. Rub the nuts in the towel to remove the skins and let them cool.

COOKIES

Almond Chocolate Chip Macaroons

4 ounces sliced or slivered blanched almonds
5 tablespoons sugar
1½ ounces bittersweet or semisweet
    chocolate, chopped very fine
2 large egg whites at room temperature
a pinch of cream of tartar
¼ teaspoon almond extract

In an electric coffee or spice grinder grind the almonds in 3 batches with a total of 3 tablespoons of the sugar until the mixture is very fine, transfer the mixture to a bowl, and stir in the chocolate. In another bowl with an electric mixer beat the egg whites with a pinch of salt until they are frothy, add the cream of tartar, and beat the whites until they hold soft peaks. Beat in the remaining 2 tablespoons sugar gradually, add the almond extract, and beat the whites until they hold stiff, glossy peaks. Stir the whites into the almond mixture, stirring until the batter is combined well, transfer the batter to a pastry bag fitted with a ½-inch star tip, and pipe it into mounds about 1½ inches in diameter and 1 inch apart on a foil-lined baking sheet. Bake the macaroons in a preheated 350° F. oven for 18 to 20 minutes, or until the edges and ridges are just golden, slide the foil off the baking sheet onto a rack, and let the macaroons cool on the foil for 5 minutes. Peel the macaroons gently from the foil and let them cool completely on the rack. *The macaroons may be made up to 2 days in advance and kept in an airtight container.* Makes about 16 macaroons.

PHOTO ON PAGE 43

Apple Cream Cheese Cookies

1 stick (½ cup) unsalted butter, softened
4 ounces cream cheese, softened
½ cup sugar plus additional for sprinkling on
   the dough
1 tablespoon Calvados
1 egg yolk
1¾ cups all-purpose flour
¼ teaspoon double-acting baking powder
¼ teaspoon baking soda
⅛ teaspoon salt, or to taste
½ cup dried apples, chopped fine

In a bowl with an electric mixer cream together the butter, the cream cheese, and ½ cup of the sugar, add the Calvados and the egg yolk, beating, and beat the mixture until it is smooth. Into the bowl sift together the flour, the baking powder, the baking soda, and the salt and combine the mixture well. Add the apples and blend the dough well. On a piece of wax paper form the dough into a log 1½ inches in diameter, using the paper as a guide. Sprinkle the log with the additional sugar, rolling the log to coat it thoroughly. Chill the log, wrapped in the wax paper and foil, for 2 hours. *The dough may be made up to 3 months in advance and kept wrapped well and frozen.* Cut the log into ⅜-inch slices with a sharp knife and bake the cookies 1 inch apart on ungreased baking sheets in a preheated 350° F. oven for 10 to 12 minutes, or until the edges are pale golden. Transfer the cookies with a metal spatula to racks to cool. Makes about 60 cookies.

Apricot Macadamia Snowballs

6 ounces dried apricots
¼ cup apricot jam
1 tablespoon sugar
1 cup macadamia nuts
1 cup packaged sweetened coconut

In a food processor blend the apricots, the jam, the sugar, and the nuts, pulsing the motor, until the mixture forms a mass. Form rounded teaspoons of the mixture into balls and roll the balls in the coconut, pressing the coconut onto them to make it adhere. Chill the "snowballs," covered loosely, for at least 1 hour or overnight. Makes about 20 "snowballs."

PHOTO ON PAGE 79

Brown Sugar Wafers

2 tablespoons unsalted butter, softened
¼ cup firmly packed light brown sugar
1 large egg white at room temperature, beaten
   lightly
5 tablespoons all-purpose flour

In a bowl with an electric mixer cream the butter with the brown sugar until the mixture is light and fluffy, add the egg white a little at a time, beating slowly, and beat the mixture for 5 seconds, or until it is smooth. Sift the flour over the mixture and fold it in thoroughly. Transfer the batter to a pastry bag fitted with a ¼-inch plain tip and pipe 2-inch lengths of it 2 inches apart on lightly greased baking sheets. Bake the wafers in the middle of a preheated 400° F. oven for 4 to 6 minutes, or until the edges are golden. Let the wafers cool on the baking sheets for 30 seconds, transfer them carefully with a metal spatula to racks, and let them cool completely. (If the wafers become too firm to remove from the baking sheets, return them to the oven for about 1 minute to soften.) *The wafers keep in an airtight container for up to 1 week.* Makes about 50 wafers.

PHOTO ON PAGE 55

Chocolate Leaf Cookies and Fruit Kebabs

4½ tablespoons butter, softened
4½ tablespoons sugar
6 tablespoons sliced blanched almonds
1 large egg, beaten lightly
½ teaspoon almond extract
¾ cup sifted all-purpose flour
9 ounces bittersweet chocolate (preferably imported), chopped
fresh fruit kebabs (such as strawberries, pineapple, and kiwi) as an accompaniment

In a bowl with an electric mixer cream the butter, add the sugar, and beat the mixture until it is light and fluffy. Beat in the almonds, the egg, the almond extract, and the flour and beat the dough until it is just combined. Lay a 4¼-inch-long leaf-shaped metal stencil (or homemade heavy cardboard stencil) on a well buttered baking sheet. With a metal spatula spread a heaping tablespoon of the dough over the stencil and press the dough smoothly and evenly through the stencil onto the sheet, scraping off the excess dough. Lift the stencil straight up, leaving the leaf cookie on the sheet, wipe the stencil clean, and make leaves with the remaining dough in the same manner. Bake the cookies in a preheated 300° F. oven for 10 to 15 minutes, or until the edges are just golden, transfer them to a rack, and let them cool completely. In a bowl set over barely simmering water melt the chocolate, stirring, and transfer it to a flat plate. Working with 1 cookie at a time lay one side flat down on the chocolate, coating it, and holding the leaf near its pointed top lift the cookie out of the chocolate at an angle so that the chocolate drips down to the base, forming ridges like the veins of a leaf. Transfer the dipped cookies chocolate side up to a rack set on a baking sheet and chill them for 30 minutes, or until the chocolate is hardened. *The cookies may be made up to 3 days in advance and kept chilled in an airtight container.* Serve the cookies with the fruit kebabs. Makes 24 chocolate leaf cookies.

Double Chocolate Peanut Butter Cookies

1½ sticks (¾ cup) unsalted butter, softened
1 cup sugar
½ cup chunky-style peanut butter
2 large eggs
1 cup all-purpose flour
¾ cup unsweetened cocoa powder
1 teaspoon double-acting baking powder
½ teaspoon baking soda
¼ teaspoon salt
7 ounces semisweet chocolate, chopped coarse

In a bowl with an electric mixer cream together the butter, the sugar, and the peanut butter and beat in the eggs. Into the bowl sift together the flour, the cocoa powder, the baking powder, the baking soda, and the salt and combine the mixture well. Add the chocolate and blend the dough well. On a piece of wax paper form the dough into a log 2 inches in diameter, using the paper as a guide. Chill the log, wrapped in the wax paper and foil, for 2 hours. *The dough may be made up to 3 months in advance and kept wrapped well and frozen.* Cut the log into ¼-inch slices with a sharp knife and bake the cookies 1 inch apart on ungreased baking sheets in a preheated 350° F. oven for 10 to 12 minutes, or until they are just firm to the touch. Transfer the cookies with a metal spatula to racks to cool. Makes about 50 cookies.

Coconut Tuiles

½ stick (¼ cup) unsalted butter, softened
½ cup sugar
2 large egg whites, beaten lightly
3 tablespoons all-purpose flour
about 2 cups sweetened shredded coconut, toasted lightly

In a bowl with an electric mixer cream the butter, add the sugar, and beat the mixture until it is light and fluffy. Add the egg whites gradually, beating slowly, and beat the mixture for 5 seconds, or until it is smooth. Sift the flour over the mixture and fold it in with 1½ cups of the coconut. Spoon rounded teaspoons of the mixture 3 inches apart onto buttered baking sheets, with the back of a fork dipped in cold water flatten them into 2-inch rounds, and sprinkle about ½ teaspoon of the remaining coconut on the center of each round. Bake the rounds in the middle of a preheated 400° F. oven for 6 to 9 minutes, or until the edges are golden. Let the *tuiles* stand on the sheets for 30 seconds, or until they are just firm enough to hold their shape, transfer them with a metal spatula to a rolling pin, and curve them top side up around the pin. (If the *tuiles* become too firm to remove from the baking sheet return them to the oven for a few seconds to soften.) Let the *tuiles* cool completely on racks. *The* tuiles *may be made up to 4 days in advance and kept in airtight containers.* Makes about 40 *tuiles*.

PHOTO ON PAGE 37

Ladyfingers with Mocha Ganache

⅓ cup semisweet chocolate chips
1½ teaspoons instant espresso powder
¼ cup plus 3 tablespoons heavy cream
6 ladyfingers
1 teaspoon coffee beans, crushed fine with a
    rolling pin between sheets of plastic wrap

In a small metal bowl combine the chocolate chips and the espresso powder. In a small saucepan scald 3 tablespoons of the cream, pour it over the chocolate chips, and whisk the mixture until the chocolate is melted. With an electric mixer beat the *ganache* set in a bowl of ice and cold water until it is firm. Spread 1 rounded teaspoon of the *ganache* inside each ladyfinger, arrange 3 filled ladyfingers in spoke patterns on each of 2 dessert plates, and chill them, covered, for 10 minutes. In a small saucepan combine the remaining ¼ cup cream, the remaining *ganache*, and the crushed coffee beans and heat the mixture over moderate heat, whisking, until the *ganache* is melted. Let the mocha *ganache* cool slightly and spoon it around the ladyfingers. Serves 2.

Tangy Lemon Cookies

1½ sticks (¾ cup) unsalted butter, softened
1 cup sugar
1 teaspoon vanilla
1½ tablespoons freshly grated lemon rind
    (about 3 lemons)
¼ cup fresh lemon juice
1½ cups all-purpose flour
1½ teaspoons double-acting baking powder
½ teaspoon baking soda
¼ teaspoon salt
confectioners' sugar for sifting over the cookies

In a bowl with an electric mixer cream together the butter and the sugar, add the vanilla, the rind, and the lemon juice, beating, and beat the mixture until it is smooth. Into the bowl sift together the flour, the baking powder, the baking soda, and the salt and blend the dough well. On a piece of wax paper form the dough into a log 1½ inches in diameter, using the paper as a guide. Chill the log, wrapped in the wax paper and foil, for 2 hours. *The dough may be made up to 3 months in advance and kept wrapped well and frozen.* Cut the log into ⅛-inch slices with a sharp knife and bake the cookies 2 inches apart on ungreased baking sheets in a preheated 350° F. oven for 8 to 10 minutes, or until the edges are just golden. Transfer the cookies with a metal spatula to racks to cool and sift the confectioners' sugar lightly over them. Makes about 50 cookies.

Peanut Butter Chocolate Chip Cookies

½ stick (¼ cup) unsalted butter, softened
¼ cup vegetable shortening
½ cup smooth peanut butter
½ cup granulated sugar
½ cup firmly packed light brown sugar
1 large egg, beaten lightly
1 teaspoon vanilla
1 cup all-purpose flour
½ teaspoon baking soda
¼ teaspoon salt
½ cup finely chopped semisweet chocolate
    (about 2 ounces)
⅓ cup salted roasted peanuts, crushed coarse

In a bowl with an electric mixer cream together the butter, the shortening, and the peanut butter, add the granulated sugar and the brown sugar, and beat the mixture until it is combined well. Beat in the egg and the vanilla, add the flour, the baking soda, and the salt, and blend the dough well. Stir in the chocolate and the peanuts and chill the dough, covered, for 30 minutes. Roll level tablespoons of the dough into balls and arrange the balls 3 inches apart on lightly greased baking sheets. Flatten the balls into 1½-inch rounds with the tines of a fork, forming a crosshatch pattern in the center of each round, and bake the cookies in the middle of a preheated 375° F. oven for 8 to 10 minutes, or until the edges are golden. Let the cookies cool for 2 minutes, transfer them with a metal spatula to racks, and let them cool completely. Transfer the cookies to a portable container. The cookies keep in an airtight container for up to 4 days. Makes about 40 cookies.

PHOTO ON PAGE 50

Pecan Sand Tarts

½ stick (¼ cup) unsalted butter, softened

¼ cup vegetable shortening

⅓ cup confectioners' sugar

1 teaspoon vanilla

1 cup all-purpose flour

½ teaspoon salt

¼ teaspoon double-acting baking powder

½ cup pecan halves, ground fine in a food processor or blender, plus additional pecan halves (about 25) for garnish

1 large egg white, beaten lightly

In a bowl with an electric mixer cream together the butter, the shortening, and the confectioners' sugar until the mixture is combined well and beat in the vanilla. Into the bowl sift together the flour, the salt, and the baking powder and combine the mixture well. Add the ground pecans, blend the dough well, and chill it, wrapped in plastic wrap, for at least 1 hour or overnight.

Roll out the dough ¼ inch thick between sheets of wax paper, with a 1⅛-inch round cutter cut out rounds, and arrange them 2 inches apart on greased baking sheets. (If the dough becomes too soft chill it on a flat surface in the freezer or refrigerator until it is firm enough to work with.) Brush the tops of the rounds with the egg white, put 1 of the pecan halves on each round, and brush the pecans with the egg white. Gather the scraps, reroll the dough, and make more rounds in the same manner. Bake the cookies in the middle of a preheated 325° F. oven for 15 to 20 minutes, or until the tops are pale golden. Let the cookies cool for 2 minutes, transfer them with a metal spatula to racks, and let them cool completely. Transfer the cookies to a portable container. The cookies keep in an airtight container for up to 4 days. Makes about 25 cookies.

PHOTO ON PAGE 50

German Spice Cookies

¼ cup raisins, chopped fine

2 tablespoons dark rum

1½ sticks (¾ cup) unsalted butter, softened

½ cup granulated sugar

¼ cup firmly packed dark brown sugar

¼ cup light cream

2 cups all-purpose flour

½ teaspoon baking soda

½ teaspoon salt

1 teaspoon cinnamon

¾ teaspoon aniseed, ground in a spice grinder

¼ teaspoon ground cloves

2 ounces semisweet chocolate, chopped fine

In a small bowl let the raisins soak in the rum for 15 minutes. In a bowl with an electric mixer cream together the butter, the granulated sugar, and the brown sugar, add the cream, and beat the mixture until it is smooth. Into the bowl sift together the flour, the baking soda, the salt, the cinnamon, the aniseed, and the cloves and blend the mixture well. Add the chocolate and the raisin mixture, blend the dough well, and on a piece of wax paper form it into a log 2 inches in diameter, using the paper as a guide. Chill the log, wrapped in the wax paper and foil, for 2 hours. *The dough may be made up to 3 months in advance and kept wrapped well and frozen.* Cut the roll into 3/16-inch slices with a sharp knife and bake the cookies 1 inch apart on ungreased baking sheets in a preheated 350° F. oven for 10 to 12 minutes, or until they are just firm to the touch. Transfer the cookies with a metal spatula to racks to cool. Makes about 55 cookies.

Shortbread Cookies with Amaretto Cream Filling and Strawberries

⅓ cup all-purpose flour

1 tablespoon cornstarch

1 tablespoon superfine sugar

3 tablespoons cold unsalted butter, cut into bits

For the sauce

½ cup sliced strawberries

1½ teaspoons superfine sugar

½ cup chopped strawberries

1½ teaspoons Amaretto di Saronno

⅓ cup heavy cream

1 tablespoon confectioners' sugar

4 teaspoons sour cream

¼ cup sliced blanched almonds, toasted lightly, reserving 8 toasted almond slices

4 small strawberries, sliced thin lengthwise

In a bowl combine the flour, the cornstarch, and the sugar, blend in the butter until the mixture resembles coarse meal, and form the dough into a ball. Quarter the dough, pat each piece into a 4- by 2½-inch rectangle on a well buttered baking sheet, smoothing the tops and sides with a knife, and bake the shortbread cookies in a preheated 350° F. oven for 13 to 15 minutes, or until the edges are golden. Transfer the cookies to a rack and let them cool to room temperature.

Make the sauce while the cookies are baking: In a blender purée the sliced strawberries with the sugar, scraping down the sides.

In a small bowl combine well the chopped strawberries and 1 teaspoon of the Amaretto. In a chilled bowl beat the heavy cream until it holds soft peaks. Beat in the confectioners' sugar, the sour cream, and the remaining ½ teaspoon Amaretto, beating the mixture until it just holds stiff peaks, and transfer the mixture to a pastry bag fitted with a small decorative tip. (Alternatively, the mixture can be spread onto the cookies.)

Arrange 1 of the cookies on a dessert plate and pipe some of the cream mixture onto it. Spoon half the chopped strawberry mixture carefully over the cream mixture and sprinkle half the almonds over it. Top the almonds with 1 of the remaining cookies and pipe more of the cream mixture decoratively on the cookie. Arrange the sliced strawberries and 4 of the reserved almonds decoratively on the cream mixture and spoon half the sauce around the dessert. Assemble another dessert with the remaining cookies, cream mixture, chopped strawberry mixture, almonds, strawberries, and sauce in the same manner. Serves 2.

oven for 30 minutes, or until it is golden. While the shortbread is still warm, cut it in the pan into 16 wedges and let the shortbread cool completely in the pan. Makes 16 wedges.

J. Oliver

Spiced Shortbread

1 stick (½ cup) unsalted butter, softened
¼ cup plus 1 tablespoon sugar
¼ teaspoon vanilla
1 cup all-purpose flour
¼ teaspoon salt
½ teaspoon ground cardamom
½ teaspoon cinnamon
¼ teaspoon freshly grated nutmeg, or to taste

In a bowl with an electric mixer cream the butter, add ¼ cup of the sugar and the vanilla, and beat the mixture until it is light and fluffy. Into another bowl sift together the flour, the salt, the cardamom, the cinnamon, and the nutmeg and add the mixture to the butter mixture, stirring until the dough is just combined. Pat the dough evenly into an ungreased 9-inch pie pan, prick it all over with a fork, and sprinkle it with the remaining 1 tablespoon sugar. Bake the dough in a preheated 350° F.

Walnut Shortbread Balls

1 stick (½ cup) unsalted butter, softened
¼ cup confectioners' sugar plus additional for dusting the cookies
1 teaspoon vanilla
1 cup all-purpose flour
1 cup walnuts, chopped fine

In a bowl cream the butter, sift in ¼ cup of the sugar, and beat the mixture until it is light and fluffy. Add the vanilla and the flour, blend the mixture well, and stir in the walnuts. Roll rounded teaspoons of the dough into balls and bake them 1 inch apart on lightly buttered baking sheets in a preheated 300° F. oven for 20 minutes, or until they are golden. Transfer the cookies to racks, while they are still warm sift the additional sugar over them, and let them cool. The cookies keep for up to 2 weeks in an airtight container. Makes about 40 cookies.

Sugar Cookies

⅓ cup vegetable shortening, softened
⅓ cup sugar plus additional for sprinkling
   the cookies
1 large whole egg, beaten lightly
1 teaspoon vanilla
1 cup all-purpose flour
1 teaspoon double-acting baking powder
½ teaspoon salt
1 large egg white

In a bowl stir together the shortening and ⅓ cup of the sugar, stir in the whole egg and the vanilla, and combine the mixture well. Sift in the flour with the baking powder and the salt and combine the dough well. Halve the dough, flatten it slightly, and chill it between sheets of wax paper for 30 minutes. Working with one half at a time, roll out the dough ⅛ inch thick between sheets of wax paper. Remove the top sheet of wax paper and with a 2- to 2½-inch fluted cutter cut the dough into cookies, but do not remove the cookies or the dough scraps from the paper. Chill the dough on the paper for 30 minutes, remove the dough scraps, reserving them, and transfer the cookies carefully to a baking sheet. Make cookies with the reserved dough scraps in the same manner. Brush the cookies lightly with the egg white, beaten lightly, sprinkle them with the additional sugar, and bake them in a preheated 375° F. oven for 10 to 12 minutes, or until the edges are pale golden. Transfer the cookies with a metal spatula to racks and let them cool. The cookies keep, separated by sheets of wax paper, in an airtight container for several days. Makes about 30 cookies.

PIES, TARTS, AND PASTRIES

Apple Cheddar Tart

For the shell
Cheddar pastry dough (recipe follows)
raw rice for weighting the shell
For the filling
1½ pounds (about 3) Golden Delicious apples
2 ounces sharp Cheddar, grated fine
   (about ¾ cup)
⅓ cup sugar
¾ teaspoon freshly grated lemon rind

½ stick (¼ cup) cold unsalted butter,
   sliced thin

2 tablespoons apple jelly

Make the shell: Roll out the dough ⅛ inch thick on a lightly floured surface, fit it into a tart pan with a removable fluted rim, 10½ inches across the bottom and 1 inch deep, and trim the edge level with the rim. Fold the edge of the dough over onto itself to form a side half as high as the rim of the pan, prick the shell lightly with a fork, and chill it for 30 minutes or freeze it for 15 minutes. Line the shell with foil, fill the foil with the rice, and bake the shell in the lower third of a preheated 425° F. oven for 15 minutes. Remove the rice and foil carefully, bake the shell for 5 to 7 minutes more, or until it is golden, and let it cool in the pan on a rack.

Make the filling: Peel and halve the apples lengthwise, core them with a melon-ball cutter, and slice them very thin crosswise. Sprinkle the Cheddar evenly over the bottom of the shell and on it arrange the apple slices decoratively, overlapping them closely. Sprinkle the apples evenly with the sugar and the rind and cover them with the butter.

Bake the tart in the middle of a preheated 375° F. oven for 45 minutes, cover it with foil, and bake it for 15 minutes more, or until the apples are tender. Transfer the tart in the pan to a rack. In a small saucepan melt the apple jelly over moderate heat, stirring, and brush it over the apples while the tart is still warm. Serve the tart warm or at room temperature.

Cheddar Pastry Dough

1¼ cups all-purpose flour plus additional for
   dusting the dough
¾ stick (6 tablespoons) cold unsalted butter,
   cut into bits
1 tablespoon cold vegetable shortening
¼ teaspoon salt
2 ounces sharp Cheddar, grated fine
   (about ¾ cup)
1 tablespoon cider vinegar

In a large bowl blend 1¼ cups of the flour, the butter, the shortening, and the salt until the mixture resembles meal and toss the mixture with the Cheddar, the vinegar, and 2 to 3 tablespoons ice water, or enough to form a dough. Knead the dough lightly with the heel of the hand against a smooth surface, distributing the fat evenly, for a few seconds and form it into a ball. Dust the dough with the additional flour, flatten it slightly, and chill it, wrapped in wax paper, for at least 1 hour or overnight.

Chocolate Coconut Phyllo Triangles with Vanilla Ice Cream

4 ounces semisweet chocolate, chopped
¼ cup sweetened grated coconut, toasted lightly
¼ cup blanched almonds, toasted lightly
1 stick (½ cup) unsalted butter, softened
6 sheets of *phyllo*, halved crosswise, stacked between 2 sheets of wax paper, and covered with a dampened kitchen towel
vanilla ice cream as an accompaniment

In a food processor chop the chocolate fine, add the coconut, the almonds, and ½ stick of the butter, and blend the mixture until it is smooth. In a small saucepan melt the remaining ½ stick butter. Working with 1 strip of *phyllo* at a time, arrange it on a work surface with a short side facing you and brush it lightly with some of the butter. Put a heaping tablespoon of the chocolate mixture in the upper right-hand corner of the strip, fold the *phyllo* in half lengthwise, covering the filling, and brush it lightly with some of the butter. Fold down the top righthand corner of the *phyllo* to form a triangle and continue to fold the triangle over onto itself, maintaining the triangular shape, until the *phyllo* strip is wrapped completely around the filling. Brush the triangle with some of the remaining butter and transfer it to a baking sheet. Form 11 more triangles with the remaining *phyllo* and filling in the same manner. *The triangles may be prepared up to this point 2 weeks in advance and kept wrapped well and frozen.* Bake the triangles in a preheated 400° F. oven for 8 to 12 minutes, or until they are golden, and serve them hot with the ice cream. Makes 12 triangles, serving 6.

Chocolate Dacquoise

For the meringue layers
3 ounces blanched whole almonds, toasted lightly and cooled
2 teaspoons cornstarch
1¼ cups plus 1 tablespoon sugar
6 large egg whites at room temperature

⅛ teaspoon salt
¼ teaspoon cream of tartar
For the filling
¼ cup unsweetened cocoa powder
2 tablespoons sugar
1 cup well chilled heavy cream
For the buttercream
⅔ cup sugar
¼ cup unsweetened cocoa powder
6 large egg yolks at room temperature
1½ sticks (¾ cup) unsalted butter, softened

about 2 tablespoons silver dragées (available at specialty foods shops and many supermarkets) for garnish
½ cup lightly ground toasted almonds
unsprayed holly sprigs for garnish if desired

Line 2 baking sheets with foil, trace two 11- by 3¾-inch rectangles on each sheet of foil, and oil them lightly.

Make the meringue layers: In a food processor grind together fine the almonds, the cornstarch, and 1 tablespoon of the sugar, being careful not to grind the mixture to a paste, transfer the mixture to a bowl, and stir in ½ cup of the remaining sugar. In a large bowl beat the egg whites with the salt until they are frothy, add the cream of tartar, and beat the whites until they hold soft peaks. Add the remaining ¾ cup sugar, a little at a time, beating, beat the meringue until it holds stiff glossy peaks, and fold in the nut mixture. Transfer the meringue mixture to a pastry bag fitted with a ½-inch plain tip and pipe it onto the prepared foil, filling in the rectangles. Smooth the tops and bake the meringues in a preheated 250° F. oven, turning the baking sheets around after 30 minutes, for 1 hour to 1 hour and 15 minutes, or until they are dry. Invert the meringues onto racks, peel off the foil carefully, and let the meringues cool. Trim the meringues with a small sharp knife so that the edges are even and reserve the trimmings. *The meringues may be made up to 1 day in advance and kept in an airtight container.*

Make the filling: In a bowl stir together the cocoa powder, the sugar, and the cream and chill the filling, covered, stirring occasionally, for 30 minutes.

Beat the filling until it just holds stiff peaks and spread one third of it on one of the meringue layers. Top the filling with a second meringue layer, spread one half of the remaining filling on the meringue, and top the filling with a third meringue layer. Spread the remaining filling on the meringue layer and top it with the remaining meringue layer, smooth side up. Keep the cake covered and chilled.

Make the buttercream: In a small saucepan combine the sugar and the cocoa powder with ⅓ cup water, bring the mixture to a boil, covered, stirring occasionally to dissolve the sugar, and boil the syrup, uncovered and undisturbed, until a candy thermometer registers 238° F. (tilt the pan so that the thermometer can register). While the syrup is cooking, in a bowl with an electric mixer beat the egg yolks until they are thick and pale. Add the syrup to the yolks in a stream, beating constantly, and beat the mixture until it is cooled to room temperature. Beat in the butter, 1 tablespoon at a time, adding each new tablespoon after the previous one has been absorbed completely, and beat the buttercream until it is fluffy.

Spread the buttercream on the top and sides of the cake and arrange the dragées decoratively on the top. Crumble the reserved meringue trimmings, combine them with the almonds, and pat the mixture gently onto the sides of the cake. Chill the *dacquoise*, covered loosely, for at least 4 hours and up to 1 day. Let the *dacquoise* stand at room temperature for 20 minutes before serving and garnish it with the holly if desired.

PHOTO ON PAGE 79

Coffee Dacquoise Hearts

For the meringue
27 hazelnuts, toasted and skinned
  (procedure on page 212)
1 teaspoon cornstarch
¾ cup plus 1 teaspoon sugar
3 large egg whites at room temperature
a pinch of cream of tartar
For the buttercream
¼ cup sugar
2 teaspoons instant espresso powder
2 large egg yolks at room temperature
¾ stick (6 tablespoons) unsalted butter,
  softened

27 hazelnuts, toasted and skinned and
  chopped

Cover a baking sheet with foil, with a 3½-inch-wide heart-shaped cutter (or a 3½-inch-wide heart-shaped cardboard template) as a guide trace 6 heart shapes on the foil, and oil them lightly.

Make the meringue: In a spice grinder or blender grind together fine the hazelnuts, the cornstarch, and 1 teaspoon of the sugar, being careful not to grind the mixture to a paste, transfer the mixture to a bowl, and stir in ¼ cup of the remaining sugar. In a large bowl beat the egg whites with a pinch of salt until they are frothy, add the cream of tartar, and beat the whites until they hold soft peaks. Add the remaining ½ cup sugar, a little at a time, beating, beat the whites until they hold stiff glossy peaks, and fold in the nut mixture. Fill a pastry bag fitted with a ⅜-inch plain tip with the meringue mixture and in the traced heart areas pipe out 4 solid hearts and 2 hearts with a heart-shaped space in the center (make drop-shaped meringue cookies with the extra meringue if desired). Bake the meringues in a preheated 250° F. oven, turning the baking sheet around after 30 minutes, for 1 hour to 1 hour and 15 minutes, or until they are dry. Peel off the foil carefully and transfer the meringues to a rack. *The meringues may be made 1 day in advance and kept in an airtight container.*

Make the buttercream: In a very small saucepan combine the sugar and the espresso powder with 2 tablespoons water, bring the mixture to a boil, covered, stirring occasionally to dissolve the sugar, and boil the syrup, uncovered, until a candy thermometer registers 238° F. (tilt the pan so the thermometer can register). While the syrup is cooking, in a bowl with an electric mixer beat the egg yolks until they are thick and pale. Add the syrup to the yolks in a stream, beating constantly, and beat the mixture until it is cooled to room temperature. Beat in the butter, 1 tablespoon at a time, adding each new tablespoon after the previous one has been absorbed completely, and beat the buttercream until it is light and fluffy.

Spread about 1 tablespoon of the buttercream evenly on 1 of the solid meringue hearts, top it with another solid heart, and spread the top heart with about 1 tablespoon of the remaining buttercream. Top the last layer of buttercream with 1 of the open hearts, spread about 1 tablespoon of the remaining buttercream around the sides of the *dacquoise* heart, and sprinkle the sides with 1 tablespoon of the chopped hazelnuts. Make another *dacquoise* heart in the same manner with the remaining ingredients and chill the *dacquoise* hearts for at least 30 minutes or up to 4 hours. Let the hearts stand at room temperature for 15 minutes before serving. Serves 2.

PHOTO ON PAGE 18

Cranberry Tart with Rum Cream and Chocolate

For the shell
cream cheese pastry dough (recipe follows)
raw rice for weighting the shell
an egg wash, made by beating 1 large egg
    with 1 teaspoon water
For the filling
⅓ cup semisweet chocolate chips
1 cup rum pastry cream (recipe this page)
2½ teaspoons unflavored gelatin
⅔ cup sugar
2½ cups cranberries, picked over

Make the shell: Roll out the dough ⅛ inch thick on a lightly floured surface and fit it into a scallop-edged 10½-inch-diameter flan form set on a baking sheet or a tart pan with a removable fluted rim measuring 9½ inches across the bottom, leaving a ¾-inch overhang. Fold the overhang inward onto the side of the shell and press it firmly against the flan form. Crimp the edge decoratively, prick the bottom lightly with a fork, and chill the shell for 30 minutes or freeze it for 15 minutes. Gather the scraps of dough into a ball, flatten the dough slightly, and chill it, wrapped in wax paper, for 30 minutes. Line the shell with foil, fill the foil with the rice, and bake the shell in the lower third of a preheated 425° F. oven for 12 minutes. Remove the rice and foil carefully and bake the shell for 5 to 7 minutes more, or until it is golden. Let the shell cool completely in the flan form on the baking sheet and transfer it to a serving plate.

While the shell is baking roll out the remaining dough ⅛ inch thick on a lightly floured surface, cut out eighteen 1¼- to 1½-inch-long leaves, and chill or freeze them on a flat surface for 5 to 10 minutes, or until they are firm. Score the leaves decoratively with a knife and arrange them, overlapping, pressing them together lightly, in a 4-inch circle on an ungreased baking sheet. Brush the leaf decoration with the egg wash, bake it in the preheated 425° F. oven for 8 to 10 minutes, or until it is golden, and let it cool completely on the baking sheet.

Make the filling: Spread the chocolate, melted, in the bottom of the shell and chill the shell for 15 minutes. Spread the pastry cream evenly over the chocolate and chill the tart, covered loosely with plastic wrap. In a metal bowl sprinkle the gelatin over 3 tablespoons cold water and let it soften for 5 minutes. In a saucepan combine the sugar and ½ cup water, bring the mixture to a boil, stirring until the sugar is dissolved, and add the cranberries. Bring the mixture to a boil and simmer it

for 1 minute. Pour the mixture over the gelatin mixture, stir the mixture until the gelatin is dissolved, and set the bowl in a larger bowl of ice and cold water. Let the cranberry mixture stand, stirring occasionally, until it is cool to the touch and thickened slightly and spoon it over the pastry cream.

Chill the tart for 2 hours, or until the filling is set. *The tart may be made 1 day in advance and kept covered loosely with foil and chilled after the filling is set.* Garnish the tart with the leaf decoration and let it stand at room temperature for at least 30 minutes before serving.

PHOTO ON PAGE 73

Cream Cheese Pastry Dough

¾ stick (6 tablespoons) cold unsalted butter,
    cut into bits
4 ounces cold cream cheese, cut into bits
1 cup all-purpose flour
½ teaspoon salt

In a food processor blend the butter, the cream cheese, the flour, and the salt, pulsing the motor, until it just begins to form a ball, form the dough into a ball, and flatten it slightly. Dust the dough with flour and chill it, wrapped in plastic wrap, for 1 hour. *The dough may be made 1 day in advance and kept wrapped well and chilled.*

PHOTO ON PAGE 73

Rum Pastry Cream

2 large egg yolks
¼ cup sugar
1½ tablespoons all-purpose flour
1½ tablespoons cornstarch
⅔ cup milk
1 tablespoon softened unsalted butter
1½ tablespoons dark rum, or to taste

In a heatproof bowl whisk together well the egg yolks, the sugar, the flour, and the cornstarch and add the milk, scalded, in a stream, whisking. In a saucepan bring the custard to a boil over moderate heat, whisking constantly, remove the pan from the heat, and add the butter and the rum, stirring until the butter is incorporated. Force the pastry cream through a fine sieve into a bowl, lay a round of buttered wax paper on it, and chill it, covered, for 1 hour, or until it is cold. *The pastry cream may be made 2 days in advance and kept covered and chilled.* Makes about 1 cup.

PHOTO ON PAGE 73

Fruit and Pecan Caramel Tartlets

For the shells
8 graham crackers (5 by 2½ inches each),
   broken into pieces
1 cup pecans
¼ cup sugar
¼ teaspoon salt
½ stick (¼ cup) unsalted butter, cut into pieces
   and softened
For the filling
1 cup dried apricots, chopped coarse
⅓ cup golden raisins
½ cup pitted prunes, chopped coarse
⅓ cup dried currants
½ cup cranberries, picked over
½ cup pecans, chopped coarse
For the caramel
1 cup sugar
1 tablespoon unsalted butter
½ cup heavy cream at room temperature

whipped cream or ice cream as an
   accompaniment if desired

Make the shells: In a food processor grind fine the graham crackers and the pecans with the sugar and the salt, add the butter, and blend the mixture until it is combined well. Divide the mixture among six 4½-inch fluted tartlet tins with removable rims, press it evenly into the bottom and sides, and bake the shells on a baking sheet in a preheated 350° F. oven for 10 to 12 minutes, or until they are colored lightly. Let the shells cool completely in the tins on racks.

Make the filling: In a bowl toss together the apricots, the raisins, the prunes, the currants, the cranberries, and the pecans and divide the filling among the shells.

Make the caramel: In a heavy skillet cook the sugar over moderately high heat, stirring constantly with a fork, until it is melted completely and a golden caramel, remove the skillet from the heat, and swirl in the butter. Add the cream, stirring, (the mixture will spatter and seize up slightly) and cook the caramel over moderate heat, stirring, until it is smooth.

Drizzle the tartlets with the caramel and chill them, covered, for at least 30 minutes or overnight. Loosen the shells with the tip of a paring knife, remove the rims, and slide the tartlets onto dessert plates. Serve the tartlets with the whipped cream or ice cream if desired. Makes 6 tartlets.

Lime Curd Tartlets with Fresh Fruit

1 stick (½ cup) unsalted butter, cut into bits
½ cup sugar
2 tablespoons freshly grated lime rind
⅓ cup fresh lime juice
2 large eggs, beaten lightly
pâte brisée (recipe follows)
fresh fruit such as raspberries, melons,
   nectarines, plums, and grapes, sliced if
   necessary, for garnish

In a small heavy saucepan combine the butter, the sugar, the rind, the lime juice, and the eggs and cook the mixture over moderately low heat, stirring, until the curd is thick enough to coat the back of a wooden spoon, but do not let it boil. Transfer the curd to a bowl, let it cool, covered with a buttered round of wax paper, and chill it for 1 hour. *The curd may be made up to 2 days in advance and kept covered and chilled.*

Roll out the *pâte brisée* ⅛ inch thick on a lightly floured surface and cut and fit the dough into sixteen 4¼-inch-long *barquette* molds. Prick the shells lightly with a fork and chill them for 1 hour. Line the shells with foil and bake them on a baking sheet in the lower third of a preheated 425° F. oven for 15 minutes. Remove the foil and bake the shells for 3 to 5 minutes more, or until they are just golden. Remove the shells from the molds and let them cool on a rack. Fill each shell with about 1 tablespoon of the curd and garnish the tartlets with the fruit. Makes 16 tartlets.

PHOTO ON PAGE 43

Pâte Brisée

1¼ cups all-purpose flour
¾ stick (6 tablespoons) cold unsalted butter,
   cut into bits
2 tablespoons cold vegetable shortening
¼ teaspoon salt

In a large bowl blend the flour, the butter, the vegetable shortening, and the salt until the mixture resembles meal. Add 3 tablespoons ice water, toss the mixture until the water is incorporated, and form the dough into a ball. Knead the dough lightly with the heel of the hand against a smooth surface for a few seconds to distribute the fat evenly and re-form it into a ball. Dust the dough with flour and chill it, wrapped in wax paper, for 1 hour.

Gingered Pear Sour Cream Pie

For the shell
pâte brisée (page 222)
raw rice for weighting the shell
For the streusel
¼ cup all-purpose flour
½ stick (¼ cup) cold unsalted butter,
　　cut into bits
3 tablespoons firmly packed
　　light brown sugar
½ teaspoon ground ginger
1 cup walnuts, chopped fine
For the filling
¾ cup sour cream
2 large eggs, beaten lightly
½ cup firmly packed light brown sugar
2 tablespoons all-purpose flour
1½ teaspoons ground ginger
1½ teaspoons fresh lemon juice
1½ pounds pears

Make the shell: Roll out the dough ⅛ inch thick on a lightly floured surface, fit it into a 9-inch (1-quart) pie pan, 1½ inches deep, and crimp the edge decoratively. Prick the shell lightly with a fork and chill it for 30 minutes or freeze it for 15 minutes. Line the shell with foil, fill the foil with the rice, and bake the shell in the lower third of a pre-heated 425° F. oven for 18 minutes. Remove the rice and foil carefully, bake the shell for 5 minutes more, or until it is golden, and let the shell cool in the pan on a rack.

Make the streusel: In a bowl blend the flour, the butter, the brown sugar, the ginger, and a pinch of salt until the mixture resembles very coarse meal, add the walnuts, and toss the mixture well.

Make the filling: In a large bowl whisk together the sour cream, the eggs, the brown sugar, the flour, the ginger, and the lemon juice until the mixture is smooth, stir in the pears, peeled, cored, and sliced thin, coating them with the mixture, and transfer the filling to the shell.

Sprinkle the streusel evenly over the filling, covering it completely, and bake the pie in the middle of a pre-heated 425° F. oven for 15 minutes. Reduce the oven temperature to 350° F. and continue to bake the pie for 30 minutes more, or until the top of it is puffed and golden. Let the pie cool in the pan on a rack. Serve the ginger pear sour cream pie while it is still warm or at room temperature.

Pear Mincemeat Tartlets with Lemon Hard Sauce

For the tartlets
cream cheese pastry dough (page 221)
about 1½ cups pear mincemeat
　　(recipe follows)
For the hard sauce
3 tablespoons unsalted butter, softened
½ cup confectioners' sugar
¼ teaspoon finely grated fresh lemon rind
Special equipment needed
16 miniature brioche molds measuring 2½
　　inches across the top (available at
　　kitchenware shops and by mail order from
　　Bridge Kitchenware Corporation, 214 East
　　52nd Street, New York, New York 10022)

Make the tartlets: Roll tablespoons of the dough into 16 balls, set 1 ball in each miniature brioche mold, and press the dough evenly into the bottom and up the sides of the molds. Set the molds in a jelly-roll pan and chill them for 30 minutes or freeze them for 15 minutes. Fill the shells with the mincemeat, mounding it slightly, and bake the tartlets in the middle of a preheated 425° F. oven for 20 to 25 minutes, or until the pastry is golden. Let the tartlets cool in the molds on racks for 10 minutes and remove them from the molds. *The tartlets may be made 1 day in advance and kept in one layer in airtight containers at room temperature.*

Make the hard sauce: In a small bowl cream the butter with the sugar, sifted, until the mixture is light and fluffy and blend in the lemon rind. With a pastry bag fitted with a small plain tip or with a small spoon put a dollop of the hard sauce on each tartlet. Makes 16 tartlets.

PHOTO ON PAGE 73

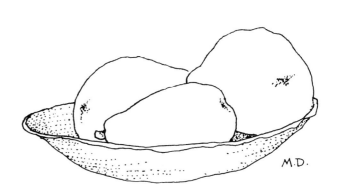

Pear Mincemeat

2 firm pears (about 1 pound)
1 tablespoon fresh lemon juice
¼ navel orange including the rind and pith, cut
    into 1-inch pieces
¼ cup golden raisins
3 tablespoons dried currants
⅓ cup firmly packed light brown sugar
¼ teaspoon cinnamon
¼ teaspoon allspice
⅛ teaspoon mace or freshly grated nutmeg
½ cup walnuts, toasted lightly
    and chopped fine
2 tablespoons brandy, or to taste

Peel, quarter, and core the pears, toss them with the lemon juice, and in a food processor chop them coarse with the orange. In a heavy saucepan combine the pear mixture with the raisins, the currants, the brown sugar, the cinnamon, the allspice, the mace, and 1 cup water, bring the mixture to a boil, stirring, and simmer it, stirring occasionally, for 40 to 50 minutes, or until it is thick. Stir in the walnuts and the brandy, transfer the mixture to a bowl, and let it cool. *The mincemeat may be used immediately but it will improve in flavor if allowed to stand, covered and chilled, for at least 1 day and up to 2 weeks*. Makes about 2 cups.

PHOTO ON PAGE 73

Plum Almond Tart

For the shell
pâte brisée (page 222)
raw rice for weighting the shell
For the filling
½ cup blanched whole almonds
1 tablespoon all-purpose flour
½ stick (¼ cup) unsalted butter,
    softened
3 tablespoons sugar
1 large egg, beaten lightly
¼ teaspoon almond extract
¼ teaspoon salt

½ pound firm red or purple plums, quartered,
    pitted, and sliced thin
about 1 tablespoon melted unsalted butter
2 tablespoons sugar

Make the shell: Roll out the dough ⅛ inch thick on a floured surface, fit it into a 10-inch tart pan with a removable fluted rim, and prick the shell lightly with a fork. Chill the shell for 30 minutes, line it with foil, and fill the foil with the rice. Bake the shell in the lower third of a preheated 425° F. oven for 15 minutes, remove the rice and foil carefully, and bake the shell for 5 to 8 minutes more, or until it is golden. Let the shell cool completely in the pan on a rack.

Make the filling: In a food processor grind fine the almonds with the flour and transfer the mixture to a bowl. In the food processor blend the butter and the sugar until the mixture is smooth, add the egg, the almond extract, and the salt, and blend the mixture well. Add the almond mixture and blend the filling until it is just combined. Spread the almond filling evenly in the cooled tart shell.

Arrange the plum slices decoratively over the almond filling, overlapping them slightly, brush them lightly with the butter, and sprinkle them evenly with the sugar. Bake the tart in the middle of a preheated 375° F. oven for 40 minutes. Let the tart cool in the pan on a rack for 15 minutes. Remove the rim and transfer the tart carefully to a serving plate. Serve the tart warm or at room temperature.

Raspberry Almond Tuile Tortes

⅓ cup well chilled heavy cream
½ teaspoon *eau-de-vie de framboise*
    (raspberry brandy) or vanilla
½ teaspoon sugar
6 flat almond *tuiles*
    (recipe follows)
½ pint raspberries

In a chilled bowl beat the cream with the *eau-de-vie de framboise* and the sugar until it holds stiff peaks and transfer the mixture to a pastry bag fitted with a small fluted tip. Put 1 almond *tuile* on each of 2 dessert plates and cover it with some of the raspberries interspersed with rosettes of the whipped cream. Top the filling with another *tuile* and cover the *tuile* with another layer of raspberries and whipped cream rosettes. Cover the filling with the remaining *tuiles* and top each dessert with 3 raspberries surrounding a rosette of whipped cream. Serves 2.

PHOTO ON PAGE 55

Flat Almond Tuiles

¼ cup sugar
1½ tablespoons unsalted butter
1 tablespoon honey
1½ tablespoons heavy cream
⅛ teaspoon almond extract
1 tablespoon all-purpose flour
⅓ cup sliced almonds

In a small heavy saucepan combine the sugar, the butter, the honey, and the cream, bring the mixture to a boil over moderate heat, stirring, and boil it, stirring, for 5 minutes. Remove the pan from the heat, stir in the almond extract, the flour, and the almonds, and let the mixture cool for 3 minutes. (The mixture will thicken and harden as it cools. If it becomes too firm to work with reheat it over moderately low heat, stirring.) Spoon rounded teaspoons of the mixture 3 inches apart onto baking sheets lined with parchment paper and bake the *tuiles* in the middle of a preheated 400° F. oven for 5 to 8 minutes, or until they are golden brown. Slide the parchment paper with the *tuiles* onto a rack and let the *tuiles* cool completely before peeling them carefully from the paper. *The tuiles may be made up to 2 days in advance and kept in an airtight container.* Makes about 15 *tuiles*.

PHOTO ON PAGE 55

Walnut Crust with Pastry Cream and Apricots

1 cup all-purpose flour
¾ cup walnut pieces
¾ stick (6 tablespoons) cold unsalted butter,
    cut into bits
½ teaspoon cinnamon
½ teaspoon vanilla
1 cup pastry cream (page 255)
a 17-ounce can apricot halves packed in
    syrup, drained and patted dry
½ cup apricot glaze (recipe follows)
⅓ cup walnuts, chopped fine and toasted
    lightly

In a food processor blend the flour, the walnut pieces, the butter, the cinnamon, and the vanilla until the mixture just forms a ball. Pat the mixture evenly into a 9-inch tart pan with a removable fluted rim, prick the bottom of the shell lightly, and freeze the shell for 15 minutes, or until it is firm. Bake the shell in a pre-heated 375° F. oven for 20 minutes, or until it is browned lightly, and let it cool in the pan on a rack. Remove the fluted rim, put the shell on a serving dish, and spread the pastry cream in it. Arrange the apricots cut side down on the pastry cream, brush them with the glaze, and sprinkle the chopped walnuts on top.

Apricot Glaze

½ cup apricot preserves, strained
1 tablespoon Cognac

In a saucepan combine the preserves and the Cognac, bring the mixture to a boil, and simmer it, stirring, for 1 minute. Makes ½ cup.

PUDDINGS AND CUSTARDS

Bread Pudding with Pineapple and Pecans

1 large egg
¼ cup granulated sugar
1 cup milk
⅓ cup pecans, chopped coarse and toasted
    lightly
½ cup drained canned chunk pineapple
2 tablespoons raisins
3 cups torn homemade-type white bread
1½ tablespoons unsalted butter, cut into bits
¼ cup well chilled heavy cream
2 tablespoons confectioners' sugar
½ teaspoon dark rum

In a bowl whisk together the egg, the granulated sugar, and the milk, stir in the pecans, the pineapple, the raisins, and the bread, and stir the mixture until the bread has absorbed most of the milk mixture. Transfer the bread mixture to a 10-inch (2-cup) gratin dish, dot it with the butter, and bake it in a preheated 375° F. oven for 20 to 25 minutes, or until it is golden. While the pudding is baking, in a small bowl whisk the cream until it is thickened, add the confectioners' sugar and the rum, and whisk the sauce until it makes a slightly rounded shape when dropped from the whisk. Serve the pudding warm or at room temperature with the sauce. Serves 2.

Plum and Mango Bread Pudding

12 slices of homemade-type white bread, crusts removed
½ stick (¼ cup) unsalted butter, melted, plus additional melted butter for brushing the fruit
3 plums, pitted and sliced thin lengthwise
1 mango, peeled, the flesh cut from the pit in 2 thick slices and sliced thin crosswise
1½ cups milk
½ cup heavy cream
¼ cup granulated sugar
½ vanilla bean, slit lengthwise, or 1 teaspoon vanilla extract
3 large egg yolks
3 large whole eggs
confectioners' sugar for sprinkling the pudding
maple syrup as an accompaniment

Brush one side of the bread slices lightly with ½ stick of the melted butter and halve the bread diagonally. Toast the bread buttered side up on a baking sheet in a preheated 400° F. oven for 8 minutes, or until the edges are just golden. Reserving about 16 plum slices, spread the remaining plum slices on the bottom of a buttered 14-inch gratin dish, top them with alternating toast slices, the reserved plum slices, and the mango slices, and brush the fruit with the additional melted butter.

In a saucepan combine the milk, the cream, the granulated sugar, and the vanilla bean or the vanilla extract and heat the mixture over moderate heat, stirring, until the sugar is dissolved and the liquid is hot. Remove the vanilla bean if used and scrape the seeds into the milk mixture, reserving the vanilla bean for another use. In a large bowl whisk together the egg yolks and the whole eggs until they are combined, add the milk mixture in a stream, whisking, and whisk the mixture until it is just combined. Pour the mixture carefully over the bread and fruit, put the dish in a baking pan, and add enough hot water to the pan to reach halfway up the sides of the dish. Bake the pudding in a preheated 350° F. oven for 20 to 30 minutes, or until the custard is just set, sprinkle the top with the confectioners' sugar, and serve the bread pudding with the maple syrup. Serves 6.

Ginger Custards with Cinnamon-Sugar Tortillas

5½ teaspoons sugar
½ teaspoon ground ginger
¾ cup heavy cream
2 large egg yolks, beaten lightly
¼ teaspoon cinnamon
vegetable oil for frying
two 4-inch flour tortillas, cut from two 8-inch tortillas

In a bowl stir together 4½ teaspoons of the sugar and the ginger until the mixture is combined well, add the cream and the egg yolks, and stir the mixture until it is combined. Divide the mixture between 2 buttered ¾-cup ramekins and steam the custards, covered with 1 large round of wax paper, on a steamer set over boiling water for 10 to 12 minutes, or until a knife inserted in the center comes out clean. Let the custards cool on a rack for 3 minutes and chill them in a shallow pan of ice and water for 10 to 15 minutes, or until they are cool.

In a small bowl combine well the remaining 1 teaspoon sugar and the cinnamon. In a large skillet heat ½ inch of the oil over moderately high heat until it is hot but not smoking and in it fry the tortillas, turning them once, for 50 seconds to 1 minute, or until they are golden. Transfer the tortillas to paper towels to drain, sprinkle them with the cinnamon sugar, and transfer them to 2 plates. Run a thin knife around the edges of the custards and unmold them onto the tortillas. Serves 2.

Kahlúa Coffee Jelly with Cinnamon Cream

For the jelly
2 teaspoons unflavored gelatin
¾ cup hot strong coffee
1½ tablespoons sugar
3 tablespoons Kahlúa
For the cinnamon cream
¼ cup well chilled heavy cream
1 teaspoon honey
⅛ teaspoon cinnamon

2 candied violets (available at specialty foods shops) for garnish if desired

Make the jelly: In a small saucepan let the gelatin soften in 2 tablespoons water for 5 minutes, heat the mixture over low heat, stirring, until the gelatin is dissolved, and remove the pan from the heat. In a metal bowl combine the coffee and the sugar, stirring until the sugar is dissolved, and stir in the Kahlúa and the gelatin mixture. Set the bowl in a larger bowl of ice and cold water and stir the mixture occasionally until it is the consistency of raw egg white. Pour ¼ cup of the jelly into each of 2 stemmed glasses and chill it, covered, for 20 minutes.

Beat the remaining coffee jelly with an electric mixer until it is pale and frothy, spoon it into the glasses, and chill it, covered, for 2 hours, or until it is set. *The coffee jelly may be made up to 2 days in advance and kept covered and chilled.*

Make the cinnamon cream: In a chilled small bowl beat the cream with the honey and the cinnamon until it just holds soft peaks.

Spoon dollops of the cinnamon cream onto the jelly and garnish each dessert with a candied violet if desired. Serves 2.

PHOTO ON PAGE 55

FROZEN DESSERTS

Espresso Tortoni with Chocolate-Covered Coffee Beans

1 large egg white at room temperature
a pinch of cream of tartar
4 tablespoons sugar
1 cup well chilled heavy cream
1 tablespoon instant espresso powder
2 tablespoons Kahlúa
3 tablespoons finely chopped *amaretti* (Italian almond macaroons, available at specialty foods shops and some supermarkets)
2 ounces semisweet chocolate, chopped
about 24 espresso coffee beans
6 thin strips of lemon rind, tied in knots

In a bowl with an electric mixer beat the egg white with a pinch of salt until it is frothy, add the cream of tartar, and beat the white until it holds soft peaks. Add 1 tablespoon of the sugar, a little at a time, beating, and beat the white until it just holds stiff peaks. In a chilled bowl with the electric mixer beat the cream with the espresso powder until it begins to thicken, add the remaining 3 tablespoons sugar and the Kahlúa, and beat the cream until it just holds stiff peaks. Stir one third of the whipped cream mixture into the egg white mixture and fold in the remaining whipped cream mixture with 2½ tablespoons of the *amaretti* crumbs gently but thor-

oughly. Spoon the mixture into six ½-cup ramekins, dishes, or espresso cups, smoothing the tops, sprinkle the tops with the remaining 1½ teaspoons *amaretti* crumbs, and freeze the tortonis, covered tightly, for at least 2 hours and up to 2 days.

In a small heatproof bowl set over barely simmering water melt the chocolate. Invert a large-holed sieve on a plate. Insert a pin into each coffee bean, dip the beans carefully into the chocolate, coating them completely, and insert the heads of the pins at an angle into the sieve. (Reserve the remaining chocolate for another use.) Freeze the chocolate-covered coffee beans for at least 15 minutes or overnight and garnish each dessert with 3 or 4 of them and a lemon knot. Serves 6.

PHOTO ON PAGE 68

Rum Apple Walnut Ice Cream

2 tablespoons firmly packed light brown sugar
a pinch of cinnamon
¾ cup coarsely chopped Golden Delicious apple
¼ cup chopped walnuts, toasted lightly
1 tablespoon dark rum
1½ cups slightly softened vanilla ice cream

In a small saucepan stir together the brown sugar, the cinnamon, 3 tablespoons water, and the apple, bring the liquid to a boil, and simmer the mixture for 8 to 10 minutes, or until the liquid is reduced to about 1 teaspoon. Stir in the walnuts and the rum, transfer the mixture to a metal bowl, and let it stand until it is cool. Add the softened ice cream and with an electric mixer beat the mixture until it is combined well. Serves 2.

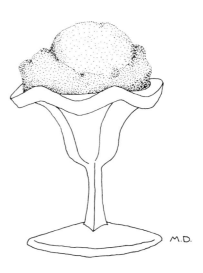

Pineapple Mint Sherbet

1 large pineapple, peeled, cored, and cut into
   1-inch pieces (about 4 cups)
½ cup firmly packed fresh mint leaves
2 tablespoons strained fresh lime juice
6 tablespoons superfine sugar
1 large egg white at room temperature

In a blender purée in batches the pineapple and the mint and transfer the purée to a bowl. Stir in the lime juice and the sugar and stir the purée until the sugar is dissolved. Freeze the purée in an ice-cream freezer according to the manufacturer's instructions until it is almost frozen but still slushy. In a bowl beat the egg white until it holds soft peaks, add it to the sherbet, and freeze the sherbet in the ice-cream freezer until it is frozen but not firm. Remove the dasher and continue to freeze the sherbet, covered, until it is firm. Makes about 1 quart.

Strawberry Ice Cream

2 pints strawberries, hulled and sliced, plus
   1 cup chopped
¾ cup sugar
2 tablespoons fresh lemon juice
4 large eggs
¼ teaspoon salt
2 cups heavy cream
1 teaspoon vanilla

In a bowl sprinkle the sliced strawberries with ¼ cup of the sugar and the lemon juice, stir the mixture until it is combined, and let it stand for 30 minutes. In a food processor purée the mixture until it is smooth.

In another bowl with an electric mixer beat the eggs until they are thick and pale, beat in the salt and the remaining ½ cup sugar, a little at a time, and beat the mixture for 1 minute. In a heavy saucepan heat the cream until it is hot and add it to the egg mixture in a stream, beating. In the saucepan cook the custard over moderately low heat, stirring constantly, until wisps of steam begin to rise from it and it is thickened. Transfer the custard to a metal bowl, set the bowl in a bowl of ice water, and stir until cool. Stir in the vanilla and the purée and freeze in an ice-cream freezer according to the manufacturer's instructions until the ice cream is firm but not frozen solid. Remove the dasher, stir in the chopped berries, and freeze the ice cream, covered, until it is firm enough to scoop. Makes about 1½ quarts.

FRUIT FINALES

Baked Apple Slices
with Pecan Sauce

1 Golden Delicious apple, peeled, cored, and
   cut into ½-inch slices
1 teaspoon fresh lemon juice
1 tablespoon dark rum
⅛ teaspoon cinnamon
⅓ cup heavy cream
1½ tablespoons firmly packed dark brown
   sugar
1 teaspoon unsalted butter
2 tablespoons chopped pecans,
   toasted lightly

In a baking pan large enough to hold the apple slices in one layer whisk together the lemon juice, 2 teaspoons of the rum, the cinnamon, and ¼ cup water, add the apple slices, and turn them to coat them with the rum mixture. Arrange the apple slices in one layer and bake them in a preheated 375° F. oven for 18 to 20 minutes, or until they are tender. In a heavy saucepan combine the cream and the brown sugar and cook the mixture over moderate heat, stirring, for 6 to 8 minutes, or until it is thickened. Stir in the butter, the remaining 1 teaspoon rum, and the pecans, stir the mixture until the butter is melted, and pour the sauce over the apple slices. Serves 2.

Amaretto Apricot Fool

4 ounces (a scant cup) dried apricots
2 tablespoons sugar
2 tablespoons Amaretto di Sarono
1 cup chilled heavy cream

In a saucepan combine the apricots and 1 cup water, bring the water to a boil, and simmer the apricots, covered, for 15 to 20 minutes, or until they are soft. Add the sugar and simmer the mixture, mashing it with a spoon, for 3 to 5 minutes, or until it is thickened. Transfer the mixture to a bowl, stir in the Amaretto, and chill the mixture, covered, for 1 to 2 hours, or until it is cold. In a chilled bowl beat the cream until it holds stiff peaks and fold it into the apricot mixture gently but thoroughly. Divide the fool among stemmed dessert glasses and serve it immediately or chill it, covered, overnight. Serves 6.

Banana Fool

¾ cup mashed ripe banana (about 2 bananas)
2 tablespoons firmly packed dark brown sugar
2 teaspoons fresh lemon juice, or to taste
¾ cup chilled heavy cream

In a bowl mash together the banana, the sugar, and the lemon juice. In a chilled bowl beat the cream until it holds stiff peaks and fold it into the banana mixture gently but thoroughly. Divide the fool among stemmed dessert glasses and serve it immediately or chill it, covered, overnight. Serves 4.

Summer Berries in Honey Rum Sauce

¾ cup blueberries, picked over and rinsed
1 pint strawberries, hulled and sliced thin
1 tablespoon fresh lime juice
½ cup honey
¼ cup dark rum
3 tablespoons unsalted butter, cut into pieces

In a bowl combine the blueberries and the strawberries with the lime juice. In a small saucepan heat the honey, the rum, and the butter over moderate heat, stirring, until the butter is melted and let the mixture cool for 15 minutes. Toss the berries gently with the honey rum sauce and serve the mixture over vanilla or strawberry ice cream or lemon sherbet. Makes about 3 cups.

Blueberry Crisp

¼ teaspoon grated orange rind
1 tablespoon fresh orange juice
2 teaspoons sugar
½ teaspoon cornstarch
1¾ cups blueberries (about ¾ pint),
  picked over
For the topping
¼ cup firmly packed light brown sugar
3 tablespoons all-purpose flour
2 tablespoons old-fashioned rolled oats
½ teaspoon cinnamon
⅛ teaspoon salt
2 tablespoons cold unsalted butter,
  cut into bits
sour cream as an accompaniment if desired

In a small bowl combine well the rind, the juice, the sugar, and the cornstarch and add the blueberries. Toss the blueberries to coat them with the orange mixture and transfer the mixture to a 7½-inch (2½-cup) gratin dish.

Make the topping: In another small bowl combine the brown sugar, the flour, the oats, the cinnamon, the salt, and the butter, blend the mixture until it resembles meal, and sprinkle it evenly over the blueberry mixture. Bake the blueberry crisp in a preheated 350° F. oven for 10 minutes, increase the heat to 400° F., and bake the crisp for 10 minutes more, or until the blueberry mixture is bubbling around the edge of the dish and the top is golden. Let the blueberry crisp cool slightly and serve it with the sour cream if desired. Serves 2.

Blueberry, Green Grape, and Nectarine Compote in Lime Syrup

2 limes
½ cup sugar
1 pint blueberries
2 cups seedless green grapes
3 nectarines

Remove the rind from the limes in thin strips with a vegetable peeler, reserving the limes, and in a food processor blend the rind with the sugar for 2 minutes, or until it is minced very fine. In a small saucepan combine the sugar mixture with 1 cup water, bring the mixture to a boil, stirring until the sugar is dissolved, and simmer the syrup for 5 minutes. Put the blueberries in a heatproof bowl, pour the hot syrup over them, and let the mixture cool to room temperature. Chill the mixture, covered, for 1 to 2 hours, or until it is cold.

Squeeze the juice from the reserved limes, stir it into the blueberry mixture, and add the grapes. Halve, pit, and cut the nectarines into ½-inch pieces, working over the bowl to catch any juices. Add the nectarines to the blueberry mixture and toss the compote gently. Serves 6.

Figs Poached in Red Wine with Oranges and Mascarpone Cream

4 cups dry red wine

½ cup granulated sugar

2 pounds dried figs

1 tablespoon fresh lemon juice, or to taste

¾ pound *mascarpone* (Italian triple-cream cheese) at room temperature

3 tablespoons light brown sugar

1½ cups sour cream

8 navel oranges, peel and pith cut away with a serrated knife and the oranges sliced horizontally

In a large saucepan combine the wine and the granulated sugar, bring the mixture to a boil, and simmer it, stirring, until the sugar is dissolved. Add the figs, simmer the mixture, covered, for 35 minutes, or until the figs are very tender, and add the lemon juice. Transfer the figs with a slotted spoon to a bowl and boil the liquid until it is syrupy. Pour the poaching liquid over the figs and let the mixture cool to room temperature. In a bowl with an electric mixer beat the *mascarpone* with the brown sugar until it is fluffy and beat in the sour cream. Arrange the orange slices around the edge of a large platter, mound the figs in the center, and pour the syrup over them. Serve the dessert with the *mascarpone* cream. Serves 12.

Spirited Green Fruit Compote

2 cups seedless green grapes

2 kiwis, peeled, halved lengthwise, and sliced thin crosswise

3 Anjou pears, halved, cored, and cut into ½-inch pieces

½ cup chilled Sauternes

¼ cup Grand Marnier

In a bowl combine the grapes, the kiwis, and the pears, add the Sauternes and the Grand Marnier, and toss the compote gently. Serves 6.

PHOTO ON BACK JACKET

Mixed Fruit Compote with Honey and Rum

½ cup honey

¼ cup light rum

2 pounds pears

2 tablespoons fresh lime juice

½ cup blueberries

½ cup raspberries

½ cup sliced peeled kiwi

½ cup halved orange segments

fresh mint sprigs for garnish if desired

In a small saucepan combine the honey and the rum, heat the mixture over low heat, stirring, until it is combined, and let it cool for 10 minutes. Peel, core, and cut the pears into ½-inch pieces. In a bowl toss the pears with the lime juice and the honey rum syrup, add the blueberries, the raspberries, the kiwi, and the oranges, and toss the compote gently. Serve the compote garnished with the mint if desired. Serves 6.

PHOTO ON BACK JACKET

Orange Fruit Compote with Cognac

4 nectarines, cut into ½-inch pieces

2 papayas or mangoes, peeled, seeded, and cut into ½-inch pieces

⅓ cup fresh orange juice

1 tablespoon freshly grated orange rind

½ cup sugar

2 tablespoons Cognac

1 ounce bittersweet chocolate if desired, chopped coarse

In a bowl combine the nectarines and the papayas, add the orange juice, the orange rind, the sugar, and the Cognac, and toss the compote gently. Serve the compote sprinkled with the chocolate if desired. Serves 6.

PHOTO ON BACK JACKET

Buttered Rum Fruit Kebabs

1 large firm banana, cut into 8 pieces

1 small navel orange, ends trimmed and the orange cut into 4 wedges

8 pieces fresh pineapple, 2 by 2 by 1 inch

8 pieces pound cake, 2 by 2 by 1 inch, buttered lightly

½ cup fresh lemon juice

1 stick (½ cup) unsalted butter

½ cup firmly packed dark brown sugar

½ cup dark rum

1 teaspoon cinnamon

⅓ cup slivered almonds, toasted lightly

vanilla ice cream or whipped cream as an accompaniment

In a shallow dish let four 12-inch wooden skewers soak in water to cover for 1 hour. Thread the banana, the orange, and the pineapple on the skewers, alternating them in a decorative pattern, thread the cake on the ends of the skewers, and arrange the kebabs in a jelly-roll pan. In a small saucepan stir together the lemon juice, the butter, the brown sugar, the rum, the cinnamon, and a pinch of salt, bring the mixture to a boil, and simmer it for 2 minutes. Brush the kebabs with the rum mixture and broil them under a preheated broiler about 4 inches from the heat, basting them often with the rum mixture and turning them once, for 10 minutes, or until the fruit is glazed. (Cover the cake with foil when it is golden brown.) Serve the kebabs sprinkled with the almonds and drizzled with the pan juices and any additional rum mixture. Serve the kebabs with the ice cream or whipped cream. Serves 4.

Grape, Raisin, and Vanilla Compote

4 cups dry white wine
½ cup sugar
1 vanilla bean, halved crosswise and slit
    lengthwise, or 2 teaspoons vanilla extract
6 cups seedless green grapes
1 cup raisins
sour cream or vanilla ice cream as an
    accompaniment if desired

In a saucepan combine the wine, the sugar, and the vanilla bean if using, bring the liquid to a boil, and simmer the mixture, covered, for 15 minutes. Add the grapes and the raisins, simmer the mixture for 5 min-
utes, and transfer the fruit with a slotted spoon to a serving bowl. Scrape the seeds from the vanilla bean, if used, into the liquid in the pan, reserving the vanilla bean for another use if desired, boil the liquid until it is reduced by two thirds, and stir in the vanilla extract if using. Pour the syrup over the fruit, let the compote cool to lukewarm, and chill it, covered, for at least 4 hours and up to 3 days. Serve the compote with the sour cream or ice cream if desired. Serves 6.

Flambéed Grapes

¼ cup sugar
a 2-inch cinnamon stick
1 tablespoon fresh lemon juice
1 cup seedless green grapes
2½ teaspoons cornstarch
¾ cup seedless red grapes
2 tablespoons dark rum
vanilla ice cream as an accompaniment

In a small skillet combine the sugar, the cinnamon stick, ¾ cup water, the lemon juice, and ¼ cup of the green grapes, chopped coarse, bring the liquid to a boil, stirring occasionally, and simmer the mixture for 5 minutes. Strain the mixture through a fine sieve set over a bowl, pressing hard on the solids, and return the syrup to the skillet. Whisk in the cornstarch and bring the syrup to a simmer, whisking. Stir in the remaining ¾ cup green grapes and the red grapes, cook the mixture over moderately high heat, stirring, for 5 minutes, and remove the skillet from the heat. Add the rum, warmed, and ignite it, shaking the skillet gently until the flames go out. Serve the grapes over the ice cream. Serves 2.

Honey-Glazed Pink Grapefruit
with Pink Grapefruit Curd

3 large pink grapefruit, rind and pith cut away
   with a serrated knife, reserving the rind
   from ¼ grapefruit and cutting it into
   julienne strips
¼ cup sugar
For the curd
½ cup strained fresh pink grapefruit juice
2½ tablespoons sugar
½ stick (¼ cup) unsalted butter, cut into bits
1 large egg

½ cup honey

In a small saucepan combine the reserved rind with
½ cup water, boil it for 1 minute, and drain it. Repeat the
procedure and reserve the rind. In the pan combine the
sugar with ⅓ cup water and cook the mixture, covered,
over moderately low heat, stirring occasionally, until
the sugar is dissolved. Add the reserved rind and simmer the mixture until the sugar syrup is very thick and
the rind is translucent.

Make the curd: In another small saucepan boil the
juice until it is reduced to about 2 tablespoons, add the
sugar and the butter, and simmer the mixture, stirring,
until the sugar is dissolved. In a small bowl beat the egg,
add the hot liquid in a slow stream, whisking, and return
the mixture to the pan. Cook the mixture over moderately low heat, stirring, until it is thickened to the consistency of hollandaise, but do not let it boil. *The curd may
be made 1 day in advance, kept covered with a buttered
round of wax paper, and chilled.*

Dip the grapefruit, sectioned and the membranes discarded, in the honey to coat it, arrange the sections in
one layer on a baking sheet, and broil them under a preheated broiler about 4 inches from the heat for 5 minutes, or until they are translucent. Divide the sections
among 4 dessert plates, arranging them in pinwheels,
spoon some of the curd in the center, and top it with the
candied rind. Serves 4.

PHOTO ON PAGE 26

Melon Balls with Port and Lime Syrup in
Melon Shells

a 2½- to 3-pound cantaloupe
a 2½- to 3-pound honeydew
3 tablespoons fresh lime juice
¼ cup sugar
2 tablespoons Tawny Port
2 teaspoons grated lime rind plus additional
   for garnish

Cut each melon lengthwise into 3 wedges, discard the
seeds, and with a melon-ball cutter scoop the melon into
balls, transferring them to a bowl. Toss the melon balls
with the lime juice. Discard 1 cantaloupe wedge and
1 honeydew wedge and with a spoon scrape away any
remaining melon in the remaining 4 wedges to form
smooth shells. To make a bow, begin at a pointed end·of
1 of the melon shells and with a small sharp knife cut a
⅛-inch-wide strip along the edge of the shell, cutting to
within ¼ inch of the center. Beginning at the other
pointed end make a similar cut, cutting to within ¼ inch
of the center and leaving ½ inch attached between the
cuts. Bend each strip back and under itself to form a
bow. Make bows with the remaining 3 melon shells in
the same manner.

In a small saucepan combine the sugar and 2 tablespoons water, bring the mixture to a boil, stirring until
the sugar is dissolved, and simmer it for 2 minutes. Remove the pan from the heat, stir in the Port and 2 teaspoons of the rind, and pour the syrup over the melon
balls, combining the mixture well. Let the melon balls
macerate, covered and chilled, stirring occasionally,
for 20 minutes.

Put each melon shell on a plate, divide the melon
balls among the shells, spooning some of the syrup over
them, and sprinkle each serving with some of the additional rind. Serves 4.

PHOTO ON PAGE 33

Melon Compote with Lemon Granita

2 cups ¾-inch watermelon balls
2 cups ¾-inch honeydew melon balls
2 cups ¾-inch cantaloupe balls
about 1 quart lemon granita (recipe follows)

Chill the melon balls in separate bowls, covered, for
1 to 2 hours, or until they are cold. Form balls of the
granita with a ¾-inch melon-ball scoop and freeze them
in one layer in a metal baking pan until they are firm.
(Dipping the scoop into hot water before scooping each
ball will facilitate the procedure.) In a large bowl combine the melon balls and spoon them into stemmed
glasses with the granita. Serves 6 to 8.

Lemon Granita

1 cup fresh lemon juice
4 teaspoons freshly grated lemon rind
1½ cups sugar
½ cup dry white wine
1 large egg white, beaten until frothy

In a bowl combine the lemon juice, the lemon rind, the sugar, the wine, 1½ cups cold water, and the egg white and stir the mixture until the sugar is dissolved. Transfer the mixture to an ice-cream freezer and freeze it according to the manufacturer's instructions. Transfer the granita to a metal baking pan and continue to freeze it until it is firm enough to scoop. Makes about 1 quart.

Nectarine Mousse with Oatmeal Cookie Crumbs

1 cup chopped nectarine
2 tablespoons sugar
1½ teaspoons fresh lemon juice
1 teaspoon dark rum, or to taste
½ cup well chilled heavy cream
⅓ cup coarsely crumbled Irish oatmeal cookies

In a small saucepan combine the nectarine, the sugar, and the lemon juice, bring the liquid to a boil, stirring, and simmer the mixture, stirring occasionally, for 8 to 10 minutes, or until the nectarine is tender and the liquid is reduced to about 2 tablespoons. Stir in the rum, transfer the mixture to a bowl set in a bowl of ice and cold water, and stir it until it is cold. In a food processor or blender purée half the nectarine mixture. In a chilled bowl beat the cream until it just holds stiff peaks, add the nectarine purée, the chopped nectarine mixture, and the cookie crumbs, and fold the mixture together gently but thoroughly. Divide the mousse between 2 wineglasses. The mousse keeps, covered and chilled, for up to 2 hours. Serves 2.

Chunky Pear Applesauce with Ginger

2 ripe pears, peeled reserving the peels, cored, and sliced thin
2 McIntosh apples, peeled reserving the peels, cored, and sliced thin
1 tablespoon sugar, or to taste
2 teaspoons minced crystallized ginger (available at specialty foods shops and some supermarkets)

In a heavy saucepan combine the reserved pear and apple peels with 2 cups water, simmer the mixture until the liquid is reduced to about ¼ cup, and strain the liquid into a bowl, discarding the peels. Return the liquid to the pan and add the pears, the apples, and the sugar. Bring the liquid to a boil and simmer the mixture, covered, stirring occasionally, for 10 minutes. Remove the lid and simmer the mixture, stirring, for 5 minutes, or until it is thickened. *The pear applesauce may be made up to this point 2 days in advance and kept covered and chilled.* Just before serving, in a bowl sprinkle the pear applesauce with the ginger and serve it warm or at room temperature. Serves 2.

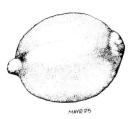

MAVRIDIS

Port-Poached Pears and Cantaloupe Compote

2 firm pears (about 1 pound)
½ lemon
1 cup dry red wine
½ cup Ruby Port
a 3-inch cinnamon stick
4 whole cloves
two 3- by 1-inch strips of fresh lemon rind
¼ cup sugar
½ cantaloupe, scooped into balls with a ½-inch melon-ball cutter and chilled

Peel the pears and put them in a bowl of cold water acidulated with the juice of the lemon. With a ½-inch melon-ball cutter scoop as many balls as possible from the pears and keep them in the acidulated water. In a small saucepan combine the red wine, the Port, the cinnamon stick, the cloves, and the rind, bring the liquid to a boil, and boil the mixture for 5 minutes. Add the sugar and simmer the syrup, stirring, until the sugar is dissolved. Add the pear balls, drained, and simmer them for 5 to 7 minutes, or until they are tender. Let the pear balls cool completely in the syrup. *The pear balls may be prepared up to this point 1 day in advance and kept covered and chilled in the syrup.* Divide the pear balls and the cantaloupe balls among 4 bowls and spoon some of the syrup over each serving. Serve the compote at room temperature. Serves 4.

Ananas en Surprise
(Pineapples Filled with
Pineapple Ice Cream and Meringue)

4 miniature pineapples (each about 1¼
    pounds) or two 3-pound pineapples, halved
    lengthwise, cored, and the flesh cut out and
    reserved for pineapple ice cream (recipe
    follows), leaving ¼-inch-thick shells
about 2 quarts pineapple ice cream
    (recipe follows)
4 large egg whites at room temperature
⅔ cup granulated sugar
confectioners' sugar for sifting over the
    meringue

Pat the pineapple shells dry with paper towels and
freeze them, wrapped well in plastic wrap, for 1 hour.
Pack the shells with the ice cream, mounding the ice
cream and smoothing the surface, and freeze the filled
pineapples, covered with plastic wrap, for at least 4
hours or up to 24 hours.

In a metal bowl combine the egg whites and the granulated sugar, set the bowl over a pan of simmering water, and stir the mixture until the sugar is dissolved.
Remove the bowl from the heat and with an electric
mixer beat the meringue until it holds stiff glossy peaks.
Working quickly, cover the ice cream in each pineapple
with a smooth layer of meringue. Transfer the remaining meringue to a pastry bag fitted with a small star tip
and pipe it decoratively over the pineapples. Sift the
confectioners' sugar lightly over the meringue, broil the
pineapples in batches if necessary on a baking sheet under a preheated broiler about 4 inches from the heat for
30 seconds to 1 minute, or until the meringue is golden,
and serve them immediately. Serves 8.

PHOTO ON PAGE 37

Pineapple Ice Cream

3 cups finely chopped fresh pineapple
1½ cups sugar
½ cup dark rum, or to taste
6 large eggs
3 cups milk
3 cups well chilled heavy cream

In a large saucepan combine the pineapple, ½ cup of
the sugar, and 6 tablespoons of the rum, bring the mixture to a boil over moderate heat, stirring until the sugar
is dissolved, and simmer it for 5 minutes. Strain the
pineapple mixture through a fine sieve into a bowl, reserving the liquid and the pineapple solids separately.

In another bowl whisk together the eggs and the remaining 1 cup sugar, add the milk, scalded, in a stream,
whisking, and transfer the mixture to a saucepan. Cook
the custard over moderately low heat, stirring constantly, until it is thickened slightly, but do not let it boil,
transfer it to a metal bowl, and set the bowl in a larger
bowl of ice and cold water. Add the reserved pineapple
liquid, let the custard cool, stirring occasionally, and
chill it, covered, until it is cold. *The custard may be prepared up to this point 1 day in advance and kept covered
and chilled.* Stir in the cream and the remaining 2 tablespoons rum and freeze the custard in batches if
necessary in an ice-cream freezer according to the
manufacturer's instructions until it is almost frozen but
still soft. Add the reserved pineapple solids and freeze
the ice cream in the ice-cream freezer until it is frozen
but not firm. Remove the dasher and continue to freeze
the ice cream until it is firm. *The ice cream keeps, covered tightly and frozen, for up to 1 week.* Makes about 2
quarts.

Poached Plums with Zabaglione

¼ cup sugar
¼ teaspoon vanilla
2 large plums (about ½ pound), cut into 8
    slices
For the zabaglione
2 large egg yolks
2 tablespoons sugar
2 tablespoons Marsala

In a saucepan combine the sugar, the vanilla, and 1½
cups water, bring the liquid to a boil, and simmer the
mixture, covered, for 5 minutes. Add the plums and
simmer them for 6 to 8 minutes, or until they are tender.
Transfer the plums with a slotted spoon to a metal bowl
set in a bowl of ice and cold water, stir them gently until
they are cool enough to handle, and discard the skins.
Bring the poaching liquid to a boil, boil it until it is reduced to about ½ cup, and add it to the plums. Stir the
mixture until it is cool and chill it, covered, while making the zabaglione.

Make the zabaglione: In a metal bowl with an electric
mixer beat together the egg yolks and the sugar for 3
minutes, or until the mixture is thick and pale, and beat
in the Marsala. Set the bowl over a saucepan of simmering water and beat the mixture for 3 to 5 minutes, or un-

til it just holds soft peaks and is warm to the touch. Set the bowl in the bowl of ice and cold water and beat the mixture for 1 minute, or until it is cold. Divide the plums between 2 serving dishes, pour some of the poaching liquid over them, and spoon the zabaglione over the plums. Serves 2.

Prune Fool

1 cup pitted prunes
½ cup dry red wine
a 3-inch cinnamon stick
two 3- by 1-inch strips of fresh lemon rind
3 tablespoons sugar, or to taste
1 cup chilled heavy cream

In a saucepan combine the prunes, the wine, the cinnamon stick, the rind, and ½ cup water, bring the liquid to a boil, and simmer the mixture, covered, for 20 minutes. Stir in the sugar and simmer the mixture, uncovered, stirring occasionally, for 5 minutes, or until it is thickened. Discard the cinnamon stick and the rind and chill the mixture in a bowl, covered, for 1 to 2 hours, or until it is cold. In a food processor purée the mixture and transfer the purée to the bowl. In a chilled bowl beat the cream until it holds stiff peaks and fold it into the prune purée gently but thoroughly. Divide the fool among stemmed dessert glasses and serve it immediately or chill it, covered, overnight. Serves 4 to 6.

Raspberry Chocolate Swirl Fool

two 10-ounce packages frozen raspberries in
   syrup, thawed and drained, reserving the
   liquid
3 ounces semisweet chocolate, chopped
1 cup chilled heavy cream

In a saucepan bring the reserved raspberry liquid to a boil and boil it, stirring occasionally, until it is thick and syrupy and reduced to about ¼ cup. Transfer the syrup

to a bowl and let it cool. In a food processor purée the raspberries and force the purée through a fine sieve set over the bowl of raspberry syrup, scraping and pressing hard on the solids to separate as much pulp from the seeds as possible. Whisk the raspberry mixture until it is blended and chill it, covered, for 1 to 2 hours, or until it is cold.

In the top of a double boiler set over barely simmering water melt the chocolate with 3 tablespoons water, stirring until it is smooth, remove the top of the double boiler from the heat, and let the chocolate cool to room temperature.

In a chilled bowl beat the cream until it holds stiff peaks and fold it into the raspberry mixture gently but thoroughly. Drizzle the chocolate over the fool and fold it in lightly, swirling it in but being careful not to mix it in completely. Divide the fool among stemmed dessert glasses and serve it immediately or chill it, covered, for up to 2 hours. Serves 6.

Strawberry Fool

1 cup sliced strawberries (about ½ pint)
3 tablespoons sugar
1½ teaspoons balsamic vinegar, or to taste
   (available at specialty foods shops and
   many supermarkets)
¾ cup chilled heavy cream

In a small saucepan combine the strawberries, the sugar, the vinegar and 1 tablespoon water, bring the mixture to a boil over moderately low heat, stirring, and cook it at a slow boil, stirring, for 4 minutes. Chill the mixture in a bowl, covered, for 1 to 2 hours, or until it is cold. In a food processor or blender purée the mixture with the vinegar and transfer the purée to the bowl. In a chilled bowl beat the cream until it holds stiff peaks and fold it into the strawberry purée gently but thoroughly. Divide the fool among stemmed dessert glasses and serve it immediately or chill it, covered, overnight. Serves 4.

ZOÉ MAVRIDIS

BEVERAGES

ALCOHOLIC BEVERAGES

Apricot Toddy

⅓ cup finely chopped dried apricots
½ cup bourbon
2 tablespoons sugar
¼ cup fresh lemon juice
½ cup apricot brandy

In a small bowl let the apricots soak in the bourbon for 2 hours. In a saucepan combine the sugar, the lemon juice, and 2 cups water and bring the mixture to a boil, stirring until the sugar is dissolved. Add the apricot mixture and the brandy, heat the mixture over moderate heat, stirring, until it is hot, and divide it among 4 heated mugs. Makes 4 drinks.

Beaujolais Kir

2 teaspoons *crème de cassis*
⅓ cup Beaujolais, chilled well

In a wine glass stir together the *crème de cassis* and the Beaujolais and add several ice cubes if desired. Makes 1 cocktail.

Champagne Pineapple Cocktail

3 tablespoons chilled unsweetened
  pineapple juice
⅓ cup chilled Champagne

In a Champagne flute combine the pineapple juice and the Champagne and stir the cocktail once. Makes 1 cocktail.

Cranberry-Orange Vodka Spritzers

4 cups strained fresh orange juice, chilled
2 cups cranberry juice, chilled
1 cup vodka
2 cups seltzer or club soda, chilled

In a large pitcher combine the orange juice, the cranberry juice, and the vodka, add the seltzer, and stir the mixture. Makes 9 cups.

PHOTO ON PAGE 33

Hot Buttered Rum

½ cup firmly packed dark brown sugar
1 stick (½ cup) unsalted butter, cut into pieces
1 teaspoon cinnamon plus additional for
  garnish
1 teaspoon freshly grated nutmeg, or to taste
¼ teaspoon ground cloves, or to taste
⅔ cup dark rum

In a saucepan combine the brown sugar, the butter, 1 teaspoon of the cinnamon, the nutmeg, the cloves, and 2 cups water and bring the mixture to a boil, whisking constantly. Simmer the mixture for 5 minutes and stir in the rum. Divide the mixture among 4 heated mugs and sprinkle each drink with some of the additional cinnamon. Makes 4 drinks.

Hot Irish Mocha

1 tablespoon unsweetened cocoa powder
1 tablespoon sugar
1 tablespoon milk
5 cups strong coffee
⅓ cup orange-flavored liqueur
1 cup Baileys Original Irish Cream

In a saucepan combine the cocoa powder, the sugar, and the milk, stirring until the mixture is smooth. Add the coffee and heat the mixture over moderately low heat, stirring, until the cocoa powder and the sugar are dissolved and the mixture is hot, but do not let it boil. Stir in the liqueur and the Baileys Irish Cream, heat the mixture over moderate heat, stirring, until it is hot, but do not let it boil, and divide it among 6 heated mugs. Makes 6 drinks.

Hot Mexican Cider

5 cups apple cider
¼ cup fresh lemon juice
½ teaspoon salt
1⅔ cups tequila
⅓ cup orange-flavored liqueur
8 lemon slices for garnish

In a saucepan combine the cider, the lemon juice, and the salt, bring the mixture to a simmer, and skim it. Add the tequila and the liqueur and heat the mixture over moderate heat, stirring, until it is hot. Divide the mixture among 8 heated mugs and garnish each drink with 1 of the lemon slices. Makes 8 drinks.

Hot Molasses Milk Punch

1 tablespoon sugar
1 tablespoon unsulfured dark molasses
¼ teaspoon ground ginger
2 cups milk
½ cup dark rum
freshly grated nutmeg for garnish

In a small saucepan combine the sugar, 1 tablespoon water, the molasses, and the ginger and bring the mixture to a simmer, stirring. Add the milk in a stream, whisking, and heat the mixture over moderate heat, stirring, until it is hot, but do not let it boil. Stir in the rum, divide the mixture between 2 heated mugs, and sprinkle each drink generously with some of the nutmeg. Makes 2 drinks.

Hot Peppermint Flip

1 large egg
⅔ cup heavy cream
1 tablespoon sugar
½ cup peppermint schnapps
½ cup Cognac
3 cups hot espresso
3 peppermint sticks, halved, for garnish

In a blender combine the egg, the cream, the sugar, the schnapps, and the Cognac and blend the mixture at high speed for 10 seconds. With the motor running add the espresso in a stream and blend the mixture until it is frothy. Divide the mixture among 6 heated coffee cups and garnish each drink with 1 of the peppermint sticks. Makes 6 drinks.

Hot Sangría

¼ cup sugar
½ cup fresh orange juice
1 bottle dry red wine
¼ cup orange-flavored liqueur
4 lemon slices
4 orange slices,
    1 slice stuck with 4 cloves

In a saucepan combine the sugar, the juice, and ½ cup water and simmer the mixture, stirring, for 5 minutes. Stir in the wine, the liqueur, the lemon slices, and the orange slices and heat the mixture over moderate heat, stirring, until it is hot. Discard the lemon and orange slices and divide the mixture among 4 heated mugs. Makes 4 drinks.

Kir Royales

4 teaspoons *crème de cassis* plus additional in
    a shallow dish for dipping the rims of the
    glasses
sugar in a shallow dish for dipping the rims of
    the glasses
1 half-bottle (12.7 ounces) Champagne,
    chilled

Dip the rims of 2 Champagne glasses into the additional *crème de cassis*, letting the excess drip off, and dip them in the sugar. Pour 2 teaspoons of the *crème de cassis* into each glass and fill the glasses with the Champagne. Makes 2 drinks.

PHOTO ON PAGE 54

Mint Julep Slush

15 fresh large mint leaves plus 1 fresh mint
    sprig for garnish
1 tablespoon sugar
2 ounces (2 ponies) bourbon

In a blender blend together the mint leaves, the sugar, the bourbon, and 3 cups ice cubes, cracked, stopping the machine and stirring the mixture several times, until the mixture is smooth. Pour the cocktail into a highball glass and garnish it with the mint. Makes 1 cocktail.

Negroni

2 ounces (2 ponies) gin
2 ounces (2 ponies) Campari
1 ounce (1 pony) sweet vermouth
2 tablespoons strained fresh orange juice

In a cocktail shaker combine the gin, the Campari, the vermouth, the orange juice, and ½ cup ice cubes, shake the cocktail until it is chilled, and strain it into a glass. Makes 1 cocktail.

PHOTO ON PAGE 30

Peach Champagne Cocktails

2 to 4 tablespoons peach schnapps, or to taste
1 half-bottle (12.7 ounces) Champagne, chilled
2 thin peach slices for garnish if desired

Divide the peach schnapps between 2 Champagne glasses, fill the glasses with the Champagne, and garnish each drink with a peach slice if desired. Makes 2 drinks.

PHOTO ON PAGE 54

Sake Martini

1 teaspoon *sake*, chilled well
2 ounces (2 ponies) vodka, chilled well
1 cucumber ball, cut with a small melon-ball cutter

In a Martini glass combine the *sake* and the vodka and garnish the cocktail with the cucumber ball. Makes 1 cocktail.

PHOTO ON PAGE 29

Spiked Hot Chocolate

4 cups milk
3 ounces unsweetened chocolate, chopped
¾ cup sugar
½ teaspoon cinnamon
½ cup dark rum
½ cup Frangelico (hazelnut-flavored liqueur)
whipped cream for garnish

In a saucepan combine the milk, the chocolate, the sugar, and the cinnamon and heat the mixture over moderate heat, stirring, until the chocolate is melted and the sugar is dissolved. Add the rum and the Frangelico and heat the mixture, stirring, until it is hot. Divide the mixture among 6 heated mugs and top each drink with some of the whipped cream. Makes 6 drinks.

Spring Fever
(Rum Lime Tonic)

2 ounces (2 ponies) white rum
1½ ounces (1 jigger) Rose's lime juice
chilled tonic water
lime slices for garnish

In a highball glass filled with ice cubes stir together the rum and the Rose's lime juice, fill the glass with the tonic water, and garnish the cocktail with the lime. Makes 1 cocktail.

PHOTO ON PAGE 31

White Sangría

2 bottles dry white wine
¼ cup Grand Marnier
2 tablespoons sugar
¼ cup halved seedless red grapes
¼ cup halved seedless green grapes
5 orange slices, halved
½ red Delicious apple, unpeeled, cored, and sliced thin

In a pitcher combine the wine, the Grand Marnier, and the sugar and stir the mixture. Add the grapes, the orange slices, and the apple slices and chill the sangría, stirring occasionally, for 2 hours. *The sangría may be made up to 24 hours in advance and kept covered and chilled.* Serve the sangría over ice in wineglasses. Serves 6 to 8.

PHOTO ON PAGE 57

White-Wine Spritzer

¾ cup dry white wine
¼ cup club soda, or to taste
a twist of lemon

In a tumbler filled with ice cubes combine the wine, the club soda, and the lemon. Makes 1 drink.

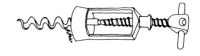

Watermelon Lime Daiquiris

4 pounds watermelon
¾ cup light rum
6 tablespoons fresh lime juice
¼ to ½ cup superfine sugar
3 thin lime slices, halved, for garnish

Cut six ¼-inch-thick small rectangular slices from the watermelon, cut off and discard the rind, and reserve the fruit for garnish. Cut off and discard the rind from the remaining watermelon and discard the seeds. Chop the watermelon and in a bowl freeze it, covered, for 1 hour, or until it is frozen solid. In a blender in batches purée the watermelon with the rum, the lime juice, and ¼ cup of the sugar, transferring the mixture as it is puréed to a pitcher. Stir the mixture well and add the remaining ¼ cup sugar if desired. Pour the mixture into 6 well chilled 6-ounce stemmed glasses and garnish each glass with a reserved watermelon slice and a lime slice. Makes about 4½ cups, serving 6.

NONALCOHOLIC BEVERAGES

Café au Lait

1 cup milk
1 cup strong freshly brewed French-roast
    coffee

In a saucepan scald the milk and strain it into a heated pitcher. Pour the milk and the coffee simultaneously into each of 2 coffee cups. Makes 2 cups.

PHOTO ON PAGE 16

Date Peanut Malteds

⅔ cup milk
2 tablespoons malt powder (available at
    specialty foods shops), or malted milk
    powder
1 pint vanilla ice cream, softened slightly
½ cup pitted dates, chopped
¼ cup unsalted dry-roasted peanuts plus
    2 teaspoons chopped fine for garnish

In a blender blend the milk, the powder, the ice cream, the dates, and ¼ cup of the peanuts until the mixture is combined well, pour the malted into two 12-ounce glasses, and sprinkle the chopped peanuts over the malteds. Makes 2 drinks.

Iced Ginger "Tea"

½ cup thinly sliced peeled fresh gingerroot
¼ cup honey, or to taste
lemon wedges and mint sprigs for garnish

In a saucepan combine the gingerroot and the honey with 7 cups water, bring the liquid to a boil, stirring, and simmer the mixture for 15 minutes. Strain the mixture into a pitcher and chill the "tea" for 30 minutes, or until it is cold. *The ginger tea may be made up to 2 days in advance and kept covered and chilled.* Just before serving stir in about 2 cups ice cubes and garnish the iced ginger tea with the lemon wedges and the mint sprigs.

Lemonade

2¼ cups strained fresh lemon juice
1½ to 2 cups sugar
2 lemons, cut into paper-thin slices,
    and mint sprigs for garnish

In a pitcher combine the lemon juice, 1½ cups of the sugar, and 5 cups cold water, stir the mixture until the sugar is dissolved, and add more sugar if desired. *The lemonade may be made up to 1 day in advance and kept covered and chilled.* Just before serving stir in about 2 cups ice cubes and garnish the lemonade with the lemon slices and the mint sprigs. Makes about 8 cups.

PHOTO ON PAGE 41

Raspberry Cooler

two 10-ounce packages frozen
    raspberries in light syrup, thawed
⅓ cup cider vinegar
¼ cup honey
2 tablespoons sugar, or to taste
lime slices for garnish

In a bowl mash the raspberries in the syrup and force the mixture through a fine sieve set over a pitcher, pressing and scraping the solids to separate the pulp from the seeds. Stir in the vinegar, the honey, the sugar, and 8 cups water and stir the mixture until the sugar is dissolved. Strain the liquid through a fine sieve lined with a double thickness of rinsed and squeezed cheesecloth into another pitcher and chill it, covered, until it is chilled well. Transfer the cooler to a portable container. Serve the cooler over ice in tall glasses and garnish it with the lime slices. Makes about 10 cups.

PHOTO ON PAGE 51

A GOURMET ADDENDUM: PROVISIONS AND PROVISOS

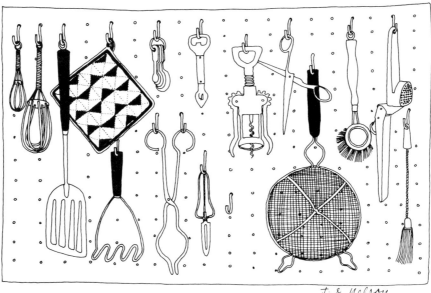

J. S. Nelson

The Gourmet Addendum is a variation on the Gourmet's Pantry column in the magazine, which contains basic recipes called for in each issue. In similar fashion, the following procedures and recipes are called for in other recipes in the book. As a bonus, we have then used these basic recipes—chicken stock, for example—to create a surprising variety of brand-new combinations. From a simmering pot of chicken stock, we have proceeded to a lustrous consommé garnished with spring vegetables, then to a veal stew whose sauce is based on that same stock, and finally to a curry sauce that is served with poached eggs and smoked salmon.

This year we begin the Addendum with procedural recipes: how to shuck clams and oysters. In each instance all you will need is the bivalves themselves, a sturdy, sharp knife, and a steady hand. Proceed with caution, though. Next is a procedure for poaching eggs. Then comes a first: a short primer on stockmaking that includes the recipe not only for chicken stock but for brown stock and white fish stock as well—all in one place, all with compelling variations.

Trusting that a supply of eggs, sugar, flour, and butter is almost always at hand, we advance quickly into desserts, beginning with a basic recipe for *génoise* batter that can be used in some remarkable combinations such as English trifle, orange tea cakes with chocolate glaze, and chocolate mocha ice-cream roll. With the same ingredients, but with the addition of milk or cream, we conclude the Addendum with a recipe for pastry cream that acts as the foundation for a noticeably light chocolate buttercream (used in the tea cake recipe); and when made with no flour, the basic recipe for pastry cream is transformed into crème anglaise—the foundation custard sauce and the basis of ice cream; finally, when made with a slight alteration (the addition of gelatin), it becomes the filling for a celebratory raspberry Bavarian cream.

In all, there are thirty-three new recipes in this Addendum, ranging from comforting brunch combinations to more formal entrée suggestions to a sublime selection of desserts—a full array of choices to work into your culinary repertoire.

TO SHUCK HARD-SHELLED CLAMS AND OYSTERS

The following procedures for shucking hard-shelled clams and oysters require a certain amount of practice, but even more than that, a sizable measure of caution. Do be careful. A sharp knife is a requisite, and sometimes it has a way of slipping.

To Shuck Hard-Shelled Clams

Working over a bowl to reserve the liquor hold each clam in the palm of the hand with the hinge against the heel of the palm. Force a strong, thin, sharp knife between the shells, cut around the inside edges to sever the connecting muscles, and twist the knife slightly to open the shells.

If the clams are not to be served raw they may be opened in the oven: Arrange the clams in one layer in a baking pan and put the pan in a preheated 450° F. oven for 3 to 5 minutes, or until the shells have opened. Reserve the liquor and discard any unopened clams.

Clams Casino

12 hard-shelled clams, shucked but still on the
    half shell (procedure above)
rock salt
½ stick (¼ cup) unsalted butter, softened
¼ cup minced green bell pepper
¼ cup minced jarred pimiento
1 tablespoon minced fresh parsley leaves
1 garlic clove, minced fine
2 teaspoons fresh lemon juice
1 tablespoon dried bread crumbs
3 strips bacon, cut into 12 pieces

Cover the bottom of 2 individual 6-inch gratin dishes with the rock salt, patting the salt into a layer, sprinkle each layer with 1 tablespoon water, and heat the dishes in a preheated 500° F. oven for 5 minutes. Remove the dishes from the oven and let them cool.

Arrange 6 clams on the half shell on each dish, pressing the shells into the salt.

In a bowl combine 3 tablespoons of the butter, the green pepper, the pimiento, the parsley, the garlic, the lemon juice, the salt and pepper to taste and divide the mixture among the clams, spreading it over each clam until it is covered completely. Sprinkle the clams with the bread crumbs, top them with the remaining 1 tablespoon butter, cut into bits, and put 1 piece of bacon on each clam. Bake the clams in the preheated oven for 8 to 10 minutes, or until the bacon is golden brown and clams are just firm, and put them under a preheated broiler until the bacon is crisp. Serves 2 as a first course.

Manhattan Clam Chowder

24 hard-shelled clams, shucked (procedure on
    this page) and chopped coarse, reserving the
    liquor
2 cups minced onion
1 cup diced celery
3 tablespoons unsalted butter
a 2-pound 3-ounce can tomatoes, drained and
    chopped, reserving the liquid
2 cups diced boiling potatoes
2 garlic cloves, minced, or to taste
white fish stock (page 250) or bottled clam
    juice as needed
1 teaspoon dried basil
½ teaspoon dried thyme
1 bay leaf
⅔ cup minced fresh parsley leaves

In a large saucepan cook the onion and the celery in the butter over moderate heat, stirring occasionally, until the vegetables are soft. Add the tomatoes, the potatoes, and the garlic and cook the mixture, stirring, for 2 minutes. Measure the reserved tomato liquid and add enough of the reserved clam liquor, strained, to measure 8 cups. (If the clam liquor is too salty, replace it with fish stock or a combination of clam juice and water.) Add the basil, the thyme, the bay leaf, and pepper to taste, bring the soup to a boil, skimming, and simmer it, skimming occasionally, for 20 minutes. Stir in the clams and parsley and heat the soup over moderate heat, stirring, for 2 minutes, or until the clams are firm. Remove the bay leaf before serving. Makes about 12 cups, serving 6.

Clam and Scallion Dipping Sauce

12 hard-shelled clams, shucked (procedure on
    page 241), chopped fine
1 garlic clove, minced fine
8 ounces whipped cream cheese
¼ cup sour cream
2 whole scallions, sliced thin
2 teaspoons fresh lemon juice
⅛ teaspoon cayenne, or to taste

In a non-stick skillet stir the clams with the garlic over
moderate heat until the clams are just firm. Remove the
skillet from the heat, let the mixture cool, and chill it,
covered.

In a bowl combine the cream cheese with the sour
cream and beat the mixture until it is smooth. Stir in the
clams, drained well, the scallions, the lemon juice, the
cayenne, and salt to taste. Serve the dipping sauce with
raw vegetables, chips, or crackers. Makes about 2 cups.

Linguine with Clam Sauce

36 hard-shelled clams, shucked (procedure on
    page 241), reserving the liquor
½ cup olive oil
1 tablespoon minced garlic, or to taste
½ cup minced Italian parsley leaves
2 tablespoons minced fresh basil leaves
¼ to ½ teaspoon red pepper flakes, or to taste
12 ounces hot cooked *linguine*

Strain the clam liquor through a fine sieve lined with
cheesecloth into a bowl and combine it with enough water to measure 1⅓ cups. (Taste for saltiness and dilute it
with additional water if necessary.) Chop the clams.

In a large saucepan heat the oil over moderate heat
until it is hot. Add the garlic and cook it, stirring, until it
is golden. Add the clam liquor mixture, the parsley, the
basil, and the red pepper flakes and simmer the mixture,
covered, for 5 minutes. Add the clams and cook the
mixture over moderate heat, stirring, for 1 or 2 minutes,
or until the clams are just firm. Add the *linguine* and toss
the mixture until it is combined well. Serves 4 as a main
course or 6 as a first course.

To Shuck Oysters

Scrub the oysters thoroughly with a stiff brush under
running cold water. Hold each oyster in a dish towel in
the palm of the hand with the hinged end away from
you, force an oyster knife between the shells at the
hinged end, pressing down on the knife to pop open the
shell, and slide the blade against the flat upper shell to
cut the large muscle and free the upper shell. If the shell
crumbles and cannot be opened at the hinge, insert the
knife between the shells at the curved end of the oyster,
pry the shells open, and sever the large muscle. Break
off and discard the upper shell and slide the knife under
the oyster to release it from the bottom shell.

Leek and Oyster Soup

18 oysters, shucked (procedure on this page;
    about 3 cups oysters), reserving the liquor
¼ pound smoked slab bacon, cut into dice
2 tablespoons unsalted butter
3 cups finely chopped leeks (white part only)
1 onion, minced
1 large potato (about 10 ounces), diced
2 garlic cloves, minced
5 cups white fish stock (page 250)
a cheesecloth bag containing 12 parsley stems,
    ½ teaspoon dried thyme, 1 bay leaf, and 8
    peppercorns
1 cup heavy cream
1 cup thinly sliced scallion greens

In a large saucepan of boiling water blanch the bacon
for 5 minutes and drain it. In the pan cook the bacon in
the butter, stirring, until it is crisp, transfer it to paper
towels to drain, and reserve it. Pour off all but 2 tablespoons of the fat from the pan, add the leeks, the onion,
and salt and pepper to taste, and cook the vegetables
over moderate heat, stirring occasionally, until they are
soft. Add the potato and the garlic and cook the mixture,
stirring, for 1 minute. Add the fish stock, the cheesecloth bag, and salt and pepper, bring the liquid to a boil,
and simmer the soup, covered, for 30 minutes. Remove
the cheesecloth bag. In a food processor or blender purée the soup in batches, return it to the saucepan, and stir
in the cream. Add the reserved bacon to the saucepan,
season the soup with salt and pepper, and bring it to a
simmer.

In another saucepan gently heat the oysters in the oyster liquor, strained, over moderate heat just until they
are plump. With a slotted spoon transfer the oysters, 1
cup of the liquor, or to taste, and the scallion greens to
the soup and heat the soup over moderate heat, stirring,
until it is hot but do not let it boil. Serve the soup immediately. Makes about 10 cups, serving 6.

The Peacemaker
(Fried Oysters in Italian Bread)

12 large oysters, shucked (procedure on page 242; about 2 cups oysters) and drained
a 10-inch loaf of Italian bread
2 tablespoons unsalted butter, softened
2 tablespoons snipped fresh chives or scallion greens
cayenne to taste
flour for dredging the oysters
1 large egg
2 tablespoons milk
1½ cups fresh bread crumbs
vegetable oil for deep-frying the oysters

For the sauce
½ cup bottled chili sauce
2 tablespoons bottled horseradish, drained
Tabasco and Worcestershire sauce to taste

shredded lettuce

Split the bread in half horizontally and remove the crumb, leaving a ½-inch shell. Spread the cut sides of the bread with the butter and sprinkle them with the chives, salt, and cayenne to taste. Arrange the bread halves on a baking sheet and bake them in a preheated 350° F. oven for 15 minutes.

Dredge the oysters in the flour, shaking off the excess. In a small bowl combine the egg with the milk and beat the mixture until it is combined well. Dip the oysters, 1 at a time, into the egg mixture, letting the excess drip off, and coat them with the bread crumbs. Chill the oysters in one layer on a plate, covered, for 30 minutes. In a deep-fat fryer or heavy saucepan heat enough vegetable oil to cover the oysters to 375° F. Fry the oysters in batches, turning them, for 1 to 2 minutes, or until they are golden brown, and transfer them with a slotted spoon to paper towels to drain.

Make the sauce: In a small bowl combine the chili sauce, the horseradish, and the Tabasco and the Worcestershire sauce to taste and spread the mixture on the cut sides of the bread. (The sandwich may be garnished with tartar sauce instead of the chili sauce if desired.)

Cover the bottom half of the loaf with shredded lettuce, top it with the oysters, and arrange the remaining bread on top. Cut the loaf into 4 pieces. Makes 2 sandwiches.

Deviled Oysters

12 oysters, shucked (procedure on page 242; about 2 cups) reserving the liquor
1 cup minced onion
1 cup diced celery
¾ stick (6 tablespoons) unsalted butter
¼ cup minced fresh parsley leaves
2 teaspoons Dijon-style mustard
cayenne to taste
2 cups crushed unsalted crackers

Drain the oysters over a bowl and strain the liquor through a fine sieve lined with a double thickness of cheesecloth into another bowl. In a skillet cook the onion and the celery in 2 tablespoons of the butter with salt and pepper to taste over moderate heat, stirring occasionally, for 5 to 7 minutes, or until the vegetables are soft. Add the oysters and cook them, stirring, for about 1 minute, or until they are just firm. Stir in the parsley, the mustard, the cayenne, and salt to taste.

Spoon one third of the crushed crackers into a buttered 10-inch oval gratin dish, top them with one half of the oyster mixture, and sprinkle the mixture with enough of the reserved oyster liquor to moisten the crumbs. Dot with 2 tablespoons of the remaining butter, cut into bits, and arrange one third of the cracker crumbs over the top. Add the remaining oyster mixture and sprinkle it with enough of the reserved oyster liquor to moisten the crumbs. In the skillet melt the remaining 2 tablespoons butter over moderate heat, add the remaining cracker crumbs, and toss them in the butter until they are coated. Spoon the crumbs over the top of the oyster mixture, spreading them into a layer that covers the oyster mixture completely, and bake the mixture in a preheated 400° F. oven for 8 to 10 minutes, or until the top is golden. Serves 4.

Oyster and Pecan Stuffing

12 oysters, shucked (procedure on page 242;
   about 2 cups) cut into bite-size pieces
2 cups chopped onion
1½ cups chopped celery
1 stick (½ cup) unsalted butter
1 cup pecan pieces, chopped coarse
3 garlic cloves, minced
½ teaspoon dried thyme
½ teaspoon sage leaves, crumbled
6 cups toasted bread cubes
⅔ cup minced fresh parsley leaves
½ to 1 cup oyster liquor
6 to 8 slices bacon

In a skillet cook the onion, the celery, and salt and pepper in the butter over moderate heat, stirring occasionally, until the onion is golden. Add the pecans, the garlic, the thyme, and the sage and cook the mixture, stirring, for 2 minutes.

In a large bowl combine the bread cubes, the parsley, the oysters, the cooked vegetables, and salt and pepper and transfer it to a buttered 2-quart baking dish. Add enough of the reserved oyster liquor to moisten the bread, cover the stuffing with the bacon slices, and bake the stuffing in a preheated 350° F. oven for 1 hour. Check the stuffing after 30 minutes and if the bacon is crisp cover the dish with foil and continue cooking the stuffing. Remove the bacon from the dish, cut it into 1-inch slices, and gently stir it into the stuffing. Serve the stuffing with roast poultry or game and baked or grilled fish. Serves 6.

TO POACH EGGS

Poached eggs are one of the most satisfying solutions to any brunch menu, and can easily solve the dilemma of a Sunday night supper as well. Not only can they be served hot, as in that comforting favorite eggs Benedict, they can also be served chilled, as two of our recipes—poached eggs with herb mayonnaise and poached eggs in aspic—demonstrate. Moreover, the sheer simplicity of a well-poached egg is only to be enhanced by a wonderful sauce—a *bourguignonne* or a curry, as examples, each of which begins with one of the stock recipes that appears in the next section of this Addendum.

To Poach Eggs

2 tablespoons distilled white vinegar
very fresh eggs at room temperature

Fill a wide 3-inch-deep pan three fourths full with water. Add the vinegar, bring the liquid to a rolling boil over high heat, and reduce the heat so that the liquid barely simmers. Break and drop in as many eggs as needed. Or break the eggs, 1 at a time, into a saucer and slide them into the pan. As each egg is dropped in, push the egg white back immediately toward the yolk with a large slotted spoon, moving the egg gently. Simmer the eggs for 3 minutes, transfer them with the slotted spoon to a pan of cold water, and let them stand until they are needed. Drain the eggs carefully in the slotted spoon, blot them carefully with paper towels, and trim them. If poached correctly the yolk will be covered completely by the white and the egg will have returned approximately to its original oval shape. To serve the poached eggs hot, heat them in a saucepan of simmering water to cover for 30 seconds, or until they are heated through.

Eggs Benedict

For the sauce
3 large egg yolks
1½ tablespoons fresh lemon juice, or to taste
2 sticks (1 cup) unsalted butter, melted and
   cooled

6 large poached eggs (procedure on this page)
6 slices Canadian bacon
2 tablespoons unsalted butter
3 English muffins, split, toasted, and buttered
2 tablespoons snipped fresh chives for garnish

Make the sauce: In a food processor or blender combine the egg yolks, the lemon juice, and salt to taste. With the motor running add the butter in a stream. Transfer the sauce to a saucepan or heatproof bowl and keep it warm, covered with a round of buttered wax paper, in a pan of warm water.

In a skillet cook the Canadian bacon in the butter over moderate heat, turning it, until it is heated through. Heat the eggs in a saucepan of simmering water for 30 seconds, or until they are heated through, and blot each egg dry. Arrange the bacon on the muffins, top each muffin with a poached egg, and spoon the sauce over the eggs. Garnish the eggs with the chives. Serves 6.

Poached Eggs with Corned Beef Hash

4 large poached eggs (procedure on page 244)
3 cups finely diced corned beef
2 cups finely diced boiled potatoes
1 cup finely chopped onion
¾ stick (6 tablespoons) unsalted butter
¼ cup minced fresh parsley leaves
2 tomatoes, sliced
4 slices toast, buttered and halved diagonally

In a bowl combine the corned beef and the potatoes. In an ovenproof skillet cook the onion in 2 tablespoons of the butter with salt and pepper to taste over moderate heat, stirring occasionally, until it is golden. Add the onion to the corned beef mixture, stir in the parsley, and add salt and pepper to taste. In the skillet heat 2 tablespoons of the butter over moderate heat until it is hot, spoon in the hash, patting it into an even layer, and cook it over moderately low heat for 20 to 25 minutes, or until it is crisp on the bottom. Dot the top of the hash with the remaining 2 tablespoons butter and put the skillet under a preheated broiler until the top of the hash is golden brown.

Warm the poached eggs by heating them in a saucepan of simmering water to cover for 30 seconds, or until they are heated through. Blot the eggs dry. Cut the hash into 4 wedges and arrange each wedge on a heated plate. Top each wedge with a poached egg and garnish each plate with some of the tomatoes and the toast slices. Serves 4.

Poached Eggs in Bourguignonne Sauce

4 large eggs
1½ cups brown stock (page 249) or canned
   beef broth
1 cup dry red wine
For the bourguignonne sauce
½ pound sliced bacon, cut into 1-inch pieces
16 small white onions
a cheesecloth bag containing 1 small bay leaf,
   ¼ teaspoon dried thyme, 6 peppercorns,
   2 cloves, and 12 parsley stems
1 garlic clove, minced
2 teaspoons tomato paste
8 large mushrooms, quartered
beurre manié made by combining into a paste
   2 tablespoons unsalted butter, softened,
   with 1 tablespoon flour
1 to 2 teaspoons red currant jelly if desired

4 slices French bread, cut ½ inch thick,
   toasted and buttered
1 tablespoon minced fresh parsley leaves

Follow the procedure on page 244 for poaching eggs, substituting brown stock and red wine for the poaching liquid. With a slotted spoon transfer the eggs as they are done to a plate and reserve the poaching liquid.

Make the bourguignonne sauce: In a sauté pan cook the bacon over moderate heat, stirring, until it is golden brown, transfer it with a slotted spoon to a plate lined with paper towels to drain, and pour off all but 1 tablespoon of the fat from the pan. Add the onions to the pan and cook them, swirling the pan, until they are golden brown. Add the reserved poaching liquid, the cheesecloth bag, the garlic, and the tomato paste, bring the liquid to a boil, and simmer the sauce, partially covered, for 10 minutes. Add the mushrooms and simmer the sauce for 5 minutes more, or until the onions are tender. Remove the cheesecloth bag. Bring the liquid in the pan to a boil and whisk in the *beurre manié*, a little at a time, until the sauce is thickened slightly. Stir in the currant jelly, if desired, and the bacon.

Heat the eggs in a saucepan of simmering water for 30 seconds and blot each egg dry. On each plate arrange each egg on a slice of the French bread and nap the eggs with the sauce, dividing it equally. Garnish the eggs with the parsley. Serves 4.

Poached Eggs with Smoked Salmon and Curry Sauce

4 large poached eggs (procedure on page 244)
For the curry sauce
½ cup minced onion
3 tablespoons unsalted butter
1 tablespoon curry powder, or to taste
2 tablespoons flour
2½ cups chicken stock (page 247) or canned chicken broth
1 bay leaf
½ cup heavy cream
fresh lemon juice to taste
2 tablespoons minced fresh coriander leaves

2 split mini *pita* breads, toasted and buttered
4 slices smoked salmon

Make the curry sauce: In a saucepan cook the onion in the butter over moderate heat, stirring, until it is softened. Add the curry powder and the flour and cook the *roux*, stirring, for 3 minutes. Add the chicken stock in a stream, whisking, bring the liquid to a boil, and add the bay leaf. Simmer the sauce, stirring occasionally, for 30 minutes. Add the cream and reduce the sauce until it is thickened slightly. Remove the bay leaf and stir in the lemon juice and the coriander.

Heat the poached eggs in a saucepan of simmering water for 30 seconds and blot each egg dry. Divide the *pita* toasts among 4 heated plates, top each *pita* with a slice of smoked salmon and a poached egg, and nap the eggs with the curry sauce. Serves 4.

Poached Eggs with Herb Mayonnaise

6 large poached eggs (procedure on page 244), thoroughly chilled
For the herb mayonnaise
1 large egg
1 large egg yolk
1 tablespoon fresh lemon juice
1 tablespoon rice vinegar
1 tablespoon dry vermouth
1 teaspoon Dijon-style mustard, or to taste
½ cup olive oil
½ cup vegetable oil
2 tablespoons minced fresh dill
2 tablespoons minced fresh parsley leaves
1 tablespoon snipped fresh chives
1 tablespoon minced fresh tarragon

2 tablespoons sour cream
3 large tomatoes
1 cup sliced white onion
1 tablespoon olive oil
¼ cup rice vinegar
lettuce leaves for lining the plates

Make the herb mayonnaise: In a food processor or blender combine the egg, the egg yolk, the lemon juice, the vinegar, the vermouth, the mustard, and salt and pepper to taste. With the motor running add the olive and vegetable oils in a stream. Transfer the mayonnaise to a bowl and stir in the fresh herbs, the sour cream, and salt and pepper to taste.

Halve the tomatoes and with a teaspoon remove some of the pulp from each, leaving a ½-inch shell. In a small skillet cook the onion in the olive oil over moderate heat, stirring, until it is softened, add the rice vinegar, and reduce the liquid to 1 teaspoon.

Line 6 plates with the lettuce leaves, arrange a tomato half on each plate, and spoon a little of the onion mixture into each tomato half, dividing it among the halves. Arrange a poached egg on each tomato half and spoon some of the herb mayonnaise over each egg. Serve the remaining herb mayonnaise separately. Serves 6.

Poached Eggs in Aspic

6 large poached eggs (procedure on page 244), chilled
1 recipe hot chicken consommé (page 248, without the vegetable garnish)
3 tablespoons unflavored gelatin
small fresh basil leaves
romaine lettuce, cut into shreds, for garnish
herb mayonnaise (recipe on this page) as an accompaniment if desired

Rinse six ½-cup oval molds with cold water and chill them thoroughly.

In a small bowl sprinkle the gelatin over 1 cup of the consommé and let it soften for 10 minutes. Set the bowl in a larger bowl of hot water, stir the mixture until the gelatin is dissolved, and stir the mixture into the remaining consommé. Let the aspic cool completely and chill it, stirring occasionally, until it is cold but not thickened. Into each of the molds ladle enough of the cold aspic to measure ¼ inch and chill the molds until the aspic is set.

Dip the basil leaves in the liquid aspic to moisten

them, arrange them decoratively in the mold, and ladle enough of the liquid aspic over them to measure ⅛ inch, being careful not to disturb the design. Chill the molds until the aspic is just set. Arrange a chilled poached egg, patted dry, in each mold, ladle enough liquid aspic around and over the eggs to cover them, and chill the molds for 2 hours, or until the aspic is completely set.

Run a thin knife around the edge of each mold, dip each mold in hot water for a few seconds, and invert it onto a cold plate. Garnish the plates with the shredded lettuce and serve the eggs with herb mayonnaise as an accompaniment if desired. Serves 6.

TO MAKE STOCK

With a supply of well-made stock on hand, the culinary possibilities are truly almost limitless. To begin with, you've soup at the ready. It can be simple or complex, but the base is there. With some extra effort, and ingredients, you also have a stew or fricassée in the works because the sauce for that stew begins with—what else?—stock. And then there are such unexpected delights as creamy Italian risotto, dependent on cups of hot stock and imported long-grain rice.

This short primer on stockmaking includes recipes for chicken stock, brown stock, and white fish stock, as well as intriguing recipes based on those stocks, and a procedure for clarifying stock. A somewhat longer clarifying process appears in the recipe for *consommé printanière* and is included to show how the addition of certain vegetables contributes in fortifying a stock's intensity.

While there certainly are alternatives to homemade stock, none can replicate the flavors of one simmering slowly in your own stockpot.

Chicken Stock

a 4-pound fowl
the neck and giblets (excluding the liver),
    chopped
1 large onion stuck with 2 cloves
2 leeks, halved lengthwise and washed well
2 carrots
1 rib of celery, halved
2 teaspoons salt
a cheesecloth bag containing 6 sprigs of
    parsley, ½ teaspoon dried thyme, 1
    unpeeled garlic clove, and 1 bay leaf

In a kettle combine the fowl, the neck and the giblets, and 12 cups cold water, bring the water to a boil, and skim the froth. Add ½ cup cold water, bring the mixture to a simmer, and skim any froth. Add the onion, the leeks, the carrots, the celery, the salt, and the cheesecloth bag and simmer the mixture, skimming the froth, for 2 hours. Remove the fowl from the kettle, remove the meat and skin from the carcass, and reserve the meat for another use. Chop the carcass, return it and the skin to the kettle, and simmer the stock, adding boiling water if necessary to keep the ingredients barely covered, for 2 hours more. Strain the stock through a fine sieve into a bowl, pressing hard on the solids, and let it cool. Chill the stock and remove the fat. The stock may be frozen. Makes about 6 cups.

To Clarify Stock

8 cups cool liquid stock, fat removed
the crushed shells of 4 large eggs
4 large egg whites, beaten lightly
4 scallions, chopped

In a kettle combine the stock, the shells, the egg whites, the scallions, and, if necessary, salt and pepper to taste. Bring the liquid to a boil, stirring, simmer the stock, undisturbed, for 20 minutes, and ladle it through a fine sieve lined with a double thickness of rinsed and squeezed cheesecloth into a bowl. Makes about 6 cups clarified stock.

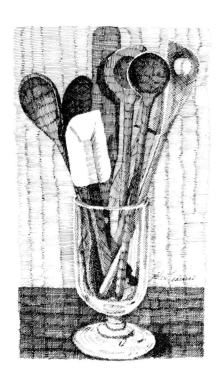

Consommé Printanière
(Chicken Consommé with Spring Vegetables)

6 cups chicken stock (page 247)
the crushed shells of 3 large eggs
3 large egg whites, beaten lightly
1 rib of celery, chopped fine
1 leek including the green top, washed well
 and chopped fine
1 cup chopped tomato
¼ cup finely chopped carrot
a cheesecloth bag containing 1 teaspoon dried
 basil, 6 peppercorns, ¼ teaspoon dried
 thyme, and a bay leaf
⅓ cup chopped fresh basil leaves
¼ cup chopped fresh parsley leaves

For the vegetable garnish
2 carrots, cut into 1½-inch pieces
1 turnip, halved and cut into thin slices
12 snow peas, cut into julienne strips
6 fresh basil leaves, cut into shreds

In a large saucepan combine the chicken stock, the egg shells, the egg whites, the celery, the leek, the tomato, the carrot, the cheesecloth bag, the basil, the parsley, and salt to taste, bring the liquid to a boil, stirring, and simmer the mixture, undisturbed, for 30 minutes. Ladle the stock through a fine sieve lined with a double thickness of rinsed and squeezed cheesecloth into a clean saucepan and skim any fat from the surface of the consommé.

Prepare the vegetable garnish: In a saucepan of boiling salted water simmer the carrots for 6 minutes, add the turnip, and continue to simmer the vegetables for 2 to 3 minutes more, or until the vegetable are just tender. Add the snow peas, bring the liquid to a simmer, and drain the vegetables. Refresh the vegetables under cold running water and pat them dry. Before serving, combine the consommé and the vegetables and simmer the soup until the vegetables are heated through. Divide the soup and vegetables among 4 bowls and garnish each bowl with some of the fresh basil. Serves 4.

Blanquette de Veau
(Veal Stew with Onions and Mushrooms)

6 cups chicken stock (page 247) or canned
 chicken broth
3 pounds boneless veal shoulder, cut into
 2-inch pieces

1 onion studded with 3 whole cloves
1 carrot, quartered
1 rib of celery, sliced
3 whole garlic cloves
a cheesecloth bag containing 12 parsley stems,
 1 teaspoon dried thyme, ¼ teaspoon
 peppercorns, and 1 bay leaf
½ pound mushrooms, quartered
5 tablespoons unsalted butter
1 tablespoon fresh lemon juice with additional
 lemon juice to taste
24 small white onions
4 tablespoons flour
½ cup heavy cream
½ cup sour cream
3 egg yolks
freshly grated nutmeg to taste
3 tablespoons minced fresh parsley leaves

In a casserole cover the veal with cold water, bring the water to a boil, and simmer the mixture for 3 minutes. Drain the veal, rinse it under cold water, and put it into a casserole. Add the stock, the onion, the carrot, the celery, the garlic, the cheesecloth bag, salt to taste, and, if necessary, enough water to cover the veal and vegetables by 1 inch. Bring the liquid to a simmer, skimming, and simmer the stew, partially covered, skimming occasionally, for 1 hour and 30 minutes, or until the veal is tender.

In a saucepan cover the mushrooms with 1 cup water, add 1 tablespoon of the butter, the lemon juice, and salt and pepper to taste, and simmer the mushrooms for 5 to 7 minutes, or until they are firm. Transfer the mushrooms with a slotted spoon to a large bowl and reduce the mushroom cooking liquid to ½ cup. Add the reduced mushroom liquid to the veal stew.

In another saucepan cover the small white onions with water, add 1 tablespoon of the butter and salt and pepper to taste, and simmer the onions, covered, for 20 to 25 minutes, or until they are tender. Transfer the onions with a slotted spoon to the bowl containing the mushrooms and reduce the onion cooking liquid to ½ cup. Add the reduced onion liquid to the veal stew.

With a large fork transfer the veal to the bowl containing the mushrooms and onions, strain the cooking liquid, discarding the vegetables, and return it to the casserole. Reduce the liquid over moderate heat to 3 cups. In a saucepan melt the remaining 3 tablespoons butter over moderately low heat, add the flour, and cook the *roux*, whisking, for 3 minutes. Add the cooking liquid to the saucepan and simmer the mixture, stirring and skimming occasionally, for 15 minutes. Rinse out the casserole, return the veal, mushrooms, and onions to it, and add the sauce. Simmer the stew for 5 minutes, or until it is heated through.

In a bowl whisk together the heavy cream, the sour cream, and the egg yolks and add 1 cup of the sauce in a stream, whisking. Stir the cream mixture into the stew and warm the stew over moderately low heat, stirring, but do not let it boil. Add lemon juice, nutmeg, and salt and pepper to taste and garnish the stew with the parsley. Serves 6.

Brown Stock

2 pounds meaty beef shanks, sawed into
   1-inch slices
2 pounds meaty veal shanks, sawed into
   1-inch slices
2 unpeeled onions, quartered
1 carrot, quartered
2 ribs of celery
1½ teaspoons salt
a cheesecloth bag containing 4 sprigs of
   parsley, ½ teaspoon dried thyme, and
   1 bay leaf

Spread the beef shanks, the veal shanks, the onions, and the carrot in a flameproof baking pan, brown them well in a preheated 450° F. oven, and transfer them to a kettle. Add 2 cups water to the pan, deglaze the pan over high heat, scraping up the brown bits, and add the liquid to the kettle with 14 cups cold water, the celery, the salt, and the cheesecloth bag. Bring the water to a boil and skim the froth. Add ½ cup cold water, bring the mixture to a simmer, and skim any froth. Simmer the mixture, adding boiling water to keep the ingredients barely covered, for 5 to 6 hours, or until the stock is reduced to about 8 cups. Strain the stock through a fine sieve into a bowl, pressing hard on the solids, and let it cool. Chill the stock and remove the fat. The stock may be frozen. Makes about 8 cups.

Onion Soup Gratinée

For the soup base
6 cups brown stock (recipe above)
1¼ pounds onions, sliced thin
2 tablespoons unsalted butter
1 tablespoon olive oil

a pinch of sugar
2 tablespoons flour
⅓ cup dry vermouth
a cheesecloth bag containing ½ teaspoon dried
   thyme, 12 parsley stems, 8 peppercorns,
   and a bay leaf
2 tablespoons Cognac
Worcestershire sauce to taste

8 to 10 slices of French bread, cut 1 inch thick
½ stick (¼ cup) unsalted butter, melted
1 garlic clove
1 cup grated Swiss cheese
½ cup grated Parmesan

Make the soup base: In a large saucepan cook the onions in the butter and the oil with the salt and pepper to taste over moderately low heat, covered, stirring occasionally, until they are soft. Add the sugar and cook the onions over moderate heat, uncovered, stirring occasionally, until they are golden brown. Add the flour and cook the mixture, stirring, for 3 minutes. Add the stock, the vermouth, the cheesecloth bag, and salt and pepper to taste and cook the soup, partially covered, skimming occasionally, for 30 minutes. Season the soup with the Cognac, the Worcestershire sauce, and salt and pepper to taste.

Arrange the slices of bread on a baking sheet, brush both sides of them with some of the melted butter, and bake the slices in a preheated 350° F. oven, turning them once, for 15 minutes, or until they are golden. Rub the slices of bread with the garlic clove.

Transfer the soup base to an ovenproof soup tureen or deep baking dish and cover the top of it completely with the toasted bread slices. Sprinkle the bread slices with the Swiss and Parmesan cheeses and drizzle the remaining melted butter on top. Bake the soup in the preheated oven for 15 to 20 minutes, or until it is simmering, and put the dish under a preheated broiler until the cheese is golden. Makes about 6 cups, serving 4.

Braised Beef in Red Wine

3 cups brown stock (page 249)
a 4-pound chuck roast or bottom round roast beef
3 cups dry red wine
1 large onion, chopped
1 carrot, sliced thick
1 rib of celery, sliced thick
3 garlic cloves, chopped
1 teaspoon salt
a cheesecloth bag containing 1 teaspoon dried thyme, 1 teaspoon dried rosemary, 8 whole peppercorns, 4 cloves, 12 parsley stems, and 1 bay leaf
2 tablespoons unsalted butter
1 tablespoon olive oil
1 tablespoon tomato paste
3 tablespoons Sercial Madeira
2 tablespoons cornstarch

In a large ceramic or glass bowl combine the roast with 1 cup of the stock, the wine, the onion, the carrot, the celery, the garlic, the salt, and the cheesecloth bag and let it marinate, covered and chilled, turning it occasionally, overnight.

Drain the roast and the vegetables, reserving the marinade and the cheesecloth bag, and pat the roast dry. In a large stainless steel or enameled casserole brown the roast in the butter and the oil over moderately high heat and remove it to a plate. Add the reserved vegetables to the casserole and cook them over moderate heat, stirring, for 5 minutes. Add the reserved marinade, the remaining stock, the roast, the tomato paste, the reserved cheesecloth bag, and enough water to just cover the roast, bring the liquid to a boil, and braise the mixture, covered, in a preheated 325° F. oven for 3 hours, or until the roast is tender. Transfer the roast to a platter, skim the fat from the braising liquid, and strain the liquid into another casserole. Reduce the liquid for 3 to 5 minutes, or until it tastes full-bodied. In a small bowl combine the Madeira and the cornstarch and whisk it into the simmering sauce, a little at a time, until the sauce is just thick enough to coat the back of a spoon. Cut the roast into slices and nap the slices with some of the sauce. Serve the remaining sauce separately. Serves 6.

If desired, the roast may also be served chilled and the stock tranformed into an aspic. Before adding the Madeira and cornstarch mixture to the sauce, simply let the roast come to room temperature and chill it and the stock overnight. Slice the roast and arrange the slices overlapping slightly in a gratin dish. A vegetable garnish may be added, if desired, such as cooked carrots, turnips, or peas. If necessary, soften enough gelatin in 2 to 3 tablespoons Sercial Madeira to thicken the stock, using the proportions on the gelatin box, heat the stock, and add the gelatin mixture to it, stirring, until it is completely dissolved. Stir the aspic over the ice until it is cold and pour it over the roast and vegetables. Chill the dish until the aspic is set. Serve the roast with a flavored mayonnaise or horseradish cream if desired.

White Fish Stock

1 pound bones and trimmings of any white fish such as sole, flounder, or whiting, chopped
1 cup sliced onion
12 parsley stems
2 tablespoons fresh lemon juice
½ teaspoon salt
½ cup dry white wine

In a well buttered heavy saucepan combine the fish bones and trimmings, the onion, the parsley, the lemon juice, and the salt and steam the mixture, covered, over moderately high heat for 5 minutes. Add 3½ cups cold water and the wine, bring the liquid to a boil, skimming the froth, and cook the stock over moderate heat for 25 minutes. Strain the stock through a fine sieve into a bowl, pressing hard on the solids, and let it cool. The stock may be frozen. Makes about 3 cups.

Cioppino

4 cups white fish stock (recipe above)
2 cups chopped onion
⅓ cup olive oil
1 green bell pepper, cut into strips
4 garlic cloves, minced
3 cups chopped tomatoes
1 cup chopped fresh parsley leaves
½ cup dry white wine
3 tablespoons tomato paste
1 teaspoon dried thyme leaves
1 teaspoon dried basil
1 bay leaf
½ teaspoon dried orégano
½ teaspoon red pepper flakes, or to taste
1 pound firm-fleshed fish such as striped bass or red snapper, cut into 1½-inch thick pieces

½ pound sea scallops, halved if large
1 pound shrimp, shelled and deveined
6 clams, scrubbed
6 mussels, scrubbed and beards removed
¼ cup minced fresh basil leaves or parsley
　leaves for garnish

In a casserole cook the onion in the olive oil over moderate heat, stirring occasionally, until it is golden. Add the green pepper and the garlic and cook the mixture, stirring occasionally, until the pepper is softened. Add the chopped tomatoes, the fish stock, the parsley, the white wine, the tomato paste, the thyme, the basil, the bay leaf, the orégano, the red pepper flakes, and salt to taste, bring the mixture to a simmer, stirring, and simmer it, covered, for 45 minutes. Bring the soup to a boil and add the bass, the scallops, and the shrimp. Bring the soup back to a boil, stirring gently, add the clams and mussels, and simmer the soup, stirring occasionally, until the clams and mussels have opened and the fish just flakes. Discard the bay leaf and any unopened clams or mussels. Spoon the soup into heated bowls and garnish each bowl with the basil or parsley. Serves 6.

Seafood Risotto

8 to 9 cups white fish stock (page 250)
7 tablespoons unsalted butter
½ pound sea scallops, halved if large
½ pound shrimp, shelled and deveined
　1 small garlic clove, minced fine
　1 cup minced onion

½ cup dry white wine
2 cups Arborio rice (available at specialty
　foods shops) or long-grain rice
⅔ cup freshly grated Parmesan

In a non-stick skillet heat 1 tablespoon of the butter over moderate heat until it is hot, add the scallops, the shrimp, the garlic, and salt and pepper to taste and toss the mixture. Cover the skillet and cook the mixture over moderately low heat, shaking the pan, for 2 to 3 minutes, or until the seafood is just firm. Remove the pan from the heat and let the seafood cool, uncovered.

In a saucepan bring to a boil the fish stock and keep it at a bare simmer. In a large heavy saucepan cook the onion in 4 tablespoons of the butter over moderate heat, stirring, until it is soft, add the Arborio rice, and cook the mixture, stirring, for 1 minute, or until the rice is well coated with the butter. Add the wine and cook the mixture at a vigorous simmer, stirring, until the wine is absorbed. Add ⅔ cup of the stock to the pan and cook the mixture at a vigorous simmer, stirring, for 3 to 5 minutes, or until the stock is absorbed. Continue to cook the risotto in the same manner, adding the stock ⅔ cup at a time until the rice begins to soften, or for about 12 to 15 minutes. Then begin adding the stock ½ cup at a time and continue to cook the risotto in the same manner until the mixture is creamy but the rice remains *al dente*. Stir in the seafood, including any juices that have accumulated, and cook it, stirring, until it is heated through. Remove the pan from the heat, stir in the Parmesan and the remaining 2 tablespoons butter, and serve the risotto immediately. Serves 6.

Barbara Fiori

Poached Rainbow Trout
with Watercress Sauce

For the sauce

3 tablespoons unsalted butter
3 tablespoons flour
3 cups white fish stock (page 250)
a cheesecloth bag containing 12 parsley stems,
 ½ teaspoon dried thyme, and 1 bay leaf
1 tablespoon minced shallots
½ cup dry white wine
½ cup heavy cream
freshly grated nutmeg to taste

four 12-ounce rainbow trout, cleaned
1 tablespoon minced shallot
about 1 cup white fish stock (page 250)
1 cup coarsely chopped watercress leaves with
 sprigs of fresh watercress for garnish
2 tablespoons unsalted butter,
 cut into bits
fresh lemon juice to taste

Make the sauce: In a saucepan melt the butter, add the flour, and cook the *roux* over moderately low heat, whisking, for 3 minutes. Add the fish stock in a stream, whisking, the cheesecloth bag, and salt and pepper to taste and simmer the sauce, whisking occasionally, for 30 minutes. If necessary, reduce the sauce to 1½ cups and strain it through a fine sieve into a bowl. In another saucepan combine the shallots and the wine, reduce the liquid to 1 tablespoon, and add the strained fish sauce. Stir in the heavy cream, the nutmeg, and salt and pepper to taste and simmer the sauce for 5 minutes. Let the sauce stand, covered with a buttered round of wax paper, while preparing the trout.

Arrange the trout in a buttered heatproof gratin dish, sprinkle it with the shallot, and pour in enough fish stock to come halfway up the fish. Bring the liquid to a simmer on top of the stove and bake the fish, covered with buttered wax paper, in a preheated 350° F. oven for 12 to 15 minutes, or until it flakes easily when tested with a fork. Transfer the fish to a cutting board and remove the skin. Bring the sauce to a simmer and stir in the chopped watercress leaves. Bring the sauce back to a simmer, stirring, and add the butter and lemon juice to taste. Arrange the fish on heated individual serving plates, spoon the sauce over the fish, and arrange the sprigs of watercress decoratively on the plates. Serves 4.

GÉNOISE BATTER

Génoise, a particularly light French spongecake, is predicated upon a batter of basic ingredients—eggs, sugar, flour, butter—but with an extraordinary amount of air beaten in. As such, it makes for a most adaptable layer cake. *Génoise* also absorbs flavor readily and combines well with other ingredients, making it the perfect base for trifle and for charlotte molds. It is also sturdy enough but still sufficiently ephemeral to act as the case for an enticing ice-cream roll, such as the one on page 254.

Génoise Batter

6 large eggs
1 cup sugar
1 cup all-purpose flour
¾ teaspoon salt
1½ teaspoons vanilla
6 tablespoons clarified butter (page 92),
 melted and cooled to lukewarm

In a metal bowl whisk together the eggs and the sugar, set the bowl over a pan of simmering water, and stir the mixture until it is warm and the sugar is dissolved. Remove the bowl from the pan and with an electric mixer beat the mixture at moderate speed for 10 to 15 minutes, or until it is triple in volume and cooled to room temperature. While the eggs are being beaten sift the flour with the salt onto a sheet of wax paper and in a bowl combine the vanilla and the clarified butter. Sift and fold the flour mixture in batches into the egg mixture until the mixture is just combined, stir one fourth of the mixture into the butter mixture, and fold the butter mixture quickly into the batter.

English Trifle

1 recipe *génoise* batter (recipe above)
1 teaspoon grated lemon rind
1 pound strawberries, hulled
1 recipe caramel crème anglaise (page 256)
3 tablespoons Cognac
1 tablespoon fresh lemon juice
2 tablespoons sugar
½ cup sieved strawberry jam
1 cup heavy cream, whipped
½ cup sliced almonds, toasted

Line the bottom of 2 buttered 8-inch round cake pans with wax paper, butter the paper, and dust the pan with flour, shaking out the excess. Add the lemon rind to the *génoise* batter, pour the batter into the pans, smoothing the tops, and bake the layers in the middle of a preheated 350° F. oven for 20 to 25 minutes, or until a cake tester inserted in the centers comes out clean. Let the layers cool in the pans on a rack for 10 minutes, turn them out onto the rack, and let them cool completely.

Reserve 6 whole strawberries for decorating the trifle and cut the remaining berries into slices. In a bowl toss the berries with the Cognac, the lemon juice, and the sugar and chill them, covered, for 30 minutes.

Have ready the caramel crème anglaise.

Halve the cake layers horizontally and spread the cut side of 3 of the halves with the jam. Quarter two of the jam-coated halves, making 8 triangular-shaped pieces, and arrange the triangles jam side out around the sides of a 2-quart bowl. Arrange the uncoated half in the bottom of the bowl cut side up and cover it with half of the berries, including all of their juice. Ladle half the caramel crème anglaise over the berries and top it with the remaining jam-coated layer jam side up. Top the cake with the remaining berries, the remaining crème anglaise, and sprinkle half of the almonds on it. Chill the trifle for 2 to 3 hours or overnight. Before serving, spoon the whipped cream over the top of the trifle, smoothing it into an even layer, and decorate the trifle with the reserved whole berries and remaining toasted almonds.

Orange Tea Cakes with Chocolate Glaze

1 recipe *génoise* batter (page 252)
1 tablespoon grated orange rind
½ recipe light chocolate buttercream (page 255)
½ cup sugar
2 tablespoons orange-flavored liqueur
For the glaze
1⅔ cups sugar
1½ cups unsweetened cocoa powder, sifted
1 cup heavy cream
1 stick (½ cup) unsalted butter, melted
2 tablespoons orange-flavored liqueur

Line the bottom of a buttered 13- by 9- by 2-inch rectangular cake pan with wax paper, butter the paper, and dust the pan with flour, shaking out the excess. Add the orange rind to the *génoise* batter, pour the batter into the pan, smoothing the top, and bake the cake in the middle of a preheated 350° F. oven for 15 to 20 minutes, or until a cake tester inserted in the center comes out clean. Let the cake cool in the pan on a rack for 10 minutes, turn it out on the rack, and let it cool completely.

Have ready the chocolate buttercream.

In a small saucepan combine the sugar with ½ cup water and stir the mixture over moderate heat until it is clear. Let the syrup cool and stir in the orange-flavored liqueur.

Divide the cake into 2 cakes by cutting it in half lengthwise and cut each half horizontally into 2 layers. Sprinkle the bottom layers with some of the syrup and divide enough of the buttercream between the layers to form a smooth and even layer about ¼ inch thick. Sprinkle the top layers cut side up with the syrup and invert them onto the buttercream-coated bottom layers. Wrap the cakes in plastic wrap and chill them for at least 2 hours or overnight.

Make the glaze: In a saucepan combine the sugar, the cocoa, and a pinch of salt. Beat in the heavy cream and the butter in a stream and cook the glaze over moderate heat, whisking, until it is smooth and of pouring consistency. Whisk in the liqueur. Set the pan in a pan of hot water to keep it warm enough to pour.

Work with 1 cake at a time, keeping the other cake chilled. Cut the cake into 1½- by 2-inch rectangles with a serrated knife and arrange the rectangles on a large cake rack over a baking pan. Ladle the glaze over the cake pieces, completely coating the top and sides of each. (If necessary, use a spatula to apply the glaze smoothly on the uncoated sections.) Scrape the excess glaze from the baking pan back into the saucepan and reheat it, stirring, until it is of pouring consistency. Chill the cakes on the rack. Cut and glaze the remaining cake in the same manner and chill both cakes until the glaze has hardened slightly. Scrape any extra glaze into a bowl and let it cool to frosting consistency. Transfer the glaze to a pastry bag fitted with a small fluted tip and decorate the tops of the cakes. Makes 24 cakes.

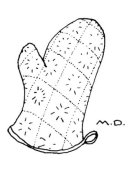

Raspberry Charlotte Mold

1 recipe *génoise* batter (page 252)
confectioners' sugar for dusting the wax paper
a 1-pound jar raspberry preserves, sieved
1 recipe raspberry Bavarian cream (page 257)
1 cup heavy cream, whipped
fresh whole raspberries for decoration

Line the bottom of a buttered 15½- by 10½- by 1-inch jelly-roll pan with wax paper, butter the paper, and dust it with flour, shaking out the excess. Pour the batter into the pan, smoothing the top, and bake the cake in the middle of a preheated 350° F. oven for 15 to 20 minutes, or until a cake tester inserted in the center comes out clean. Let the cake cool in the pan for 5 minutes, run a thin knife around the sides to loosen it, and invert it onto a sheet of wax paper dusted with the confectioners' sugar. Peel off the top layer of wax paper, spread the cake with the jam, and, starting with a long side, roll up the cake jelly-roll fashion, lifting it with the wax paper and finishing it with the seam side down. Wrap the cake in wax paper and chill it overnight.

Cut the cake into 20 slices and arrange the slices cut side down on the bottom and around the sides of a buttered 2-quart bowl, reserving the extra slices for the base of the charlotte. Chill the bowl, covered.

Have ready the raspberry Bavarian cream. Pour the cream into the mold and top it with the extra cake slices. Chill the charlotte, covered, for 2 hours. (The charlotte may be chilled overnight.) Dip the bowl into hot water, run the point of a thin knife around the inside edge of the bowl, and invert the charlotte onto a platter. Transfer half of the whipped cream to a pastry bag fitted with a fluted tip and decorate the charlotte with the cream and the raspberries. Serve the remaining cream separately.

Chocolate Mocha Ice-Cream Roll

1 recipe *génoise* batter (page 252), substituting
  ½ cup all-purpose flour combined with
  ⅓ cup unsweetened cocoa powder for the
  1 cup all-purpose flour in the master recipe
confectioners' sugar for dusting the wax paper
1 recipe chocolate mocha ice cream (page
  256), soft enough to spread
½ cup sugar
2 tablespoons Kahlúa liqueur
1 ounce semisweet chocolate, grated
sifted confectioners' sugar for garnish

Line the bottom of a buttered 15½- by 10½- by 1-inch jelly-roll pan with wax paper, butter the paper, and dust it with flour, shaking out the excess. Pour the batter into the pan, smoothing the top, and bake the cake in the middle of a preheated 350° F. oven for 15 to 20 minutes, or until a cake tester inserted in the center comes out clean. Transfer the pan to a rack, let the cake cool for 5 minutes, and run a knife around the sides of the pan to release the wax paper. Dust a sheet of wax paper with the confectioners' sugar and invert the cake onto it. Peel off the top layer of wax paper and lay the paper loosely on the top of the cake. Let the cake cool to just warm and roll it up in the wax paper.

Have ready the chocolate mocha ice cream.

In a small saucepan combine the sugar with ½ cup water and cook the mixture over moderate heat, stirring, until it is clear. Let the syrup cool and stir in the Kahlúa.

Unroll the cake, sprinkle the top of the cake with the syrup, and spread the ice cream over the cake, leaving a 1-inch border. Starting with a long side, roll up the cake jelly-roll fashion, lifting it with the wax paper and finishing it with the seam side down. Wrap the roll in wax paper and freeze it for at least 4 hours, or until the ice cream is frozen. To serve, cut the roll into slices, arrange them on a platter, and garnish them with the grated chocolate and confectioners' sugar.

Génoise Peach Tart

an 8-inch round baked *génoise* cake or
  leftover *génoise* cake
½ stick (¼ cup) unsalted butter, softened
4 to 5 ripe peaches or nectarines, peeled,
  pitted, and sliced
2 tablespoons sugar
⅛ teaspoon ground cinnamon
2 tablespoons honey
1 teaspoon fresh lemon juice
2 tablespoons skinned pistachio nuts, sliced
  toasted almonds, or toasted ground hazelnuts
sour cream or whipped cream as an
  accompaniment if desired

Cut the cake into 4 wedges and cut each wedge horizontally in half. Spread the wedges with 2 tablespoons of the butter and arrange them in concentric circles on the bottom of a buttered 10-inch tart pan, overlapping them slightly. Completely cover the cake with the peaches, sprinkle the fruit with the sugar and cinnamon, and dot it with the remaining butter. Bake the tart in a preheated 450° F. oven on a baking sheet for 20 to 25 minutes, or until the edges of the cake are golden.

In a small saucepan heat the honey with the lemon juice and brush it over the fruit. Garnish the *croûte* with the nuts and accompany it with the sour or whipped cream if desired.

PASTRY CREAM

Pastry cream, another straightforward combination, this time of egg yolks, sugar, flour, milk or cream, and flavoring, is actually basic custard. When made with no flour and additional cream or half-and-half, it becomes crème anglaise, the silky custard sauce so appropriate on poached fruit or as an accompaniment to any number of other desserts. And when gelatin is added, you are on your way to a Bavarian cream. Lastly, and perhaps most surprisingly, these simple ingredients for basic custard are the foundation for making ice cream.

Pastry Cream

3 large egg yolks
⅓ cup sugar
2 tablespoons cornstarch
2 tablespoons all-purpose flour
1 cup milk
1 teaspoon vanilla

In a large bowl with an electric mixer beat the egg yolks until they are combined, add the sugar, a little at a time, beating, and beat the mixture until it is light and lemon colored. Add the cornstarch and the flour, a little at a time, beating, and beat the mixture until it is smooth. Add the milk, scalded, in a stream, beating, and beat the mixture until it is combined well. In a heavy saucepan bring the mixture to a boil, stirring, and simmer it, stirring, for 3 minutes. The mixture will be thick and custardlike. Remove the pan from the heat and beat in the vanilla. Strain the pastry cream into a bowl and chill it, covered with a buttered round of wax paper, for 1 hour, or until it is chilled well. Makes 1 cup.

Strawberry Frangipane Tart

1 recipe pastry cream (recipe above)
1 tablespoon Amaretto, or to taste
¼ teaspoon almond extract
1 recipe *pâte brisée* (page 222)
dried beans or raw rice for weighting the shell

½ cup whole blanched almonds, toasted and ground
½ cup heavy cream, whipped
½ cup red currant jelly
2 pints strawberries or other seasonal fruit

Beat the Amaretto and the almond extract into the pastry cream and chill the pastry cream, covered with a buttered round of wax paper, for 1 hour.

Roll the *pâte brisée* into a round ⅛ inch thick on a floured surface, fit it into a 10-inch tart pan with a removable bottom, and set the pan on a baking sheet. Crimp the edge decoratively, prick the bottom lightly with a fork, and chill the shell for 30 minutes. Line the shell with wax paper, fill the paper with the beans, pushing the beans against the sides to support the sides, and bake the shell in the lower third of a preheated 425° F. oven for 15 minutes. Remove the beans and the paper carefully, lower the oven temperature to 375° F., and continue to bake the shell for 10 to 15 minutes more, or until it is golden. Let the shell cool in the pan on the baking sheet for 10 minutes. Remove the shell from the pan carefully, transfer it to a rack, and let it cool completely. In a small saucepan heat the currant jelly over moderate heat, stirring, until it is smooth and brush the bottom of the shell with some of it.

In a bowl combine the pastry cream and the ground nuts. Stir one third of the whipped cream into the pastry cream mixture and fold in the remaining cream gently but thoroughly. Spoon the cream into the bottom of the shell, smoothing it into an even layer, and arrange the strawberries or other fruit on top. If the jelly has hardened, heat it until it has melted and brush it over the strawberries. Chill the tart until ready to serve.

Light Chocolate Buttercream

2 recipes pastry cream (recipe this page)
  substituting 2 ounces semisweet chocolate,
  melted, for the vanilla
¾ stick (6 tablespoons) unsalted butter at room
  temperature

Have the pastry cream at room temperature. In a large bowl with an electric mixer beat the pastry cream until it is smooth. With the mixer running add the butter, a little at a time, and continue to beat the cream until it is smooth. Transfer the buttercream to a bowl and chill it, covered, until it has hardened but is still of spreading consistency. Use the buttercream as a filling for cakes and pastries. Makes about 2½ cups.

Gingered Pear Puff

1 cup milk
¼ cup chopped crystallized ginger
3 large eggs, separated
½ cup sugar
2 tablespoons cornstarch
2 tablespoons all-purpose flour
2 tablespoons dark rum
2 teaspoons vanilla
½ cup heavy cream, whipped
3 ripe pears, peeled, cored, and sliced
3 tablespoons apricot jam, melted
½ teaspoon grated lemon rind
sifted confectioners' sugar for garnish

In a blender or a food processor combine the milk and the ginger and blend the mixture until it is combined well. Tranfer the mixture to a heavy saucepan and bring it to just a simmer.

In a large bowl with an electric mixer beat the egg yolks until they are combined, add ¼ cup of the sugar a little at a time, beating, and beat the mixture until it is light and lemon colored. Add the cornstarch and the flour a little at a time, beating, and beat the mixture until it is smooth. Add the milk mixture in a stream, beating, and beat the mixture until it is combined well. Transfer the mixture to a heavy saucepan, bring it to a boil, whisking, and simmer it, whisking, for 3 minutes. The pastry cream will be thick and custardlike. Remove the pan from the heat and beat in the rum and the vanilla.

In a large bowl with an electric mixer beat the egg whites until they are frothy. Add a pinch of salt and beat the whites until they hold soft peaks. Add the remaining sugar, a little at a time, and beat the whites until they hold stiff peaks but are not dry. Stir one third of the whites into the pastry cream and fold in the remaining whites gently. Fold in the whipped cream.

In a bowl toss the pear slices with the apricot jam and the grated lemon rind. Spoon a layer of the pastry cream mixture into a buttered 10-inch gratin dish, cover it with the pears, and spoon the remaining pastry cream mixture over them. Bake the gratin in the upper third of a preheated 400° F. oven for 30 to 35 minutes, or until the cream is puffed and golden brown. Sprinkle the pear puff with the confectioners' sugar and serve at once.

Caramel Crème Anglaise

8 large egg yolks
⅔ cup sugar
2 tablespoons flour
3 cups half-and-half, scalded
1 teaspoon vanilla

In a bowl with an electric mixer beat the egg yolks with ¼ cup of the sugar and a pinch of salt until the mixture is thick and pale. Beat in the flour. Add the cream to the yolk mixture in a stream, stirring constantly. Tranfer the mixture to a heavy saucepan and cook the custard over moderate heat, stirring constantly, until it is thickened, but do not let it boil. Strain the custard into a metal bowl set in a bowl of cracked ice, stir in the vanilla, and let it cool, stirring occasionally.

In a small heavy saucepan combine the remaining sugar with 2 tablespoons water and melt it over moderate heat, stirring and washing down any sugar crystals clinging to the sides with a brush dipped in cold water, until it begins to color slightly. Cook the syrup, swirling the pan and being careful not to let it burn, until it is amber-colored. Add 2 tablespoons boiling water immediately, bring the mixture to a boil, stirring, and cook it, stirring, until the caramel is dissolved completely. Let the caramel cool and stir it into the custard. If not using the sauce immediately, chill it, covered with a round of wax paper. Makes about 4 cups.

Chocolate Mocha Ice Cream

1 cup sugar
1 cup unsweetened cocoa powder
¼ cup instant espresso powder
3 cups half-and-half
6 large egg yolks
2 tablespoons Kahlúa
2 teaspoons vanilla

In a heavy saucepan combine the sugar, the cocoa, the espresso powder, and the half-and-half and scald the mixture over moderate heat, whisking. In a large bowl with an electric mixer beat the egg yolks until they are pale and thick. Pour the hot half-and-half mixture through a fine sieve into the bowl in a stream, stirring. Transfer the mixture to another heavy saucepan and cook it over moderately low heat, stirring, until it thickens and coats the spoon. Stir in the Kahlúa and the vanilla. Transfer the custard to a metal bowl set in a bowl of cracked ice, let it cool, covered with a round of wax paper, and chill it in the refrigerator for 2 hours. Freeze the custard in an ice-cream freezer according to the manufacturer's instructions. Makes about 1 quart.

Raspberry Bavarian Cream

a 10-ounce package frozen raspberries in
   syrup
1 cup milk
1 envelope unflavored gelatin
3 large egg yolks
¼ cup sugar
1 tablespoon *eau-de-vie de framboise*
   (raspberry liqueur)
2 teaspoons fresh lemon juice
½ teaspoon vanilla
1 cup heavy cream
fresh raspberries for decoration
raspberry sauce as an accompaniment if
   desired (recipe follows)

Strain the raspberries through a sieve, purée them in a food processor or blender, and strain the purée into a bowl. (There should be ½ cup raspberry purée.)

In a saucepan scald the milk. In a small heatproof bowl sprinkle the gelatin over 2 tablespoons water and let it soften for 10 minutes. In a bowl with an electric mixer beat the egg yolks until they are combined, beat in the sugar a little at a time, and beat the mixture until it is thick and pale. Add the milk in a stream, stirring, transfer the custard to a heavy saucepan, and cook it over moderately low heat, stirring constantly, until it is thick enough to coat the back of the spoon, but do not let it boil. Transfer the custard to a large bowl and stir in the raspberry purée, the *eau-de-vie*, the lemon juice, and the vanilla.

Put the bowl of gelatin in a pan of simmering water, stir the gelatin mixture until the gelatin is dissolved, and stir it into the custard. Set the bowl of custard in a bowl of ice and stir the custard until it is thick, being careful not to let it set. In a chilled bowl beat the cream until it holds soft peaks, stir one fourth of it into the custard, and fold in the remaining cream gently but thoroughly.

Spoon the cream into a chilled decorative 3-cup mold, oiled with vegetable oil, rap the mold on a hard surface once or twice to expel any air bubbles, and chill the cream, covered, for 3 hours, or until it is set. (Or use the cream as a filling for raspberry charlotte mold [page 254].) Run a thin knife around the edge of the mold, dip the mold into a bowl of hot water for 3 seconds, and invert a platter over it. Invert the dessert onto the platter, garnish it with the fresh raspberries, and serve it with the raspberry sauce if desired.

Raspberry Sauce

a 10-ounce package frozen raspberries,
   thawed, reserving the juice
1 tablespoon fresh lemon juice
sugar to taste

In a food processor or in a blender purée the raspberries with the reserved juice and the lemon juice, add the sugar if desired, and strain the sauce through a fine sieve into a serving bowl, pressing hard on the solids. Makes about 1 cup.

GUIDES TO THE TEXT

GENERAL INDEX

INDEX OF 45-MINUTE RECIPES

*Starred entries can be prepared in 45 minutes or less
but require additional unattended time

INDEX OF RECIPE TITLES

Page numbers in *italics* indicate color photographs

TABLE SETTING ACKNOWLEDGMENTS

To avoid duplication below of table setting information within the same menu, the editors have listed all such credits for silverware, plates, linen, and the like in its most complete form under "Table Setting."

Any items in the photographs not credited are privately owned.

Front Jacket: Tomato, basil, and cheese tart on an Italian ironstone footed cake stand from Wolfman ● Gold & Good Company, 484 Broome Street, New York City. "Marseilles Matelasse" 100 percent cotton fabric available through decorator at Brunschwig & Fils, 979 Third Avenue, New York City.

Back Jacket: "Provence" crystal sorbet glasses from Baccarat, Inc., 55 East 57th Street, New York City.

Frontispiece: "Volumetric" porcelain dinner plates designed by Steven Holl for Swid Powell—Bloomingdale's, 1000 Third Avenue, New York City. Italian "Novocento" silver-plate flatware; Italian "Cartoccio" crystal water goblets and wineglasses by Carlo Moretti—Avventura, 463 Amsterdam Avenue, New York City. German cotton jacquard napkins—Frank McIntosh at Henri Bendel, 10 West 57th Street, New York City. Flower arrangement—Mädderlake, 25 East 73rd Street, New York City. "The White Furniture" hand-carved birch table and chairs from a design by Eliel Saarinen, circa 1910 (available through decorator)—ICF, Inc., 305 East 63rd Street, New York City.

The Menu Collection

Table Setting (page 8): Photographed at the Old Merchants House, New York City. "Directoire" hand-painted porcelain dinner plates; "Chrysanthemum" sterling flatware; Orrefors "Prelude" crystal wineglasses; crystal fruit bowl; Baccarat crystal candelabra; crystal nut baskets; Italian crystal footed compotes—Tiffany & Company 727 Fifth Avenue, New York City. Linen place mats and napkins—Léron, Inc., 745 Fifth Avenue, New York City. English cut glass open salts, circa 1830—Bardith, Ltd., 901 Madison Avenue, New York City. English nineteenth-century sterling salt spoons—F. Gorevic & Son, Inc., 660 Lexington Avenue, New York City. Flower arrangement—Mädderlake, 25 East 73rd Street, New York City.

A New Year's Day Buffet

Buffet Setting (page 11): Hand-thrown Inc., 46 East 57th Street, New York City. Italian linen napkins—Frank McIntosh at Henri Bendel, 10 West 57th Street, New York City. Wedgwood "Basalt" candlesticks, circa 1820; French bloodstone and bronze candlestick on jasper base, circa 1830; French bronze "Cupid" candlestick on marble base, circa 1820—Vito Giallo Antiques, 966 Madison Avenue, New York City. Italian Florentine-style inlaid marble tabletop—Frederick P. Victoria & Son, Inc., 154 East 55th Street, New York City. Flower arrangement—Mädderlake, 25 East 73rd Street, New York City. English silk taffeta fabric (available through decorator)—Cowtan & Tout, 979 Third Avenue, New York City.

Oysters and Clams with Mignonnette Sauce (page 12): Hand-forged sterling bowl; "Torchon" sterling oyster forks—Buccellati, Inc., 46 East 57th Street, New York City. "Black Diplomat" porcelain plates—Céralene, Inc., 55 East 57th Street, New York City. "Dom Pérignon" crystal Champagne flutes—Baccarat, Inc., 55 East 57th Street, New York City. Gorham sterling Champagne bucket, circa 1870—Vito Giallo Antiques, 966 Madison Avenue, New York City.

Stuffed Breast of Veal, Gratin of Celery Root and Potato (page 13): Porcelain platter—Lee Bailey at Henri Bendel, 10 West 57th Street, New York City.

Super Bowl Supper

Walnut Orange Cake (page 14): Hand-thrown porcelain plate by Steven Stewart—Gordon Foster, 1322 Third Avenue, New York City. French cotton canvas tablecloth by Patrick Frey—Frank McIntosh at Henri Bendel, 10 West 57th Street, New York City.

Curried Shrimp, Chicken, and Vegetable Stew, Indian-Style Fried Bread (page 15): Hand-formed platinum-glazed earthenware tureen and stand and plate by Lyn Evans—Gordon Foster, 1322 Third Avenue, New York City.

Valentine's Day

Breakfast Setting (page 17): Hand-thrown and hand-painted pottery plates and bowls and hand-painted tile trays on pine stands by Aletha Soulé; English mohair throw and 8′ by 10′ wool rug designed by Elizabeth Eakins—Elizabeth Eakins, Inc., 1053 Lexington Avenue, New York City. "Queen Anne" English silver-plate flatware; Flossie Designs cotton piqué napkins with lace trim; "Spring Bouquet" hand-thrown cups and saucers by Janet Schneider—Creative Resources, Inc., 24 West 57th Street, New York City. English silver-plate café au lait set—Garrard, The Crown Jewelers, 112 Regent Street, London, England. Martex "Thundercloud" cotton and Dacron polyester sheets, comforter, dust ruffle, pillowcases, and curtains—Westpoint Pepperell, 1221 Avenue of the Americas, New York City.

Roast Duck Bourguignonne (page 18): Copeland earthenware platter, circa 1870—La Cuisinière, Inc., 968 Lexington Avenue, New York City.

Coffee Dacquoise Heart (page 18): Wedgwood earthenware dessert plate, circa 1820—Ages Past Antiques, 1030 Lexington Avenue, New York City.

Dinner Setting (page 19): "Ochre" hand-painted French porcelain dinner plates by M. Le Tallec; Christofle "Marly" silver-plate flatware—Barneys New York, Seventh Avenue and Seventeenth Street, New York City. "Nancy" crystal water goblets, wineglasses, and Champagne flutes—Baccarat, Inc., 55 East 57th Street, New York City. Linen and lace napkins, circa 1900—Françoise Nunnallé Fine Arts, 105 West 55th Street, New York City. Christofle silver-plate salt and pepper shakers; Lalique "Saint Cloud" crystal vase—Cardel, Ltd., 621 Madison Avenue, New York City. English Sheffield-plate candlesticks, circa 1780—James Robinson, 15 East 57th Street, New York City. Reproduction French glass and gold leaf over steel table; Italian embossed leather 4-panel screen, circa 1870 (both available through decorator)—Yale R. Burge, 305 East 63rd Street, New York City. French upholstered armchairs, circa 1860—Lenox Court Antiques, 972 Lexington Avenue, New York City. French needlepoint rug, circa 1830—Coury Rugs, Inc., 515 Madison Avenue, New York City.

An All-American Sunday Dinner

Cider-Braised Pork Loin with Sautéed Apples, Rutabaga Potato Purée, Quick Cloverleaf Rolls (page 21): English ironstone platter, circa 1870—La Cuisinière, 968 Lexington Avenue, New York City.

Easter Dinner

Table Setting (page 23): Limoges porcelain service plates and dinner plates; Taitù "Uno" porcelain salad plates—Mayhew, 509 Park Avenue, New York City. Georg Jensen "Bernadotte" silver-plate flatware—Royal Copenhagen Porcelain/Georg Jensen Silversmiths, 683 Madison Avenue, New York City. Milk-glass goblets—Lord & Taylor, Fifth Avenue and Thirty-eighth Street, New York City. Cotton napkins—Frank McIntosh at Henri Bendel, 10 West 57th Street, New York City. Sterling saltshaker and pepper mill—Tiffany & Company, 727 Fifth Avenue, New York City. Hand-painted glass vase by Billy Jarecki; flowers—Mädderlake, 25 East 73rd Street, New York City. Italian lacquer drop-leaf table—Modern Age Galleries Ltd., 795 Broadway, New York City.

Rack of Lamb Persillé, Garlic Rosemary Tuiles, Couscous Timbales (page 24): Italian silver-plate platter—S. Wyler, Inc., 713 Madison Avenue, New York City.

An Early Spring Dinner

Poached Salmon with Cumin Sauce and Deep-Fried Celery Leaves, Steamed Red Potatoes with Dill Butter, Red-Leaf Lettuce and Watercress Salad Mimosa (page 27): French "Paisley" porcelain dinner plates; Scof stainless-steel and acrylic flatware; French "City" glasses; cotton and polyester place mats and napkins—Bergdorf Goodman, 754 Fifth Avenue, New York City. Mikasa glass salad bowl by Laslo—Bloomingdale's, 1000 Third Avenue, New York City.

A Cocktail Party

Sake Martinis, Steamed Vegetables, Kalamata Dipping Sauce, Chipotle Dipping Sauce (page 29): Hand-built porcelain tray and sauce dishes by Barbara Takiguchi; wire glass and anodized aluminum tray by Peter Hand-

ler—Rogers & Tropea, Inc., 1351 Third Avenue, New York City. "Clarity" Martini glasses—Hoya Crystal Gallery, 450 Park Avenue, New York City.

Negronis, Baked Camembert with Hazelnut Crust, Sausage and Mushroom Phyllo Twists, Cheese Lace Crackers (page 30): Slip-cast stoneware plates and bowl by Jean-Pierre Shu—Rogers & Tropea, Inc., 1351 Third Avenue, New York City. "Vision" Martini glasses—Orrefors Crystal Gallery, 58 East 57th Street, New York City. French marble-top bistro table—Le Bris Antiques, 510 Broome Street, New York City. Italian wicker armchairs by Valentino—Valentino, 451 North Robertson Boulevard, Los Angeles, California. "Roman Stripe" and "Roman Stripe Paisley" cotton fabrics (available through decorator)—Brunschwig & Fils, Inc., 979 Third Avenue, New York City.

Spring Fevers, Scallops in Saffron Mayonnaise, Pastry Seashells with Salmon Roe (page 31): Hand-built and hand-thrown multicolored porcelain plate by Judith Poe of Live Oak Design; slip-cast porcelain plate by Dan Levy—Rogers & Tropea, Inc., 1351 Third Avenue, New York City.

Brunch For Four

Poached Eggs on Potato and Bacon Pancakes, Watercress Hollandaise (page 32): Hand-made porcelain plate by Barbara Cahn—Downtown Potter's Hall, 113 Mercer Street, New York City.

Kitchen Setting (page 33): Hand-made porcelain plates by Barbara Cahn; hand-thrown white porcelain mugs, spatterware tumblers, and footed bowl by Sylvia Finkle; earthenware shell by Carol Richman—Downtown Potter's Hall, 113 Mercer Street, New York City. "Kimberly" stainless steel flatware; acrylic-handled butter knife; wire trays; glass pitcher; silverstone griddle; 8-cup "Chambord" *cafetière* by Bodum—Ad Hoc Housewares, 842 Lexington Avenue, New York City. Handmade wicker basket—Bloomingdale's, 1000 Third Avenue, New York City.

Anniversary Dinner

Hearts of Palm Salad with Lamb's-Lettuce (page 34): "Flora Danica" porcelain salad plate—Royal Copenhagen Porcelain/Georg Jensen Silversmiths, 683 Madison Avenue, New York City.

Table Setting (page 35): Royal Copenhagen "Flora Danica" porcelain dinner plates—Tiffany & Company, 727 Fifth Avenue, New York City. "Albany" silver-plate flatware by Mappin & Webb, circa 1880—S. Wyler, Inc., 713 Madison Avenue, New York City. "Marennes" hand-cut crystal water glasses and wineglasses; "Massena" crystal open salt and pepper with ivory spoons—Baccarat, Inc., 55 East 57th Street, New York City. Hand-embroidered organdy place mats and napkins—D. Porthault & Co., 18 East 69th Street, New York City. Sterling candlesticks, 1931—J. Mavec & Company Ltd., 52 East 76th Street (3rd floor), New York City. Sterling basket by Peter and Anne Bateman, London, 1793—F. Gorevic & Son, Inc., 660 Lexington Avenue, New York City. Flowers—Mädderlake, 25 East 73rd Street, New York City. English mahogany two-pedestal dining table, 1790-1800; English rosewood chiffonier, 1805-1810; English nineteenth-century glass plates and berry bowl with stand; English eighteenth-century glass rummers; Italian nineteenth-century carved walnut columns—Florian Papp Inc., 962 Madison Avenue, New York City. Mahogany side chairs and armchairs, circa 1820—Stair & Company, Inc., 59 East 57th Street, New York City. "Hope Cottage" wallpaper (available through decorator)—Clarence House, 211 East 58th Street, New York City.

Roast Capon with Tarragon Sauce, Confetti Rice, Buttered Green Beans (page 36): "Flora Danica" porcelain platter—Royal Copenhagen Porcelain/Georg Jensen Silversmiths, 683 Madison Avenue, New York City. Sterling sauceboat and stand by Reed & Barton; sterling entrée dish (cover not shown); sterling vegetable dish—F. Gorevic & Son, Inc., 660 Lexington Avenue, New York City.

Ananas en Surprise, Coconut Tuiles (page 37): Oriental silver tray—F. Gorevic & Son, Inc., 660 Lexington Avenue, New York City.

A May Luncheon

Raspberry Hazelnut Savarin (page 38): Thomas porcelain plate—Mayhew, 509 Park Avenue, New York City.

Green Pea Consommé, Onion Toasts, Terrine de Coquilles Saint-Jacques with Spring Tomato Sauce (page 39): Riedel crystal soup bowls; Val St. Lambert crystal plates—Cardel, Ltd., 621 Madison Avenue, New York City. Mottahedeh earthenware plates (adapted from a nineteenth-century Creil plate)—Mottahedeh, 225 Fifth Avenue, New York City.

Afternoon Croquet Tea Parties

Tea Sandwiches in a Bread Basket (page 40): English silver-plate salver with fern design, circa 1870—S. Wyler, Inc., 713 Madison Avenue, New York City.

Tea Setting (page 41): Coalport "Chinese Willow" bone china dessert plates and cups and saucers—Cardel, Ltd., 621 Madison Avenue, New York City. English "Feather Edge" hand-forged sterling dessert forks and teaspoons—James Robinson, Inc., 15 East 57th Street, New York City. English engraved silver-plate teapot, sugar, and creamer (coffeepot not shown), circa 1870; English engraved glass bowls with silver-plate ladles and stand (stand not shown), circa 1880; English nineteenth-century woven silver-plate basket; English miniature croquet set, circa 1910—James II Galleries, Ltd., 15 East 57th Street, New York City. Cotton napkins with crocheted edges; cotton and lace runner—Cherchez, 862 Lexington Avenue, New York City. Krosno glass pitcher; "Tall Iced Tea" glasses—The Pottery Barn, 117 East 59th Street, New York City. French wicker tables, armchair, and side chairs, circa 1920—J. Garvin Mecking Antiques, 72 East 11th Street, New York City. Skowhegan croquet set—Hammacher Schlemmer, 147 East 57th Street, New York City.

Mustard Tarragon Stuffed Eggs, Ham Cornets with Apple Horseradish Filling (page 42)—French porcelain platter, circa 1860—S. Wyler, Inc., 713 Madison Avenue, New York City. Hand-embroidered linen tea cloth, circa 1890—Cherchez, 862 Lexington Avenue, New York City.

Layered Walnut Yogurt Terrine (page 42): Gorham sterling tray with Greek key border, circa 1850—F. Gorevic & Son, Inc., 660 Lexington Avenue, New York City.

Cinnamon Toast Rolls, Almond Chocolate Chip Macaroons, Lime Curd Tartlets with Fresh Fruit (page 43): English nineteenth-century tole cake stand—James II Galleries, Ltd., 15 East 57th Street, New York City.

A Graduation Dinner

Creamy Lemon Chive Pasta with Asparagus (page 44): Italian earthenware plate—Frank McIntosh at Henri Bendel, 10 West 57th Street, New York City.

Boiled Lobsters with Tomato Basil Beurre Blanc, Romaine with Anchovy Caper Vinaigrette, Garlic Pepper Pita Toasts (page 45): Slip-cast porcelain dinner plates, salad plates, and bowl by Dan Levy—Rogers-Tropea, Inc., 1351 Third Avenue, New York City. Supreme "Epoch" stainless steel flatware; Sasaki crystal beer glasses; Boston Warehouse china ramekins—Ad Hoc Housewares, 842 Lexington Avenue, New York City. Linen napkins—Cherchez, 862 Lexington Avenue, New York City.

Fourth of July Alfresco

Corn Soup, Corn Bread Thins (page 46): "Morning Glory Pink" stoneware soup bowl and butter plate—Bennington Potters, Inc., P.O. Box 199, Bennington, Vermont.

Table Setting (page 47): "Morning Glory Pink" stoneware dinner plates and pitcher—Bennington Potters, Inc., P.O. Box 199, Bennington, Vermont. Gorham "Fairfax" sterling flatware—Gorham Division of Textron Inc., 333 Adelaide Avenue, Providence, Rhode Island. Lenox "Antique" glass goblets—Bloomingdale's, 1000 Third Avenue, New York City. Hand-embroidered linen napkins with cutwork; wicker armchairs, circa 1895—Pamela Scurry's The Wicker Garden, 1318 Madison Avenue, New York City.

"Bridgewater Blue and White" cotton fabric (available through decorator)—Hinson & Company, 979 Third Avenue, New York City.

Grilled Salmon, Shrimp, and Scallop Kebabs, Glazed Sugar Snap Peas, Sautéed Tomatoes with Mint Butter, Egg Noodles with Buttered Crumbs (page 48): "Morning Glory Blue" stoneware platter—Bennington Potters, Inc., P.O. Box 199, Bennington, Vermont.

Chocolate Layer Cake with Chocolate-Dipped Cherries (page 49): Wicker armchair, circa 1900—Pamela Scurry's The Wicker Garden, 1318 Madison Avenue, New York City.

Picnic at the Beach

Pecan Sand Tarts, Peanut Butter Chocolate Chip Cookies, Assorted Fruit (page 50): Bamboo trays designed by Lisa Desti—Desti Imports, Inc., 225 Fifth Avenue, New York City.

Spicy Fried Chicken, Onion Sandwiches, Grated Carrot, Radish, and Chive Salad, Pasta Shells with Tomatoes, Olives, and Basil, Raspberry Cooler (page 51): Hand-decorated wood serving bowl and plates designed by Phillip Mueller for Sigma—B. Altman & Company, Fifth Avenue and Thirty-fourth Street, New York City. Bamboo box (lid not shown), bamboo tray, and cloth-lined picnic basket designed by Lisa Desti—Desti Imports, Inc., 225 Fifth Avenue, New York City. Plastic tumbler—Lee Bailey at Henri Bendel, 10 West 57th Street, New York City. Cotton napkins—Bloomingdale's, 1000 Third Avenue, New York City. Teak chaise and folding table designed by Kipp Stewart for Summit Furniture (available through decorator)—Luten Clarey Stern Inc., 1059 Third Avenue, New York City.

Terrace Dinners For Two

Chilled Cucumber Soup with Mint Ice (page 52): Viking glass bowl—Mayhew, 507 Park Avenue, New York City.

Table Setting (page 53): "Volumetric" porcelain dinner plates designed by Steven Holl for Swid Powell—Bloomingdale's, 1000 Third Avenue, New York

City. Italian "Novocento" silver-plate flatware; Italian "Cartoccio" crystal water goblets and wineglasses by Carlo Moretti—Avventura, 463 Amsterdam Avenue, New York City. German cotton jacquard napkins—Frank McIntosh at Henri Bendel, 10 West 57th Street, New York City. Alabaster hurricane lamp designed by Angela Cummings for Arita—Marshall Field's, 111 North State Street, Chicago, Illinois. Flower arrangement—Mädderlake, 25 East 73rd Street, New York City. "The White Furniture" hand-carved birch table and chairs from a design by Eliel Saarinen, circa 1910 (available through decorator)—ICF, Inc., 305 East 63rd Street, New York City.

Peach Champagne Cocktail, Kir Royale, Prosciutto Radish Toasts, Tapenade Toasts (page 54): Lalique "Ange" crystal Champagne glasses—Cardel, Ltd., 621 Madison Avenue, New York City. Riedel "Optic" and "Dimension" glass plates—Mayhew, 507 Park Avenue, New York City.

Grilled Filet Mignon, Rosemary Potato Balls, Summer Squash with Basil and Parmesan, Garlic and Pimiento Mayonnaise (page 54): Romanian crystal jar (lid not shown)—Mayhew, 507 Park Avenue, New York City.

Kahlúa Coffee Jelly with Cinnamon Cream, Brown Sugar Wafers, Raspberry Almond Tuile Tortes (page 55): "Spring Crocus" crystal Pilsner glasses; "Sumikiri" square crystal plates—The Hoya Crystal Gallery, 450 Park Avenue, New York City. English engraved glass plates, circa 1850—James Robinson, 15 East 57th Street, New York City. Hand-painted *faux marbre* table with cast-iron base—Pamela Scurry's The Wicker Garden, 1318 Madison Avenue, New York City.

Lunch from a Cool Kitchen

White Sangría, Sesame Ginger Toasts, Lemon and Basil Poached Chicken Breasts, Smoked Mozzarella and Tomato Salad (page 57): Riedel "Coil" crystal platter—Tiffany & Co., 727 Fifth Avenue, New York City. French handmade rattan and *rilsan* table and armchair by Drucker Inc.—T & K French Antiques, Inc., 65 Wooster Street, New York City.

An Early Autumn Weekend

Dinner Setting (page 59): Moustiers "Rose Ferrat" faience service plates; "Le Ballon de Gonesse" cotton fabric—Pierre Deux, 870 Madison Avenue, New York City. Ricci "Modigliani" silver-plate flatware; Biot water goblets and wineglasses—Barneys New York, Seventh Avenue and 17th Street, New York City. English oak barley twist candlesticks and brass measures, both circa 1870; Russian brass wall sconce, circa 1880—Bob Pryor Antiques, 1023 Lexington Avenue, New York City. Nineteenth-century French pine dining table; nineteenth-century Norwegian pine cupboard—Howard Kaplan Antiques, 827 Broadway, New York City. Nineteenth-century English brass spice box—James II Galleries, Ltd., 15 East 57th Street, New York City.

Red Snapper with Artichoke Lemon Sauce, Sautéed Napa Cabbage and Swiss Chard, Red Potatoes with Prosciutto and Chives (page 60): "Flores" faience dinner plate—Mayhew, 507 Park Avenue, New York City.

Duck Salad with Raspberries, Oranges, Arugula, and Cracklings, Two-Grain Salad with Green Beans and Pine Nuts (page 61): Italian ceramic platter and serving dish—Bergdorf Goodman, 754 Fifth Avenue, New York City.

Elegant But Easy Chicken Dinners

Spinach-Stuffed Chicken Breasts with Madeira Sauce, Zucchini and Carrot Julienne, Saffron Rice Timbale (page 62): "Swan Service" porcelain dinner plate by Vista Alegre for Mottahedeh—Mayhew, 507 Park Avenue, New York City. "Torchon" hand-forged sterling flatware—Buccellati, Inc., 46 East 57th Street, New York City. "Nancy" crystal wineglass—Baccarat, Inc., 55 East 57th Street, New York City. Silver-plate pierced basket—F. Gorevic & Son, Inc., 660 Lexington Avenue, New York City. Italian cut-work linen tablecloth, circa 1890—Françoise Nunnallé Fine Arts, 105 West 55th Street, New York City.

Blasted Cornish Hens with Basil Couscous Stuffing, Tomatoes Stuffed with Squash, Feta, and Olives, Steamed

Green and Wax Beans (page 63): English Davenport ironstone platter, circa 1880—Hubert des Forges, 1193 Lexington Avenue, New York City.

October Dinner

Smoked Swiss Cheese, Apple, and Celery Salad (page 64): Pickard "Gold" porcelain salad/dessert plate—Cardel, Ltd., 621 Madison Avenue, New York City.

Table Setting (page 65): "Framboise Rose" hand-painted porcelain dinner plates—Tiffany & Company, 727 Fifth Avenue, New York City. Kirk Stieff "Paramount" sterling flatware—The Kirk Stieff Company, 800 Wyman Park Drive, Baltimore, Maryland. Lobmeyr "Ambassador" crystal wineglasses and water goblets—Mayhew, 507 Park Avenue, New York City. French vermeil candlesticks, circa 1830; English sterling salt cellars, circa 1830; American coin silver salt spoons, circa 1850—Vito Giallo Antiques, 966 Madison Avenue, New York City. Nineteenth-century Swedish Biedermeier maple armchairs—Lenox Court Antiques, 972 Lexington Avenue, New York City. Nineteenth-century German Biedermeier cherry wood veneer table with ebonized wood legs; nineteenth-century German Biedermeier cherry wood mirror with contrasting fruitwood inlay—Angus Wilkie, 96 Grand Street, New York City. Italian engraving of Etruscan masks, circa 1780, in Whistler-style wood and gesso frame (one of a pair; available through decorator); nineteenth-century engravings in marbleized wood frames (available through decorator)—Yale R. Burge, 305 East 63rd Street, New York City. Aubusson rug, circa 1870—Coury Rugs, Inc., 515 Madison Avenue, New York City. "Marlborough Stripe" wallpaper (available through decorator)—Cowtan & Tout, 979 Third Avenue, New York City.

Pork with Mustard Seed Sauce, Broccoli Rabe with Lemon and Garlic, Buttered Noodles with Crisp Browned Shallots (page 66): Sterling tray by Dominick & Haff; sterling bowl by Gorham; sterling brandy warmer by Robert Sharp, London, 1802; sterling sauce ladle by Solomon Hougham, London, 1794—F. Gorevic & Son,

Inc., 635 Madison Avenue, New York City.

Apricot Cheesecake (page 67): English silver-plate salver, circa 1870—S. Wyler, Inc., 713 Madison Avenue, New York City. English Davenport pottery baskets and stands, circa 1800—Bardith, Ltd., 901 Madison Avenue, New York City.

Meals To Make Ahead

Espresso Tortoni with Chocolate-Covered Coffee Beans (page 68): Italian "New Wave Geometric" hand-painted earthenware espresso cups and saucers designed by Rosanna Imports—Panache, 1015 Western Avenue, Seattle, Washington.

Spicy Lamb Stew with Sweet Potato Rosettes (page 69): Le Creuset enameled iron casserole—Bloomingdale's, 1000 Third Avenue, New York City. "Pliniana" cotton fabric (available through decorator)—Donghia Textiles, 485 Broadway, New York City.

A Country Thanksgiving

Golden Creamed Onions, Buttered Brussels Sprouts, Root Vegetable Purée (page 70): Wedgwood creamware platter, vegetable dish, and dinner plates (from a service for 12), circa 1862—Bardith Ltd., 901 Madison Avenue, New York City. English brass candlesticks—Ages Past Antiques—1030 Lexington Avenue, New York City.

Table Setting (page 71): Wedgwood creamware dinner plates (from a service for 12), circa 1862—Bardith Ltd., 901 Madison Avenue, New York City. Puiforcat "Cardinal" silver-plate dinner knives and forks and "Richelieu" sterling oyster forks—Neiman-Marcus (all stores). St. Louis "Iriana" crystal wineglasses—Pavillon Christofle, 680 Madison Avenue, New York City. English lignum vitae pail with brass handle, circa 1800; English nineteenth-century brass castor; French Art Deco glass candlestick; English brass-bound wood ale jug, circa 1840; English brass and copper tea caddies, circa 1860; English eighteenth-century elm wood high chair—James II Galleries, Ltd., 15 East 57th Street, New York City. English brass candlesticks, circa 1850—Ages Past Antiques, 1030

Lexington Avenue, New York City. Portuguese linen hemstitched napkins—Léron, Inc., 745 Fifth Avenue, New York City. "New Ravenna" cotton fabric (available through decorator)—Brunschwig & Fils, Inc., 979 Third Avenue, New York City. English mahogany chairs (from a set of 6), circa 1780—Florian Papp Inc., 962 Madison Avenue, New York City. American brass fender, circa 1900; brass and iron fire tools and andirons, circa 1800—Wm. H. Jackson Company, 3 East 47th Street, New York City.

Boned Turkey with Sausage Hazelnut Stuffing and Madeira Gravy (page 72): English pewter and porcelain hot-water platter, circa 1870—Bob Pryor Antiques, 1023 Lexington Avenue, New York City. Wedgwood creamware gravy boat (cover not shown, from a service for 12), circa 1862—Bardith Ltd., 901 Madison Avenue, New York City. "Hanoverian" English silver-plate serving fork and spoon, circa 1875—S. Wyler, Inc., 713 Madison Avenue, New York City.

Cranberry Tart with Rum Cream and Chocolate, Pear Mincemeat Tartlets with Lemon Hard Sauce (page 73): English pottery dessert plates by Neale & Co., circa 1784; Scottish majolica leaf plate, circa 1870—Bardith Ltd., 901 Madison Avenue, New York City. Christofle silver-plate pastry tongs—Pavillon Christofle, 680 Madison Avenue, New York City.

Thanksgiving for a Small Gathering
Pumpkin Soup with Sage Croutons (page 74): "Bountiful" stoneware soup bowl and dinner plate by Epoch, a division of Noritake—available at Sears stores nationwide. Jean Couzon Orfèvre stainless steel flatware— Bloomingdale's, 1000 Third Avenue, New York City.

Christmas Dinner

Smoked Salmon Christmas Trees, Radish and Parsley Butter Wreaths (page 76): English sterling tray, circa 1870—James II Galleries, Ltd., 15 East 57th Street, New York City.

Table Setting (page 77): Bernardaud "Consulat" porcelain dinner plates designed by Clarence House; polka dot linen damask napkins (from a set of 12), circa 1940—Barneys New York, Seventh Avenue and 17th Street, New York City. Christofle's Cardeilhac "Brienne" sterling flatware—Pavillon Christofle, 680 Madison Avenue, New York City. "Massena" crystal wineglasses—Baccarat, Inc., 55 East 57th Street, New York City. British colonial sterling salt and pepper shakers by Pittar & Co., Calcutta, circa 1840—F. Gorevic & Son, Inc., 635 Madison Avenue, New York City. English silver-plate and crystal epergne, circa 1810; Irish sterling candlesticks by Issac D'Olier, 1755—S. Wyler, Inc., 713 Madison Avenue, New York City. "Dover" cotton fabric (available through decorator)—Cowtan & Tout, 979 Third Avenue, New York City. English nineteenth-century mahogany chairs; American leaded-glass panel (one of a pair), circa 1890 (available through decorator)—Newel Art Galleries, Inc., 425 East 53rd Street, New York City. French bronze wall sconces, circa 1820 (available through decorator)—Marvin Alexander, Inc., 315 East 62nd Street, New York City.

Roast Tenderloin of Beef with Wild Mushroom Sauce, Spinach, Pea, and Red Pepper Timbales, Pommes Lorette (page 78): Silver-plate tray; sterling vegetable dish by Black, Starr & Frost—F. Gorevic & Son, Inc., 635 Madison Avenue, New York City. English nineteenth-century silver-plate sauceboat and ladle—James II Galleries Ltd., 15 East 57th Street, New York City.

Chocolate Dacquoise, Apricot Macadamia Snowballs (page 79): Engraved sterling tray by Dominick & Haff, New York, 1904—F. Gorevic & Son, Inc., 635 Madison Avenue, New York City. English ivory-handled cake knife, circa 1870; English footed cut-crystal dishes, circa 1840—James II Galleries, Ltd., 15 East 57th Street, New York City. Tharaud "Crown Jewels" hand-cut crystal wineglasses—Cardel, Ltd., 621 Madison Avenue, New York City. English inlaid rosewood chess table, circa 1820 (available through decorator)—Yale R. Burge, 305 East 63rd Street, New York City.

A Tree-Trimming Party

Baked Alaska (page 80): Stainless steel platter—Bridge Kitchenware Corporation, 214 East 52nd Street, New York City.

Sun-Dried Tomato and Provolone Bread with Smoked Turkey; Hot Crab, Artichoke, and Jalapeño Dip with Pita Triangles; Radish- and Celery-Stuffed Endive Leaves (page 81): Italian silver-plate tray; English silver-plate chafing dish by Hukin & Heath, 1875—S. Wyler, Inc., 713 Madison Avenue, New York City. Wedgwood majolica compote and shell dish, both circa 1880; English majolica covered bowl, circa 1880—J. Garvin Mecking Antiques, 72 East 11th Street, New York City. Wedgwood "Napoleon Ivy" china dinner plates—Tiffany & Company, 727 Fifth Avenue, New York City. Italian hand-painted ceramic candlesticks—Portantina, 886 Madison Avenue, New York City. English decoupage screen in mahogany frame, circa 1870 (available through decorator)—Yale R. Burge, 305 East 63rd Street, New York City.

The Recipe Collection

Noodles and Smoked Salmon with Dill Sauce (page 82): "Mist" porcelain luncheon plate designed by Gwathney Siegel for Swid Powell—Frank McIntosh at Henri Bendel, 10 West 57th Street, New York City.

If you are not already a subscriber to *Gourmet* magazine and would be interested in subscribing, please call *Gourmet's* toll-free number, 800-247-2160.